RESEARCH MANUAL IN CHILD DEVELOPMENT

Second Edition

RESEARCH MANUAL IN CHILD DEVELOPMENT

Second Edition

Lorraine Nadelman
University of Michigan

2004

Lawrence Erlbaum Associates, Publishers
Mahwah, New Jersey   London

Copyright © 2004 by Lawrence Erlbaum Associates, Inc.

Lawrence Erlbaum Associates, Inc. Publishers
10 Industrial Avenue
Mahwah, New Jersey 07430-2262

Cover design by Kathryn Houghtaling Lacey

Library of Congress Cataloging-in-Publication Data

ISBN: 8058-4041-9
CIP information for this book can be obtained by contacting the Library of Congress.

Books published by Lawrence Erlbaum Associates
are printed on acid-free paper, and their bindings are
chosen for strength and durability.

Printed in the United States of America

10 9 8 7 6 5 4 3 2 1

To our grandchildren
Aaron Noah Kara Jacob Max Micah Ryan Gabriel

CONTENTS

Preface

Goals for this book and its audience remain constant, so some of the earlier preface is repeated in this updated reprint/revision.

Twenty years ago, student demand for research training courses in child development exceeded the supply of such courses. Today, that situation has improved, but not sufficiently. University faculty prefer to teach research by having students act as assistants in faculty research projects. College and Junior College instructors recognize the value of a traditional, comprehensive, hands-on laboratory course, but are reluctant to take on the hassle and workload which, indeed, are formidable: obtaining human subjects review approval, lining up subjects and signed permission slips, choosing projects, preparing lectures, and creating stimuli, instructions, data sheets, collation charts, bibliographies, and choosing appropriate statistics for each project. I can't provide the institutional review board approvals, or the children, but this manual does significantly reduce the "hassle" component and thereby encourage the addition of hands-on research experiences to students' training in child development. Students who have had actual experience with research processes and writing will derive a long-term benefit, regardless of their eventual career choice.

The instructor can use this manual in a variety of ways. I have taught the lab course as an introduction to experimental psychology, as an advanced undergraduate laboratory course, and as an early graduate course. It is not intended as a student do-it-yourself manual; supervision and feedback are crucial. Dedicated teachers are not yet out of style, and individualized attention continues to be the keystone of a superior training experience.

Most programs tend to denigrate the data-collection process. Because our archival journals do not always include sufficient methodological detail to replicate published experiments, the Method sections in this book are meticulously detailed. An insistence on adherence to these details, much practice to establish reliability, and a critical discussion of each methodological detail in class may help to rid students of naive notions of the definition and collection of appropriate data.

The projects that follow are grouped by topics similar in organization to the more heavily-used child psychology textbooks. The experiments cover different content areas, several theoretical paradigms, and various statistical techniques; the measures vary in validity and amount of inference; some effects are robust and others are not (as in real life). I should have liked to order the projects for the researcher from easiest to hardest, but the difficulty levels of the data-collection, the statistics, and the constructs often vary independently. For what it is worth, students seem to find the following projects the simplest to assimilate: self-esteem, the two sex-role studies, reaction time, and interference proneness. Appendix A (Notes for the Instructor), which is based on many years of experience, will help the researcher in deciding which projects best suit their varied purposes, and offers many practical suggestions. How many experiments are run in a term depends on one's goals. We have varied between three and eight, with the number affected by decisions on number of subjects, amount and kind of statistics, kind of write up, and extent of student involvement in design modifications.

For this edition, six experiments and the statistics chapter were dropped. Projects added include Theory of Mind, Language, Sibling Relationships, plus suggestions for cross-cultural and neuropsychology investigations. The observation chapter was expanded with a TV project. Background essays, introductions, discussions, and bibliographies have been revised and expanded.

Former contributors—Scott Miller, Keith Stanovich, and Robert Wozniak—are welcomed back, and joined by new colleagues—Sandra Graham-Bermann, John Coley and Susan Gelman.

Perhaps a historical and autobiographical note is in order here. My first involvement with this course began in April, 1951, when the incoming chairman of the Psychology and Education Department at Mount Holyoke College, Stuart Stoke, interviewed potential assistant professors interested in initiating an Experimental Child Psychology course and program. The immediate rapport and challenge were irresistible, and four exciting and productive years followed.

Influenced by my new Skinnerian and psychophysical psychology colleagues, the course was fairly "hard-nosed," but broad. An eclectic rigorous point of view derived from the earlier and long association at New York University with Theodore Schneirla, Herbert Birch, Ralph Gilbert, Elsa Robinson, Presley Stout, and Marian Jenkins. Many fine honors projects and independent research studies conducted by the student "graduates" of that pioneer course added to the intellectual pleasure.

After four years at Mount Holyoke College, I temporarily withdrew from academia to start a family, and resumed teaching at the University of Michigan seven years later. I introduced the laboratory course in developmental psychology at the University of Michigan in 1967, after a stimulating year as a National Science Foundation Fellow at Tavistock Clinic, London, under the sponsorship of John Bowlby. The developmental aspect was more strongly emphasized, and infant observation projects were added.

The course continues to evolve, reflecting changes in the field of developmental psychology, but retaining some classic and historically important projects. With the aid of a small grant from the Center for Research on Learning and Teaching, I added elderly subjects and a life-span orientation, with the enthusiastic help of Ann Zubrick.

ACKNOWLEDGEMENTS

Above all, I am grateful to the hundreds of families in South Hadley and Ann Arbor who cooperated with this program over many decades. From 1970–1980, the University of Michigan had no laboratory nursery or school, and without the cheerful and steady aid of the children, families, and public schools' administrators and staffs, training in developmental research would have been curtailed. Special thanks to Burns Park School families, and UM Children's Center.

Graduate students who acted as my teaching assistants were young colleagues, sharing the joys and frustrations and work. Those who assisted me for three or more semesters were Ellen Reese, Frederick McNelly, and Joanne Quarfoth. Their intellectual and emotional companionship are cherished memories. My competent, hard-working, and valued laboratory assistants are acknowledged with gratitude in the accompanying list. I happily acknowledge again the contribution of drawings by Glenda (Vogt) Revelle for Experiment 11. We used pictures lent by Akira Kobasigawa and Barbara Moely for Experiment 6 for several years in our lab course, these are redrawn here. John Coley supplied the drawings for Experiment 7. Copyrighted material is acknowledged in the conventional manner in the appropriate locations.

Keith Smith, David Krantz, and Dan Weintraub were early caring colleagues, who offered generous and prompt statistical assistance and occasional design criticisms. Stuart Stoke, my Mount Holyoke College chair, taught me, by his example, that much could be accomplished if you didn't care who received the credit. I wish that I had made clearer to Theodore Schneirla and Herbert Birch, while they were still alive, how intellectually stimulating and long-lasting their influence was. Ted Schneirla was an influential presence from the first undergraduate introductory psych course to chairman of my Ph. D. thesis. Barbara Graham and Bari Goldman, undergraduate students, performed the library searches needed to update this book; they were competent and valued assistants. A very special note of appreciation to Valerie Wood who, over many years, has been turning my legal pad manuscript into computer disks. As much as her painstaking and competent work, I appreciate her concern and friendship. My thanks to Lawrence Erlbaum, who agreed to publish this manual, and to my editors, Bill Webber and his associates for their patience and sympathy with my medical delays, and to Nancy Proyect for making the manuscript page-ready. Special thanks to Judi Amsel for her good suggestions for updating this edition. Above all, my patient and supportive husband, Sidney Warschausky, survived the overlong and difficult gestation of the 1982 book with our mutual love and respect intact. I am deeply grateful that we survived this edition similarly. Given his neatness and clean desk, his tolerance for my decades of incredible clutter (even beyond the confines of my study) has been remarkable. He has been indispensible to my finishing this book. Our grown children, Seth, Judith, Carl, and their spouses, have been unfailingly supportive, and have supplied welcome, stimulating distractions, as listed in the dedication. If this book enables more students to enjoy learning how to be a researcher in child development, and how to appreciate and evaluate empirical efforts, I am satisfied.

—*Lorraine Nadelman*

Teaching Assistants

Amy Aberbach
Stanley Alexander
Mita Banerjee
Catherine Biderman
Chuansheng Chen
Carol Claflin
John Coley
David Cross
Ann Cunningham
Donna Dumm
Panfang Fu
Gail Gottfried
Jean Graham*
Grant Gutheil
Tam Halle
Kirby Heller
Paula Hill
Raelyn Janssen
Robert Kail
Phillip Kingsley
Babette Kronstadt
Lynn Liben
Susan Livingston
Douglas Mac Iver
Elizabeth Mazur
Julia McAdoo
Frederick McNelly

John Meacham
Christy Miller-Buchanan
Missi Nadeau
Richard Newman
Kathleen Patusky
Pam Puro
Joanne Quarfoth
Steve Rawson
Meda Rebecca
Ellen Reese*
Glenda (Vogt) Revelle
Ruth Sabo
Carolyn Schult
Bettina Schwethelm
Jane Sheldon
Jennifer Smith
Catherine Sophian
Keith Stanovich
Randy Stiles
Marianne Taylor
Ann Watson
Sharon Wilcox
Joy Wolfe
Jacqui Wooley
Robert Wozniak
Bruce Yovitz
Ann Zubrick

* Mount Holyoke College

PART ONE

INTRODUCTION—RESEARCH CONSIDERATIONS

A

A Primer of Scientific Research

SECTION 1
AN INTRODUCTION TO PSYCHOLOGICAL RESEARCH

Robert Wozniak

When Sara, a 3-month-old infant, accidentally brushes a rattle with her hands, the sound that follows surprises her. For a small baby, events such as this are unpredictable and unknown. A few months later, when Sara sees the rattle, picks it up, and shakes it to hear the noise, she has brought a bit of order into her world. She has learned to relate a visual experience, an action, and feelings of grasping and shaking to the occurrence of a sound.

To "know" is to construct such relationships between events; and to "understand" is to fit such relationships into more comprehensive organized systems. Thus, although 7-month-olds may be aware of rattles and rattling sounds, they will not really understand much about them for some years. They will not, for example, connect the relationship between the rattle and the sound it makes to knowledge of a general class of sounds made by hollow containers that enclose loose objects. Yet, eventually, despite the fact that they may never see a rattle that has been broken open, they will come to think of a rattle as a hollow container enclosing a number of very small objects that produce their characteristic sound by bouncing off the walls of the container. The simple relationship between the visual image, the motion of a baby's arm, the feeling of the rattle in her hand, the feeling of movement, and the resulting sound, will become embedded in a complex system of relationships (much broader, of course, than that just described). Then the child may be said to "understand" something about the occurrence of the rattling sound. Often the level of this understanding continues to increase well into adulthood. It may quite possibly increase for the rest of the person's life (if, for example, the individual becomes an expert in acoustics) as the simple relationship is continually incorporated into wider and wider systems of knowledge.

What each of us as individuals does on a personal level, science attempts to achieve on a transpersonal level. The goals of science will be to "know" the event: to relate its occurrence to the occurrence of other events that accompany it, a process generally termed *description*; and to "understand" the event: to incorporate these descriptive relationships into the systematically organized body of knowledge about such occurrences that the science already possesses. Only this will allow the scientist to *explain* why certain accompanying conditions and not others are those under which the phenomena of interest appear. The building of a systematic body of knowledge requires both description and explanation.

Method—The Means to Achieving Understanding

Although, in practice, there is variation among the sciences in the way in which knowledge and understanding are achieved, there are, nonetheless, general characteristics of the scientific approach that show up in one way or another in the work of all scientists. These are outlined briefly here, and then each of the key elements of the process is discussed individually in more detail.

In general, scientists begin with a *question* concerning the conditions surrounding the occurrence of some phenomenon that they do not yet understand. In research in child development, as a rule, such questions arise from one of three sources: (a) the observation of children's activity; (b) implications drawn from theoretical statements; or (c) logical or methodological criticism of previous research.

After a question has been identified, the researcher generally proceeds to *review the information* already available concerning the phenomena with which the question is involved. When the available information is the product of *observation*, it is referred to as *data*. From a review of the available data, the researcher formulates a descriptive statement or *hypothesis* concerning the conditions under which the phenomena of interest might be regularly observed.

Hypotheses usually lead to *investigation*, that is, to further observation designed to determine whether the phenomena of interest will appear under the conditions specified by the hypothesis. Investigation generates new data; from data the scientist draws conclusions about the suitability of the hypothesis. This may lead to the acceptance, rejection, or, most often, reformulation of the hypothesis.

The process of reformulation typically continues until the hypothesis has been so stated that further data repeatedly suggest that the hypothesis is a fair statement of the conditions under which the phenomena can be observed. When this occurs, the hypothesis attains the status of law; furthermore, when in the course of the development of a science a number of laws have been articulated concerning interrelated phenomena, then a *theory* concerning the relationship among these laws may be constructed. The theory, if it is well formulated, in turn suggests new combinations of conditions under which particular phenomena ought to be observable (i.e., new hypotheses may be formulated), and the process begins anew with the important additional characteristic that now the evaluation of hypotheses also implies the acceptance, rejection, or modification of a theory.

Questions and Their Sources

The starting point of any program of research is the articulation of a question. A *psychological question* is a statement concerning the occurrence of some mental or behavioral event that ought to be incorporated into the systematic body of psychological theory but for which the psychologist is unable to give a satisfactory psychological explanation.

1. *Direct observation.* Perhaps the best source of questions for the researcher interested in children is the direct observation of children's activity, although interesting scientific questions about children may also originate from other sources (see below). Sometimes, formulating these questions requires naturalistic observation of children in the everyday environment. Often, however, the activity of children in the controlled setting of the experimental laboratory itself yields important and interesting questions for investigation.

2. *Implications from theory.* A second source of psychological questions is theory. The nature and role of theory in psychology will be discussed later. For now, it is sufficient to note that *theories* are systems of interrelated statements concerning classes of phenomena and their relationships. Theories are attempts to understand.

    The nature of theory is such that it must have implications that are testable. It must yield statements of the form—*if A, then B*. Theory must suggest that one or another phenomena, previously unobserved in a particular context, will occur given some set of conditions. It must, in other words, generate questions for research. Indeed, this is one of the characteristics of good theory. All things being equal, the more a theory is productive of research questions, the better the theory.

    One important point that must not be overlooked in research on children is that theory, which is neither good nor bad in and of itself, is but a tool for the understanding the child. Consequently, theory-generated research questions should be tied closely to the original phenomena that the theory set out to explain. When the results of investigations suggested by a theory are interpreted, they should be interpreted with an eye to implications for understanding the original phenomena that prompted the theory to begin with.

Keeping this in mind helps the researcher resist the temptation to let theory replace the child as the subject of research.

3. *Revision and extension of prior research.* Research questions may also be generated by logical or methodological criticism of previous research. An important variable may have been inadequately controlled or overlooked. An interpretation that does not follow from the data may have been offered or alternative interpretations slighted. An overly specific set of experimental conditions may have been employed and the results generalized to too wide a context. Such occurrences typically suggest questions that need to be answered before the conclusions of the original research can be accepted.

Review of the Available Data and Formulation of Hypotheses

When a particular question has been selected, the researcher proceeds to gather whatever information is known about the phenomena in question. This information may come from any of several sources: (a) published journals and books; (b) unpublished sources such as master's theses, doctoral dissertations, convention papers, and unpublished manuscripts; (c) personal communication with coworkers in the area; and (d) experience with one's own previous research.

Published Sources. Journals that publish the results of child development research on a wide variety of topics and ages include *Child Development, Developmental Psychology, Monographs of the Society for Research in Child Development, British Journal of Developmental Psychology, International Journal of Behavioral Development, Journal of Experimental Child Psychology, Journal of Genetic Psychology, Genetic Psychology Monographs, Human Development,* and *Merrill-Palmer Quarterly.* More specialized journals focus on narrower ranges of topics or particular periods of development. These include *Infancy, Infant Behavior and Development, Journal of Child Language, Journal of Family Psychology, Early Education and Development, Developmental Neuropsychology, Journal of Applied Developmental Psychology, Cognitive Development, Journal of Cognition and Development, Journal of Clinical Child Psychology, Development and Psychopathology, Journal of Research on Adolescence,* and *Social Cognition.* In addition, the Society for Research in Child Development publishes a valuable reference work entitled *Child Development Abstracts and Bibliography,* which provides subtopical indexes of newly published books and articles in child psychology. See THREE D for a description of information retrieval systems.

Unpublished Material. Information relevant to the researcher's question may also reside in unpublished sources such as dissertations, convention papers, and unpublished manuscripts. Dissertations are usually abstracted and indexed in a reference manual entitled the *Dissertation Index* and are often available on microfilm or through interlibrary loan. Convention papers are, of course, listed in convention programs (sometimes with abstracts), and, along with unpublished manuscripts, they are often indexed in the reference lists of published articles. Unpublished work can usually be obtained by writing directly to the author.

Personal Communication. As a rule, the researcher working in a given area is not the only worker in that area. Often the researcher has a number of colleagues whose interests center around the same general class of problems. They may maintain contact with one another through correspondence, mutual attendance at symposia, or through acting as occasional consultants to one another's research. This leads to an informal exchange of ideas, which is one of the most important factors in the progress of the field. Such personal communications with often provide the researcher with information useful in articulating a question.

Prior Experience. Except in instances where the researcher turns attention to a new area of investigation, an important source of information relevant to the research question will typically be one's own past research. Data from previous investigators may bear directly on some aspect of the problem at hand. Or, at least, the researcher will have a fund of experience in observing and thinking about children in situations somewhat similar to that with which the present question is involved. This experience often plays a major role in helping the researcher to formulate the specific new hypotheses and design the particular new investigations.

Hypotheses

When all of the already accumulated data that bear on the research question have been gathered and examined, they are employed in formulating hypotheses about the conditions under which the phenomena of interest will appear. For example, a researcher might notice that whenever a 5-month-old baby catches sight of the mother's face, the baby smiles. This could lead to the following hypothesis: *If* a baby sees a face, *then* the baby smiles. Such a hypothesis, however, leaves a great deal to be desired. Anyone who hears this hypothesis might almost immediately be inclined to ask the following: What do you mean by a *baby*? Is a 3-year-old a baby? What sort of face do you mean? Does it have to be a real face? Will a photo do? Can it be anyone's face? Will the child smile at a stranger's face, or must the face be someone with whom the child is familiar, or must it be the child's mother? What do you mean by a smile? and so on. These questions must be answered, and the hypothesis must be clarified and made much more specific before it will be possible to design a study to test it. Often, as we will see, the way to narrow down the hypothesis is to embed many of these questions into the design of the investigation that the hypothesis suggests.

Design and Conduct of Psychological Research

Psychologists assume that all psychological phenomena, like other types of natural phenomena, depend in some way on the conditions that accompany them. Psychological research is, essentially, a method of searching for *relationships* that exist between the occurrence of *psychological events* and some critical subset of *conditions accompanying those events*.

1. Psychological Events

Anyone who has ever spent time observing a child is usually certain of at least one thing: As long as the child is awake, activity never ceases and it never ceases to change. One minute a child may be sitting at a table, lifting a spoonful of cereal to eat, and the next minute the milk has spilled and the child is down on the floor trying to feed the cereal to the dog. While these actions may seem to be discrete, an observant researcher would note that while lifting the spoon with one hand, the child is reaching for the milk glass with the other hand, eyeing the dog, and moving one foot toward the floor.

The problem that faces the researcher interested in exploring this behavior is that of defining a psychological event for investigation. Psychological events are both complex and continuous. It is often difficult to isolate and describe *an* occurrence of *a* psychological event so that it can be investigated and the results of the investigation can be properly communicated. To help assure adequate definition of a psychological event, psychologists subscribe to a number of general guidelines.

External versus Internal Events. Roughly speaking, psychological events fall into two broad categories: external and internal. External events are public. They can, at least in principle, be described by more than one person. An infant shaking a rattle or visually scanning a design, a toddler crying at the approach of a stranger, a preschooler grabbing a toy from another child, an 8-year-old running on the playground, or an adolescent calling a friend on the telephone are all examples of external events. Internal events, on the other hand, are private. Some, such as visual images, sensations of pain or hunger, and verbal thoughts, can be observed only by the experiencing person. Others, such as memory storage or retrieval processes, the operation of syntactic, semantic, or phonological systems in the production of meaningful speech, or processes involved in the coordination of goal-directed movement are unavailable even to the observation of the individual in whom they are taking place.

Because external events are open, at least in principle, to public inspection, one might think that their observation would be relatively straightforward. In practice, however, the *scientific* observation of external psychological events takes great skill and involves either the careful choice of naturalistic or design of experimental situations to maximize the opportunity to observe the events in question and relate them to other variables. These issues will be addressed shortly. In addition, in the observation of external events, researchers concern themselves with two important principles: precision and reliability. A *precise* observation is one that clearly distinguishes the event in question from other events of the same general type. Thus, for example, "Johnny is being aggressive" is imprecise relative to "Johnny hit Tommy on the head with the red fire engine." *Reliable* observations require that different people observing the same event agree among themselves as to its occurrence and description. External events that cannot be reliably described, cannot become the subject of scientific research. The movements of unidentified flying objects and certain phenomena in extrasensory perception are examples of events that have not generally been given the status of scientific events because reports lack sufficient reliability.

By its nature, the occurrence of internal events is not something subject to interpersonal agreement. In order to become subject matter for research, internal events must be indirectly made available to investigation. In the case of internal events open to the observation of the experiencing person, this is done through verbal report. In the case of internal events inaccessible to anyone's observation, it is done through inference from that which is observable.

Verbal report is the experiencing person's verbal description of an internal event such as a visual image or verbal thought. Verbal report can take many forms and like descriptions of external events can be more or less precise (e.g., "I am visualizing an apple" vs. "I am visualizing a small red apple sitting in a fruit dish surrounded by pears"). Because observers vary widely in their ability and motivation to observe their own internal events, verbal reports cannot be taken as definitive evidence of the occurrence of the events they represent. This is especially true with young children, who are often unable to describe even the simplest and most obvious of their own internal events (e.g., "What are you thinking about?" "What do you think will happen?"). Used with caution, however, verbal report, especially with older children, can serve as a helpful index of the occurrence and sometimes even of the nature of internal events.

Inference from observables is employed when the researcher wishes to study internal processes that are unavailable to observation by anyone, even by the experiencing person. This is often the case in the study of cognitive development, when processes of knowing constitute the subject matter for investigation. Indeed, studies of the development of what children know about objects, about other people (including other people's thought processes), and about themselves constitute one of the most important areas of developmental research. To study such processes, researchers typically present the child with a variety of different but related tasks and observe the child's pattern of activity (sometimes including verbal report) in response to the tasks. A set of rules that might describe the "knowledge" of someone who exhibits one rather than some other pattern of activity across the respective tasks is then constructed. The inference is then made that the workings of the cognitive system of the child who adopts such a response pattern conforms to these rules. Further research is then typically carried out to assess predictions, based on this inference, about the child's activity in other, related situations.

Representation of the Psychological Event. Researchers must be able to represent the occurrence of a psychological event by some means that will be relatively permanent. This record, referred to as *data*, may be close to the original event (such as audio or video recordings) or relatively far removed from it (such as computerized storage of numbers read from a time clock). Whatever its relationship to the actual event, however, data must at least represent the occurrence of the event; usually it will represent one or another characteristic of the event as well.

A characteristic of an event chosen for representation is called a *property* of the event. Sets of properties that are mutually exclusive and usually, though not always, related in some fashion are referred to as *variables*. When a child is given a bag of red, blue, and green marbles and told to choose the marbles liked best, the color choice *blue* is one possible property of the event class *color choice*. The three properties *red*, *blue*, and *green* make up a variable, and the name of each of three properties is referred to as a *value* on that variable.

2. Accompanying Conditions

The activity of a child does not occur in a vacuum. On the contrary, it is integral part of a complex set of social and physical events all occurring simultaneously. While our young friend was lifting the cereal spoon, the dog was entering the room, wagging its tail and whining. The cereal was going "crack, snapple, and pop." The child's mother was leaving the room for a moment to put away a magazine she had finished reading; and the second hand was moving swiftly around the clock face. The list of events accompanying the psychological events with which the researcher is interested is, of course, infinite. Researchers must consequently proceed on the assumption that only a very small subset of these events is really critical for the occurrence of the psychological event of interest. It is the scientist's task to determine which of these accompanying conditions are critical by searching for the relationships that might exist between the presence of such conditions and the occurrence of the psychological event.

Experimental Design

Because actual psychological events are fleeting, the researcher must seek relationships between variables (variables representing the psychological event and variables representing accompanying conditions). If such relationships are found in the data, corresponding relationships between real behavioral events and accompanying conditions may possibly be inferred. The validity of such inference, however, depends entirely on how the data were obtained, how they relate to the properties of the event, how they were manipulated in the process of searching for relationships, and, of course, the particular inference that the researcher attempts to draw. Roughly grouped together, these various factors may be referred to as characteristics of *experimental* design.

Classification and Measurement. The process by which the psychologist converts the occurrence of psychological events into data is called *classification*. The simplest classification scheme is a rule assigning observations to categories in such a way that observations that fall into the same category are considered equivalent, and observations that fall into different categories are considered nonequivalent. This type of simple classification is termed *nominal classification*. It generates a type of scale of values of variables that is called a *qualitative* (or *nominal*) *scale*, because the values on the scale differ among themselves on the basis of their quality (i.e., they are different in kind). The color-choice situation referred to above, in which the child's choice of a marble was represented by assigning it to either the *red*, *blue*, or *green* name categories is an example of a situation generating a nominal scale.

When the classification of events involves the assignment of *numbers* to properties, classification is referred to as *measurement*, and the scales that result are referred to as *quantitative scales*, since the numbers reflect the quantity of the property possessed by the event. Two such measurement scales generally in use in psychology are the ordinal scale and the interval scale.

An *ordinal* scale is generated when the psychologist assigns numbers to properties of events so that only the relative rank-order of the magnitudes of the observed properties is preserved. For example, ordinal data may indicate that boys prefer stereotypically masculine toys most, neutral toys second, and stereotypically feminine toys least.

The fact that ordinal data preserve only the rank-order of magnitudes constrains the inferences made from relationships in these data to relationships in reality. In the example given, these ordinal data do not permit the psychologist to say *how much* boys prefer stereotypically masculine toys to neutral or stereotypically feminine toys.

An *interval* scale is generated by a measurement procedure that preserves rank-order and in which numerically equal differences between ranks represent equal quantities on the measured dimension. Units are equal throughout the length of the scale. The difference in ball bounces between Sara, who bounced 10, and Keith who bounced 15, is equal to the difference between Steve (25) and Ann (30). A second example is a negative one—an example where the measurement scale is *not* truly an interval one. In most intelligence tests, the difference between an IQ of 100 and 105 (an interval of 5) is not equal to the difference between 140 and 145, nor is a child with 120 IQ twice as bright as a child with 60 IQ (since there is no true 0 to the scale).

A *ratio* scale has the characteristics of increasing order of magnitude and equal intervals, as above, but also has a meaningful zero point. This can be difficult to achieve, although the fractionation method—"Make this light one-half as bright as this one," "Make this circle one-third the size of this one," and so on—has been used in attempts to obtain ratio scales in psychology.

Conditions of Measurement. The characteristics of the situation that the researcher chooses as the context for observing and classifying psychological events are referred to as the *conditions* of the investigation. Two major types of conditions are naturalistic and experimental. The differences between them have important implications for the inferences about relationships that can be drawn from the measurements that are made. It may be helpful first to clarify what is meant by a relationship.

A *relationship* may be said to exist between two variables when knowledge of the measurement of an event on one variable allows the psychologist to predict the measurement of the event on a second variable with greater accuracy than is possible without such knowledge. Some relationships are of the nature of *what?* (what is related to what?), and some deal with *how?* (how is *A* related to *B*?). The *what* study is typically called *factorial*; the *how* study is typically called *functional*. If one asks, "Is noise related to psychomotor performance?" and tests children on a psychomotor task with or without noise present, that is a factorial design. If, however, one manipulates the decibel (db.) level of the noise over, say, 5 values between 60 db. and 90 db., that is a functional design.

Naturalistic Observation. Observing activity in a natural setting, without intervening in or manipulating the antecedents of the activity, is called *naturalistic observation*. Naturalistic studies have the advantage of ecological validity (generalizability to other real-life settings) and may be the only ethical method to obtain information (e.g., in studies of children's reaction to death, anxiety, or pain).

One important form of naturalistic investigation is the *correlational* study. Studies that investigate the relation between two variables neither of which is manipulated by the researcher are correlational. It has been a familiar maxim that correlation does not imply causation. If *A* and *B* are related, we don't know from a conventional correlation design if *A* leads to *B*, *B* leads to *A*, or both were affected by a third unstated variable. No matter how high the correlation between *A* and *B*, we were unable to draw causal interpretations.

There were beginning cautious attempts in the 1970s to draw causal suggestions from correlations taken at different times (e.g., Clarke-Stewart, 1973). This was superseded by newer statistical techniques called latent variable path analysis (LVPA), used increasingly by clinical researchers (Kline, 1991).This helped answer questions like: If a correlation is found, what is the direction of this effect? What other variables mediate the relationship? What is the pattern of indirect and direct effects? More frequently referred to now as structural equation modeling, these complex techniques provide a way of investigating hypothesized causal relationships via computer programs like LISREL (Hayduk, 1987; Morris, Bergan, & Fulginiti, 1991).

Comments and critiques abound on these techniques (e.g., Bentler, 1987; Freedman, 1987), and discussions about causation continue (White, 1990), but causal modeling remains important, particularly in family research (Godwin, 1988).

Experimental Investigations. Certain changes may be deliberately introduced into a variable while a second variable is observed in search of concomitant change. The variable deliberately manipulated by the researcher is the *independent variable*. The variable left free to change and observed for the effects of manipulating the independent variable is the *dependent variable*. The values of the independent variable may be referred to as the *experimental conditions*. The variation observed in the dependent variable is of three types:

primary variance—systematic variation that occurs as a result of manipulating the independent variable;

secondary variance—systematic variation resulting from extraneous factors (ones the experimenter is not primarily interested in, just then); and

error variance—random variation resulting from extraneous factors.

The basic nature of experimental research is to control variance so as to maximize the primary variance, control the secondary variance, and minimize the error variance.

Analyzing the Data. The procedures most often employed for analysis and interpretation of data are statistical. The importance of statistics as a tool for the research psychologist cannot be overemphasized.

While we mainly use in this manual measures of central tendency, measures of variability, *chi* squares, correlations, and analysis of variance, there are many other statistical techniques used in our professional journals. Keep your statistics textbook handy!

Laws and Theories

When an hypothesis has been repeatedly investigated and confirmed, it attains the status of a law. Because hypotheses are never completely and perfectly confirmed, laws, too, are never absolutely certain: They are probabilistic, and they are hypotheses about which researchers have a high degree of confidence.

Theories. Laws, like "if *A* then *B*," are essentially descriptions of relationships between events. They represent things that science and the scientist know. In order to convert such knowledge to the level of understanding, laws must be fit into more comprehensive organized systems of relationships. This is the process of scientific explanation, and it involves the construction of theories. A theory is a set of interrelated statements that include definitions of the basic theoretical concepts, descriptions of the interconnections among such concepts, and statements about the relation of these concepts to the class of actual events they are supposed to explain. A major function of theory is to integrate existing facts and to organize these facts in such a way as to give them meaning. Another major function of theory is to provide the basis for testable ideas, that is, to provide the source for deductions that are then capable of being empirically confirmed or rejected.

There are several criteria that may be applied in evaluating the worth of a theory: internal consistency, heuristic value, generality, parsimony.

1. A theory must be *internally consistent*. It must interrelate statements concerning events and relationships in a way that conforms to the principles of logic. If the theory fails to meet this criterion, it will also be unable to meet the second criterion.

2. A theory must have some *heuristic value*. It must be capable of generating further logically consistent statements concerning events and relationships among events that have not yet been observed. To the extent that it succeeds at this, it provides the scientist with research questions. The answers to these research questions then reflect back upon theory and lead to further confirmation or alteration or rejection.

3. Given the two previous criteria, the more *general* the theory, the better. Generality refers to the breadth of the set of event classes that the theory incorporates into its explanatory structure. The more phenomena that theory is capable of interrelating, the better the theory.

4. *Parsimony* refers to the economy of initial assumptions and propositions that a theory requires to complete the interrelation among concepts that it sets out to achieve.

The scientist strives for the smallest number of principles and the largest generality.

SECTION 2
DEVELOPMENTAL RESEARCH[1]

Definitions: The Concept of Development

Performing experiments with children rather than pigeons, rats, or college students may earn you the label of experimental child psychologist, but not necessarily of developmental psychologist. What then is meant by development and what does the developmental psychologist do?

Development implies change. Reese and Lipsitt (1970) carefully noted that there are two kinds of change: the unfolding or development of behavior within an individual organism as he or she or it ages, and the evolutionary development of behavioral capacities of a species. Those interested in the former are called *developmental psychologists*; those interested in the latter are called *comparative psychologists*.

A brief, but limited, traditional statement of the developmental viewpoint is that behaviors or responses are a function of factors that change with age:

$$R = f(A)$$

with the proviso that the responses can be extremely varied in kind, and that age includes calendar age, physiological age, mental age, perceived age (self-concept of age). The study of development includes (a) the search for regular relationships between behavior and age, and very importantly (b) the analysis of such relationships to provide precise and effective ways of understanding and predicting behavior. Theories of development are systems of proposals about the processes that lie behind changes or lack of changes in behavior with age.

Given this concept of development and the task of the developmental psychologist, it should be no surprise that the core issues of development (and ones that characterize differences in theories) revolve about (a) the activity or passivity of the child's role in development, (b) heredity/environment (nature/nurture), (c) continuitydiscontinuity (are behavior changes quantitative additions or qualitative emergences?).

Viewpoints

Brief surveys of the history of child psychology usually appear in the first chapter of most textbooks for child psychology courses, and more comprehensive recent coverage is available from Kimble, et al. (1995, 1996); Koch and Leary (1992); Parke, Ornstein, Riesser, and Zahn-Waxler (1994); and Smuts and Hagen (1985).

The child development field grew out of *relevance*—out of external pressures in the nineteenth and early 20th century to better the health, rearing, education, legal, and occupational treatment of children. Joined by scientists from various disciplines, including the young psychology departments (but also medicine, dentistry, anthropology), the child development field experienced a burgeoning of activity between the two World Wars, in two directions: clinical and research. The emphasis of the early researchers was normative (descriptive: what is the average, modal behavior at certain ages in specified populations?) and somewhat atheoretical (notable exceptions were Piaget and Freudians). After World War II, the emphasis shifted from naturalistic methods toward experimental research (although descriptive studies of infancy abound); and theoretical advances in cognition, learning, perception, and linguistics provided impetus for theory-based investigations that aim at explanations of behavior changes. Core issues mentioned earlier remain, and theoretical viewpoints still diverge.

Consider some current theories, like behaviorist learning theory, Piaget's cognitive theory, psychoanalytic dynamic theories (Freud or Erikson). We can ask where they stand on some basic philosophic positions: (a) To what extent do they stress innate characteristics (*pre-formed* characteristics present at birth)? Think about learning theories' basic drives, Piaget's notions of adaptation and organization, and Freud's id and libidinal energy. (b) To what extent do they believe that development is an ordered *sequence of stages* depending on progress

---

[1] Sections 2 and 3 were written by Lorraine Nadelman.

11

through earlier stages (Piaget and Freud)? (c) To what extent do they rely on *empiricist* position—that development is controlled by experiences with the environment? All theories, to differing extents, include learning.

The social development of Heather, a young friend of Cooper, provides a delightful introductory example for our next point.

> When she was a young infant she would smile at almost anyone, if she were happy. Smiling was a global response which was not used selectively for particular people or situations. At nine or ten months she began to differentiate among people, smiling at those she knew well and being shy toward others. As she grew older, her behavior became even more differentiated. Some people were given smiles from four or five feet away, some received them from a closer distance and were spoken to, and some of us were lucky enough to receive hugs. Heather also took the setting into account in deciding which response was appropriate. In her own home, she seemed more open and responsive than in strange territory. Thus the components from differentiation among people, differentiation in types of social responses, and differentiation of social settings were integrated into a complex system of social responding. (Cooper, 1977, p. 2)

The differentiation and integration processes involved in Heather's development are accounted for differently by different theories with respect to the core issues mentioned earlier: First, with regard to the child's role in these processes, the Piagetian theory sees the child as more *active* than do the other two. Werner's (1957) and Schneirla's (1957) organismic theories are also good examples of older theories that saw the child as a relatively active responder to the environment. To be fair to learning theories, the information processing approach also appears to be according the child a more active role with the recent stress on "strategies" of remembering, for example. Second, although all theories adopt an interactionist position to some extent and recognize that *heredity and environment* necessarily act together, there is more emphasis on *interaction* in Piaget, Freud, Erikson, Werner, or Schneirla than in most learning theories, which stress the environmental determinants of behavior. An interactionist stresses the interdependence and dynamic relationship between maturation (nature, heredity) and experience (environment, stimulation). The effects of experience are limited by the organism's maturation level. The maturation level, in turn, is affected by the organism's experiences. Third, the *continuity-discontinuity* issue strongly divides theories. Stage theories like Piaget's or Freud's see development as including complex changes in organization that depend on but are qualitatively different from (and not reducible to) earlier stages. Lerner (1976) attempted to unmuddy the waters by phrasing the issue in terms of whether the *laws* involved in behavioral development remain the same (continuity) or change (discontinuity). A Skinnerian learning theorist would presumably argue for continuity (and universality) of the laws of learning. Stage theorists generally maintain that *both* continuities and discontinuities are important in development.

There are other ways to group theories than the ones we have used. Lerner (1976), who shares my organismic, interactionist views, summarizes four types of theories or *approaches* to the conceptualization of psychological development: the learning approach (e.g., Skinner, Bijou, Baer, Gewirtz); stage theory (e.g., Piaget, Kohlberg, Freud); the differential approach (Kagan and Moss), and the ipsative approach (Thomas, Chess, Birch, Hertzig, Korn). Although various theories are presented in context later in our book[2], and are consequently not described in detail in this chapter, the differential and ipsative approaches are characterized briefly now.

The *differential approach* does not tie its practitioners to a particular theory. The interest lies in how people sort into subgroups over the course of development and how selected status (e.g., age, sex. race) and behavioral (e.g., extroversion–introversion, aggression–passivity) attributes interrelate. A differential, longitudinal investigation like the Kagan and Moss study (1962) can turn up *sleeper effects*—a behavior or event measured early in a child's life may not show its effects until much later. One provocative (and debatable) find-

---

[2] There are a number of relatively contained theories in this manual with which you will be working. These, however, can be considered as less broad or general than the viewpoints or approaches or paradigms from which they emerged. The organismic-developmental viewpoint is exemplified by Piagetian theory, (see the section entitled Cognitive Development), with its emphasis on qualitative changes, inferred psychological structures, and the child as an active contributor to development. An application of this point of view to sex identity appears in the introduction to Experiments 9 and 10, in the description of Kohlberg's theory. The psychodynamic viewpoint (e.g., Freud, Erikson), is very lightly touched, but can be related to the infant observations in Chapter 2-B. The observations in natural habitats suggested in Chapters 2-B and C, and the emphasis on attachment and reciprocal behaviors of mother and child stem from an ethological approach. The reaction-time study (3: E-1) fits a stimulus-response paradigm, as well as the more modern information-processing theories. Social learning theories abound in the section entitled The Socialized Child.

ing was that maternal protection of girls during their first three years was related to withdrawal from stress as adults.

The *ipsative approach* emphasized the importance of intraindividual laws—the need for understanding the contributions that an organism's individuality makes towards its own development. The so-called "same" environment is not the same environment for any two children. One of my favorite older studies, the New York Longitudinal Study (Thomas et al., 1963; Thomas, Chess, & Birch, 1968) derived measures of temperament (reaction patterns) from observations of the infant and interviews of the parents and found marked individual differences in temperament, some of which were stable over several years, and were not systematically related to the parents' personality and child rearing methods. There are both theoretical and practical implications in being able to characterize youngsters as "easy," "difficult," or "slow-to-warm-up."

Developmental Research Today

Celia Fisher analyzed the topics of the studies published in *Child Development* and found that the decade of the 1930s was marked by studies of physical and physiological development, the 1950s by social-emotional development, the 1970s by cognitive development, and the 1980s by both cognitive and social-emotional development. Developmental research is now in an exciting period of maturation and expansion.

Old issues still survive, in sophisticated versions. The nature/nurture question is not asked in terms of which is more important in the development of a specific behavior, but instead—how do nature (genes, biology, constitution) and nurture (environment, family, culture) dynamically interact (Brauth, Hall, & Dooling, 1991; Gazzaniga, 1992; Plomin, 1994; Plomin & McLearn, 1993; Rowe, 1993; Wachs & Plomin, 1991)?

Similarly, the continuity/change problem persists and is investigated in various domains by various methods (Bornstein & Krasnegor, 1989; Brauth, Hall, & Dooling, 1991; Caspi & Bem, 1990; Collins & Horn, 1991; Elder, Modell, & Parke, 1993; Funder, et al., 1993; Magnuson, Bergman, Rudinger, & Torestad, 1992; Rutter & Rutter, 1993).

The big change is the attention to context and culture and interdisciplinary research. Developmental science is now a multidisciplinary field, utilizing differing perspectives, methodologies, cultures, and populations. Bronfenbrenner (1979), Hinde (see Bateson, 1991), Vygosky (1978) and others saw early on that behavior is a joint function of psychological and biological attributes of a person and the physical, social, cultural features of the environment. To understand behavior, it now seems necessary to study the process from different perspectives—e.g., ethology, behavioral ecology, neuroscience, developmental psychology, psychiatry. Human development can be considered a social construction, occurring in specific environments, in specific historical times, and in continuous transformation (Elder, Modell, & Parke, 1993; Hwang, Lamb, & Sigel, 1996; Wertsch, del Rio, & Alvarez, 1995). There is spreading acceptance of the belief that psychological functioning is specific to its social context and is dependent on the mastery of culturally defined modes of speaking, thinking, and acting (Forman, Minick, & Stone, 1993).

Within psychology, there is now recognized overlaps *between* domains, for example, cognitive/social–emotional development (Bandura, 1986; Bennett, 1993; Dunn, 1995; Fletcher & Fitness, 1995; Nelson, 1993; Resnick, Higgins, & LeVine, 1993; Wertsch, del Rio, & Alvarez, 1995); developmental/clinical, now called developmental psychopathology (Sameroff, 1993, 1995; *Journal of Development and Psychopathology*); personality/social (Cantor & Kihlstrom. 1987).

Psychologists now interact with researchers in other disciplines, like biology (Bates & Wachs, 1994, Gazzaniga, 1992; Rowe, 1993; Worthman, 1995), neuroscience, pediatrics, cardiology, physical medicine, surgery.

The bibliography at the end of this chapter may seem overwhelmingly long, but it is only a sample of the burgeoning literature. The interest in the profound effects of the cultural, social, and contextual settings on human development and functioning appear throughout the list, from Bornstein to Wozniak and Fischer.

One can safely predict that developmental research will continue an interest in context effects, ethnic minorities (Greenfield & Cocking, 1994), stressors (Sameroff, 1993), poverty (McLoyd & Flanagan, 1990), violence, and social class. Policy-relevant research, dealing with interventions and transitions, is and will be increasingly prominent. Note the new journal, *Current Directions in Psychological Science*.

A brief quote from Sameroff (1993) can end this section appropriately: "An understanding of the developmental process requires an appreciation of the transactions between and among individuals, their biological inner workings, and their social outer workings. Continuities and discontinuities are a function of three systems, the genotype, the phenotype, and the environtype" (p. 11).

Methodological Strategies and Problems

The conventional data collection strategies used by developmental researchers (and others) involve (a) cross-sectional designs, (b) longitudinal designs, and less frequently (c) time-lag designs. An investigator doing all her testing in 1980, and working with a group of newborns, 20-, 40-, 60-, 80-year-olds is doing a cross-sectional study. If she takes only those children born in the year 2000 and follows them (with the aid of younger colleagues) until they are 80, testing them at 20-year intervals, she is doing longitudinal research. Concerned with the effect of being born at different times in history, she may even limit herself to one age group, i.e., 80-year-olds, and test a group of 80-year-olds in 1960, another group of 80-year-olds in 1980, et cetera; in other words, a time-lag experiment. There are obvious advantages and disadvantages to each design, and most unfortunately the data resulting from each design do not always seem to agree.

Concerned with worrisome discrepancies, culture-centered and historically parochial research (Reigel, 1972), and lack of control of error sources like selective sampling and survival dropout, repeated-testing effects, and generation differences, a number of developmental psychologists have pressed for more complex research designs that may help to demonstrate and/or disentangle the effects of age, cohort (generation, when born), and time of testing (Nesselroade & Baltes, 1974; Schaie, 1965). The sequential strategies suggested are successions of either cross-sectional or longitudinal studies. The experimenter who did the cross-sectional study in 1980, for example, would repeat her study in the year 2000, with new groups of newborns, 20-, 40-, 60-, 80-yearolds, thereby performing a cross-sectional sequential study. Nadelman (1970, 1974) studied sex identity in English and American children in the mid-1960s. Given the passage of three decades, the women's movement, TV, family changes, labor force adjustments, et cetera, it would be foolish to assume the same findings still stand, without retesting for the effects of historical change. A provocative example of an early two year, sequential-longitudinal study is Nesselroade and Baltes' investigation (1974), in which the relationship between ontogenetic (individual) and sociocultural (historical) change *differed* for personality versus ability development of adolescents over the 1970–1972 period. Gatz and Karel (1993) used cross-sectional, longitudinal, and sequential strategies to look at individual change in perceived control over 20 years.

The complexity, the demands on the experimenter's time and money, the involved mathematical issues, the problems of substantive interpretation all combine to slow down wholesale acceptance of these sequential designs, but they raise issues that require serious thought by the development researcher.

Even adopting sequential designs would not eliminate all *methodological problems*. McCandless (1967) described several that still require caution and handling:

1. *Contamination.* One of my colleagues hires bright housewives to collect her data, training them well, but telling them nothing about her research program nor hypotheses, nor more about the measuring instruments than necessary for reliable data collection. She is trying thereby to avoid the contamination that may result when the person with the hypothesis is the person who collects the data (particularly if the data are rather subjective). This, of course, does not prevent the data-collector nor the subjects from forming their own self-generated hypotheses, which are seldom formally assessed!

   In most of the studies you will perform in this course, your last words to the children, in addition to fervent thank you's, are pleas not to tell their classmates for a specified while what they did or saw (a subject-to-subject contamination). In other words, you are trying to ensure that the next child's responses are being influenced by the variables under investigation rather than by a classmate's information (extraneous variables).

   Many researchers try to control or balance the race and sex of the data-collector in order not to find their data contaminated by those experimenter effects. Rosenthal and his colleagues have made us wary of the contamination possibilities of experimenter effects, interpersonal expectations, and other artifacts (Rosenthal, 1966; Rosenthal & Rosnow, 1969).

2. *Reconstruction through retrospection.* All this imposing phrase means is that the investigator asked the respondents to think back and relate specific information about themselves or their children from that far-back period. What with forgetting, lack of frankness, and desire to present oneself as a competent or "with-it" parent, the data gathered in this fashion are questionable. Pinning the respondent to "this week," or "yesterday" and asking for concrete detailed descriptions of the act works a bit better.

3. *Faulty logic.* Suppose one studies colicky babies and their mothers and finds the mothers are tense, anxious, and low in esteem. If the conclusion is drawn that the babies' colic are due to the mothers, that may be a fallacious causal inference. Perhaps the mothers' tenseness and so on are due to the babies' colic! Or perhaps both the babies' colic and the mothers' state are due to a third variable. All three conclusions show the need for further clarifying studies. Good reasoning is needed for good research.

4. *Poor definition of concepts.* Translating concepts (abstractions) into observable events can be very difficult. How, for example, can aggression be defined so that it can be measured reliably and validly? If observers are rating aggression in preschool children, how can aggression be operationally defined so that sex stereotypes on the part of the observers don't interfere with their ratings of aggression in boys and girls? Aggression measured by self-report, aggression measured by projective tests, and aggression measured by observation may result in noncomparable findings. Readers need to know exactly what the experimenter intends to include and exclude in his or her definition of concepts.
I once boasted of an exceptionally "easy and fast delivery" until I discovered that our gynecologist considered a very short delivery "hard" from the infant's point of view.

5. *Sampling problems.* These are an inescapable fact of life for the psychologist. With the ethics rules, research subjects are, in effect, volunteers, and because volunteers differ in unspecified ways from nonvolunteers, our samples are biased to some extent. In a nonbiased random sample, each member of the population under consideration has an equal chance of being chosen for the sample. Even with an inescapably biased sample, the experimenter can be vary cautious and assign the subjects truly randomly to the experimental conditions.

6. *Unsound generalization.* A good background in comparative psychology made me wary, very early, of a psychology based on rats, pigeons, and introductory psychology students. A finding based on one population should not, without further investigation, be applied to another population. Even within the same population, behavior may be situation specific, and findings should not be generalized from one set of circumstances to another without confirmation. The child who tests as distraction-prone in a school setting may focus his attention for an uninterrupted six hours fixing his bicycle at home. A third kind of unsound generalization according to McCandless (1967) is "writing or speaking as though findings were more significant or clear-cut than they are" (p. 73). Some of the class differences in child-rearing practices, while statistically significant, are based on very small differences in mean scale values, and should be quoted with far more caution than they generally are. With regard to the sex identity study mentioned earlier, Nadelman (1974) found several statistically significant findings relating to knowledge of masculine and feminine items which—while very gratifying on theoretical grounds—seemed to her to require restraint in generalizing their significance, since out of 40 items, the mean differences involved only one (or part of one) item.

Before looking at some of the additional problems posed by using children as subjects, let us consider briefly some research designs used by psychologists. As indicated earlier, psychologists look for relationships between variables in an attempt to answer such questions as: Is *A* related to *B*? How is *A* related to *B*? To what degree is *A* related to *B*? They are primarily interested in the systematic variation in behavior which results from their experimental manipulation of the independent variable, and they need to control any other variation. *Different research designs* vary in terms of which types of variables are controlled and how well they are controlled:

In *one-group* experimental designs, subjects act as their own controls. They undergo all the conditions of the experiment. For example, in an investigation of the effect of several different noise levels on psychomotor performance, each child performs the psychomotor task under each of the noise levels. But what then of the possible practice and/or fatigue effects? What about he possible effects of having sound level X preceding sound level Y? If subjects are each to be observed under two or more treatment conditions, a rotation method is frequently employed. That is, the order of the conditions is counterbalanced, either by measuring conditions *A, B, B, A* in that order for each child, or by presenting half the group with the AB sequence and the other half *BA*.

In *two-group* designs, the experimental group receives some level of the independent variable and the control group receives none. Subjects may be randomly assigned to the experimental or control group, or the two groups may be matched on some characteristic (like IQ or socioeconomic status) which might influence the results but which is not the experimenter's present concern. This design characteristic (random assignment vs. matching) affects the statistics that may be used.

In the before-after two-group design, the random assignment of subjects to the experimental and control groups is followed by a pretest to measure the initial performance level. If the random assignment was effective, the two groups start out equivalent. Then any difference between them after the experimental group has been "treated" can be attributed to the treatment. If the control and experimental groups are not equivalent before beginning the experimental treatment, this needs to be taken into account when statistically handling the after data.

Multiple treatment designs involve more than two levels of an independent variable, or more than one independent variable, or both. Designs containing all possible combinations of the levels of two or more independent variables are called *factorial designs*. They are favored by many psychologists because they permit simultaneous collection of data from each subject about the effects of several variables, and because they make it possible to discover whether the effects of one variable depend upon (interact with) the effects of the other variable.

Watch for the use of each of the above designs in the experiments in this manual.

A sophisticated example of a multiple treatment design is the Solomon four group design. This is a factorial design which combines random assignment of groups, treatment versus no treatment conditions, and pretesting versus no pretesting (which itself is a variable that may have an effect):

Pretest	Experimental Group	Control Group
Yes	I	III
No	II	IV

Such a design enables the researcher to determine the possible effects of pretesting, the effects of the independent variable, and the effects of an interaction of the pretest with the independent variable (Solomon & Lessac, 1968). This kind of design and control is useful in developmental research which involves pretesting and is aimed at evaluating the effect of deprivation or compensatory treatment.

One of the problems frequently overlooked in designs that deal with only two values of an independent variable is the often unstated assumption of a linear progression between two points. What, however, if the relation is curvilinear, instead of linear? For example, suppose you give children a very easy task, and a very hard task, and measure their achievement motivation, and find no difference. Can you then conclude that achievement motivation is not related to task difficulty, or does it occur to you that including a moderately challenging task might change the picture?

SECTION 3
CHILDREN AS SUBJECTS

The problems listed in the preceding section plague research with any subject population, not just children. Children, however, raise additional problems for a researcher, which must be considered in designing, running, and interpreting research.

The lack of docility of young children to verbal procedures is a major problem. With adults, we can structure the test situation via verbal instructions and request verbal answers to verbal stimuli, if we wish. This is more difficult to do with children, and prescribing or limiting the psychological situation for the child requires much ingenuity and sensitivity by the psychologist.

"Please sit here." "I want to look out of the window."
"Don't talk to each other when we start." "But Mary is my best friend."
"Now you do it by yourself like I just did." "Show me again." or "Help me,
  help me" (accompanied by a tug on your shirt sleeve).

Interpreting the child's response is another problem:

"Now you say the words I just said." "Hey, did you see on TV yesterday when..."
"The next thing we'll do..." "I think I'll go now" (interruption followed by exit).
"Choose the picture you like best." "I don't like this game."
"What do you think of that?" Silence.

Is the child's failing to respond in the form requested an indication of cognitive level, or a loss of interest or task orientation, or a run of free association?

Deception

One of the thorniest issues in research with humans, deception becomes a particularly sensitive technique in research with children. Arguments can be made for ceasing to do research that involve any deception. Certainly the kind of deception that heightens anxiety or depresses the child or involves explicit lying would need to be both heavily justified by the value of the research and the clear demonstration of unavailability of other techniques before being considered by a clearance committee, and would rarely be approved. The kind of deception that is more frequently pursued is the failure to tell all in advance. For example, the experimenter is honest about describing specific measures and techniques, but does not indicate until later that differences between boys' and girls' performance is the main focus. Another common example is not indicating whether the subject is in the experimental or control group. These kinds of less than total information are judged for individual projects and often deemed neutral or benign.

Webb, Campbell, Schwartz, and Sechrest (1966) cleverly surveyed methods of obtaining research data without the use of interview or questionnaire. The multiple methods examined involve physical traces (e.g., selective erosion of floor tiles in from of museum exhibits), archives (e.g., actuarial records of births, marriages, deaths; frequencies of suicides, city budgets for welfare; newspapers), and nonparticipant observation (e.g., of seating patterns, conversation samples). While the measures are unobtrusive and avoid express manipulation of subjects, they do not all meet full disclosure and high moral standards (i.e., eavesdropping procedures), as the authors point out.

Rapport and Techniques

Nothing takes the place of experience in working with children. And even experience is ineffective if your personality is inappropriate for working with children. If you're an unusually impatient person, or a constant put-downer, or not really interested in children (just another publication), or highly insensitive to interpersonal cues, child research may not be your field.

There are specific suggestions that can maximize your rapport with the child and aid in the collection of reliable data. First of all, let the child become familiar with you and the setting. If possible, help around the classroom and let your voice and appearance become familiar. If that's not possible, do some chatting and strolling on the way to the research room. Did the school just have a Halloween parades? "What was your costume?" Is it close to the winter recess? "Are you going away for Christmas (recess)?" "Can you ice-skate?" Is it early fall? Ask about vacation happenings. Offer information about yourself. Once in the testing room, give the child an opportunity to see the view (if any), look at your physical setup, and see the apparatus (to the extent that this does not interfere with the study). Notice that I did *not* say "Tell him/her about your study" on the way to the test room. That information needs to be standardized and presented to all children in the same specified manner, as part of your test procedure.

Try to use your normal voice and manner when talking with children. Many of us suffer from an attack of saccharinity when confronted with a young child, and the younger the child the higher and more sugary the voice quality and content. Species-specific-innate considerations aside, this syndrome is perceived negatively by many middle-years elementary school children.

Don't touch! While some preschoolers respond well to pats and hugs and even prefer holding hands walking down unfamiliar corridors, most elementary-schoolers do not want strangers invading their personal space. This caution is especially important in cross-sex pairings of experimenter and child.

There are many nonverbal cues that can affect your data collection as much as your verbal instructions. Nods of the head after each of the child's answers, smiles, enthusiastic "That's good!" after particular responses all can operate on the child's performance. Some consideration must be given to recognizing and coping with these influences, whether there is one experimenter or multiexperimenters.

To pay or not to pay? Thanking a child for acting as a subject, by giving money, is often unacceptable to the community (and beyond the experimenter's budget). Giving candy or food is also disapproved of by many parents. We have, for some years, thanked the children with small school-related items from which they choose: pads, millimeter rulers, colored pencils, small sharpeners, et cetera. It should be recognized, however, that the parent who does not wish to give permission may perceive even these tokens as social pressures and unfair inducements.

Subject Pools, Feedback, and Quid Pro Quo

Obtaining subjects is a major hurdle, and involves a good deal more than settling a research trailer in a busy park and waving M&Ms out the windows to attract children.

Children are frequently obtained through nursery-schools, day-care centers, public and private schools, recreation programs, scout programs, YMCA or YWCA children's classes, Sunday schools connected with religious institutions, summer camps, hospitals, et cetera. Infants are solicited through Lamaze, LaLeche, child study groups, pediatricians' offices, Well Baby clinics, supermarket bulletin boards, newspaper birth announcements.

The first step is obtaining the approval of a human subject research committee. This is a *sine qua non* for federally sponsored research, and for research under most universities' auspices. Someone, other than the involved researcher, needs to determine that the procedures will not be harmful to the subject and that minimum deception is employed, permissions properly obtained, feedback provided, confidentiality preserved, et cetera.

If the research is taking place in a school-setting, even if after school hours, the central school administration or its research committee usually needs to review your study. After that, the principal of the specific school has to approve, and in many cases, so do the teachers whose children will be involved. It is courteous to inform the PTA or PTSA (parent-teacher-student associations) of your plans even if that group may not have the veto power of the foregoing groups and individuals.

The initial contact with the child may be a verbal pitch to whole classrooms of children if principal and teachers permit, followed in any case by written requests to individual families for *written* permission for the children to participate. Telephone soliciting or explaining is an additional, not a substitute, technique. The children and families have to understand that their participation is voluntary and may be terminated whenever they wish. They need to be told in advance as much about the research as will not ruin the study, and provided with feedback after the study. (See Section D.)

Whether the feedback applies to individual or group results needs to be resolved before soliciting subjects or collecting data. In either event, confidentiality of data is a major issue. One can promise not to show Susie's responses to her teacher or principal. Will her parents sign the permission slip if Susie wants her responses kept private even from them? That is where good public relations with your community and care with the initial letter to families and promise of detailed feedback on group performance help. Susie herself is entitled to feedback about her own responses. The child and family need to resolve the feedback issue themselves; this is not an issue with younger children, usually, but can be with older elementary school grades. The experimenter does not lie: Information is not divulged beyond the initially agreed-on recipient.

Feedback can be written or verbal. A copy of the formal report on group data can be filed with the school; abstracts can be sent to individual teachers. A parents' meeting can be held, or written summaries (in layman language) sent to participating families. In older grades, an educational classroom visit is of value.

Quid pro quo, aside from the rewards mentioned earlier, and classroom lectures, may consist of free speeches to various parent or teacher groups, and columns in PTA newsletters. There are many ways of acting as a professional resource, limited only by the researcher's time and personality.

Ethics

Many of the ethical issues in human research have already been mentioned: honesty, full disclosure, volunteer aspect, feedback, confidentiality. Division 7 (Developmental) of the American Psychological Association and the Society for Research in Child Development play an active role in establishing the new guidelines for research with human subjects, particularly children. The ethical principles published by the APA in 1973, 1982, 1992, and 1995 are periodically in revision, and several publications discuss emerging issues (Fisher & Tyron, 1990; Stanley, Seiber, & Melton (1996).

Hetherington and Parke (1993) outlined a children's bill of research rights and protections as follows, using as their sources American Psychological Association ethics rules, and the SRCD Committee on Ethical Conduct in Child Development Research (1990):

1. *The right to be fully informed*: Each child participant has the right to full and truthful information about the purposes of the study and the procedures to be employed.

2. *The right to informed and voluntary consent of participation*: Each child participant has the right either verbally or in written form to agree to participate in a research project. In the case of children who are too young to understand the aims and procedures and to make an informed decision about participation, parental consent should always be secured.

3. *The right to voluntary withdrawal*: Each child participant has the right to withdraw at any time from continued participation in any research project.

4. *The right to full compensation*: Each child participant has the right to be fully compensated for his or her time and effort as a research subject, even if he or she withdraws and does not complete participation in the project.

5. *The right to nonharmful treatment*: Each child participant has the right to expect that he or she will not experience any harmful or damage-producing events during the course of the research procedure.

6. *The right to knowledge of results*: Each child participant has the right to new information concerning the results of the research project. In the case of young children, their parents have the right to be provided this information. Often this information will take the form of the group scores on a task, rather than the individual participant's own score.

7. *The right to confidentiality of their research data*: Each child participant has the right to expect that personal information gathered as part of the research project will remain private and confidential. Nor will any information about individual research participants be available to any other individuals or agencies.

8. *The right to beneficial treatments*: Each child participant has the right to profit from the beneficial treatments provided to other participants in the research project. If experimental treatments are believed to be beneficial (for example, participation in a program to enhance reading or math skills), children in control groups, who do not originally receive this treatment, have the right to alternative beneficial treatments at some later time.

Selected Bibliography

American Psychological Association. (1992). Ethical principles of psychologists and code of conduct. *American Psychologist, 47*, 1597–1611.

American Psychological Association. (2001). *Publication Manual of the American Psychological Association* (5th ed.). Washington, DC: American Psychological Association.

Bandura, A. (1986). *Social foundations of thought and action: A social cognitive theory*. Englewood Cliffs, NJ: Prentice Hall.

Bates, J. E., & Wachs, T. D. (Eds.). (1994). *Temperament: Individual differences at the interface of biology and behavior*. Washington, DC: American Psychological Association.

Bateson, P. (Ed.). (1991). *The development and integration of behavior: Essays in honor of Robert Hinde*. New York: Cambridge University Press.

Bennett, M. (Ed.). (1993). *The development of social cognition: The child as psychologist*. New York: Guilford.

Bentler, P. M. (1987). Structural modeling and the scientific method: Comments on Freedman's critique. *Journal of Educational Research, 12*, 151–157.

Betancourt, H., & Lòpez, S. R. (1993). The study of culture, ethnicity, and race in American psychology. *American Psychologist, 48*, 629–637.

Bigner, J. J. (1994*). Individual and family development: A life-span interdisciplinary approach.* Englewood Cliffs, NJ: Prentice Hall.

Bjorklund, D. F., & Pellegrini, A. D. (2002). *The origins of human nature*: *Evolutionary developmental psychology*. Washington, DC: American Psychological Association.

Bornstein, M. H. (Ed.). (1991). *Cultural approaches to parenting*. Hillsdale, NJ: Lawrence Erlbaum Associates.

Bornstein, M. H., & Krasnegor, N. A. (Eds.). (1989). *Stability and continuity in mental development: Behavioral and biological perspectives*. Hillsdale, NJ: Lawrence Erlbaum Associates.

Bornstein, M. H., & Lamb, M. E. (Eds.). (1999). *Developmental psychology: An advanced textbook* (4th ed.). Mahwah, NJ: Lawrence Erlbaum Associates.

Brauth, S. E., Hall, W. S., & Dooling, R. J. (Eds.). (1991). *Plasticity of development*. Cambridge, MA: MIT Press, Bradford Books.

Breakwell, G. M., Hammond, S., & Fyfe-Schaw, C. (Eds.). (2000). *Research methods in psychology* (2nd Ed.). Thousand Oaks, CA: Sage.

Bronfenbrenner, U. (1979). *The ecology of human development*. Cambridge, MA: Harvard University Press.

Cairns, R. B., & Elder, G. H. (Eds.). (1996). *Developmental science*. New York: Cambridge University Press.

Cantor, N., & Kihlstrom, J. (1987). *Personality and social intelligence*. Englewood Cliffs, NJ: Prentice Hall.

Caspi, A., & Bem, D. J. (1990). Personality continuity and change across the life course. In L. A. Pervin (Ed.), *Handbook of personality: Theory and research* (pp. 549–575). New York: Guilford.

Cole, M. (1996). *Cultural psychology: A once and future discipline*. Cambridge, MA: Harvard University Press.

Collins, L. M., & Sayer, A. G. (Eds.). (2001). *New methods for the analysis of change*. Washington, DC: American Psychological Association.

Cook, T. D., & Campbell, D. T. (1979). *Quasi-experimentation*: *Design and analysis issues for field settings*. Boston: Houghton-Mifflin.

Cooper, H., Dorr, N, & Bettencourt, B. A. (1995). Putting to rest some old notions about social science. *American Psychologist, 50*(2), 111–112.

Cooper, R. G. (1977). *Principles of development*. Westwood, MA: The Paper Book Press.

Dent-Read, C., & Zukow-Goldring, P. (Eds.). (1997). *Evolving explanations of development: Ecological approaches to organism-environment systems*. Washington, DC: American Psychological Association.

Dunn, J. F. (Ed.). (1995). *Connections between emotion and understanding in development*. (A special issue of *Cognition and Emotion*). Mahwah, NJ: Lawrence Erlbaum Associates.

Elder, G. H. Jr., Modell, J., & Parke, R. D. (Eds.). (1993). *Children in time and place: Developmental and historical insights*. New York: Cambridge University Press.

Emde, R. N. (1994). Individuality, context, and the search for meaning. *Child Development, 65*, 719–737.

Fisher, C. B. & Tryon, W. W. (Eds.). (1990). *Ethics in applied developmental psychology: Emerging issues in an emerging field*. Norwood, NJ: Ablex.

Fisher, C. B. (1993). Integrating science and ethics in research with high-risk children and youth. *Social Policy Report, Society for Research in Child Development, VII*(4), 27pp.

Fisher, C. B. (1994). *Reporting and referring child and adolescent research participants*. A special issue of *Ethics & Behavior, 4*(2). Hillsdale, NJ: Lawrence Erlbaum Associates.

Flavell, J. H., Miller, P. H., & Miller, S. (1993). *Cognitive development*. Englewood Cliffs, NJ: Prentice-Hall.

Fletcher, G. (1995). *The scientific credibility of folk psychology*. Mahwah, NJ: Lawrence Erlbaum Associates.

Fletcher, J. O., & Fitness, J. (Eds.). (1995). *Knowledge structures in close relationships: A social psychological approach*. Mahwah, NJ: Lawrence Erlbaum Associates.

Ford, D. H., & Lerner, R. M. (1992). *Developmental systems theory: An integrative approach and the living systems framework*. Thousand Oaks, CA: Sage.

Forman, E. A., Minick, N., & Stone, C. A. (1993). *Contexts for learning: Sociocultural dynamics in children's development*. New York: Oxford University Press.

Freedman, D. A. (1987). As others see us: A case study in path analysis. *Journal of Educational Statistics, 12,* 101–128.

Friedman, S. L., & Haywood, H. C. (Eds.). (1995). *Developmental follow-up: Concepts, domains, and methods.* San Diego, CA: Academic Press.

Friedman, S. L., & Wachs, T. D. (Eds.). (1999). *Measuring environment across the life span: Emerging methods and concepts*. Washington, DC: American Psychological Association.

Funder, D. C., Parke, R. D., Tomlinson-Keasey, C. A., & Widaman, K. (Eds.). (1993). *Studying lives through time: Personality and development*. Washington, DC: American Psychological Association.

Gatz, M., & Karel, M. J. (1993). Individual change in perceived control over 20 years. *International Journal of Behavioral Development, 16*(2), 305–322.

Gazzaniga, M. G. (1992). *Nature's mind: The biological roots of thinking, emotions, sexuality, language and intelligence*. New York: Basic Books.

Godwin, D. D. (1988). Causal modeling in family research. *Journal of Marriage and the Family, 50,* 917–927.

Goodnow, J. J., Miller, P. J., & Kessel, F. (Eds.). (1995). *Cultural practices as contexts for development. New directions in child development, 67*. San Francisco, CA: Jossey-Bass.

Greenfield, P. M., & Cocking, R. R. (Eds.). (1994). *Cross-cultural roots of minority child development*. Hillsdale, NJ: Lawrence Erlbaum Associates.

Halpern, D. F., & Nummendal, S. G. (Eds.). (1995). *Psychologists teach critical thinking*. (A special issue of *Teaching of Psychology*). Mahwah, NJ: Lawrence Erlbaum Associates.

Hartup, W. W. (2000). Developmental science at the millenium. *International Journal of Behavioral Development, 24*(1), 2–4.

Hartup, W. W., & Weinberg, R. A. (Eds.). (2002). *Child psychology in retrospect and prospect: In celebration of the 75th anniversary of the Institute of Child Development*. Mahwah, NJ: Lawrence Erlbaum Associates.

Hayduk, L. A. (1987). *Structural equation modeling with LISREL*. Baltimore: Johns Hopkins University Press.

Hetherington, E. M. (1998). Relevant issues in Developmental Science: Introduction to the special issue. *American Psychologist, 53,* 93–94.

Heatherton, T. F., & Weinberger, J. L. (Eds.). (1994). *Can personality change?* Washington, DC: American Psychological Association.

Hoagwood, K., Jensen, P. S., & Fisher, C. (1996). *Ethical issues in mental health research with children and adolescents*. Mahwah, NJ: Lawrence Erlbaum Associates.

Hock, R. R. (1992). *Forty studies that changed psychology: Explorations into the history of psychological research*. Englewood Cliffs, NJ: Prentice Hall.

Horowitz, F. D. (1987). *Exploring developmental theories: Toward a structural/behavioral model of development*. Hillsdale, NJ: Lawrence Erlbaum Associates.

Hwang, C. P., Lamb, M. E., & Sigel, I. E. (Eds.). (1996). *Images of childhood*. Mahwah, NJ: Lawrence Erlbaum Associates.

Kagitçibasi, C. (1996). *Family and human development across cultures: A view from the other side*. Mahwah, NJ: Lawrence Erlbaum Associates.

Kazdin, A. E. (Ed.). (2000). *Encyclopedia of psychology*. Washington, DC: American Psychological Association.

Kimble, G. A., Boneau, C. A., & Wertheimer, M. (1996). *Portraits of pioneers in psychology*, Vol. II; Vol. III, 1998; Vol. IV, 2000. Mahwah, NJ: Lawrence Erlbaum Associates.

Kimble, G. A., Wertheimer, M., & White, C. L. (Eds.). (1991). *Portraits of pioneers in psychology*. Washington, DC: American Psychological Association.

Kitayama, S., & Markus, H. R. (Eds.). (1994*). Emotion and culture: Empirical studies of mutual influences*. Washington, DC: American Psychological Association.

Kline, R. B. (1991). Latent variable path analysis in clinical research: A beginner's tour guide. *Journal of Clinical Psychology, 47*(4), 471–484.

Koch, S., & Leary, D. E. (Eds.). (1992). *A century of psychology as a science*. Washington, DC: American Psychological Association.

Koslowski, B. (1996). *Theory and evidence: The development of scientific reasoning.* Cambridge, MA: MIT Press.

Lee, Y. (1994). Why does American psychology have cultural limitations? *American Psychologist, 49,* 524.

Lerner, R. M. (2002). *Concepts and theories of human development* (3rd ed.). Mahwah, NJ: Lawrence Erlbaum Associates.

LeVine, R. A., Miller, P. M., & West, M. M. (Eds.). (1994). *Parental behavior in diverse societies.* San Francisco: Jossey-Bass.

LeVine, G., & Parkinson, S. (1994). *Experimental methods in psychology.* Mahwah, NJ: Lawrence Erlbaum Associates.

Magnusson, D., Bergman, L. R., Rudinger, G., & Torestad, B. (Eds.). (1992). *Problems and methods in longitudinal research: Stability and change.* New York: Cambridge University Press.

Magnusson, D., & Casaer, P. (Eds.). (1993). *Longitudinal research on individual development: Present status and future perspectives.* New York: Cambridge University Press.

Mays, V. M., Rubin, J., Sabourin, M., & Walker, L. (1996). Moving towards a global psychology: Changing theories and practice to meet the needs of a changing world. *American Psychologist, 51*(5), 485–487.

McCandless, B. R. (1967). *Children: Behavior and development* (2nd ed.). New York: Holt, Rinehart and Winston.

McLoyd, V. C., & Flanagan, C. A. (Eds.). (1990). *Economic stress: Effects on family life and child development.* San Francisco: Jossey-Bass.

Meltzoff, J. (1998). *Critical thinking about research: Psychology and related fields.* Washington, DC: American Psychological Association.

Messick, S. (1995). Validity of psychological assessment: Validation of inferences from persons' responses and performances as scientific inquiry into score meaning. *American Psychologist, 50*(9), 741–749.

Miller, P. H. (1993). *Theories of developmental psychology* (3rd ed.). New York: Freeman.

Miller, S. A. (1987). *Developmental research methods.* Englewood Cliffs, NJ: Prentice-Hall.

Moen, P., Elder, G. H. Jr., & Lüscher, K. (Eds.). (1995*). Examining lives in context: Perspectives on the ecology of human development.* Washington, DC: American Psychological Association.

Morris, R. J., Bergan, J. R., & Fulginiti, J. V. (1991). Structural equation modeling in clinical assessment research with children. *Journal of Consulting and Clinical Psychology, 59*(3), 371–379.

Morse, J. R., Stephenson, N., & van Rappard, H. (Eds.). (2001). *Theoretical issues in psychology.* New York: Kluver Academic/Plenum Publishers.

Nadelman, L. (1968). Training laboratories in developmental psychology. *Psychological Reports, 23,* 923–931.

Nadelman, L. (1970). Sex identity in London children: Memory, knowledge and preference tests. *Human Development, 13,* 28–42.

Nadelman, L. (1974). Sex identity in American children: Memory, knowledge and preference tests. *Developmental Psychology, 10,* 413–417.

Nadelman, L. (1990). Learning to think and write as an empirical psychologist: The laboratory course in developmental psychology. *Teaching of Psychology, 17*(1), 45–48.

Nadelman, L., Morse, W., & Hagen, J. (1976). Developmental research in educational settings: Description of a seminar/practicum. *Teaching of Psychology, 3,* 21–24.

Nelson, C. A. (Ed.). (1993*). Memory and affect in development: The Minnesota Symposia on Child Psychology,* Vol. *26.* Hillsdale, NJ: Lawrence Erlbaum Associates.

Nelson, K. (Spring, 1999). Whither Developmental Science? *Developmental Psychologist,* Div. 7, APA, *Newsletter, 16.*

Nesselroade, J. R., & Baltes, P. B. (1974). Adolescent personality development and historical change: 1970–1972. *Monographs of the Society for Research in Child Development, 39*(1, Serial No. 154).

Parke, R. D., & Kellam, S. G. (Eds.). (1994*). Exploring family relationships with other social contexts.* Hillsdale, NJ: Lawrence Erlbaum Associates.

Parke, R. D., Ornstein, P. A., Reiser, J. J., & Zahn-Waxler, C. (Eds.). (1994). *A century of developmental psychology.* Washington, DC: American Psychological Association.

Pickren, W. E., & Dewsbury, D. A. (Eds.). (2002). *Evolving perspectives on the history of psychology.* Washington, DC: American Psychological Association.

Plomin, R. (1994). *Genetics and experience: The interplay between nature and nurture.* Thousand Oaks, CA: Sage Publications.

Plomin, R., & McClearn, G. E. (Eds.). (1993). *Nature, nurture, and psychology.* Washington, DC: American Psychological Association.

Reese, H. W., & Lipsitt, L. P. (1970). *Experimental child psychology.* New York: Academic Press, chapter 1.

Resnick, L. B., Higgins, E. T., & Levine, J. M. (1993). Social foundations of cognition. In M. Rosenzweig and L. Porter (Eds.), *Annual Review of Psychology* (*Vol. 44*, pp. 585–612). Palo Alto, CA: Annual Reviews, Inc.

Richardson, K. (2000). *Developmental psychology: How nature and nurture interact.* Mahwah, NJ: Lawrence Erlbaum Associates.

Riegel, K. F. (1972). The influence of economic and political ideology upon the development of developmental psychology. *Psychological Bulletin, 78,* 129–141.

Rosenthal, K. (1966). *Experimenter effects in behavioral research.* New York: Appleton-Century-Crofts.

Rosenzweig, M., & Pawlik, K. (Eds.). (1995). *Origins and development of psychology: Some national and regional perspectives.* A special issue of the *International Journal of Psychology.* Hillsdale, NJ: Lawrence Erlbaum Associates.

Rowe, D. C. (1993). *The limits of family influence: Genes, experience, and behavior.* New York: Guilford.

Rutter, M. (2002). Nature, nurture, and development: From evangelism through science toward policy and practice. *Child Development, 73*(1), 1–21.

Rutter, M., & Rutter, M. (1993). *Developing minds: Challenge and continuity across the lifespan.* New York: Basic Books.

Sales, B. D., & Folkman, S. (Eds.). (2000). *Ethics in research with human participants.* Washington, DC: American Psychological Association.

Sameroff, A. (1975). Transactional models in early social relations. *Human Development, 18*(12), 65–79.

Sameroff, A. J. (1993). Models of development and developmental risk. In C. H. Zeanah (Ed.), *Handbook of infant mental health* (pp.3-13). New York: Guilford Press.

Sameroff, A. J. (1995). General systems theories and developmental psychopathology. In D. Cicchetti & D. Cohen (Eds.), *Manual of developmental pyschopathology,* (*Vol. 1*, pp. 659–695). New York: Wiley.

Scarr, S. (1993). Biological and cultural diversity: The legacy of Darwin for development. *Child Development, 64,* 1333–1353.

Schneirla, T. S. (1957). The concept of development in comparative psychology. In D. B. Harris (Ed.), *The concept of development* (pp. 78–108). Minneapolis: University of Minnesota Press.

Schneirla, T. S., & Rosenblatt, J. S. (1963). "Critical periods" in the development of behavior. *Science, 139,* 1110–1115.

Segal, N. L., Weisfeld, G. E., & Weisfeld, C. C. (Eds.). (1997). *Uniting psychology and biology: Integrative perspectives on human development.* Washington, DC: American Psychological Association.

Simpson, J. A., & Kenrick, D. (Eds.). (1996). *Evolutionary social psychology.* Mahwah, NJ: Lawrence Erlbaum Associates.

Smuts, A. B., & Hagen, J. W. (Eds.). (1985). History and research in child development. *Monographs of the Society for Research in Child Development, 50* (4–5, Serial No. 211).

Solomon, R. L., & Lessac, M. S. (1968). A control group design for experimental studies of developmental processes. *Psychological Bulletin, 70,* 145–150.

Stanley, B. H., Seiber, J. E., & Melton, G. B. (Eds.). (1996). *Research ethics: A psychological approach.* Lincoln, NE: University of Nebraska Press.

Stanovich, K. E. (1989). *How to think straight about psychology* (2nd ed.). Glenview, IL: Scott, Foresman.

Stern, P. C., & Kalof, L. (1996). *Evaluating social science research* (2nd ed.). New York: Oxford University Press.

Sternberg, R. J., & Grigorenko, E. L. (2001). Unified psychology. *American Psychologist, 56*(12), 1069–1079.

Street, W. R. (1994). *A chronology of noteworthy events in American psychology.* Washington, DC: American Psychological Association.

Super, C. M., & Harkness, S. (1986). The developmental niche: A conceptualization at the interface of child and culture. *International Journal of Behavior Development, 9,* 545–569.

Thomas, R. M. (2000). *Recent theories of human development.* Thousand Oaks, CA: Sage.

Thomas, A., Chess, S., & Birch, H. G. (1968). *Temperament and behavior disorders in children.* New York: New York University Press.

Thomas, A., Chess, S., Birch, H. G., Hertzig, M., & Korn, S. (1963). *Behavioral individuality in early childhood.* New York: New York University Press.

Vygotsky, L. S. (1978). *Mind in society.* Cambridge, MA: Harvard University Press.

von Eye, A., & Clogg, C. C. (Eds.). (1996). *Categorical variables in developmental research: Methods of analysis.* San Diego, CA: Academic Press.

Wachs, T. D. (2000). *Necessary but not sufficient: The respective roles of single and multiple influences on individual development.* Washington, DC: American Psychological Association.

Wachs, T. D., & Plomin, R. (Eds.). (1991). *Conceptualization and measurement of organism-environment interaction*. Washington, DC: American Psychological Association.

Webb, E. J., Campbell, D. T., Schwartz, R. D., & Sechrest, L. (1966). *Unobtrusive measures: Non-reactive research in the social sciences*. Chicago: Rand McNally.

Werner, H. (1957). The concept of development from a comparative and organismic point of view. In D. B. Harris (Ed.), *The concept of development* (pp. 125-148). Minneapolis: University of Minnesota Press.

Wertsch, J. V., del Rio, P., & Alvarez, A. (Eds.). (1995). *Sociocultural studies of mind*. New York: Cambridge University Press.

White, P. A. (1990). Ideas about causation in philosophy and psychology. *Psychological Bulletin, 108*, 3–18.

Worthman, C. W. (1995). Biocultural interactions in human development. In M. E. Pereira & L. A. Fairbanks (Eds.), *Juvenile primates: Life history, development and behavior* (pp. 339–358). New York: Oxford University Press.

Wozniak, R., & Fischer, K. W. (Eds.). (1993). *Development in context: Acting and thinking in specific environments*. Hillsdale, NJ: Lawrence Erlbaum Associates.

PART TWO

OBSERVATIONAL STUDIES

We have at least three major research strategies available to us: (1) we can study exclusively what an organism *can do*—test for all his abilities, competencies by intervening into his life by various artificial means—as has been done in psychometric and experimental work, or (2) we can study exclusively what an organism actually *does do* without any kind of, or a minimum amount of, intervention on our part—as has been done in the few naturalistic observational studies of human behavior that now exist, or (3) we can study him in both ways back and forth. If we did the latter we would be able to generate a foundation of data that would both produce a comprehensive and coherent picture of the phenomena as well as have maximum applicability and impact on areas dealing with social problems."

—Charlesworth (1973)

From about 1890 to 1960, only 8% of the published empirical studies on children and adolescents were observational studies of naturally occurring events; of that relatively small number, 94% dealt with preschool children, with nursery schools the favored settings—56% (Wright, 1960). The field-based observational procedures fashionable in the 1930s and 1940s gave way in the 1950s to nonnaturalistic-observational techniques (like interviews), and these in turn shifted to laboratory experiments in the early 1960s (Parke, 1979). Interest in observational studies appears to be rising during these last decades, and common now are studies combining naturalistic observation with laboratory experiments.

The reasons are not difficult to discern. In the previous chapter, the issue of *ecological validity* was raised—a concern with generalizing findings from one setting to a different setting (i.e., laboratory to home or classroom or supermarket). The federal government's interest in funding applied research that has relevance to pressing social problems makes the issue of generalizability a practical one. A second, related reason has to do with *construct validity*, which we touched on earlier in discussing the difficulty of defining concepts, in English and operationally. Is the mild anger that the experimenter may elicit from the subject as a result of some brief blocking maneuvers in a laboratory task qualitatively the same as the rage that so many Blacks report they live with daily? Is the lowered self-esteem following failure-feedback in a laboratory test the same as life-long low self-esteem? A rose is a rose is a rose is a shaky assumption for a scientist, and the same name given to an acute, reactive form of a variable does not guarantee its equivalence to the chronic version of that variable.

Partly because of the above issues; partly because of a shift in interest from a unidirectional model where children are the passive receivers of stimulation to one that emphasizes children's active contribution to their development; partly because the current Zeitgeist applauds the study of reciprocal interaction between the child and another person, there is now explicit pressure for a multimethod research strategy. Parke (1979) described, with many examples, how laboratory and field-observation approaches can be intermeshed even in the same study, with the independent variable and the dependent variable occurring in the field *or* the lab. The breakdown of the field-lab dichotomy plus the interest in the sequential strategies for data collection (described earlier) plus refinements in statistical analyses show promise of a more fertile period in psychology.

A study of the impact of the affective environment on young children illustrates many of these points. Zahn-Waxler, Radke-Yarrow, and King (1977) used an overlapping cohort design, in which 10-, 15-, and 20-month-old children, respectively, were studied for 9 months in their homes. The focus on emotional events occurring in the natural environment illustrates the "field" aspect. The additional simulation of affect by the mother or investigator on a predetermined schedule illustrates the "experimental" aspect. The hiring and training of the mothers as coinvestigators preserved the normality of the situation for the child and permitted contrasts to be made between the child's response to affect displayed by a mother and to affect displayed by an investigator seen at 3-week intervals. (See also Zahn-Waxler, Radke-Yarrow, & King, 1979.)

Observing children in natural contexts may lighten some concerns about relevance and validity, but the process is often neither easy nor fast, and it is characterized by problems that need careful handling. Some of these problems include observer influence, reliability of observation, instrumental recording aids, and descriptive categories (Wright, 1960).

Observer Influence

When students are being trained as observers, the instruction is usually to be a nonparticipant observer—friendly but not warm or enticing, nondirective and relatively quiet. This can be very difficult when children scramble over your lap or try to see your stopwatch or solicit your approval or attention or notice your earjack. Fortunately, your novelty wears off for most young children, and their behavior generally reverts to normal. The adult being observed in interaction with the child presents a more difficult problem, and many adults probably never behave with the child in the known presence of an observer exactly as they would without an observer.

Reliability of Observation

Do simultaneous independent observers agree on what they see and report? Agreement or consistency is not synonymous with accuracy (or veridicality) of observation (both observers could be similarly wrong!), but agreement has to be demonstrated and disagreements resolved before data can be analyzed. Here, once again, defining the specific behaviors to be observed is an early necessity.

Instrumental Recording Aids

Is the observer to sit with a clipboard and pen and paper? With a stopwatch? With an auditory prompter? Or is the observer going to whisper into a small microphone? Are videotapes or movies going to be made? Silent or sound? Each technique has advantages and disadvantages, and careful early consideration needs to be given to the objectives of the study, the kinds of data that will best answer those objectives, and the optimal means of recording those data. An instrumental aid that is used frequently is an auditory ear prompter. This can be a self-contained unit that fits in a pocket or hangs from one's belt, with an earjack, or it can be a tape recorder with prerecorded time signals. In either event, a noise is heard by the observer every *x* seconds. The DOT (Device for Observation Timing) that we used can alternate two tones at preset intervals to indicate *Ready* and *Go*, or *Start* and *Stop*.

Descriptive Categories

A naive observer, released in a nursery setting to "look and see and learn about children" can easily be overwhelmed and bewildered: "What shall I look at first?" "Too much happens all at once." "What do you mean, I'm doing 'too much interpreting and not enough describing'?" The investigator has to decide whether molar or reductive bits of behavior are to be recorded; whether "facts" (the subject's face pinkened, the brow furrowed, the left foot stamped) or inferences (the subject was angry) are the data; whether the observer records things and events as the observer sees them or as the observer thinks the child sees them. An observer can be told to record "attention seeking"; or more specifically, "positive attention-seeking behaviors" and "negative attention-seeking behaviors"; or still more specifically, "shouts, requests help verbally, requests help gesturally, brings product for praise" and so on.

How one resolves the above problems is related to the method one chooses for the investigation. Methods that have been used include:

1. diary description (the early baby biographies)

2. specimen description (narrative recording of behavior sequence)

3. time sampling

4. event sampling

5. field unit analysis (of successive behavior units) and

6. trait rating.

Some of these will form the exercises in the following pages and will be described in context. Each method combines a sampling plan (with regard to time units and behaviors), a recording technique, and data analysis. Pellegrini (1996) and Sackett (1978) provided useful information on methodology for observational studies.

Although observation provides a crucial source of data about child development and reveals many relationships, it rarely establishes *causal* relationships between phenomena (Cole & Cole, 1993). For that, experiments are needed. However, a good experimenter needs to be a good observer, and training in observation should be fundamental in any thorough research training program.

Selected Bibliography

Barker, R. G. (1963). *The stream of behavior*. New York: Appleton-Century-Crofts.

Bakeman, R., & Gottman, J. M. (1986). *Observing behavior*. New York: Cambridge University Press.

Barker, R. G., & Wright, H. F. (1951). *One boy's day*. New York: Harper & Row.

Boehm, A. E., & Weinberg, R. A. (1997). *The classroom observer: Developing observation skills in early childhood settings* (3rd ed.). New York: Teachers College Press.

Bronfenbrenner, U. (1989). Ecological systems theory. In R. Vasta (Ed.), *Annals of child development* (*Vol. 6*). Greenwich, CT: JAI Press.

Charlesworth, W. R. (1973, August). Ethology's contribution to a framework for relevant research. In J. E. Turnure (Chair), *The value of relevant research: Selling the unwashed to the pure*. Symposium presented at the meeting of the American Psychological Association, Montreal.

Cohen, D. H., Stern, V., & Balaban, N. (1997). *Observing and recording the behavior of young children* (4th ed.).New York: Teachers College Press.

Cole, M., & Cole, S. R. (1993). *The development of children* (2nd ed.). New York: Scientific American Books/Freeman.

Irwin, D. M., & Bushnell, M. M. (1980*). Observational strategies for child study*. New York: Holt, Rinehart & Winston.

Kerig, P. K., & Lindahl, K. M. (Eds.). (2001). *Family observation coding systems: Resources for systemic research*. Mahwah, NJ: Lawrence Erlbaum Associates.

McGrew, W. C. (1972). *An ethological study of children's behavior*. New York: Academic Press.

Medinnus, G. R. (1976). *Child study and observation guide*. New York: Wiley.

Parke, R. D. (1976). Social cues, social control and ecological validity. *Merrill-Palmer Quarterly*, *22*, 111–118.

Parke, R. D. (1979). Interactional designs. In R. B. Cairns (Ed.), *The analysis of social interactions: Methods, issues, and illustrations* (pp. 15–35). Hillsdale, NJ: Lawrence Erlbaum Associates.

Pellegrini, A. D. (1996). *Observing children in their natural worlds: A methodological primer*. Mahwah, NJ: Lawrence Erlbaum Associates.

Rosenbaum, P. R. (1995). *Observational studies*. New York: Springer-Verlag.

Sackett, G. P. (Ed.). (1978). *Observing behavior* (*Vol. II*): *Data collection and analysis methods*. Baltimore: University Park Press.

Schoggen, P. (1989). *Behavior settings: A revision and extension of Roger G. Barker's Ecological Psychology*. Stanford, CA: Stanford University Press.

Wright, H. F. (1960). Observational child study. In P. Mussen (Ed.), *Handbook of research methods in child development* (pp. 71–139). New York: Wiley.

Wright, H. F. (1967). *Recording and analyzing child behavior*. New York: Harper & Row.

Zahn-Waxler, C., Radke-Yarrow, M., & King, R. A. (1977, March). *The impact of the affective environment on young children*. Paper presented at the biennial meeting of the Society for Research in Child Development, New Orleans.

Zahn-Waxler, C., Radke-Yarrow, M., & King, R. A. (1979). Child rearing and children's prosocial initiations toward victims of distress. *Child Development*, *50*, 319–330.

B

Infant Observation

A developmental student is interested in change and, apart from prenatal development, infancy is the period of most rapid and comprehensive change. Psychologists have developed an increasing sophistication about the rapidly developing competencies of newborns and infants. Much of the research depends on good design, systematic observation, and detailed recording procedures. Prolonged familiarity with developing babies and sharpened observational skills are the initial tools of the infancy researcher.

This chapter describes an infant observation project that provides some necessary initial experiences. The opportunity to observe an infant in the child's natural context for a semester may be overwhelming because of the richness and complexity of data that can ensue, but you can hardly fail (in a supervised context) to augment your knowledge about children and to enhance your observational skills. An infant observation program of this kind generally has no difficulty in being approved by the appropriate human subjects review committee.

Sources

Cheerful announcements requesting cooperation from families of infants and toddlers can be posted in Well Baby clinics, offices of pediatricians, housing projects, supermarkets, church bulletin boards, university publications, and public libraries. Lamaze and La Leche groups and child study groups are fruitful sources. Announcements in parent–teacher organizations, school newsletters, and local nurseries often produce younger sibs. Research with tighter controls on age, socioeconomic status, race, or birth order may require different solicitation. The vital statistics records of local newspapers and hospitals provide comprehensive lists.

This initial solicitation should make clear what is being requested and why; for example:

permission for one or two students to visit the home weekly to observe the baby for one hour, for 12 weeks; or

permission for one student to administer an infant assessment measure or Piagetian task or whatever at home, x number of times; or

x number of paid or unpaid visits of the baby and parent to a specified location for a specified purpose.

Arrangements and Behavior

Interested parents call the instructor or secretary at the numbers provided, and leave their names and phone numbers. After the instructor has answered questions and received the address, sex, and birthdate of the infant, an official letter of confirmation and thanks is sent to the family. If two students are assigned to each baby, they then make a joint phone call to the mother to arrange one convenient hour a week when the baby is likely to be awake—lunch, bath, or playtime are optimal—and one or both parents are home (rather than a sitter).

Both students make the first visit to the home together, bearing cards with their names and phone numbers should the parent wish to cancel a meeting for illness or other reasons. Future visits are made singly, in alternate weeks, with occasional joint visits arranged. It is understood that no student with a cold or other illness visits.

The observation period is not an occasion for free babysitting! A student willing to babysit for free or for money *at other times* may make private arrangements to that effect. The focus of the observation is to watch the normal development of a child, longitudinally, in interaction with the child's family. The observation period is also not an occasion for entertaining. Accept a cup of coffee or cookie if you wish. Let the parents determine how and to what extent the observer fits into their household.

Rapport is needed for the parent to relax in your presence and behave naturally. Answer questions about the project cheerfully and honestly. Do not initiate questions about occupation, income, location of extended family, and so on. *Do not give advice about childrearing.* Learn not to make certain kinds of comments. For example, Marie's innocent comment, "Isn't he cute and tiny!" elicited the mother's anxious and delayed response, "Is he too small for his age?" "What a beautiful boy!" is not always a welcome comment to the ears of certain fathers.

Frequently, problems arise concerning breast-feeding, siblings, and touching. The instructor can sometimes determine during the initial telephone contact whether the mother is breast-feeding and whether she would prefer no observers at that time. If not clarified then, it should certainly be made explicit at the first meeting that there is no pressure on the mother to have her breast-feeding observed, nor is she expected to delay feeding until after the hour visit. A briefer visit can be equally fruitful. Male observers are more likely to be ousted from this situation than female observers, but by and large, breast-feeding is less of a problem in our training program than expected.

Siblings present difficulties to observers. A toddler, preschooler, or young child does not quietly sit and let an observer concentrate on the youngest sib! And trying instead to observe two children simultaneously for the whole hour may prove very tiring and frustrating to the new observer. A modus vivendi needs to be worked out that turns the difficulty into an asset or a challenge. A fairly successful ploy is to play with the older child initially during the hour, then announce, "I need to see B and mommy for a while," and remove eye contact. The baby's interaction with the older sib is properly part of the protocol, as is the parent's technique of coping simultaneously with the baby and an attention-seeking sib. Full attention can be restored to the older sib at intervals and certainly at the end of the hour. A similar technique is useful when a mother makes the visit a social occasion between you and her, with the baby a distant third. Remove eye contact with the mother and sit so that the baby is between you and the mother.

The main advice with regard to touching is *don't!* Do not pat, caress, pick up, or hug that baby until the mother offers the child to you. Most mothers will ask, in this situation, if you wish to hold the baby. This provides a good opportunity to see if the baby molds to you, to see changes in muscle tonus as the parent moves out of sight, and to see if there is any clinging or scrambling over you as you become more familiar to the baby. However, do not hesitate to say, as one male student did when offered a 4-week-old baby on his first visit, "Thank you; I want to but have never even seen a baby this young. Let me watch how you hold her for now, and I'll do it when I'm more comfortable."

Termination must be prepared carefully. The instructor's letter will have announced the calendar span of the observation periods. On the first visit, thank the family again for letting you "come from September to mid-December" (or late January to late April, etc.). On the penultimate visit, announce that the following visit is your last observation. Any friendship beyond that date is your and the family's private agreement. We stress the importance of the termination process, because of the effect that regular visits by a bright young adult may have on a lonesome young mother feeling trapped in a small apartment with a first child.

An inexpensive (carefully chosen or made) termination gift to the baby or family from the pair of students is appropriate but not mandatory. More important are written notes of appreciation.

Schedule of Visits and Reports

Many modifications are possible and easy. One schedule that works well follows:

Visit 1. *Joint visit*
       Milieu report
       five-minute sequential protocol and observer-reliability exercise
Visit 2. Topical report based on both visits

Visit 3. One memory unit sequential protocol

Visit 4. five-minute sequential protocol

Visit 5. *Joint visit*
>   five-minute sequential protocol
>   Observer-reliability exercises
>   Memory unit sequential protocol

Visit 6. Topical report, focusing on changes since Visit 2 and current status

Milieu Report

The first visit is a get-acquainted time, a time for all of you to assimilate first impressions of each other and of the setting. Because the observer is not always more comfortable in this first meeting than the observed parent, the report will probably be more accurate if it focuses on neutral non-interactional observations. The milieu report includes a general description of the home and its location, and of the stimulation that the setting provides for the infant. The description of the infant areas in the home should be as detailed as possible.

Begin this report and all others with detailed labeling: your name; child's name or code; sex; birthdate; chronological age; day, date, and time of visit; other people and animals present; location (i.e., kitchen, back porch).

Describe the *physical environment* in the home and neighborhood. Does the family live in a house, apartment, trailer? How is it furnished? Clean and ultratidy? Clean and cluttered? Dirty? Bright colors, pastels, monotones? Radio, stereo, TV, records, books, art, plants?

Where does the infant sleep? Room alone? Play area in and out of house? Where bathed? Where fed? Toys—what kind? Sex-typed? Pets? Noise level?

Describe the *social environment*. Sibs? Other relatives living there or present? Neighbors dropping in during visit? Busy phone?

Note your first impressions of *baby*: physical description, how dressed, temperament, baby's reaction to you—a stranger, baby's reaction to mother or father, or pet or sib?

Note your first impressions of *mother*: physical description if noteworthy (i.e., obese), manner to you, reserved or garrulous, offers relevant information, handling of infant, responsiveness to baby, tone of voice, use of baby talk.

Sequential Protocols

This is a detailed running account of the behaviors and events observed in sequence; it can be done on the spot (simultaneously) or later by memory. See Bick (1964) for examples of protocols from memory by psychoanalytic trainees. With practice, one can build up surprisingly detailed accuracy even for a memory protocol. The sight of a pad and pencil inhibits many people, and learning to watch carefully and to remember details until they can be written down is a very useful ability for an observer. On the schedule above, the third and fifth visits provide some practice with memory protocols.

On-the-spot sequential protocols are recorded in writing or into a small mouth microphone. You will probably be writing in this situation and will rapidly discover that you need some form of shorthand or speed writing. Practice will help you develop your personal abbreviations. Write your observations in list format. Or divide your page vertically, with baby's behaviors on one half and mother's behaviors on the other. See Clarke-Stewart (1973) for an illustration of this.

Always include all the top labeling described in the directions for the milieu report. The starting and stopping time for this five-minute period must be noted. If the sequential protocol is to serve as the basis for an observer-reliability exercise, you and your partner must be observing the same five-minute period.

One need not be a professional psychologist to recognize which of the following protocols is the better one:

M put B in highchair in kitchen. She fed him chicken, peas, milk, and applesauce. She did this neatly and quickly. Feeding—from into and out of the highchair—took eight minutes.

At 12:35 p.m., M put B in metal highchair in kitchen, adjusting safety straps and bib. She used an electric-heating dish with two compartments, on the kitchen table, to feed B with baby spoon his chicken and junior peas, alternating but not mixing food. She fed rapidly, with the next spoonful hovering near his mouth before he had swallowed the previous mouthful. When he had finished all the chicken and peas, she gave him applesauce, which had been kept out of his sight. She then gave him half a cup of milk in a two-handled cup with a safety cover. She coaxed him verbally, with a smile, to finish the milk several times. Then she said, "All done!" in a sing-song voice, unstrapped him, wiped his face with damp cloth, removed the bib, hugged him, and carried him on her hip to the nursery rug, where she sat him down near a terry-cloth ball (12:44 p.m.).

More detailed though the second protocol is, it is notably lacking in a description of the baby's behavior in this situation. Among the many comments I would put in the margin are:

Does B "adjust" physically for placement in highchair? Does B sit quietly or change position frequently or try to climb out? Where does B look—at M for food, at spoon, at observer, around the room? Facial expressions of B and M? Vocalizations? Does B anticipate by opening mouth before spoon touches lips? Is there another spoon for B to hold? Is food out of B's reach so B cannot attempt self-feeding? Does food dribble out of B's mouth? If so, what does M do? Is M responsive to signals re: satiety or pace? What are the signals? Does B like some foods better than others? How can you tell?

In these sequential protocols, focus on observable behaviors and events. Place interpretations, inferences, or speculations in brackets. To say that someone is disappointed, angry, sad, happy, likes a special food, and so on, is to make an inference from observed behavior (tears, tone of voice, tempo, gesture) and knowledge of situation. At the end of a sequential protocol, you may draw a line and give your subjective interpretation of the episode. It is important to you as an observer to try to distinguish the two.

Observer Reliability Exercise

Using the five-minute protocol (rewritten so that it is readable by the instructor), compare yours and your partner's phrase by phrase. If you both observed the same thing, score plus. If you disagree on what was or was not seen (disagreements and omissions) score minus. Write both protocols and their scores in a three-column format as follows. Don't forget the full top labeling. The percent of agreement is the number of agreements divided by the total number of agreements and disagreements, times 100.

SCORE	OBSERVER AB	OBSERVER YZ
+	B waved both arms,	B waved her arms
–,–	fisted,	and smiled.
+	and reached for the block.	She grabbed at block
–		with RH,
–	She dropped it.	And banged it on floor.
+	Looked at me and Y.	B looked at observers
–		and at M.
etc.		

$$\text{Observer reliability} = \frac{+}{+ \text{ and } -} \; X \; 100 \quad (\text{e.g.,} \; \frac{3}{8} \; X \; 100 = 37\tfrac{1}{2} \, \% \text{ agreement})$$

You can anticipate a fairly low agreement if you are both novices and trying to observe everything. Narrowing your observation to motor behavior, to language, to mother-child interaction, or to some other focused interest or specific behaviors often enhances observer agreement.

Many of the movies and videotapes shown in child psychology courses provide opportunities for practicing and scoring sequential protocols, with the advantage that the films and tapes can be rerun.

Topical Report

A topical report describes the child on a more molar level. It should give someone who has not met the child a picture of the child's present functioning in as many areas of development as possible, set in context. The child's level and pace of competencies can be compared to norms. In an academic framework, explicit links to the relevant literature are in order; in some applied settings, these may not be necessary. A perceptive comprehensive report results from the integration of observational skills, a knowledge of child development theories and findings, and a responsiveness to the interactional dynamic aspects of the observed setting.

The *organization* of the report can be idiosyncratic. Clinical students sometimes prefer a psychoanalytic framework and use organizational headings such as id, ego, beginnings of superego; oral stage, anal stage, trust/mistrust, autonomy/doubt, defense mechanisms. Students with an organismic-interactionist bent sometimes use the temperament classification of Thomas, Chess, Birch, Hertzig, and Korn (1963) and outline their report in terms of the child's activity level, quality of mood, approach/withdrawal tendencies, rhythmicity, adaptability, threshold of responsiveness, intensity of reaction, distractibility, attention span, and persistence. Some read the detailed descriptions of babies of the same age in current textbooks and adopt or adapt that outline. The most commonly used is a traditional division into (a) physical development, (b) cognitive development, (c) emotional-social development. Usually, (d) parent or family is added to encompass material in which the infant is not necessarily the specific or major focus.

These four areas are expanded below to provide indications of the content of topical reports. Generalizations should be buttressed with concrete examples of behaviors on which they were based. When possible, explicitly relate your findings and inferences to the relevant literature, that is, Piaget, Freud, Erikson, Bayley, and Ainsworth. A few of these frames of reference will be indicated briefly in the relevant section. Because humans are not conveniently divided into the categories below, it will occasionally be difficult to decide where certain behaviors or competences should be located. For example, imitation and attachment overlap the cognitive and social categories; prehension has cognitive and physical components; and so on.

A. PHYSICAL DEVELOPMENT

1. Description of size and appearance

   Classification by temperament and state (Thomas et al., 1963) or kinds of individual differences like
       motor activity, irritability, passivity
   Attractiveness, coloring

2. Locomotion
   Locomotor sequence and style: pivoting, crawling, creeping, sitting, standing, walking, climbing,
       running, hopping
   Pace, inhibition of movement
   Coordination

3. Prehension and laterality
   Sequence, timing, coordination
   Transfer
   Cross median body line
   Other-directed vs. self-directed

4. Perception: hearing, seeing, depth perception

Locomotor Development. The classic work by Shirley (1931) is still used to indicate developmental milestones in motor development, and the drawings are reproduced or adapted in many standard developmental texts. See Fig. B.1.

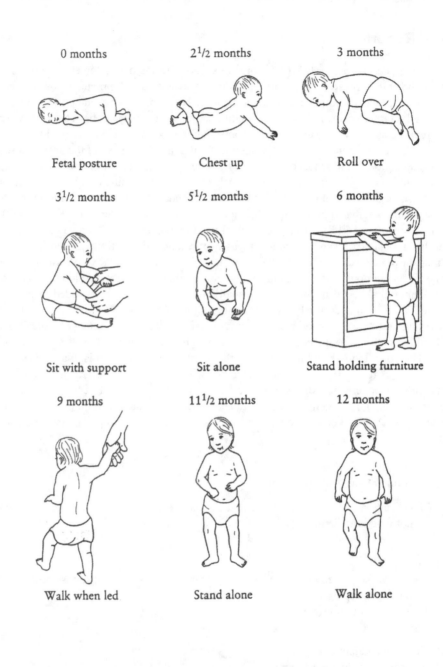

Fig. B.1. A typical sequence of motor development and locomotion in early infancy.
Note: From *Development through life: A psychosocial approach* (7th ed., p. 147) by B. M. Newman and P. R. Newman, 1999, Belmont, CA: Brooks/Cole, Wadsworth. Copyright © by Wadsworth. Reprinted with permission.

Prehension. The old Gesell child study center movie (Infant development: later stages) vividly compares and contrasts the developing prehension of an infant at different ages, for example: *12* weeks, regard; *16*, incipient approach; *20*, corral and contact; *24*, grasp one cube, transfer, inspect, bang, mouth; *28*, regard second cube, approach, rub two cubes; *40*, exploitive combining of two cubes, use of index finger, play with three cubes.

Compare the ages and sequence of this child with yours and with Hetherington and Parke's summary (1986, 1999) and figure (Fig. B2), or with other relevant norms.

TABLE B1
DEVELOPMENT OF PREHENSION DURING THE FIRST YEAR OF LIFE

16 weeks	Scratches with fingers on tabletop
	Looks at and swipes at objects
	Retains toys put into hand
	Makes no contact with objects on table
20 weeks	Contacts toys on table
	Graps block precariously
28 weeks	Bangs, shakes, and transfers toys from hand to hand
	Palmar grasp of block
	Whole hand contact of raisin
36 weeks	Finger grasp of block
	Scissors grasp of raisin
40 weeks	Holds one block in each hand
	Crude voluntary release of block
	Index finger approach to raisin
48–52 weeks	Forefinger grasp of block
	Releases block into cup
	Neat pincer grasp of raisin

Note: From *Child psychology: A contemporary viewpoint* (3rd ed.), by E. M. Hetherington and R. D. Parke, 1986, p. 203. New York: McGraw-Hill. Copyright © by McGraw-Hill. Reprinted with permission.

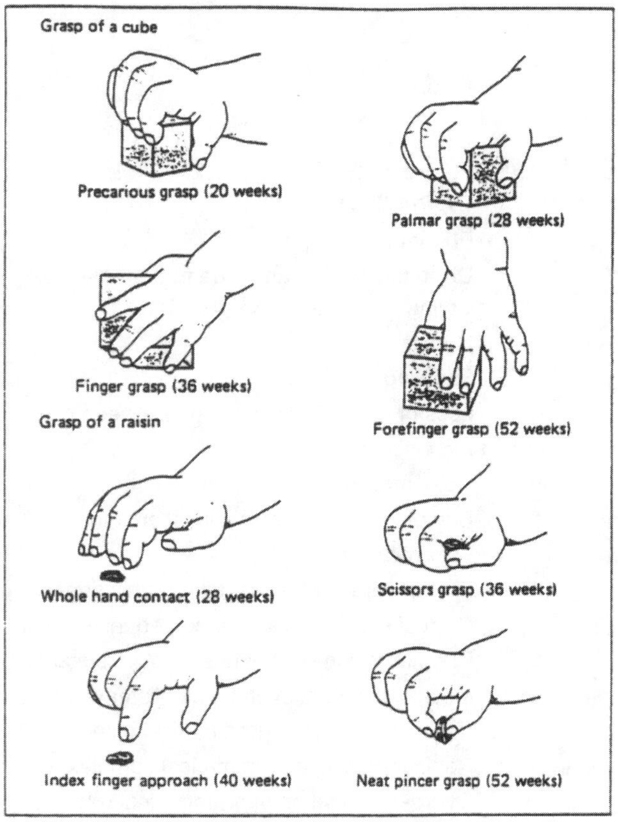

Fig. B2. Development of prehension during the first year of life.
Note: From *Child psychology: A contemporary viewpoint* (3rd ed., p. 203) by E. M. Hetherington and R. D. Parke, 1986, p. 203. New York: McGraw-Hill. Copyright © McGraw-Hill. Reprinted with permission.

B. COGNITIVE DEVELOPMENT

1. Object concept
     Piagetian substages
     Peek-a-boo, hide-and-seek games

2. Learning and problem solving
     Attention span; persistence
     Tertiary circular response: repetition, novelty, making new things happen
     Imitation
     Reversibility
     Problem solving; exploration; cause-effect
     Symbolic play
     Cognitive styles (i.e., impulsive/reflective; global/analytic)

3. Development of communication skills and language
     Vocalizations: fake crying, noncry vocalizations, babblings
     Holophrase
     Length of utterances
     Nonverbal communication
     Imitation: vocal/gesture
     Receptive and expressive
     Does parent label objects? Use expanded sentences? Baby talk?

TABLE B2
THE PROGRESS OF LANGUAGE DEVELOPMENT

Approximate Age	Typical Behavior
Birth	Phoneme perception
	Discrimination of language from nonlanguage sounds
	Crying
3 months	Cooing
6 months	Babbling
	Loss of ability to discriminate between normative phonemes
9 months	First words
	Holophrases
12 months	Use of words to attract adults' attention
18 months	Vocabulary spurt
	First 2-word sentences (telegraphic speech)
24 months	Correct responses to indirect requests ("Is the door shut?")
30 months	Creation of indirect requests ("You're standing on my blocks!")
	Modification of speech to take listener into account
	Early awareness of grammatical categories
Early Childhood	Rapid increase in grammatical complexity
	Overgeneralization of grammatical rules
Middle Childhood	Understanding the passive forms ("The balls were taken by the boys.")
	Acquisition of written languages
Adolescence	Acquisition of specialized language functions

Note: From *The development of children* (2nd ed.), by M. Cole and S. R. Cole, 1993, p. 311. New York: Scientific American Books, Freeman. Copyright © 1993 by Freeman. Reprinted with permission.

Object Concept. The substages of the Piagetian sensory-motor period from birth to 1½ or 2 years, and the substages of the development of the object concept apper in Piaget's books (1952, 1954), and more succinctly in Flavell (1963). During the third and fourth visits to the home, many parents will permit and abet small demonstrations of many of these substages: pulling the scarf over the baby's head, dropping a spoon from a high-chair, hiding a small favored toy with a tissue, barrier behavior, visibly switching hiding places, and so on. (See also Baillargeon, 1987, and Baillargeon, Spelke, & Wasserman, 1985, for their description of object permanence in 3½- to 5-month old infants.)

Communication and Language. This is currently the focus of much research and new publications. Relevant context is provided by Bates, Bretherton, Snyder (1988), Bloom (1991, 1995), Chomsky (1985), and Shatz (1994).

C. EMOTIONAL-SOCIAL DEVELOPMENT

1. Attachment
   Ainsworth's (1963) patterns of attachment behavior; see also Ainsworth (1993); Ainsworth, Blehar, Waters, and Wall (1978); Bowby (1969); Cassidy and Shaver (1999); Goldsmith and Alansky (1987); Greenspan and Thorndike Greenspan (1985); Vaughn et al. (1992).

2. Relations to sibs, peers: initiation, mood, playfulness

3. Reactions to stranger (changing reactions to observer)

4. Sex-role typing

5. Antecedents of moral development

6. Autonomy: reactions to frustration; discipline

7. Personality style: coy? charmer? flirt? sulker? whiner?

Attachment. The mother's natural movements in and out of a room, and in out of the baby's sight, as well as your own entrance and exit will provide ample opportunity to observe the baby's differential behaviors to parents and strangers, and to assess the criteria of attachment initially described by Ainsworth (1963) in her study of African children:
Discrimination of mother and differential responsiveness to her
    Differential crying
    Differential smiling
    Differential vocalization
Concern for whereabouts of mother. Use of distance receptors
    Visual-motor orientation towards the mother
    Crying when mother leaves the room
    Following
Scrambling over the parent
Burying face in lap
Mother as secure base, haven of safety
    Exploration from secure base
    Clinging
Greeting patterns after an absence
    Lifting arms
    Clapping hands

Ainsworth (1973) distinguished sequential phases in the development of attachment, with the baby moving from a phase of undiscriminating social responsiveness to a phase of discriminating social responsiveness, to a phase of active initiative in seeking proximity and contact, to a phase (at about 3 years?) of goal-corrected partnership (a more complicated and reciprocal relationship with the primary caregiver).

Publications on attachment abound. Reading these in conjunction with the ethologically oriented theory of Ainsworth (1973, 1993) and Ainsworth et al. (1978) may clarify some of the issues and implications of your observations (Bretherton, 1985; Cassidy, 1994; Clarke-Stewart, 1973; Egeland & Farber, 1984; Lamb, 1976; and Waters, Matas, & Sroufe, 1975).

Emotional Development (Affective Development). The child's emotional reactions may be difficult to categorize but are unquestionably present, as are the emotions of others in the baby's environment. The cognitive element (when, what, and how much does the child understand of other people's emotions, or even of his or her own?) is difficult to disentangle. An observational, empirical attempt to investigate emotional development in young children was described earlier (Zahn-Waxler, Radke-Yarrow, & King, 1979). See this description for suggestions for the categories of behavior to observe. Reviews of emotional development appear in publications by Brazelton and Yogman (1986), Greenspan and Greenspan (1985), Izard (1991), Izard and Malatesta (1987), Lewis and Rosenblum (1974), Lieberman (1993), Sroufe (1996).

Social Development. The literature on the effect of the parent or caregiver on the child changed slowly to recognize the child's contribution to these physical, cognitive, emotional, and social interchanges. The research focus now is on the *reciprocity* of the interactions and the ways in which the child's changing developmental status relates to changing interactions. This research may lead you to reconsider your stance on the continuity issue. The Selected Bibliography at the end of this chapter includes references on sociability and social interactions.

Temperament. The concept of temperament appears to be involved in all aspects of the child's social-emotional development. Much attention is being paid to the interaction of temperament and attachment, individual differences in temperament, its assessment by observation and questionnaires, its stability (Bates & Wachs, 1994; Carey, 1978; Goldsmith & Alansky, 1987; Kohnstamm, Bates, & Rothbart, 1989; Seifer and Sameroff, 1986; Seifer, Sameroff, Barrett, & Krafchuk, 1994; Thomas et al., 1963; Thomas & Chess, 1977; Vaughn et al., 1992; Wachs & Kohnstamm, 2001).

D. PARENT OR FAMILY

How did the various members of the family react to the observer? to each other?

Is there a difference in the way the subject baby and sibs are treated by the family? Contingent responsiveness? Expressions of affection? Appropriateness of parental behavior for children's ages and developmental levels?

Is sex-role stereotyping evidenced in parental perception of adult roles, or of sib roles, even if not observable vis-à-vis infant?

Home atmosphere: permissive? warm? stimulating? overwhelming?

What do the parents call the child (directly and indirectly); what does mother (or father) call the observer?

Comment. Some students omit this section, preferring to incorporate the material into the earlier sections. Others are struck by the large differences among families and the changing dynamics in a family system effected by an infant, and they emphasize this portion of the topical report. Lamb's reviews and bibliographies (1979 and 1998) are helpful in focusing your attention on the family context. See also Berkowski, Ramey, and Bristol-Power (2001); Bornstein (1995).

Assessment Instruments

From time to time, babies may be brought to the classroom to be tested with items from some standardized infant tests. This is done more to demonstrate competencies and individual differences than to produce an IQ or Developmental Quotient. Nonetheless, some surface familiarity with these instruments will be useful, because they appear with increasing frequency in recent empirical literature. All require intense training in administration.

Neonatal Procedures. It is unlikely that a newborn will be trundled to the classroom, but movies and videotapes are available and brief descriptions of several assessments follow. Some are fast-screening tests, some are neurological examinations, and some are behavioral assessment tests (Self & Horowitz, 1979). An example of a routinely used screening test is *Apgar's* (1953), in which the newborn is rated 1 minute after birth (and a few minutes later) on five signs: heart rate, respiratory effort, reflex irritability, muscle tone, and color. Although the Apgar scores relate to infant mortality, their correlation with later intelligence or developmental or neurological measures is still controversial.

Prechtl and Beintema (1964) devised a screening procedure that can single out the children who need the fuller neurological examinations. Their classification and assessment of six infant states are highly regarded. For example, a baby lying quietly in the crib, breathing regularly, is in State I, while a crying baby is in State V. Observations are made in the baby's resting position, then when placed supine, undressed, placed prone, and so on. Various reflexes, spontaneous activity, coloring, expressions, thresholds are assessed, and a diagnosis is made summarizing the large amount of data. Tests given from day 4 on appear to have some prognostic value.

The *Brazelton Neonatal Behavioral Assessment Scale* (1973) includes many neurological items similar to previous ones, plus behavioral scales assessing the initial and predominant state of the infant, specific behaviors, and general behaviors. The content of the assessment includes 20 reflex items tapping neurological integrity (e.g., tonic neck reflex, rooting, Babinski), several global ratings (e.g., need for stimulation), and 27 behavioral items assessing the capacity to respond to the environment (e.g., defensive movements, cuddliness, rapidity of buildup to coping state). This scale has been used in investigations of the effects of maternal obstetric medication, narcotic addiction, mother-infant interaction, and cross-cultural comparisons item by item (Als, Tronick, Lester, & Brazelton, 1979). Most reviews (Sameroff, 1979) agree that the scale does specify the contemporary behavior of the infant and demonstrates the richness of the neonates's behavioral organization. It is not, however, a predictor of later development.

Infant and Toddler Scales. Bayley Scales of Infant Development (1969, 1993) are not neonatal tests, like the ones just mentioned, but standardized scales for children, aged 1–42 months. The 1993 version (efforts extend back 63 years) was standardized on 1,700 children, stratified according to the census for sex and race, urban–rural residence, educational attainment of the head of the household, and geographic region, and distributed in 17 age groups. The Mental Scale has 178 items with results expressed as a standard score, the Mental Development Index (MDI). The Motor Scale has 111 items reflecting motor coordination and skills, and results in a Psychomotor Development Index (PDI). The Behavior Rating Scale, which is completed last by the examiner, assesses the qualitative aspects of the child's test-taking behavior, as shown by his/her activity level, approach/withdrawal tendencies, energy, emotional regulation, and so on. Bayley admits that the mental and motor indexes have limited value as predictors of later abilities. She considers their primary value to be an indication of the child's current status, a way to identify mental and motor retardation, i.e., high risk and developmentally delayed infants.

The Bayley Scales of Infant Development (BSID) attempt to provide broad coverage of the infant's response repertoire at each age and an indication of what is "normal" for that age. Accordingly, the items are arranged by the age at which 50% of the children passed a given item; in addition, estimates of the ages at which each item was passed by 5% and 95% of the children are presented.

For descriptions of other scales, and a history of infant intelligence testing and its limitations, see Honzik (1976), Reynolds and Kamphaus (1990), and St. Clair (1978).

Ethics, Again

All of the ethical issues raised earlier apply in full force to research with infants. The fact that a mother gives permission does not absolve the researcher from making as certain as possible that the planned interventions or manipulations (if any) do not have potentially harmful effects on the child. For that, decisions by less-involved colleagues are apt to be more protective and cautious than the researcher's. The history of psychological research has its share of studies that would not pass today's human research review boards. An ethical researcher strives to plan research that will not be in that company some decades hence.

Home visits seem so innocuous to some student observers that they forego privacy considerations, and amusing baby anecdotes bubble up during their meal conversations and in dorms and restaurants. Aside from the obvious caution against mentioning names publicly, it is impossible to know who may overhear and be able to recognize the family from small cues. So the injunction, again, is *don't*!

The value of observing and recording the development of an infant over the course of a semester can be enhanced by periodic classroom discussions (omitting names, of course). Aside from the areas of development highlighted in this chapter, there are issues of relevance to developmental psychologists. Did *all* the children follow the invariant sequences found in child psychology textbooks, with regard to prehension? Locomotion? Object concept? Attachment? Were the motor, cognitive, and social competencies developing at similar or variable rates for each child? Were the parents following similar child-rearing fashions or were they responsive to the individuality of the child? Discuss the theoretical and practical implications related to these issues. Do any of the usual paradigms address these issues? Do the measurement techniques or the statistical designs of most research take them into account?

Selected Bibliography

Adamson, L.B. (1996). *Communication development during infancy*. Boulder, CO: Westview Press.

Ainsworth, M. D. (1963). The development of infant–mother interaction among the Ganda. In B. M. Foss (Ed.), *Determinants of infant behavior II* (pp. 67–112). New York: Wiley.

Ainsworth, M. D. S. (1973). The development of infant–mother attachment. In B. Caldwell & H. Ricciuti (Eds.), *Review of child development research* (*Vol. 3*, pp. 1–94). Chicago: University of Chicago Press.

Ainsworth, M. D. S. (1993). Attachment as related to mother-infant interaction. In C. Rovee-Collier & L. P. Brown, *Advances in infancy research*, (*Vol. 8*). Norwood, NJ: Ablex.

Ainsworth, M. D. S., Blehar, M. C., Waters, E., & Wall, S. (1978). *Patterns of attachment: A psychological study of the strange situation*. Hillsdale, NJ: Lawrence Erlbaum Associates.

Apgar, V. A. (1953). A proposal for a new method of evaluation of the newborn infant. *Current Researches in Anesthesia and Analgesia, 32*, 260–267.

Baillargeon, R. (1987). Object permanence in 3½- and 4½- month old infants. *Developmental Psychology, 23*, 655–664.

Baillargeon, R., Spelke, E., & Wasserman, S. (1985). Object permanence in five-month-old infants. *Cognition, 20*, 191–208.

Bates, E., Bretherton, I., & Snyder, L. (1988*). From first words to grammar*. Cambridge: Cambridge University Press.

Bates, J. E., & Wachs, T. D. (Eds.). (1994). *Temperament: Individual differences at the interface of biology and behavior*. Washington, DC: American Psychological Association.

Bayley, N. (1969). *Manual for the Bayley Scales of Infant Development*. San Antonio: Harcourt Brace.

Bayley, N. (1993). *Manual for the Bayley Scales of Infant Development* (2nd ed.). New York: Psychological Corporation.

Beaty, J. J. (1990). *Observing development of the young child*, (2nd ed.). Riverside, NJ: Merrill/Macmillan Publishing Co.

Bell, R. Q. (1968). A reinterpretation of the direction of effects in studies of socialization. *Psychological Review, 75*, 81–95.

Bell, R. Q. (1971). Stimulus control of parent or caretaker behavior by offspring. *Developmental Psychology, 4*, 63–72.

Bick, E. (1964). Notes on infant observation in psychoanalytic training. *International Journal of Psychoanalysis, 45*, 558–566.

Bloom, L. (1991). *Language development from two to three*. New York: Cambridge University Press.

Bloom, L. (1995). *The transition from infancy to language: Acquiring the power of expression*. New York: Cambridge University Press.

Borkowski, J. G., Ramey, S. L., & Bristol-Power, M. (Eds.). (2001). *Parenting and the child's world: Influences on academic, intellectual, and social-emotional development*. Mahweh, NJ: Lawrence Erlbaum Associates.

Bornstein, M. H. (Ed.). (1995). *Handbook of parenting*, Vols. 1–4. *Hillsdale, NJ: Lawrence Erlbaum Associates.*

Bowlby, J. (1969). *Attachment and loss:* Vol. I. London: Hogarth.

Bowlby, J. (1973). Attachment and loss: Vol. II. Separation anxiety and anger. London: Hogarth.

Brazelton, T. B. (1973). *Neonatal Behavioral Assessment Scale*. (Clinics in Developmental Medicine, No. 50.). Philadelphia: Lippincott.

Brazelton, T. B., Als, H., Tronick, E., & Lester, B. M. (1979). Specific neonatal measures: The Brazelton Neonatal Behavior Assessment Scale. In J. D. Osofsky (Ed.), *Handbook of infant development* (pp. 185–215). New York: Wiley.

Brazelton, T. B., Koslowski, B., & Main, M. (1974). The origins of reciprocity: The early mother-infant interaction. In M. Lewis & L. Rosenblum (Eds.), *The effect of the infant on its caregiver* (pp. 49–77). New York: Wiley.

Brazelton, T. B., & Yogman, M. W. (Eds.). (1986). *Affective development in infancy*. Norwood, NJ: Ablex.

Bremmer, G., Slater, A., & Butterworth, G. (Eds.). (1997). *Infant development: Recent advances*. Bristol, PA: Psychology Press (Taylor & Francis).

Bretherton, I. (1985). Attachment theory: Retrospect and prospect. In I. Bretherton & E. Waters (Eds.), Growing points of attachment theory and research. *Monographs of the Society for Research in Child Development, 50* (1, 2).

Cairns, R. B. (1979). *Social development: The origins and plasticity of interchanges*. San Francisco: Freeman.

Carey, W. B., & McDevitt, S. C. (1978). Revision of the Infant Temperament Questionnarie. *Pediatrics, 61*, 735–739.

Cassidy, J. (1994). Emotion regulation: Influences of attachment relationships. In N. A. Fox (Ed.), The development of emotion regulation: Biological and behavioral considerations. *Monographs of the Society for Research in Child Development, 59* (2–3, Serial No. 240).

Cassidy, J., & Shaver, P. R. (Eds.). (1999). *Handbook of attachment: Theory, research, and clinical applications*. New York: Guilford Publications.

Chomsky, N. (1985). *Reflections on language*. New York: Pantheon.

Clarke-Stewart, K. A. (1973). Interactions between mothers and their young children: Characteristics and consequences. *Monographs of the Society for Research in Child Development, 38* (6–7, Serial No. 153).

Cohen, D. H., Stern, V., & Balaban, N. (1997). *Observing and recording the behavior of young children* (4th ed.). New York: Teachers College Press.

DeHart, G. B., Sroufe, L. A., & Cooper, R. G. (2000). *Child development: Its nature and course* (4th ed.). New York: McGraw-Hill.

Egeland, B., & Farber, E. A. (1984). Infant–mother attachment: Factors related to its development and changes over time. *Child Development, 55*, 753–771.

Eisenberg, N. (Ed.). (1998). *Handbook of child psychology, Vol. 3: Social, emotional, and personality development* (5th ed.). New York: Wiley.

Emde, R. N., & Hewitt, J. K. (Eds.). (2001). *Infancy to early childhood: Genetic and environmental influences on developmental change*. New York: Oxford University Press.

Field, T. (1990). *Infancy*. Cambridge, MA: Harvard University Press.

Flavell, J. H. (1963). *The developmental psychology of Jean Piaget* (chapters 3, 4). Princeton, NJ: Van Nostrand

Frankenburg, W. K., & Dodds, J. B. (1968). *Denver Developmental Screening Test*. Denver: University of Denver Press.

Goldberg, S. (2000). *Attachment and development*. New York: Oxford University Press.

Greenspan, S., & Thorndike Greenspan, N. (1985). *First feelings: Milestones in the emotional development of your baby and child from birth to age 4*. New York: Viking.

Hetherington, E. M., & Parke, R. D. (1999). *Child psychology: A contemporary viewpoint* (5th ed.). New York: McGraw-Hill.

Izard, C. E. (1991). *The psychology of emotions*. New York: Plenum.

Izard, C. E., Fantauzzo, C. A., Castle, J. M., Haynes, O. M., Rayias, M. F., & Putnam, P. H. (1995). The ontogeny and significance of infants' facial expressions in the first 9 months of life. *Development Psychology, 31*(6), 997–1013.

Izard, C. E., & Malatesta, C. Z. (1987). Perspectives on emotional development. Differential emotions theory of early emotional development. In J. D. Osofsky (Ed.), *Handbook of infant development* (2nd ed.), pp. 494–554. New York: Wiley.

Jaffe, J., Beebe, B. Feldstein, S., Crown, C., & Jasnow, M. (2001). Rhythms of dialogue in infancy: Coordinated timing in development. *Monographs of the Society for Research in Child Development, 66* (2, Serial No. 265).

Keith, T. Z., & Reynolds, C. R. (1990). Measurement and design issues in child assessment research. In C. R. Reynolds & R. W. Cabhouse (Eds.), *Handbook of psychological and educational assessment of children* (pp. 29-61). New York: Guilford.

Klaus, M. H., & Kennell, J. H. (1976). *Maternal-infant bonding: The impact of early separation or loss on family development*. St. Louis, MO: Mosby.

Kohnstamm, G. A., Bates, J. E., & Rothbart, M. K. (Eds.). (1989). *Temperament in childhood*. New York: Wiley.

Lacerda, F., vonHofsten, C., & Heimann, M. (2001). *The emerging cognitive abilities in early infancy*. Mahwah, NJ: Lawrence Erlbaum Associates.

Lamb, M. E. (Ed.). (1976). *The role of the father in child development*. New York: Wiley.

Lamb, M. E. (1979). Influence of the child on marital quality and family interaction during the prenatal, perinatal, and infancy periods. In R. M. Lerner & G. Spanier (Eds.), *Child influences on marital and family interaction: A life-span perspective* (pp. 137–163). New York: Academic Press.

Lamb, M. E. (1998). *Parenting and child development in "nontraditional" families*. Mahwah, NJ: Lawrence Erlbaum Associates.

Lamb, M., Bornstein, M. H., & Teti, D. (2002). *Development in infancy: An introduction* (4th ed.). Mahwah, NJ: Lawrence Erlbaum Associates.

Lewis, M. (Ed.). (1976). *Origins of intelligence: Infancy and early childhood*. New York: Plenum Press.

Lewis, M., & Rosenblum, L. A. (Eds.). (1974). *The effect of the infant on its caregiver. New York: Wiley.*

Lieberman, A. (1993). *The emotional life of a toddler*. New York: The Free Press.

Newman, B. M., & Newman, P. R. (1999). *Development through life*: *A psychosocial approach* (7th ed.). Belmont, CA: Brooks/Cole, Wadsworth.

Osofsky, J. D. (Ed.). (1987). *Handbook of infant development* (2nd ed.). New York: Wiley.

Parke, R. D. (1996). *Fatherhood*. Cambridge, MA: Harvard University Press.

Piaget, J. (1952). *The origins of intelligence in children*. New York: International Universities Press.

Piaget, J. (1954). *The construction of reality in the child*. New York: Basic Books.

Prechtl, H. F. R. (1977*). The neurological examination of the full-term newborn infant* (2nd ed.). Philadelphia: Lippincott.

Reynolds, C. R., & Kamphaus, R. W. (1990). *Handbook of psychological and educational assessment of children: Intelligence and achievement*. New York: Guilford.

Rosenblith, J. F. (1992). *In the beginning: Development from conception to age two*. Thousand Oaks, CA: Sage.

Rowe, D. C. (1994). *The limits of family influence*: *Genes, experience, and behavior*. New York: Guilford.

Sameroff, A. J. (Ed.). (1979). Organization and stability of newborn behavior: A commentary on the Brazelton Neonatal Behavior Assessment Scale. *Monographs of the Society for Research in Child Development*, *43* (56, Serial No. 177).

Santrock, J. W. (2000). *Children* (6th ed.). New York, NY: McGraw-Hill.

Schaffer, H. R. (2000). The early experience assumption: Past, present, and future. *International Journal of Behavioral Development*, *24*(1), 5–14.

Seifer, R., & Sameroff, A. J. (1986). The concept, measurement and interpretation of temperament: A survey of research. In M. Wolraich & D. Routh (Eds.), *Advances in developmental and behavioral pediatrics* (*Vol 1*, pp. 143). Greenwich, CT: JAI Press.

Seifer, R., Sameroff, A. J., Barrett, L. C., & Krafchuk, E. (1994). Infant temperament measured by multiple observations and mother report. *Child Development*, *65*, 1478–1490.

Shatz, M. (1994). *A toddler's life: Becoming a person*. New York: Oxford University Press.

Shirley, M. M. (1931*). The first two years. A study of twenty-five babies (Vol. 1). Postural and locomotor development*. Minneapolis: University of Minnesota Press.

Sroufe, L. A. (1996*). Emotional development: The organization of emotional life in the early years*. New York: Cambridge University Press.

Stern, D. N. (1992). *Diary of a baby*. New York: Basic Books.

Thomas, A., & Chess, S. (1977*). Temperament and development*. New York: Brunner/ Mazel.

Thomas, A., Chess, S., Birch, H. G., Hertzig, M. E., & Korn, S. (1963). *Behavioral Individuality in early childhood*. New York: New York University Press.

Van Ijzendoorn, M. H., & Sagi, A. (1999). Cross-cultural patterns of attachment: Universal and contextual dimensions. In J. Cassidy & P. R. Shaver (Eds.), *Handbook of attachment: Theory, research, and clinical applications* (pp. 713–734). New York: Guilford.

VanderZanden, J. W. (2000). *Human development* (7th ed.). New York, NY: McGraw-Hill.

Vaughn, B. E., Stevenson-Hinde, J., Waters, E., Kotsaftis, A., Lefever, G. B., Shouldice, A., Trudel, M., & Belsky, J. (1992). Attachment security and temperament in infancy and early childhood: Some conceptual clarifications. *Developmental Psychology*, *28*, 463–473.

Wachs, T. D., & Kohnstamm (Eds.). (2001). *Temperment in context*. Mahwah, NJ: Lawrence Erlbaum Associates.

Wyly, M. V. (1997). *Infant assessment*. Boulder, CO: Westview Press.

Zahn-Waxler, C., Radke-Yarrow, M., & King, R. A. (1979). Child rearing and children's prosocial initiations toward victims of distress. *Child Development*, *50*, 319–330.

C

Observation Projects

METHODS

General Comments

Once you have decided to use direct observation methods in your research, either because automated measurement techniques are not available and standard tests and questionnaires do not seem adequate, then there are decisions you have to make (Sackett, 1978):

- deciding what to observe

- deciding on a sampling strategy

- deciding whether your data are usable (reliable)

- deciding how to analyze the data and evaluate your research hypotheses.

Observation projects are not simpler, easier, or quicker than traditional experiments, but often offer information that is richer or unavailable by other techniques. The researcher preparing to use observational methods faces many problems, including the absence of control, the possibilities of observer bias and subject reactivity, and the ethical problems of invasion of privacy and informed consent (Goodwin, 1998).

In the introduction to Part Two there was a brief listing of six methods of observational child study (Wright, 1960). Several of these will be expanded now, and then some exercises and projects for training observational skills will be detailed.

Specimen Records

The sequential protocols describing infant behavior, earlier, are specimen records. The observer records everything possible of the immediate setting and situation, and behaviors exhibited. These are often made more precise by periodically jotting the time in the margin, or at the beginning and end of some action like diapering, drinking a bottle, or bathing. It is not uncommon to fill out one's hurried shorthand or speedwriting with remembered details immediately afterwards.

Such records are utilized in many ways in both clinical and research settings. They can be read through successively for frequency of behaviors like crying episodes, people-touching, object-touching, or withdrawal movements. The whole record can be divided into relatively molar behavior episodes, a techniques used by Barker and Wright (1951). These episodes have a beginning and an ending to the action; examples are "taking off wraps," "going outside," "cleaning the workspace." A good specimen record lends itself to analysis of either molecular bits or molar units, and can be used and reused.

Time Sampling

If you know precisely which behaviors you wish to observe and are interested mainly in the frequency of occurrence of these behaviors, the time-sampling technique is an appropriate one to utilize.

The observer uses a specified number of time intervals, of a specified uniform length and spacing. The observed behavior is recorded by a prearranged code notation or a checklist system of tallying. If a group of children is being observed, each child is commonly watched in rotation, that is, one minute-John, one minute-Sue, one minute-Barry, and so on. In the 70 or so years that this method has been used, a wide range of behaviors has been observed (e.g., quarrels, thumbsucking, nervous habits); the time units have varied in duration; the behavior categories have varied from molecular to molar, and objective to relatively subjective; the data have been scored and analyzed in various ways. Scores in use include

the number of time intervals during which the observed behavior occurred,

the total number of occurrences of that behavior,

the number of occurrences per interval,

the total occurrence time, and

the occurrence time per interval.

Time sampling is a controlled observation method, which systematically and reliably samples the target behaviors and limits the uncertainties (and time and effort) of the researcher. The disadvantages are that the complexity and richness of behavior in context are difficult to capture by this method, and the target behaviors need to occur frequently for this method to be feasible. Cause–effect relationships, reciprocal interactions, and the meaningful flow of behavior in context are often lost in a method that resembles still photographs rather than movies.

One can lengthen the observation time interval and use a specimen record in order to combine some of the advantages of the sequential protocol with frequent time samples. Advantages and disadvantages of various techniques need to be weighed in the context of one's research aims and constraints.

An example of an observational study that combined 10-second time-sampling with event sampling is Hall and Vecia's (1990) research on touching between couples moving through a mall.

Event Sampling

The researcher focuses attention on a unit of behavior, a single class of behavior episodes like quarrels (Dawe, 1934), greetings, going-to-bed routines, playing with pets, cooperation episodes, meeting a new teacher and so on. The kinds of notes taken vary widely from specimen records to coded checklists and time measures. The point, however, is to attempt to describe an integral action (from beginning to end) within a context: what began it, who was involved, precisely what happened, how it terminated, how long it lasted. As many such episodes are collected as possible. Dawe (1934), for example, collected 200 quarrels from the 40 preschoolers, about 3 to 4 an hour.

In a more recent study, which added a structured element to the observational study of helping behavior in young children, the researchers also added a trait rating to their event sampling (Peterson, Ridley-Johnson, & Carter, 1984). Children took turns wearing a fancy "supersuit" for four minutes; it had a large button at the back of the neck that was difficult to button or unbutton alone.

The advantage in studying an integral event in context is that the relationship between the behavior and its coexisting (and sometimes antecedent) conditions may be clarified. On the other hand, event sampling focuses on a piece of the behavior stream, and the larger stream that is picked up by specimen records is unrecorded.

Trait Rating

In most rating scales, specific observations are not recorded; instead, summaries or assessments of earlier observations are noted. Most scales do not require the rater to list or specify the observed behaviors on which the ratings were based, although some do ask for an example or two.

Rating scales differ from time sampling, event sampling, and specimen records in that what is being recorded is not being observed at the moment of recording but is the result of cumulative observation. Examples are the ratings that teachers commonly need to make about the child's adjustment to school, cooperation, motor coordination, and so on. Widely known older classic rating scales for assessing the child's home setting in terms of the parents' behavior patterns are the Fels Parent Behavior Rating Scales (Baldwin, Kalhorn, & Breese, 1945, 1949; Champney, 1941). These are characterized by many scales with many items each, with ratings made on a graphic continuum. Several scales could be grouped to measure some aspect of parent behavior, like warmth. Similarly, the Fels Child Behavior Rating Scales (early version: Richards & Simons, 1941; revision: Fels Research Institute, Yellow Springs, Ohio) focus the ratings on children of preschool through about 9 years of age. The child is rated on affectionateness, aggressiveness, competitiveness, emotional control, friendliness, vigor of activity, and so on. A more recent example of rating scales, based on much earlier research, however, is the Behavior Rating Scale, with is part of the Bayley Scales of Infant Development. These were described earlier in the Infancy section, and uses a 5-point rating scale for each item.

Checklists and rating scales abound in the psychological and educational literature, and are heavily used in school and clinical settings as well as in research. A heavily used test is the Child Behavior Checklist (CBCL), now published in two forms: a 1992 version for ages 2-3, and a 1991 version for ages 4-18. There are also related forms for the teacher and the youths. The CBCL/4-18, for example, has 113 items, which the parent or caregiver rates on a three-point scale (very true or often true, 2 points; somewhat or sometimes true, 1; not true, 0). The CBCL is the most frequently cited measure in studies of child psychopathology (Achenbach & Edelbrock, 1986; Achenbach, 1991a, b, c).

Although skilled raters can achieve high reliabilities, rating scales can be difficult for novices. How does one rate a drowsy 3-month-old for alertness if the infant is the first 3-month-old one has seen? Although ratings have the advantage of being quantifiable, they are not very helpful in clarifying cause–effect behavior. Nonetheless, rating is a heavily used technique in diagnostic assessment and research.

EXERCISES

There is so much that you can study from a one-way observation booth:

how teachers respond to boys and girls

object- vs. social-directed play

sex-typing of activity preferences

prosocial behaviors (empathy, nurturing, cooperation, sharing)

aggressive behaviors (verbal, physical)

choice of peers (same-sex or opposite-sex affiliation)

size of play group

persistence, attention span (number of different activities in X time period)

dominance/submission

positive and negative affect.

Possibilities are great. We will study now sex-typed behavior, measured two ways:

(a) Activity preferences via group time-sampling

(b) Sex-typed play of individual children

(a) Activity Preferences by Sex

The following observation, which involves time sampling, has been performed frequently by our students at campus nurseries in South Hadley, Massachusetts, and Ann Arbor since 1952. The observer merely *counts* the number of boys and girls playing at specific activities. The simplest version is limited to one age group and uses Data Sheet C2.1. One can look at age and sex differences, using Data Sheet C2.2 instead. Suppose you use the youngest nursery-school class and run these observations at the beginning and again at the end of the school year or semester. What will that tell you? You may wish, too, to compare your results with those for younger age groups (Etaugh, Collins, & Gerson, 1975; Fagot, 1974; Serbin, Moller, Gulko, Powlisha, & Colburne, 1994), as well as with results for preschoolers (Connor & Serbin, 1977; Fagot and Patterson, 1969; Weintraub et al., 1984).

Moeller and Moeller (1971), and a large group of graduate and undergraduate students, used this activity-preference observation as one part of a complex project on activity preferences, task orientation, and social interaction of first- and second- graders. The following description and instructions are largely excerpted or adapted from their paper, with permission.

The Classroom Setting. A visit should be made to the classroom where the observations will take place so as to become familiar with the room and with the location of different activities, and to decide where the observer should stand, and to let the children see him or her. During data collection, the observer should stay in the designated positions so as not to distract the children with constant movement.

If the room to be observed is occupied by children of both sexes or by children from two different grade levels, then each child should wear a large badge that clearly demonstrates grade (or age) and sex. Color can be used as a cue, for example, green badge for older males, yellow badge for older females, and so on.

The children should be told that visitors will be in the room to watch what the teacher and children do during the day or period. If the raters avoid eye contact with the children, the children will be more likely to ignore them.

Times at Which Observations Should Be Made. Observations should be scheduled so as to cover systematically the beginning, middle, and end of the activities period(s), as well as the days of the week. Conclusions drawn from behaviors observed only on late Friday afternoons cannot be generalized to apply to daily behavior.

Secondly, the observations should optimally occur over a minimum of two weeks. Observations taken during one week may be heavily influenced by a specific event, such as Halloween; in such a case, many children may choose the craft area in order to make masks.

The Number of Observations. The number of observations gathered depends on the number of raters, the number of days reserved for these observations, the amount of time spent by each observer, and the type of information one wants to obtain from the data. As a suggestion, each activity could be observed a minimum of 40 times, that is, four times a day over ten school days (which would constitute two weeks—the suggested minimum for the observation period). To gather this many observations would involve relatively little individual effort if a large number of observers were available.

The Materials Needed by the Observer. The observer should have a clipboard or some hard surface on which to write and prepared data sheets. A dark pencil is preferable to a pen because erasures can be made. The observer will also need a stopwatch or a wristwatch with a second hand. The observation sheets need to be adjusted to fit your situations by entering the list of activities in the left-hand column, as they will appear in *sequence* to an observer swiveling his or her head from one activity to its adjacent one; for example, Playhouse area, Trucks, Game table, Workbench, and so on. This list must be standardized and inserted onto the data sheet prior to the formal observation.

Collecting the Data. Because the interobserver reliability has been consistently very high on this task, it will probably be adequate and efficient to use one observer at a time in the room, after he or she runs and discards the first two observations (columns of data). The observer should stand at the designated position and count and record *all* the girls and boys, respectively, in the room. Then the observer looks at the first activity area and counts and records the boys and girls there at that moment. If a new child enters that activity area *after* the observer has counted the children, this child is not included in the tally. The observer immediately switches his or her gaze to the adjacent activity (the next row on the data sheet) and quickly repeats the counting process. And so on, until the first column is finished. The second column or round of observations is started at the designated time. For this task, three- or five-minute intervals have been feasible even for novices. If, for example, observations started at 10:00, and the cycles were to be three minutes apart, the columns would be headed 10:00, 10:03, 10:06...

A Suggested Analysis of the Data. Add the *rows* of numbers of boys and girls, and record the sums in the *Sum* column of Data Sheet C2.1. Divide by the number of columns of observations to obtain the *mean* number of boys and girls at each activity. The *proportion* can be computed by placing the mean number of boys in that activity over the total number of boys in the room; similarly for girls. If Data Sheet C2.2 is being used (both sexes, two age groups), adjust the arithmetic accordingly.

Collate the summary data from each observer, for each activity, on Master Data Sheet C2.3. At the bottom of each column, record the median proportion. These simple medians offer much information. Ignoring sex, one can see which activities attracted the most or least children. Focusing on sex, one can see for which activities the proportions of girls and boys differ most and for which activities these proportions differ least—in other words, which activities are most and least sex-typed. Utilizing the more refined age and sex data, one can discuss the preferences of younger boys, younger girls, older boys, and older girls. Activities can be rank ordered in a variety of ways, depending on questions being asked.

(b) Sex and Age Differences in Play—Sex-typed Play of Individual Children

Using naturalistic observation of one child by one observer, each, we wish to collect data to answer these questions about sex-typed play:

Is there a difference between boys and girls in the total sex-typing score?

If you used two preschool groups—younger and older—is there an age difference in the total sex-typing scores for boys and girls? (Age X Sex *F*)

Is same-sex affiliation greater than opposite-sex affiliation, that is, do girls play with girls and boys with boys more than they play in mixed-sex groups? Is there greater same-sex affiliation in older children? (Age X Sex *F* on Group Composition)

Size of group: do boys play in larger groups than girls? (Sex *F* on Mean Group Size).

Try to change these questions into hypotheses based on the research findings from articles listed in the bibliography.

INSTRUCTIONS FOR THE OBSERVATION OF ONE CHILD

Procedure

1. Sign up for an observation session. Each observation session takes half an hour but be sure to allow time to get oriented.
2. Have an individual data sheet for each child, C2.4.

Explanation for the columns on the chart.

1. *Time Column*
   a. Locate your child in the assigned room.
   b. Be familiar with the areas of the nursery; be sure the clock is in view.
   c. Begin observing at 5 minute intervals, e.g. 10:00, 10:05, 10:10, 10:15, 10:20.

2. *Where Column*
   a. Specify carefully where the child is playing at the moment of observation, for example, block section, little house section.

3. *What Column*
   a. Specify in as much detail as possible precisely what the child is doing at the moment of observation.

HINT: Watch the child the minute before in order to understand the context, for example, fixing faucet versus playing house with the blocks using one block for a mommy and another block for a daddy.

*Try to catch the language, affect (smile, frown, stomps foot)

**Specify exactly what toy the child is playing with and how he/she is playing with it. YOU MUST BE EXPLICIT.

  4. *Group Column*

    a. Count the number of children in the specific play area. *(Include* the child you are observing)

    b. Indicate the number of boys and the number of girls in that play area.

DO NOT SCORE WHILE YOU ARE OBSERVING, JUST BE AS DETAILED AS POSSIBLE.

It is important to establish observer reliability *before* collecting your formal data. To do this, have two students observe the same child simultaneously, for several rows of data. Then, they should leave the observation booth, and run the reliability check as shown in the Infant Observation, Two B. The class should decide how high a reliability number they are comfortable with—90% agreement, 85%? or what?

Scoring

1. Score columns 2, 3, 4 on your data sheet. Indicate score in the little boxes.

2. Use the following scoring

    5 most masculine
    4 somewhat masculine
    3 alone, neutral or both
    2 somewhat feminine
    1 most feminine

3. Two students should score each data sheet together. In the event of a disagreement, a third person mediates, (preferably a TA or the instructor).

4. For each time period there are 3 scores which are summed horizontally and noted in the last column labeled "score." Add the 5 scores together vertically for the total score of that (half hour) session. Write the score in the box, bottom right hand corner.

5. Also add the 5 scores in each column and indicate the score on the line under each column. Add up all the "wheres", then all the "whats", etc.

6. Total scores can range from 15 (most feminine) to 75 (most masculine). The least sex-typed child would have a score of 45.

We used the data from the previous exercise to decide the masculinity/femininity of the play areas for the Where column scoring.

The What column scoring is more ambiguous and requires discussion and consensus in the class. Aggressive acts, shouting, racing about, throwing blocks, were stereotypically considered masculine. Nurturing acts were considered feminine. Sharing was scored 3. The data from exercise (a) was helpful here too, and determined whether we could rate table play, easel painting, kitchen play as feminine.

Analysis

First enter your child's scores (where, what, group composition, total sex-typing score and mean play group size) on the master data sheet. Appropriate means are computed, and table C2.5 is the result.

There are several ways to analyze these data; we will use ANOVAs. Do a 2 age X 2 sex ANOVA for Where scores, What scores, Group Composition scores, separately. Do an ANOVA for mean Playgroup Size, and fill in Tables C.6, 7, 8, 9, 10. It is helpful, if you obtain any age X sex interactions, to draw a figure of the four means, with the scores on the ordinate, the two sexes on the abscissa, a solid line for the Young means, a dotted line for the Old means.

Discussion

Referring to your hypotheses and the table specifically relating to each, what did you find? How does it relate to the literature? Do boys and girls differ in their total sex-typing score, and are older children more sex-typed in their play as several researchers suggest? If same-sex affiliation is an aspect of sex identity, do your three-year-olds show this, as La Freniere, Strayer, and Gauthier (1984) and others find? (See Bibliography.) Is sex a more potent variable than age in determining sex-typed play?

Many of the authors listed in the Bibliography agree that there is a strong behavioral preference for same-sex playmates as young as three or four, and this preference increases in prevalence until puberty (e.g. Maccoby, 1994; Maccoby & Jacklin, 1987). They also find that boys play in larger groups than girls do. Think about the WHY of these findings. Explanations for same-sex preference include (a) direct reinforcement (social approval), (b) cognitive consonance ("same as self"), and (c) behavioral compatibility (sex differences in the behavioral repertoire, Maccoby & Jacklin, 1987). Did you see any evidence for or against these explanations? Serbin, Powlisha, and Gulko (1993, p. 9) pointed out that "even when we do see apparent behavioral enactment of sex-typed traits (e.g., dominant/submissive), it is often as much a function of the interaction partner and setting as of the individual's generalized personality." Did you see any examples of this?

(c) Television Programs as a Socialization Agent

Over the last few decades the conviction grew that violence in TV programs (and movies and records, etc.) was related to the increasing violence in real life. Becoming stronger and louder, this notion prompted much research (APA, 1994; Eron & Murray, nd; Green, 1994; Huston et al., 1992; Murray, 1980; Sparks, 1996). By 1980, Murray could review 25 years of research and controversy about television's positive and negative impact on youth, and he provided master bibliographics from 1955 on. Much of the research with young children was experimental; with adolescents it was correlational. Time-lagged studies reported in the 1970s by Lefkowitz, Eron, Huesmann, and Walder found a significant relationship between preferences for violent television programs at age eight and aggression at age 18.

A recent brief APA brochure by Eron and Murray concluded that seeing violence on television has three major effects: it may desensitize children to the pain and suffering of others; it may make children more fearful; it may lead to more aggressive, harmful behavior.

During early 1996, Congress mandated that a chip be inserted in TV sets produced in 1998 that would enable parents to cut out chosen violent TV programs. This requires a violence-rating system for programs, however; not an easy task and still ongoing. After much controversy and compromise, the Federal Communications Commission passed a resolution in August, 1996, that requires TV stations to show three hours of children's educational programming each week (sic!), and the FCC is to determine compliance. (Is a show labeled "educational" by a station really educational?) Perhaps the combined publicity and pressure and outcries are having some effect—newspapers in late 1996 reported a slight decline in juvenile violent crime.

It is important to realize that violence may not be the only effect of TV viewing. Sex and race stereotypes can be furthered (or lessened). Prosocial behavior (sharing, helping, nurturing) can be taught, as the "Barney" show and "Mr. Roger's Neighborhood" demonstrate.

The following observation project was created in the early 1990s by Carol Claflin, when she was my teaching assistant and young colleague in several child psychology and life-span development classes. It enables you to investigate the present status of children's TV programs with regard to violence, some sex and ethnic stereotypes, prosocial incidents, et cetera.

Assignment

Watch 15-minute segments from four different children's television programs. These could include Saturday morning cartoons, before or after school programs like "Sesame Street", "Mr. Roger's Neighborhood". Then, for each segment complete the first four rows in Table C2.11. In addition, complete the table for 3 of the commercials viewed during children's programming, using the last three rows. Use tally strokes while watching.

DIRECTIONS FOR COMPLETING THE TABLE

For each segment record the following:

1. Title of program or name of commercial product, and time and date.

2. Characters: Indicate the total number of male characters, female characters, and whether the main character was male or female. For nonhuman characters (i.e., animals, ghosts, Smurfs, etc.) classify as male or female if dress, hairstyle, name, et cetera, is indicative of gender.

3. Ethnicity: Indicate total number of characters represented as White, Black, Asian, Hispanic, or other (describe).

4. Family composition: Indicate whether the program identifies or represents characters as members of traditional, single/divorced, adoptive, or other family structures.

5. Home/Neighborhood: Indicate whether program setting is representative of white middle-class neighborhoods or other (describe).

6. Prosocial behavior: Record the number of episodes of prosocial behavior, for example, helping, sharing, coming to another character's aid, self-sacrificing behavior.

7. Aggression: Record the number of episodes involving:
   a. physical aggression—physical action that intentionally causes damage to a character. Action may be performed.
   b. verbal aggression—any threat, statement, or verbal response that causes psychological damage to another character (i.e. severe sarcasm or criticism, yelling, teasing, silence, etc.).

8. Violation of the laws of nature: Record the number of events where the laws of nature are violated, as in humans fly, characters bounce after falling from a cliff, character returns to previous condition after being run over by a car, body part passes through a wall, picture on cereal box comes to life, and so on.

9. Short summary of story line or main theme.

CAUTION: This is a complex assignment. It is crucial that you and another student practice on several minutes of a program and do the reliability exercise before tackling the assignment individually.

Scoring

Sum the tally marks in each column, and enter the sum in the row labeled "Total", for the programs and commercials, respectively, on your Individual Data Sheet. Then enter the sums on the master data sheets provided by the instructor. The latter information can be summarized in Table C2.12, for the class.

Discussion

What do your data say about the target behaviors? Were you surprised by any of the results? Did you find differences between the programs and commercials? Why might these exist? What socializing messages are being sent to children?

In the several classes engaged in this project in the early 1990s, we found almost three times as many males as females portrayed. The main character was a male 68–90% of the times. Commercials were a little more even handed with regard to males/females. Characters were mainly White, markedly so in commercials. Traditional family composition outnumbered the other possibilities, again even more so in commercials. When home or neighborhood was identified, it was most often White middle class. Episodes of physical and verbal aggression outnumbered episodes of prosocial behavior. Violations of nature were very common (78–86%). Commercials, on the other hand, were low in aggression and violation of nature episodes.

Now a decade later, did you find an improvement in TV *children's* programs in your data compared to ours? Adult programs may provide different results. The industry averages across TV programming *overall* indicated 57% of programs with violence, and 73% of those with unpunished violence (*APA Monitor*, April 1996). Can we assume that children do not watch adult programs?

Selected Bibliography

General

Achenbach, T. M., (1991a). *Manual for the Child Behavior Checklist/4-18 and 1991 Profile*. Burlington, VT: University of Vermont, Department of Psychiatry.

Achenbach, T. M., (1991b). *Manual for the Youth Self-Report and 1991 Profile*. Burlington, VT: University of Vermont, Department of Psychiatry.

Achenbach, T. M., (1991c). *Manual for the Teacher's Report Form and 1991 Profile*. Burlington, VT: University of Vermont, Department of Psychiatry.

Achenbach, T. M., & Edelbrock, C. S. (1986). *Child Behavior Checklist and Youth Self-Report*. Burlington, VT: Author.

Bayley, N. (1993). *Bayley Scales of Infant Development* (2nd ed.). San Antonio, TX: Psychological Corporation.

Beaty, J. J. (1990). *Observing development of the young child* (2nd ed.). Riverside, NJ: Merrill/Macmillan Publishing Co.

Baldwin, A. L., Kalhorn, J., & Breese, F. H. (1949). The appraisal of parent behavior. *Psychological Monographs*, *63*(4, Whole No. 299).

Barker, R. G. (Ed.). (1963). *The stream of behavior*. New York: Appleton-Century-Crofts.

Barker, R. G., & Wright, H. F. (1951*). One boy's day*. New York: Harper & Row.

Boehm, A. E., & Weinberg, R. A. (1997). *The classroom observer: Developing observation skills in early childhood settings* (3rd ed.). New York: Teachers College Press.

Braza, F., Braza, P., Carreras, M. R., & Munoz, J. M. (1997). Development of sex differences in preschool children: Social behavior during an academic year. *Psychological Reports*, *80*(1), 179–188.

Champney, H. (1941). The measurement of parent behavior. *Child Development*, *12*, 131–166.

Clarke-Stewart, K. A. (1973). Interactions between mothers and their young children: Characteristics and consequences. *Monographs of the Society for Research in Child Development, 38*(67, Serial No. 153).

Cohen, D. H., Stern, V., & Balaban, N. (1997). *Observing and recording the behavior of young children* (4th ed.). New York: Teachers College Press.

Dawe, H. C. (1934). An analysis of two hundred quarrels of preschool children. *Child Development*, *5*, 139–157.

Goodwin, C. J. (1998). *Research in psychology: Methods and design* (2nd ed.). New York: Wiley.

Hall, J. A., & Vecia, E. M. (1990). More "touching" observations: New insights on men, women, and interpersonal touch. *Journal of Social Psychology*, *59*, 1155–1162.

Irwin, D. M., & Bushnell, M. M. (1980). *Observational strategies for child study*. New York: Holt, Rinehart & Winston.

Moeller, T., & Moeller, J. R. (1971). *Methods for examining children's behavior with respect to classroom activities: Determining activity preferences, attentiveness, and social interaction*. Unpublished report, University of Michigan.

Pellegrini, A. D. (1996). *Observing children in their natural worlds: A methodological primer*. Mahwah, NJ: Lawrence Erlbaum Associates.

Peterson, L., Ridley-Johnson, R., & Carter, C. (1984). The supersuit: An example of children's altruism. *Journal of General Psychology*, *110*, 235–241.

Richards, T. W., & Simons, M. P. (1941). The Fels Child Behavior Scales. *Genetic Psychology Monographs*, *24*, 259–309.

Rosenbaum, P. R. (1995). *Observational studies*. New York: Springer-Verlag.

Sackett, G. P. (Ed.). (1978). *Observing behavior*, Vol II: *Data collection and analysis methods*. Baltimore, MD: University Park Press.

Wright, H. F. (1960). Observational child study. In P. Mussen (Ed.), *Handbook of research methods in child development*. New York: Wiley.

Wright, H. F. (1967). *Recording and analyzing child behavior*. New York: Harper and Row.

Play: Sex and Age Differences

Alexander, G. M., & Hines, M. (1994). Gender labels and play styles: Their relative contribution to children's selection of playmates. *Child Development*, *65*, 869–879.

Beal, C. R. (1994). *Boys and girls: The development of gender roles*. New York: McGraw-Hill.

Beere, C. A. (1990). *Gender roles: A handbook of tests and measures*. New York: Greenwood.

Benenson, J. F. (1993). Greater preference among females than males for dyadic interaction in early childhood. *Child Development, 64*, 544–555.

Bronson, W. C. (1981). *Toddler's behaviors with agemates: Issues of interaction, cognition, and affect*. Norwood, NJ: Ablex.

Connor, J. M., & Serbin, L. A. (1977). Behaviorally-based masculine and feminine activity scales for preschoolers: Correlates with other classroom behaviors and cognitive tests. *Child Development, 48*, 1411–1416.

DeRosier, M. E., Cillessen, A. H. N., Coie, J. D., & Dodge, K. A. (1994). Group social context and children's aggressive behavior. *Child Development, 65*, 1068–1079.

Ellis, S., Rogoff, B., & Cromer, C. (1981). Research reports: Age segregation in children's social interactions. *Developmental Psychology, 17*, 399–407.

Etaugh, C., Collins, G., & Gerson, A. (1975). Reinforcement of sex-typed behaviors of two-year-old children in a nursery school setting. *Developmental Psychology, 11*(2), 255.

Fagot, B. I. (1974). Sex differences in toddlers' behavior and parental reaction. *Developmental Psychology, 10*(4), 554–558.

Fagot, B. I., & Patterson, G. R. (1969). An *in vivo* analysis of reinforcing contingencies for sex-role behaviors in the preschool child. *Developmental Psychology, 1*, 563–568.

Goldstein, J. H. (1994). Sex differences in toy play and use of videogames. In J. H. Goldstein (Ed.), *Toys, play, and child development*. New York: Cambridge University Press.

Hines, M., & Kaufman, F. R. (1994). Androgen and the development of human sex-typical behavior: Rough-and-tumble play and sex of preferred playmates in children with congenital adrenal hyperplasia (CAH*). Child Development, 65*, 1042–1053.

Kuhn, D., Nash, S., & Brucken, L. (1978). Sex role concepts of two- and three-year-olds. *Child Development, 49*, 445–451.

LaFreniere, P., & Sroufe, L. A. (1985). Profiles of peer competence in preschool: Interrelations between measures, influences of social ecology, and relation to attachment theory. *Developmental Psychology, 21*(1), 56–69.

LaFreniere, P., Strayer, F. F., & Gauthier, R. (1984). The emergence of same-sex preferences among preschool peers. *Child Development, 55*, 1958–1966.

Langlois, J. H., Gottfried, N. W., & Seay, B. (1973). The influence of sex of peer on the social behavior of preschool children. *Developmental Psychology, 8*(1), 93–98.

Leaper, C. (Ed.). (1992). *Childhood gender segregation: Causes and consequences. New Directions in Child Development* (No. 65). San Francisco: Jossey-Bass.

Leaper, C. (1994). Exploring the consequences of sex segregation on social relationships. In C. Leaper (Ed.), *The development of gender and relationships* (pp. 67–86). San Francisco: Jossey-Bass.

Lever, J. (1976). Sex differences in the games children play. *Social Problems, 23*(4), 478–487.

Liben, L. S., & Signorella, M. L. (Eds.). (1987). *Children's gender schemata. New directions in child development* (*Vol. 38*). San Francisco: Jossey-Bass.

Lytton, H., & Romney, D. M. (1991). Parents' differential socialization of boys and girls: A meta-analysis. *Psychological Bulletin, 109*, 267–296.

Maccoby, E. E. (1988). Gender as a social category. *Developmental Psychology, 24*, 755–765.

Maccoby, E. E. (1994). Sex segregation in childhood. In C. Leaper (Ed.), *The development of gender and relationships* (pp. 87–98). San Francisco: Jossey-Bass.

Maccoby, E. E., & Jacklin, C. N. (1987). Gender segregation in childhood. In H. W. Reese (Ed.), *Advances in child development and behavior* (*Vol. 20*, pp. 239–287). New York: Academic Press.

Martin, C. L., Eisenbud, L., & Rose, H. (1995). Children's gender-based reasoning about toys. *Child Development, 66*(5), 1453–1471.

Martin, C. L., & Fabes, R. A. (2001). The stability and consequences of young children's same-sex peer interactions. *Developmental Psychology, 37*(3), 431–446.

Martin, C. L., & Fabes, R. A., Evans, S. M., & Wyman, H. (1999). Social cognition on the playground: Children's beliefs about playing with girls versus boys and their relation to sex segregated play. *Journal of Social and Personal Relationships, 16*, 751–772.

O'Brien, M., Huston, A. C., & Risley, T. (1983). Sex-typed play of toddlers in a day care center. *Journal of Applied Developmental Psychology, 4*, 1–9.

Pellegrini, A. D. (1996). *Observing children in their natural worlds: A methodological primer*. Mahwah, NJ: Lawrence Erlbaum Associates.

Powlishta, K. K., Serbin, L. A., & Moller, L. C. (1993). The stability of individual differences in gender typing: Implications for understanding gender segregation. *Sex Roles, 29*, 723–737.

Serbin, L. A., Moller, L. C., Gulko, J., Powlisha, K. K., & Colburne, K. A. (1994). The emergence of sex segregation in toddler playgroups. In C. Leaper (Ed.), *The development of gender and relationships* (pp. 7–18).San Francisco: Jossey-Bass.

Serbin, L. A., Poulin-Dubois, D., Colbume, K. A., Sen, M. G., Eichstedt, J. A. (2001). Gender stereotyping in infancy: Visual preferences for and knowledge of gender-stereotyped toys in the second year. *International Journal of Behavioral Development, 25*(1), 7–15.

Serbin, L. A., Powlishta, K. K., & Gulko, J. (1993). The development of sex typing in middle childhood. *Monographs of the Society for Research in Child Development, 58*(2, Serial No. 232).

Serbin, L. A., & Sprafkin, C. (1982). Measurement of sex-typed play: A comparison between laboratory and naturalistic observation procedures. *Behavioral Assessment, 4*, 225–235.

Serbin, L. A., & Sprafkin, C. (1986). The salience of gender and the process of sex-typing in three- to seven-year-old children. *Child Development, 57*, 1188–1199.

Thorne, B. (1993). *Gender play: Girls and boys in school*. Rutgers, NJ: Rutgers University Press.

Turner, P. J. (1991). Relations between attachment, gender and behavior with peers in preschool. *Child Development, 62*, 1475–1488.

Turner, P. J., & Gervai, J. (1995). A multidimensional study of gender typing in preschool children and their parents: Personality, attitudes, preferences, behavior, and cultural differences. *Developmental Psychology, 31*(5), 759–772.

Turner, P. J., Gervai, J., & Hinde, R. A. (1993). Gender-typing in young children: Preferences, behavior, and cultural differences. *British Journal of Developmental Psychology, 11*, 323–342.

Underwood, M. K., Schockner, A. E., & Hurley, J. C. (2001). Children's responses to same- and other-gender peers: An experimental investigation with 8-, 10-, and 12-year-olds. *Developmental Psychology, 37*(3), 362–372.

Vaughter, R. M., Sadh, D., & Vozzola, E. (1994). Sex similarities and differences in types of play in games and sports. *Psychology of Women Quarterly, 18*, 85–104.

Weinraub, M., Clemens, P. L., Sokoloff, A., Ethridge, T., Gracely, E., & Myers, (1984). The development of sex-role stereotypes in the third year: Relationships to gender labeling, gender identity, sex-typed toy preference, and family characteristics. *Child Development, 55*, 1493–1503.

See additional references related to sex-role in the Section entitled Sex Identity, Experiments 9 and 10.

Television

American Psychological Association. (1993). *Violence and youth: Psychology's response*. Washington, DC: American Psychological Association.

Asamen, J. K., & Berry, G. L. (Eds.). (1998). *Research paradigms, television, and social behavior*. Thousand Oaks, CA: Sage.

Bushman, B. J., & Anderson, C. A. (2001). Media violence and the American public: Scientific facts versus media misinformation. *American Psychologist, 56*(6/7), 477–489.

Clifford, B. R., Gunter, B., & McAleer, J. L. (1995). *Television and children: Program evaluation, comprehension, and impact*. Mahwah, NJ: Lawrence Erlbaum Associates.

Davies, M. M. (1996). *Fake, fact, and fantasy: Children's interpretations of television reality*. Mahwah, NJ: Lawrence Erlbaum Associates.

Durkin, K., & Nugent, B. (1998). Kindergarten children's gender-role expectations for television actors. *Sex Roles, 38*(5-6), 387–402.

Eisenberg, N. (Ed.). (1998). *Handbook of child psychology, Vol. 3: Social, emotional, and personality development* (5th ed.). New York: Wiley.

Eron, L., & Murray, J. P. (no date). *Violence on Television: What do children learn? What can parents do?* Washington, DC: American Psychological Association, Office of Public Affairs.

Eron, L. D., Gentry, J., & Schlegel, P. (Eds.). (1995). *Reason to hope: A psychosocial perspective on violence and youth*. Washington, DC: American Psychological Association.

Frederich, L. K., & Stein, A. A. (1973). Aggressive and prosocial television programs and the natural behavior of preschool children. *Monographs of the Society for Research in Child Development, 38*(Serial No. 151, No. 5).

Green, R. G. (1994). Television and aggression: Recent developments in research and theory. In D. Zillman, J. Bryant & A. C. Huston (Eds.), *Media, children and the family: Social scientific, psychodynamic, and clinical perspectives* (pp. 151–162). Mahwah, NJ: Lawrence Erlbaum Associates.

Huesmann, L. R. (1994). *Aggressive behavior: Current perspectives*. New York: Plenum Press.

Huesmann, L. R., & Eron, L. (1986). *Television and the aggressive child: Cross- national comparison*. Hillsdale, NJ: Lawrence Erlbaum Associates.

Huesmann, L. R., & Eron, L. D. (1996). *The development of aggression from infancy to adulthood*. Boulder, CO: Westview Press.

Huston, A. C., Donnerstein, E., Fairchild, H., Feshbach, N. D., Katz, P. A., Murray, J. P., Rubinstein, E. A., Wilcox, B., & Zuckerman, D. (1992). *Big world, small screen: The role of television in American society*. Lincoln, NE: University of Nebraska Press.

Murray, J. P. (1995). Children and television violence. *Kansas Journal of Law and Public Policy*.

Murray, J. P. (1980). *Television and youth: 25 years of research and controversy*. Boys Town, NE: Boys Town Center for the Study of Youth Development.

Sparks, R. (1996). Television and the well-being of children and young people. In V. Varma (Ed.), *Violence in children and adolescents*. Bristol, PA: Jessica Kingsley Publishers (Taylor & Francis).

Ward, M., & Rivadeneyra, R. (1999). Contributions of entertainment television to adolescents' sexual attitudes and expectations: The role of viewing amount versus viewer involvement. *The Journal of Sex Research, 36*, 237–249.

Weigel, R. H., & Loomis, W. (1981). Televised models of female achievement revisited: Some progress. *Journal of Applied Social Psychology, 11*(1), 58–63.

Williams, T. M. (Ed.). (1986). *The impact of television: A natural experiment in three communities*. Orlando, FL: Academic Press.

Wright, J. C., Huston, A. C., Murphy, K. C., St. Peters, M., Pinon, M., Scantlin, R., & Kotler, J. (2001). The relations of early television viewing to school readiness and vocabulary of children from low income families. The Early Window Project. *Child Development, 72*(5), 1347–1366.

C2.1 DATA SHEET FOR THE STUDY OF ACTIVITY PREFERENCES BY SEX

E: _____ Date:_____ Day:_____ Time:_____ Page:_____

Place:_____ No. Children: Start ____ M ____ F   No. Adults: Start ___ M ___ F

                                                  End ____ M ____ F   End ___ M ___ F

Partner:_____ Grade:_____

Activity	Observation Cycles and Time					Statistics		
	1	2	3	4	5	Sum	Mean	Proportion
_____	b	b	b	b	b	b		
	g	g	g	g	g	g		
						T		
_____	b	b	b	b	b	b		
	g	g	g	g	g	g		
						T		
_____	b	b	b	b	b	b		
	g	g	g	g	g	g		
						T		
_____	b	b	b	b	b	b		
	g	g	g	g	g	g		
						T		
_____	b	b	b	b	b	b		
	g	g	g	g	g	g		
						T		
_____	b	b	b	b	b	b		
	g	g	g	g	g	g		
						T		
_____	b	b	b	b	b	b		
	g	g	g	g	g	g		
						T		
_____	b	b	b	b	b	b		
	g	g	g	g	g	g		
						T		
_____	b	b	b	b	b	b		
	g	g	g	g	g	g		
						T		
_____	b	b	b	b	b	b		
	g	g	g	g	g	g		
						T		
_____	b	b	b	b	b	b		
	g	g	g	g	g	g		
						T		
_____	b	b	b	b	b	b		
	g	g	g	g	g	g		
						T		

Note: b = boys; g = girls; T = both sexes.

C2.2 OBSERVATION SHEET: ACTIVITY PREFERENCES TALLY -- Sex and Grade

Rater's Name: _____ Partner's Name: _____ Page No.: _____

Date: _____ Day: _____ Observation Time: Start: _____ Finish: _____ Total: _____ (mins.)

Name of Teacher: _____ Grade Level: _____ Number of Children: _____ M: _____ F: _____

Name of Teacher: _____ Grade Level: _____ Number of Children: _____ M: _____ F: _____

Activity	1 Time:	2	3	4	5	Sums	Means	Proportions
	M1 F1 M2 F2	M1 F1 M2 F2	M1 F1 M2 F2	M1 F1 M2 F2	M1 F1 M2 F2	M1 F1 M2 F2	M1 F1 M2 F2	M1 F1 M2 F2
	M1 F1 M2 F2	M1 F1 M2 F2	M1 F1 M2 F2	M1 F1 M2 F2	M1 F1 M2 F2	M1 F1 M2 F2	M1 F1 M2 F2	M1 F1 M2 F2
	M1 F1 M2 F2	M1 F1 M2 F2	M1 F1 M2 F2	M1 F1 M2 F2	M1 F1 M2 F2	M1 F1 M2 F2	M1 F1 M2 F2	M1 F1 M2 F2
	M1 F1 M2 F2	M1 F1 M2 F2	M1 F1 M2 F2	M1 F1 M2 F2	M1 F1 M2 F2	M1 F1 M2 F2	M1 F1 M2 F2	M1 F1 M2 F2
	M1 F1 M2 F2	M1 F1 M2 F2	M1 F1 M2 F2	M1 F1 M2 F2	M1 F1 M2 F2	M1 F1 M2 F2	M1 F1 M2 F2	M1 F1 M2 F2
	M1 F1 M2 F2	M1 F1 M2 F2	M1 F1 M2 F2	M1 F1 M2 F2	M1 F1 M2 F2	M1 F1 M2 F2	M1 F1 M2 F2	M1 F1 M2 F2
	M1 F1 M2 F2	M1 F1 M2 F2	M1 F1 M2 F2	M1 F1 M2 F2	M1 F1 M2 F2	M1 F1 M2 F2	M1 F1 M2 F2	M1 F1 M2 F2
	M1 F1 M2 F2	M1 F1 M2 F2	M1 F1 M2 F2	M1 F1 M2 F2	M1 F1 M2 F2	M1 F1 M2 F2	M1 F1 M2 F2	M1 F1 M2 F2
	M1 F1 M2 F2	M1 F1 M2 F2	M1 F1 M2 F2	M1 F1 M2 F2	M1 F1 M2 F2	M1 F1 M2 F2	M1 F1 M2 F2	M1 F1 M2 F2
	M1 F1 M2 F2	M1 F1 M2 F2	M1 F1 M2 F2	M1 F1 M2 F2	M1 F1 M2 F2	M1 F1 M2 F2	M1 F1 M2 F2	M1 F1 M2 F2
	M1 F1 M2 F2	M1 F1 M2 F2	M1 F1 M2 F2	M1 F1 M2 F2	M1 F1 M2 F2	M1 F1 M2 F2	M1 F1 M2 F2	M1 F1 M2 F2
	M1 F1 M2 F2	M1 F1 M2 F2	M1 F1 M2 F2	M1 F1 M2 F2	M1 F1 M2 F2	M1 F1 M2 F2	M1 F1 M2 F2	M1 F1 M2 F2
	M1 F1 M2 F2	M1 F1 M2 F2	M1 F1 M2 F2	M1 F1 M2 F2	M1 F1 M2 F2	M1 F1 M2 F2	M1 F1 M2 F2	M1 F1 M2 F2

Note: M = male; F = female; 1 = older group; 2 = younger group.

Directions: Look at a particular activity and record the number of children present, their ages, and their sex. For example, if at one activity there were two boys in age group 1 and three girls, two of whom were in age group 1 and one in age group 2, you would circle M1 and write a 2 beside it; and you would do the same for F1 and F2. Then go to the next activity.

C2.3 MASTER DATA SHEET

PROPORTION OR PERCENTAGE OF CHILDREN
PARTICIPATING IN EACH ACTIVITY

Activity: _____			_____			_____			_____		
Rater	B	G	T	B	G	T	B	G	T	B	G	T
1												
2												
3												
4												
.												
.												
.												
.												
n	_____			_____			_____			_____		
Median												

Activity: _____			_____			_____			_____		
Rater	B	G	T	B	G	T	B	G	T	B	G	T
1												
2												
3												
4												
.												
.												
.												
.												
n	_____			_____			_____			_____		
Median												

C2.4
INDIVIDUAL DATA SHEET (TIME SAMPLING)

E _____ Day, Date _____ Room _____ Group _____

Child _____ Birthdate _____ CA _____ Sex _____

Time begun _____ Time Ended _____ Elapsed Time _____

Time	Where	What	Group		Score	
			B			
			G			
Time	Where	What	Group		Score	
			B			
			G			
Time	Where	What	Group		Score	
			B			
			G			
Time	Where	What	Group		Score	
			B			
			G			
Time	Where	What	Group		Score	
			B			
			G			

TABLE C3.5

MEAN SEX-TYPE SCORES FOR INDIVIDUAL OBSERVATION MEASURES

Group	Where	What	Group Composition	Total	Mean Playgroup Size
3-4 Year-Olds					
Boys					
Girls					
Total					
4-5 Year-Olds					
Boys					
Girls					
Total					
Overall					
Boys					
Girls					
Total					

TABLE C2.6

2 (AGE) X 2 (SEX) ANOVA FOR WHERE SEX-TYPE SCORES

Source	Sum of Squares ÷ df = Mean Square			F	p
Age					
Sex					
Age X Sex					
Within Groups					

TABLE C2.7

2 (AGE) X 2 (SEX) ANOVA FOR WHAT SEX-TYPE SCORES

Source	Sum of Squares ÷ df = Mean Square			F	p
Age					
Sex					
Age X Sex					
Within Groups					

TABLE C2.8

2 (AGE) X 2 (SEX) ANOVA FOR GROUP COMPOSITION SEX-TYPE SCORES

Source	Sum of Squares ÷ df = Mean Square			F	p
Age					
Sex					
Age X Sex					
Within Groups					

TABLE C2.9

2 (AGE) X 2 (SEX) ANOVA FOR TOTAL SEX-TYPE SCORES

Source	Sum of Squares ÷ df = Mean Square			F	p
Age					
Sex					
Age X Sex					
Within Groups					

TABLE C2.10

2 (AGE) X 2 (SEX) ANOVA FOR MEAN PLAYGROUP SIZE

Source	Sum of Squares ÷ *df* = Mean Square			*F*	*p*
Age					
Sex					
Age X Sex					
Within Groups					

TABLE C2.11
INDIVIDUAL DATA SHEET, TV

Date and Time Title of TV Program	Characters			Ethnicity					Family Composition					Home/Neighbor-hood		Pro-Social Behav	Aggression		Viol. Law of Nature	Story/Theme
	# M	# F	Main M/F	# W	# B	# As	# Hi	# Oth	Tradi-tional	Homo-Sexual	Div/ sngle	Adopted	Oth	W Mid class	Oth		Phy	Ver	Viol. Law of Nature	Story/Theme
Totals																				
Name of Comm Product																				
Totals																				

TABLE C2.12
SUMMARY OF TV OBSERVATIONS

	Programs	Commercials
Number of segments viewed		
Total number of characters		
# male	n, (%)	
# female	n, (%)	
Number of segments where main character identified as		
male	n, (%)	
female	n, (%)	
both	n, (%)	
Not recorded	n, (%)	
Ethnicity		
White	n, (%)	
Black	n, (%)	
Asian	n, (%)	
Hispanic	n, (%)	
Other	n, (%)	
Animal	n, (%)	
Not recorded	n, (%)	
Family composition		
Traditional	n, (%)	
Divorced/ Single Parent	n, (%)	
Adopted	n, (%)	
Other-Blended, homosexual	n, (%)	

	Programs	Commercials
Number of segments where home/neighborhood identified		
White middle class	n, (%)	
Other	n, (%)	
Prosocial behavior		
# of segments	n, (%)	
# of episodes	n, (%)	
Aggression		
Overall (physical & verbal)		
# segments	n, (%)	
# episodes	n, (%)	
Physical		
# segments	n, (%)	
# episodes	n, (%)	
Verbal	n, (%)	
# segments	n, (%)	
# episodes	n, (%)	
Violation of Nature		
# segments	n, (%)	
# episodes	n, (%)	

Note: Segments refer to the number of rows (i.e., one 15 min. Observation is a segment); episodes refer to the sum of the tally marks.

PART THREE
EXPERIMENTAL STUDIES

D

General Experimental Research Procedures

In Chapter One, there was a discussion of the importance of surveying related studies and learning how an issue evolved and was handled by others. The traditional and time-consuming manual method has been to work systematically backward, year by year, using the index of *Psychological Abstracts*, and possibly *Biological Abstracts*, and certainly *Child Development Abstracts* and *Bibliography*. *Psychological Abstracts* is a print reference guide to international literature in psychology and related fields. It includes journal articles, books, and chapters in psychology and the social sciences; it appears monthly.

It was inevitable, with the rise and spread of computer technology, that much of the database in psychology should be automated for rapid, efficient search and retrieval. APA has several ways in which its information is distributed electronically: *PsycLIT* and *PsycINFO* and *PsycARTICLES*.

PsycLIT contains references from 1974 on and is usually available in university and psychology department libraries in CD-ROM form. It is user-friendly and permits unlimited searches for no fee to you.

PsycINFO is an online, comprehensive database, with journal references from 46 countries in over 30 languages, covering 1967 to the present. U.S. Dissertation citations are included. It is accessible through commercial on-line services or direct tape leasing from APA. Records dating back to 1894 have just been added to their files. Many universities have this available in their libraries.

PsycARTICLES is the database of full-text from APA journals.

PASAR (*PsycINFO* Assisted Search and Retrieval) is for those who want someone else to do the electronic search. A professional will do the search on your selected topic and give you the results in print or electronic format, for pay, after you fill out detailed request form.

PsycSCANS are quarterly publications containing current records from the *PsycINFO* database, and three prior years, on selected areas, like developmental psychology, clinical psychology, applied psychology and other areas. Issues include abstracts, index terms, and full bibliographic information.

The American Psychological Society has developed two information services accessible through the Internet: Focus On and Personal Searcher. *Focus On* searches a series of six predefined, discipline specific databases (biological, cognitive, developmental, industrial/organizational, social/personality, and clinical/treatment research). *Personal Searcher* tracks bibliographic data and author abstracts for your exact subject specifications. Both are for pay.

ERIC. The Educational Resources Information Center is a federally funded nationwide information system that disseminates published and unpublished resources and research materials in education. There are a central facility and many decentralized clearinghouses, each of which focus on a specific aspect of education. Clearinghouses relevant to developmental psychology are:

Disadvantaged
Teachers College, Columbia University
New York, New York 10027

Early Childhood Education
University of Illinois
Urbana, Illinois 61801

Information Resources
Stanford University, School of Education
Center for Research and Development in Teaching
Stanford, California 94305

In addition, ERIC sponsors a monthly announcement of all new documents, RIE (*Research in Education*).

MEDLINE. MEDLINE exists at some universities and hospitals to gain access to information stored in the National Library of Medicine. Abstracts of the *Index Medicus* from 1966 to the present are currently available through this retrieval system. Although specifically designed to track down information on nonpsychological diseases, users have had some success in obtaining both psychiatric and psychological sources.

The cost of the operation of the system is moderate. Further information and a list of index keywords can be obtained at the reference office of a medical center library.

SSIE. The Smithsonian Science Information Exchange, Inc., (Room 300, 1730 M Street, N. W., Washington, DC 20036; telephone: 202-381-5511) offers a variety of search services, for money, and is a national source for information on research in progress. The latter generally refers to projects that have been registered with the Exchange during the last two years. One can order a custom search on a specific topic, for a charge.

Their *Science Newsletter* regularly offers research information search packages on current topics, many relevant to developmental psychologists, which are considerably cheaper than the custom searches.

Outline of Data-Collection Procedures

There are a number of procedures, practices, or arrangements common to many research situations. The importance of acclimatizing the child to the test room and the researcher, and other rapport considerations, were discussed in Part ONE, Section 3, and should be reread now.

Obtaining the Subject. See Part ONE for sources of subjects and for procedures. If a pool of signed permission slips exists, assignments of child to experimenter can be made from that file. Indicate on the back of the permission slip the experimenter's name, days and date of session, and the experiment. This provides an experimental history for each child. Copy the child's name, address, telephone, grade, teacher, and room, but never remove the signed permission slip from the laboratory file. An example of a permission slip appears in Fig. D-1.

The next step is to telephone the parent. Identify yourself by name and as "a student in Professor X's child study program at the university. You signed a permission slip (last fall) (last spring) (last week) (whenever) for your son/daughter (name), (present grade) to help us in our child study course. Could (name) help (again) (day, date, time)? I'll meet (name) at (the door of his or her classroom or some convenient place)."

Try to speak to the subject as well, if the child is in the second grade or more. "May I say hello to (name), too? ...I'm a college student, (your own name); could you meet me (day, date, time, place)?"

For 3:30 p.m. (after school) appointments, tell parent and child you'll meet at the child's classroom door. Ask his or her present teacher's name and room. Verify with the parent if the child should be walked home or accompanied across intersections.

Be sure to leave your name and phone number with the parent in case the child becomes ill or has to cancel. If this happens, notify the course assistants.

Describe the study to the parent in the manner decided upon in class. If the child asks about it, also answer as previously established. Do not offer information that you are not asked. Don't use words like "experiment" or "tests." Do not telephone children after 8:00 p.m. or prior to 8:00 a.m. Be honest, frank, friendly, and grateful, even if the response is negative.

If you absolutely cannot keep an appointment already made, contact your lab assistant by phone or message promptly. Inform the child and parent, if possible! Otherwise, someone will need to be at the classroom door to cancel the appointment and to make sure the parent is home to receive the child.

Report at least 15 minutes before your appointment time to the assigned central location for check in and room assignment, and equipment. Pick up the child on time at the designated meeting place. Ask and use the child's preferred name or nickname.

Practice. Prior to working with a child, it is essential to practice thoroughly the administration of the tasks used in the experiment. Pair off with a classmate, and take turns being subject and experimenter. Say the verbal instructions with expression, handle the materials as you would in the actual test situation, and take notes on practice data sheets. Try to anticipate awkward or difficult points, and practice those particularly often until you are fluent and comfortable. Many students prefer to retype the experimental instructions on index cards to avoid fluttering pages. Sometimes instructions are short enough to be memorized. Even without memorization, the experimenter needs to be sufficiently familiar with task administration to be able to observe the child and maintain eye contact when appropriate. Supervision and feedback by the instructor or laboratory assistant are desirable, but partners should monitor each other as well.

Physical Testing Arrangements. These vary with each experiment. In most, the child and experimenter are seated across a table from one another, with the height of the table and chairs determined by the child's size. Occasionally, a catty-corner or side-by-side arrangement is needed. In any event, do not invade the child's private space. If the experimenter is moving too close to the child, there will often be small signals to indicate this: a subtle rearing away, turning of the head, or a frown or anxious look. Space needs differ for each child, some young children virtually climb into your lap.

The table is to be kept clean of everything but the immediate test stimuli. This is important. Data sheets can be on clip boards in your lap, out of the child's sight. Instructions, stopwatches, extra pencils, used or to-be-used stimuli, or other paraphernalia belong on small chairs next to you or in a semiopen drawer in front of you. In other words, distractions are kept to a minimum. In a training situation like ours, arrange the seating so that the child's back is to the door so that supervisors may observe the experimenter with least distraction to the child. With preschoolers, however, it may be better for the experimenter to sit closer to the door in order to be able to stop a child who starts a precipitate exit.

Data Sheets. Notice that individual data sheets for the experiments that follow often identify the title of the experiment with initials or abbreviations, that is, SE for self esteem, RT for Reaction Time. The data sheet should be kept out of sight, but if an alert child gets a glimpse of it, it should not reveal any more information about the nature and purpose of your study than has been given in your instructions to the child. When correct answers need to be provided on the data sheet for the experimenter, these, too, should be abbreviated. Place for totals or summary scores should be provided, and all pertinent labeling should appear: the child's name or code, experimenter's name, date, child's birthdate and chronological age, sex, grade, experimental group or condition, where tested, time of testing (when began, when finished, elapsed time), other people present, and (when needed) which specific set of apparatus was used.

An excellent exercise prior to the data-collection stage of an experiment is to plan the individual data sheet in detail, without looking at the one provided for each experiment in this manual.

The group data sheet is the place to collate data collected by each experimenter. Generally, each subject has a row, identified by the experimenter's name or initials, and a code name or number for the subject. The column headings indicate which information derived from the individual data sheet should appear in that row. Care must be taken to enter the subject's data on the appropriate group data sheet—the one for sex and grade and experimental condition. A buddy system is helpful here: Pair off with another student experimenter and check one another's arithmetic and entries on the group data sheet. There are few situations more frustrating than to perform all the group statistics, only to find data were entered in the inappropriate group data chart, or incorrect data in the right group.

Again, designing the group data sheet layout yourself will permit you to demonstrate understanding of the experimental design used and of the data needed to test the hypotheses.

Notes. In addition to the specific responses and measures called for on the individual data sheet, qualitative behavior notes are important. The experimenter should be able to reconstruct the flavor of the test situation. Did the child fidget? pay rapt attention to the stimuli? to the experimenter? Did the child speak volubly or answer minimally? Did the child initiate conversation? Did the child keep asking, "Is this the last one?" and when in the test sequence did this behavior begin? Lips moving in silent recall? Head nodding in interactional synchrony with experimenter's laying out of cards? Curious about the apparatus or the note taking? Tense and on the verge of tears? "Is my answer correct?" "How many seconds did I take?"

Work out an abbreviated fast system that will allow as much note taking as possible without sacrificing accuracy on the main experimental data. For example, (E) can mean that the experimenter used standard prompts like "Tell me more" or "What do you mean?" A (P) (for pause) or a dot (.) can mean a passage of, say, five seconds in an untimed experiment in which you wish to retain some additional notion of fluency or rhythm of response.

Taking of such notes should become habitual and rapid. These can be marked on the data sheet during the experiment. There are two reasons for developing this skill. The first is that you are learning about the development of children. Although most of this manual deals with experiments, each study provides opportunity for observing facets of the child's behavior beyond the one needed for the specific statistics. The second reason can be called serendipity[1]—discoveries made by chance. An unanticipated observation may trigger a hunch in a new direction, may suggest a new deduction to be tested, or may bring a previously unnoticed relationship into focus. The 1977 discovery that the drug ara-A (adenine arabinoside) can destroy viruses without harming the body cell itself was made serendipitously during testing of ara-A for its antibiotic (rather than antiviral) properties. Pavlov's discovery of classical conditioning in those famous dogs came in the course of physiological studies. Another unexpected discovery was Olds and Milner's "reward region" of the brain (Rosenzweig, in Postman, 1962).

Termination. Express your appreciation for the child's help sincerely but not overeffusively. Explain, if necessary, that you need to work with some of the child's classmates, and that the pictures (words, tasks, games) need to be a surprise to them, too, so that you are asking the child to keep the pictures (tasks, etc.) a secret from them until x time (specify when they can talk about the session).

If payment is being made for acting as subject, and the parent has acquiesced to this, give the child the gift, or preferably accompany the child to a central gift-dispensing location where a choice can be made. Because other children will also be choosing gifts, this ends the session on a social, cheerful note. It also gives the supervisor a chance to observe the child's emotional state and to provide additional feedback and reassurance to the child as needed. Be sure also to give gifts to children who fail the pretest and are not included in the experiment per se. If an intact class is tested as a group, children for whom permission was denied are not tested but are included in the gift giving.

Accompany the child to the location arranged by parent: classroom door or outer school door, across busy intersections, or to residence. Thank the child again.

Feedback to Experimenter. If you were observed during the data collection, be sure to obtain the supervisor's critique prior to testing another subject. The children usually take sufficient time choosing their gifts so that this information can be given to you quietly at the same time. You should be observed for (a) *general handling of the child*: for example, eye contact, clarity and pace of your speech, control of the dyadic situation, responsiveness to cues, handling of interruptions by child and others, your response to your own errors, how you put the child at ease; and (b) *test administration* per se: familiarity with instructions, physical handling of the stimulus materials, prompt timing, note taking, clear working space, unobtrusive data recording, smooth pace.

Reports

Not all the observations and experiments performed in this class will be written as full reports. Some may be performed just to familiarize you with certain tasks or measures, others to illustrate individual differences, and still others for note taking practice. Portions of reports may be assigned: a results section, or the rationale for the hypotheses. Sometimes, each of you individually will cope with the group data; sometimes the class will

---

[1] Serendip was the former name of Ceylon; serendipity is a word coined by Horace Walpole, circa 1754, from the title of a fairy tale, "The Three Princes of Serendip," whose heroes made unexpected discoveries "by accidents and sagacity, of things they were not in quest of" (Oxford English Dictionary, 1971, p. 2735).

cooperatively work out the statistical calculations; sometimes (as we do) the instructor will run the statistics on the computer and present you with finished or almost finished tables. At least twice, however, experiments should be written up as if for publication, using the style prescribed by the revised *Publication Manual* of the American Psychological Association (2001). Careful study of APA journal articles facilitates the writing of a professional report.

Experimental reports are composed of the following, in the order given: a cover sheet with title, author's name, and institutional affiliation; abstract, introduction, method, results, discussion, references. Detailed descriptions appear on pages 6–29 of the *Publication Manual*, and on pages 284–302, and only highlights are summarized here.

Title. Informative, substantive, concise.

Contrast	"An Experimental Research Project on How Children Think About Themselves and What That Might Be Related to"
with	"Self-Concepts of High- and Low-Curiosity Boys"
Contrast	"A Study of Piagetian Tasks With Variations"
with	"Responses to Class-Inclusion Questions for Verbally and Pictorially Presented Items" (longer but more informative).

Omit words like "method" or "results" or "an investigation of."

Author's Name and Affiliation. For blind grading purposes, your instructor may ask you to substitute your social security number or code number for your name. Title, name, and affiliation appear on the cover sheet.

A shortened title, the *running head*, appears at the top left of the title page, and top right corner of all other pages, near the page number. It is limited to 50 characters.

Abstract. This is a brief summary of the research, including the problem, subjects and method, results, and conclusions, all in 100–120 words, on a separate page numbered 2. It is best written last, and takes more time and thought than its brief size might indicate. It needs to be accurate, self-contained, concise, and specific. It will appear, not only in your article, but in many databases.

Introduction. Start a new page with the paper title at the top, the running head, and "3" at the top right. The introduction sets the relevant historical context briefly, defines the problem, presents the rationale for the research design and each hypothesis, and ends with a definition of variables and statements of hypotheses. It is not necessary or desirable to include every single reference you found in your arduous search of the literature; just include the ones with close theoretical and empirical relevance to your hypotheses and design decisions.

Method. Subdivisions titled *participants* (subjects), *materials* or *apparatus*, and *procedure* are appropriate and useful. Description of the subjects should include number, sex, age, demographic characteristics, how selected. If apparatus is unusual, a figure may be in order. The procedure section must make clear for possible replication the experimental conditions and control features—*what* you did and *how* you did it. Use the metric system.

Results. Summarize the statistical treatment of the data and state the findings. Present tables or state specific statistical findings that justify the conclusions being drawn. Figures may be needed to show interactions or trends. State the particular alpha level ($p = .05$, or $p = .01$) used for statistical tests.

Discussion. First, discuss the extent to which your data support or do not support the hypotheses stated in the introduction. Second, relate your findings to the literature. Third, evaluate your study—theoretical and practical implications, shortcomings and strengths, suggestions for next-step research. If there are many numbers in your discussion, you are probably repeating too much of your results. Make clear what your study contributes and how it helps resolve the original problem.

References. Every study cited in the text must appear in the reference list, following the detailed guidelines provided in pages 215–281 of the *Publication Manual* (2001). Start this list on a new page. It should include only those references cited in the text, not everything you may have read. (Most of the reading lists provided in this book include more than the references cited in the text and are, therefore, labeled bibliographies. Journals which publish research data generally require reference lists rather than bibliographies.)

The arrangement of the remainder of the manuscript is

> footnotes (new page; avoid their use)
>
> tables (one to a page)
>
> figure captions (new page)
>
> figures (one to a page; pages not numbered)

The sample manuscript, pp. 306–320 in the *Publication Manual* is very helpful.

Double space *everything*; proofread (using a dictionary); keep a xerox copy. The first paper is usually the most time consuming and difficult; you will be gratified by your rapid improvement.

(The presentation of historical contexts, painstakingly detailed procedures, and wide-ranging discussion sections that accompany the projects in this volume are for broader learning and teaching purposes. They are usually far more expansive than would be appropriate in a publishable article.)

Original Projects

In addition to performing several of the studies that follow, a worthwhile enterprise in the latter part of the term is to design an original project. This can be done as a "paper design," in which each student individually conceives, plans, and writes a detailed, full prospectus of a new study but does not run it. Or more popularly, the class breaks into two or three groups, and each group plans *and runs* an original project. The papers can then be presented, miniconvention style, at the last class session, with handouts that may include abstracts, tables, figures, and references.

Ideas come from variations in the experiments already performed, from issues raised in this or other courses, from skimming recent journals on topics of high interest, from review chapters, or from group brainstorming. Some of the experiments listed in Appendix B were group projects. Several were later pursued beyond this course as senior honors or M.A. theses. The Science Directorate of the American Psychological Association can provide a useful brochure, *Finding Information About Psychological Tests*. (Phone 202-336-6000 for a free copy.)

Selected Bibliography

American Psychological Association. (1992). Ethical principles of psychologists and code of conduct. *American Psychologist, 47*(12), 1597–1611.

American Psychological Association. (2001). Ethical principles of psychologists and code of conduct: Drafts for comment. *Monitor on Psychology, 32*(2), 77–90.

American Psychological Association. (2001). *Publication Manual* (5th ed.). Washington, DC: American Psychological Association.

Breakwell, G. M., Hammond, S., & Fife-Schaw, C. (Eds.). (2000). *Research methods in psychology* (2nd ed.). Thousand Oaks, CA: Sage.

Bronfenbrenner, U. (1986). Ecology of the family as a context for human development: Research perspectives. *Developmental Psychology, 22*, 723–742.

Burton, R. V. (1971). An inexpensive and portable means of one-way observation. *Child Development, 42*, 959–962.

Cairns, R. B., Cairns, B. D., Rodkin, P., & Xie, H. (1998). New directions in developmental research: Models and method. In R. Jessor (Ed.), *New perspectives on adolescent risk behavior* (pp. 13–40). New York: Cambridge University Press.

Denmark, F. L., Russo, N. F., Frieze, I. H., & Sechzer, J. A. (1988). Guidelines for avoiding sexism in psychological research: A report of the AdHoc Committee on Nonsexist Research. *American Psychologist, 43*, 582–585.

Fisher, C. B. (1993). Integrating science and ethics in research with high-risk children and youth. *Social Policy Report, Society for Research in Child Development, VII*(4), 27 pp.

Fisher, C. B. (1994). Reporting and referring child and adolescent research participants. A special issue of *Ethics & Behavior, 4*(2). Hillsdale, NJ: Lawrence Erlbaum Associates.

Gelfand, H., & Walker, C. J. (1990). *Mastering APA style: Instructor's resource guide*. Washington, DC: American Psychological Association.

Gelfand, H., & Walker, C. J. (1990). *Mastering APA style: Students workbook and training guide*. Washington, DC: American Psychological Association.

Nadelman, L. (1968). Training laboratories in developmental psychology. *Psychological Reports, 23*, 923–931.

Nadelman, L. (1990). Learning to think and write as an empirical psychologist: The laboratory course in developmental psychology. *Teaching of Psychology, 17*(1), 45–48.

Nadelman, L., Morse, W., & Hagen, J. (1976). Developmental research in educational settings: Description of a seminar/practicum. *Teaching of Psychology, 3*(1), 21–24.

Nicol, A. A. M., & Pexman, P. M. (1999). *Presenting your findings: A practical guide for creating tables*. Washington, DC: American Psychological Association.

Postman, L. (Ed.). (1962). *Psychology in the making: Histories of selected research problems*. New York: Knopf.

Reed, J. G., & Baxter, P. M. (1992). *Library use: A handbook for psychology* (2nd ed.). Washington, DC: American Psychological Association.

Richardson, J. (Ed.). (1996). *Handbook of qualitative research and methods for psychology and the social sciences*. Malden, MA: Blackwell.

Scott, K. (1969). The design of mobile laboratories for behavioral research with children. *Journal of Experimental Child Psychology, 7*, 143–152.

Sommer, B., & Sommer, R. (2001). *A practical guide to behavioral research: Tools and techniques.* (5th ed.). New York, NY: Oxford University Press.

Stanovich, K. E. (1989). *How to think straight about psychology* (2nd ed.). Glenview, IL: Scott, Foresman.

Sternberg, R. J. (1993). *The psychologist's companion: A guide to scientific writing for students and researchers* (3rd ed.). New York: Cambridge University Press.

Permission Form

Child's name: _____ Sex:_____ Phone Number:_____

Birthday: _____ Grade: _____ Room:_____ Teacher:_____

Address: _____

We have read the description of the research training course and understand that participation is volunary and that confidentiality will be carefully preserved.

My child has permission to cooperate, if he or she wishes, in the child study program, at school, after school hours.

Date: _____ _____
Parent's Signature

Escort service home:

1. Please walk my child home.

2. Please accompany my child over Packard or Stadium.

3. Neither of the above is necessary.

Fig. D1. An example of a permission slip.

E

Psychomotor and Perceptual Behavior—A Classic Experiment

This next section treats a very old and classic topic in psychology: reaction time. Are you wondering why a laboratory manual in developmental psychology, written in the last few years of the 20th century and early 21st century includes such a "traditional" project? Reaction time is enjoying renewed interest partly because of the information processing approach so popular now in psychology. The traveling exhibition created for the 100th anniversary of APA and now visiting museums over the country includes exhibits on both reaction time and illusions.

Courses in perceptual development in children do not seem to attract as many students as, for example, courses in personality development or psychopathology. Yet, to understand many aspects of learning, thinking, or motivation in children, one needs to understand the processes and mechanisms underlying the development of perceptual skills and judgments. Infants must perceive an object before they can slowly develop the concept of an object; they have to perceive their mother's face before they can form a scheme for that face or differentiate it from the face of a stranger. Furthermore, it is easier to trace the development of a perceptual process in a child, in whom it is still developing, than in an adult, in whom it may be full-blown. The determination of those factors that shape perceptions or alter perceptual processes has implications and applications for the social psychologist, the researcher, and the educator.

Introductory psychology textbooks distinguish sensation and perception: Sensation refers to the reception of stimulation from the environment through the senses. Perception refers to the interpretation and understanding of that stimulation. Perception has been studied in relation to its biological causes, its relation to learning and cognition, and to sociocultural contexts. Illusions, like the Müller-Lyer, are fruitful ways of investigating the misperceptions of real objects. The illusion originates in the brain, not in the retina.

Research on children's perceptual behavior may raise more questions than it answers. It is well for students of child behavior to recognize early in their careers that perception is not a "cleaner" topic than personality or social development; that complexities and problems of definition, measurement, and control of extraneous variables exist in research in all areas of child development; and that it takes much hard work by many investigators to know (i.e., understand, in a scientific sense) any facet of child development. Gibson's efforts (1991, 1992) attest to that. Perception is a facet of behavior, including the behavior involved in reaction-time experiments.

Stanovich, in his introduction to the reaction-time project, summarizes the familiar history and relevant concepts, and places reaction-time experiments in their modern context. Reaction time has reentered psychology in information processing models, in the decision-making literature, and in mathematical psychology. Reaction-time methods are used not only by experimental psychologists but by developmental psychologists and research clinicians. Richard Steffy, for example, is working extensively on reaction-time deficit in schizophrenia. For another example, developmental data appear to suggest a curvilinear progression in simple reaction time, with reaction times of young children slower than those of young adults, and with reaction times again slowing from the 20s to the 60s (Kail, 1991). Ellis and Nelson (1999) used reaction time and event-related potentials to examine how adults and 6-year-olds categorize prototypical and nonprototypical pictures of cats and dogs. Reaction time has been used to study semantic classification in autistic and normal children (Dunn, Vaughan, Kreuzer, & Kurtzberg (1999), and slowed reaction time during a continuous performance test in children with Tourette's syndrome (Shucard, Benedict, Tekok-Kilic, & Lichter, 1997), and in children with specific language impairment (Windsor, & Hwang, 1999). An interesting study of reaction time in six varied tasks given to children on Monday, Tuesday, Thursday, and Friday (cross-sectional design) indicated that performance was best on Thursday and weakest on Monday (Beau et al., 1999). In a longitudinal study of infants (3.5 months) and 4-year-olds, measures of visual anticipation and visual reaction time in infants correlated with manual reaction time and childhood IQ in four-year-olds (Dougherty, & Haith, 1997). The interpretations are often in terms of the speed of information processing, the speed of decisions, and the time taken to monitor movements.

Notice that in the experiment that follows, two characteristics of the data collection are the large number of responses to the same stimulus and the counterbalancing techniques used.

There are several psychophysical methods that can determine the relation between physical events and the child's differential reaction to these events. In the method of adjustment or reproduction, children are presented with a standard stimulus and a variable one, and they attempt to make the variable stimulus match the standard as closely as possible. In the method of limits (method of minimal change), the child needs to detect the presence of a stimulus or a change in some dimension of that stimulus. In the constant method (right and wrong cases), children are presented with a series of pairs of stimuli and need to judge whether A is greater than, equal to, or less than B. When applicable, decide which psychophysical method is being used in the projects in this manual. In all our projects, determine carefully what is being counterbalanced and how this is being done.

Bibliography

Band, G. P. H., van der Molen, M. W., Overtoom, C. C. E., & Verbaten, M. N. (2000). The ability to activate and inhibit speeded responses: Separate developmental trends. *Journal of Experimental Child Psychology, 75*(4), 263.–290.

Beau, J., Carlier, M., Duyme, M., Capron, C., & Perez-Diaz, F. (1999). Procedure to extract a weekly pattern of performance of human reaction time. *Perceptual and Motor Skills, 88*(2), 469–483.

Dougherty, T. M., & Haith, M. M. (1997). Infant expectations and reaction time as predictors of childhood speed of processing and IQ. *Developmental Psychology, 33*(1), 146–155.

Ellis, A. E., & Nelson, C. A. (1999). Category prototypicality judgments in adults and children: Behavioral and electrophysiological correlates. *Developmental Neuropsychology, 15*(2), 193–211.

Gibson, E. J. (1991). *An odyssey in learning and perception.* Cambridge, MA: MIT Press.

Gibson, E. J. (1992). How to think about perceptual learning: Twenty-five years later. In H. L. Pick, P. Van den Broek, & D. C. Knoll (Eds.), *Cognitive Psychology: Conceptual and methodological issues* (pp. 215–237). Washington, DC: American Psychological Association.

Kail, R. (1991). Developmental change in speed of processing during childhood and adolescence. *Psychological Bulletin, 109*, 490–501.

Palmeri, T. J., & Blalock, C. (2000). The role of background knowledge in speeded perceptual categorization. *Cognition, 77*(2), B45–B57.

Pick, H. (1992). E. J. Gibson's contributions to developmental psychology. *Developmental Psychology, 28.*

Shucard, D. W., Benedict, R. H. B., Tekok-Kilic, A., & Lichter, D. G. (1997). Slowed reaction time during a continuous performance test in children with Tourette's syndrome. *Neuropsychology, 11*(1), 147–155.

Windsor, J., & Hwang, M. (1999). Testing the generalized slowing hypothesis in specific language impairment. *Journal of Speech, Language, & Hearing Research, 42*(5), 1205–1218.

Weiler, M. D., Harris, N. S., Marcus, D. J., Bellinger, D., Kosslyn, S. M., & Waber, D. P. (2000). Speed of information processing in children referred for learning problems: Performance on a visual filtering test. *Journal of Learning Disabilities, 33*(6), 538–550.

Experiment 1

Age and Sex Differences in Two Reaction-Time Tasks

Keith Stanovich

Reaction time, the time between the onset of the stimulus and the subject's response, has a long and varied history. Boring (1950) and Hearst (1979) contain extended discussions of this interesting history.

Reaction time became an issue in the field of astronomy over 150 years ago. In 1796, the Astronomer Royal at the Greenwich Observatory fired an assistant because the assistant's observations of the times of star movements differed from his own observations. The method of measuring star movements at that time involved noting the time, estimated to a fraction of a second, that a star crossed a wire in the field of a telescope. The seconds were counted from the ticks of a clock. The discrepancies between the observations of the Royal Astronomer and his assistant interested Bessel, a German astronomer, some decades later.

During the 1820s, Bessel tested the ability of a number of trained observers to react to a star crossing the wire on a telescope lens. The average difference between two observers was called the personal equation. Thus, Bessel was the first to investigate differences between individuals in speed of reaction to a stimulus. The study of the *personal equation* by the astronomers led to investigations of what is now known as simple reaction time, a situation where the subject makes one response (usually a key press or a finger lift) to a single stimulus (usually a light or a tone).

In 1868 Donders, a Dutch physiologist, made an important methodological contribution. He suggested that by complicating the reaction-time task, it would be possible to measure the duration of some basic psychological processes. Donders was the first to suggest that the mental events intervening between stimulus and response might be revealed by studies using reaction time as a dependent variable. His approach was termed the *subtraction method*. It involved first estimating the subject's simple reaction time. According to Donders, the reaction to a single stimulus involves two processes: stimulus detection and response execution. The same subject then performs another reaction-time task (termed a *C-reaction*) in which there are two or more stimuli but only one to which a response is required. It was hypothesized that such a task involved three processes: stimulus detection, stimulus discrimination, and response execution. Donders claimed that by subtracting the simple reaction time from the time for a C-reaction, one would obtain the duration of the psychological process of stimulus discrimination. In a similar manner, the subject performed a choice reaction-time task where each of two or more stimuli was assigned a separate response. Such a task was presumed to require stimulus detection, stimulus discrimination, response choice, and response execution operations. By subtracting the time for a C-reaction from the time in a choice reaction-time task with the same number of stimuli the duration of the response choice process was obtained. Thus, the subtraction method makes use of two tasks. One serves as a control task that is assumed to involve a certain number of mental processes. The other task is constructed so as to involve one additional mental process. The duration of the additional mental process is obtained by looking at the difference in reaction times between the two tasks.

The logic of Donders' subtraction method was much exploited by Wundt and his colleagues in the 1880s. In fact, it was one of Wundt's students, Kulpe, who made the most telling criticism of the subtraction method. Kulpe argued that a task could not be altered so as to add or delete only one mental process. His attack on Donders' method was based on his introspection that changing a task so as to add a process does not leave other processes unchanged. For example, it can be argued that the stimulus discrimination process does not remain the same when one goes from a choice reaction-time situation to a C-reaction paradigm. In the C-reaction situation, one is looking for a particular stimulus, in contrast to the choice situation where attention is spread over all the stimuli. Thus, having to respond to each stimulus changes the stimulus discrimination process as well as adding a response-selection process.

Kulpe's criticism was one contributing factor to the diminishing interest in reaction time as a dependent measure in the first half of this century. The other major factor was the rise of behaviorism during that period (see Baars, 1986; Lachman, Lachman, & Butterfield, 1979). The behaviorists were uninterested in internal mental events and thus had no use for techniques like Donders', which attempted to examine the nature of mental processes.

The use of reaction time as a dependent variable in the investigation of psychological processes was revived during the 1950s and 1960s. Interest in the use of reaction time stemmed from several developments within the field of psychology, but most important was the growth of the metaphor of the human being as an information processor (Lachman, Lachman, & Butterfield, 1979). Such seminal works as Broadbent's *Perception and Communication* (1958) and Neisser's *Cognitive Psychology* (1967) focused on tracing the flow of information through the human mind. The emphasis was on how subjects stored, recoded, and manipulated the stimulus input in order to arrive at a response. Such ideas are related to Donders' aim, which was to trace the time course of mental events.

Another development that led to increased use of reaction time in experimental psychology was the introduction of techniques that overcame the earlier criticisms of Donders' subtraction method. Sternberg's (1969) additive factors method became one of the most popular. Unlike Donders' method, the additive factors approach does not assume the existence of a set of mental operations prior to the measurement of their duration. Instead, Sternberg's method starts at a more basic level and allows the investigator to discover the sequence of stages that are involved in performing a given task.

Briefly, the method involves manipulating a variety of factors (stimulus intensity, stimulus probability, type of response, etc.) within the context of a reaction-time task. If the effects of two factors on reaction time display additivity (do not interact in a statistical sense), it is assumed that they affect different mental operations and thus define two separate processing stages. The reasoning is that if the effect of manipulating factor A is independent of the level of factor B, then factor A must be affecting a different mental operation, or stage, than factor B. In a similar manner, two factors that interact are assumed to be tapping the same stage of processing. Thus, by running a multifactor experiment and examining the pattern of additivity and interaction among factors, it is possible to discover the sequence of mental operations that intervenes between stimulus and response. See Sternberg (1969) for a fuller discussion of this method and McClelland (1979) for a discussion of more sophisticated techniques.

The above-mentioned methodological advances, coupled with the increasing use of the information-processing approach as a framework for research (Keele, 1973; Lachman et al., 1979; Neisser, 1967; Posner, 1973), brought reaction-time experiments back into the forefront of experimental psychology. Refinements in the use of reaction time as a dependent measure are of continuing interest (see McClelland, 1979; Pachella, 1974).

The information-processing approach has also influenced research and theory within developmental psychology. A number of studies investigating the development of information-processing abilities in children, many using reaction time as a dependent measure, have been reviewed by Wickens (1974). Kail (1991) has demonstrated that the decrease in reaction time with age follows a particular mathematical function with reasonable precision. Stanovich (1978) has reviewed how reaction time techniques have been used to study the information processing capabilities of mentally retarded individuals. Other researchers have linked performance on a variety of reaction-time tasks to individual differences in components of intelligence (see Keating & Bobbitt, 1978; Vernon, 1987). As the information-processing approach has become more prevalent in developmental psychology, experiments employing reaction time have increased commensurately.

Goodenough (1935) found that the simple reaction time of children was slower than that of adults. As with experiments using adult subjects, studies of children's reaction time have moved from using the measure as a global index of performance to the utilization of reaction-time techniques in order to infer specific differences in processing across age. Elliot (1970, 1972), in a series of studies, investigated how the effects of variables like incentive, preparatory interval, and practice are modified by changes in the ages of the subjects. His interest was on the interaction of age with experimental factors that affect reaction time. Such analyses enable one to gain information about how specific mental operations change with age. Thus, researchers have moved beyond the point of merely noting the slower reaction times of children on a variety of tasks and are now concerned with elucidating which cognitive processes are responsible for the slower reaction times of children relative to adults (see Keating, List, & Merriman, 1985; Manis, Keating, & Morrison, 1980).

Problem and Hypotheses

Although Donders' subtraction method has been superseded by more sophisticated techniques, the basic reaction-time phenomena that he investigated are still objects of experimental study. One highly reliable result observed by Donders was that it took less time to make a simple reaction (one response to one stimulus, usually a light) than to execute a C-reaction, where a response is made to only one of two or more stimuli (usually lights of different colors). Because the responses in the two tasks are identical, the longer response time in the C-reaction condition is due to the additional time needed to decide which light has been lit. Thus, a simple reaction is faster because it does not require this discrimination process. A developmental study comparing these two types of reaction-time tasks is of interest owing to the fact that the relation between simple reaction time and age is firmly established in the research literature.

Goodenough (1935) found that simple reaction time decreases from age 3½ through early adolescence. More recent investigations (Grim, 1967; Elliot, 1970, 1972) have replicated the basic finding of a decrease in simple reaction time from early childhood to adulthood. In addition, Goodenough obtained a sex difference in her study. Prior to 7 years of age, boys responded faster than girls.

The development of response speed in two different reaction-time tasks will be investigated using boys and girls in two grades.

1. The simple reaction time of older children is (slower than) (equal to) (faster than) that of younger children.

2. The C-reaction time of older children is (slower than) (equal to) (faster than) that of younger children.

3. The simple reaction time of boys is (slower than) (equal to) (faster than) that of girls.

4. The C-reaction time of boys is (slower than) (equal to) (faster than) that of girls.

5. Simple reactions are (slower than) (equal to) (faster than) C-reactions.

6. The slowness or fastness of the C-reaction relative to simple reaction time (does) (does not) change with age.

Method

Subjects

Boys and girls in the first and sixth grades.

Apparatus

1 Stimulus presentation device with a subject response button and trial initiation button

1 Standard electric timer

1 Stopwatch (optional)

1 Individual Data Sheet

A reaction-time apparatus needs (a) some way of presenting the stimulus in a standardized systematic fashion to all subjects, (b) some standard way for the subject to respond, and (c) some mechanical means of measuring the subject's speed of response. A sketch of our reaction-time apparatus appears in Fig. E1-1. The wiring diagram is presented in Appendix A, Notes for the Instructor.

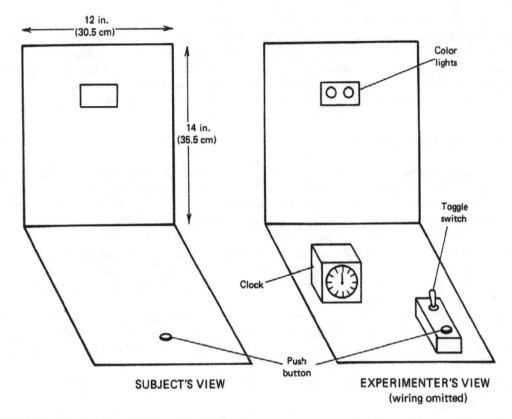

Fig. E1.1. Reaction-time apparatus.

The subject and experimenter sit on opposite sides of a 12 in. (30.5 cm) X 14 in. (35.5 cm) wooden partition. On the subject's side is a single response button, which the subject must depress. The button is 13 in. (33 cm) from the partition. When the subject is seated and depressing the button, he or she is looking directly at a 12 in. (3.8 cm) X 3 in. (7.6 cm) translucent plastic window located 3 in. (7.6 cm) from the top and in the middle of the wooden partition. Directly behind the plastic window, on the experimenter's side of the partition, are two adjacent lights, one blue and one orange. When lit, these lights illuminate the plastic window. A toggle switch, which can be moved to the left and the right, controls which light will be lit when a trial is initiated. Also on the experimenter's side of the partition are a button and the standard electric timer, which can be read to a hundredth of a second. The apparatus is wired so that the light goes on only when the child's button is being held down and the experimenter's own button is pressed. The depression of the experimenter's button simultaneously lights the light and starts the timer. The timer is stopped by the child lifting the finger holding down his or her button. The timer is placed out of view of the child.

Procedure

Design. This experiment investigates reaction times to two different tasks using a between-subjects design with half the children performing the simple reaction-time task and half, the C-reaction task. Equal numbers of subjects are randomly assigned to each of the eight groups generated by the 2 tasks X 2 grades X 2 sexes design. Because there are two stimuli involved in a C-reaction, it is advisable to counterbalance the color of light to which a response is appropriate in both tasks. Therefore, one-half of the children in each condition should be reacting to the blue light and one-half, to the orange light.

Simple Reaction Time. The child is brought in to the experimental room and seated facing the wooden partition. The experimenter says, **"Your job today is pretty easy, but you'll have to pay close attention. You're going to sit there and I'll sit over here. Which hand would you rather use to press this button?"** [Wait for child's response.]

"When I say 'ready-press,' put your finger on this button and hold it down. In a little while, you'll see a *blue* [orange] light come on over here [E points to window]. As soon as you see the light come on, turn it off by *lifting* your finger, letting go of the button as *quickly* as you can. Do you understand? I say 'ready-press' and you press down right away and hold it down. Soon you'll see the light come on, and as *fast* as you can, you *lift* your finger. I'm trying to see how *fast* you can lift your finger when you see a light, so press down when I say 'ready-press' and lift as soon as you see the light come on."

C-Reaction Time. The experimenter says, "Your job today is pretty easy, but you'll have to pay close attention. You're going to sit there and I'll sit over here. Which hand would you rather use to press this button?" [Wait for child's response.]

"When I say 'ready-press,' put your finger on this button and hold it down. In a little while, you'll see a *blue* or an orange light come on over here [E points to window]. As soon as you see the *blue* [*orange*] light come on, turn it off by *lifting* your finger, letting go of the button as *quickly* as you can. If the *orange* [*blue*] light comes on, *do not* lift your finger off the button. Just *keep pressing* until I tell you to stop. Do you understand? I say 'ready-press' and you press down right away and hold it down. Soon you'll see a light come on. If the light is *blue* [*orange*], *lift* your finger as *fast* as you can. If the light is *orange* [*blue*], just *keep pressing* until I tell you to stop. I'm trying to see how *fast* you can *lift* your finger when you see the *blue* [*orange*] light, so press down when I say 'ready-press' and lift as soon as you see the *blue* [*orange*] light come on."

For both tasks, present 40 trials in rapid sequence. The first 10 are practice, but the child is not to be aware of any difference between the first 10 and the last 30. Be sure to administer the stimuli in the sequence listed on the Individual Data Sheet. Use the first few trials to make sure the child understands the nature of the task, repeating whatever portion of the instructions seem necessary. In the C-reaction conditions, be sure the child understands that he or she is not to lift the finger when the orange (blue) light comes on.

After each trial be sure to record the reaction time to the nearest hundredth second on the data sheet, reset the timer, and make sure the toggle switch is set to display the proper stimulus on the next trial. After saying "ready-press," wait 2 seconds (measured on a running stopwatch or by saying silently "one-second, two-second"), and turn on the light by depressing your button. In the C-reaction condition, only one-half of the trials (5 practice, and 15 of the last 30) require a response by the subject. On trials when the subject is not to respond, let the child continue pressing for 3 to 4 seconds after the onset of the light before telling him or her to lift the finger.

Repeat any trials in which the child anticipates the stimulus, either by lifting the finger before the light comes on or by responding in less than .10 second. In the C-reaction condition, repeat any trials in which a finger is lifted in error to the stimulus that does not require a response. Note on the Individual Data Sheet when a trial has been repeated and why (anticipation or error). After the session, be sure to praise the child's performance.

During and after testing, qualitative notes should be taken on the child's behavior. Especially note any signs of boredom or inattentiveness (irritation, verbal comments, etc.).

Results

Scoring. On the Individual Data Sheet, calculate and record the mean, median, standard deviation, and range of the reaction times obtained in the last 30 trials. (Remember, subjects in the C-reaction conditions will have only 15 reaction times.) The mean or median reaction time of each subject's last 30 trials is the score that enters into the subsequent data analysis. In addition, record on the Individual Data Sheet the mean, median, standard deviation, and range of the reaction times for the 10 practice trials.

Data Analysis. Record the individual scores on the Master Data Sheet (from your instructor) for the appropriate task-grade-sex group. Compute the means for each grade-sex group and enter these on Table E1.1 on the Group Data Sheet provided at the end of the experiment. Complete Fig. E1.2. The data can be analyzed by running a three-way analysis of variance (two tasks X two grades X two sexes) on the mean reaction-time scores (Table E1.2). We are not analyzing for possible differences in response to different colors, although this can be done.

Does the *F* ratio for the effect of grade indicate a statistically significant difference in reaction time between the two age groups? Check the results of the analysis of variance regarding the effect of sex. Does the *F* ratio here reach the 0.05 level of statistical significance? Notice that these findings refer to the *combined* simple and C-reaction times.

Were the simple reactions faster than, equal to, or slower than the C-reactions? Does the analysis of variance (*F* for task) indicate a significant difference? Is the interaction between task type and age statistically significant? Did any other interactions reach the 0.05 level of statistical significance?

You might want to look at some other data and summary statistics that you have available. For example, was reaction time on the 10 practice trials slower than on the 30 test trials? Is the median reaction time of most individuals similar to their mean? What can you say about the variability of the reaction times in the various conditions, as indicated by the standard deviations?

Discussion

Relate your data to your first two hypotheses. Do the mean reaction times for the two age groups show the predicted differences? Have you replicated the work of previous investigators?

Look at the mean scores for boys and girls. Do you find support for hypotheses 3 and 4? Do the data support your prediction regarding the speed of a C-reaction when compared to a simple reaction (hypothesis 5)?

Examine the validity of hypothesis 6 by looking at the interaction of task type and age in the analysis of variance. Do you have evidence for a developmental change in the difference in speed of responding to these two tasks? In other words, is the difference in reaction time to simple and C-reaction tasks as large in the sixth grade as in the first? If we assume, as did Donders, that the difference between a C-reaction and a simple reaction is the lack of a discrimination process in the latter, what can you say about the development of this discrimination process based on the results from your experiment? This relates specifically to hypothesis 6 and to the interaction between task type and age. Hypothesizing a change in the discrimination process with age would lead you to predict statistical significance for this interaction. Is this what you obtained? If so, look at Table E1.2. What type of interaction have you observed? Is the speed of the discrimination process increasing or decreasing with age? What are your general conclusions regarding the development of the processes that are tapped by reaction-time tasks?

You might want to think about whether complicating these reaction-time tasks could lead to further conclusions about the development of certain cognitive processes. Are experiments involving more complicated stimuli warranted? What about increasing the complexity and/or number of responses? Issues such as these are of continuing interest to cognitive and developmental psychologists.

Selected Bibliography

Baars, B. J. (1986). *The cognitive revolution in psychology*. New York: Guilford Press.

Boring, E. G. (1950). *A history of experimental psychology* (2nd ed.). New York: Appleton-Century-Crofts.

Broadbent, D. E. (1958). *Perception and communication*. New York: Pergamon Press.

Elliot, R. (1970). Simple reaction time: Effects associated with age, preparatory interval, incentive shift, and mode of presentation. *Journal of Experimental Child Psychology, 9*, 86–104.

Elliot, R. (1972). Simple reaction time in children: Effects of incentive, incentive shift, and other training variables. *Journal of Experimental Child Psychology, 13*, 540–557.

Goodenough, F. L. (1935). The development of the reactive process from early childhood to maturity. *Journal of Experimental Psychology, 18*, 431–450.

Grim, P. F. (1967). A sustained attention comparison of children and adults using reaction time set and GSR. *Journal of Experimental Child Psychology, 5*, 26–38.

Hearst, E. (1979). One hundred years: Themes and perspectives. In E. Hearst (Ed.), *The first century of experimental psychology* (pp. 1–37). Hillsdale, NJ: Lawrence Erlbaum Associates.

Kail, R. (1991). Developmental change in speed of processing during childhood and adolescence. *Psychological Bulletin, 109*, 490–501.

Keating, D. P., & Bobbitt, B. L. (1978). Individual and developmental differences in cognitive-processing components of mental ability. *Child Development, 49*, 155–167.

Keating, D. P., List, J. A., & Merriman, W. E. (1985). Cognitive processing and cognitive ability: A multivariate validity investigation. *Intelligence, 9*, 149–170.

Keele, S. W. (1973). *Attention and human performance*. Pacific Palisades, CA: Goodyear Publishing.

Krupski, A., & Boyle, P. R. (1978). An observational analysis of children's behavior during a simple-reaction-time task: The role of attention. *Child Development, 49*, 340–347.

Lachman, R., Lachman, J. L., & Butterfield, E. C. (1979). *Cognitive psychology and information processing: An introduction*. Hillsdale, NJ: Lawrence Erlbaum Associates.

Landauer, A. A., Armstrong, S., & Digwood, J. (1980). Sex differences in Choice Reaction time. *British Journal of Psychology, 71*, 551–555.

McClelland, J. L. (1979). On the time relations of mental processes: An examination of systems of processes in cascade. *Psychological Review, 86*, 287–330.

Manis, F. R., Keating, D. P., & Morrison, F. J. (1980). Developmental differences in the allocation of processing capacity. *Journal of Experimental Child Psychology, 29*, 156–169.

Neisser, U. (1967). *Cognitive psychology*. New York: Appleton-Century-Crofts.

Pachella, R. G. (1974). The interpretation of reaction time in information processing research. In B. Kantowitz (Ed.), *Human information processing: Tutorials in performance and cognition*. Potomac, MD: Lawrence Erlbaum Associates.

Posner, M. I. (1973). *Cognition: An introduction*. Glenview, IL: Scott, Foresman, and Company.

Stanovich, K. E. (1978). Information processing in mentally retarded individuals. In N. R. Ellis (Ed.), *International review of research in mental retardation* (*Vol. 9*, pp. 29–60). New York: Academic Press.

Sternberg, S. (1969). The discovery of processing stages: Extensions of Donders' method. In W. Koster (Ed.) *Attention and performance* (*Vol. 2*). Amsterdam: North-Holland.

Vernon, P. A. (Ed.). (1987). *Speed of information-processing and intelligence*. Norwood, NJ: Ablex.

Wickens, C. D. (1974). Temporal limits of human information processing: A developmental study. *Psychological Bulletin, 81*, 739–755.

INDIVIDUAL DATA SHEET

Title: Reaction Time   **Group:** *Simple RT, C-RT*

E: _____   **Day and Date:** _____   **S–Sex:** *M or F*   **Grade:** _____
S: _____   **Birthdate:** _____   **CA:** _____

Time Begun: _____   **Time Ended:** _____   **Elapsed Time:** _____   **Room:** _____

Practice Stimulus Sequence			Last 30 Trials Stimulus Sequence			Notes
Trial	(C-RT Only)	RT	Trial	(C-RT Only)	RT	
1.	B	____	1.	O	____	
2.	O	____	2.	B	____	
3.	B	____	3.	O	____	
4.	B	____	4.	B	____	
5.	O	____	5.	B	____	
6.	B	____	6.	O	____	
7.	O	____	7.	B	____	
8.	B	____	8.	O	____	
9.	O	____	9.	B	____	
10.	O	____	10.	B	____	
			11.	O	____	
10 Practice Trials			12.	O	____	
Σ X			13.	B	____	
Σ X^2			14.	B	____	
Mean			15.	O	____	
Median			16.	O	____	
SD			17.	O	____	
Range			18.	B	____	
			19.	B	____	
Last 30 Trials			20.	B	____	
Σ X			21.	B	____	
Σ X^2			22.	O	____	
Mean			23.	O	____	
Median			24.	B	____	
SD			25.	O	____	
Range			26.	O	____	
			27.	B	____	
			28.	O	____	
			29.	B	____	
			30.	O	____	

97

Title: Reaction Time

E: _____   **Day and Time:** _____

Hypothesis:

Method and Procedure: (as described in text with following modifications, if any)

Group Results and Analysis:

TABLE E1.1
MEAN AND STANDARD DEVIATION OF REACTION TIMES OF FIRST AND SIXTH GRADERS

	Simple RT				*C-Reaction*			
	10 Practice		*30 Trials*		*10 Practice*		*30 Trials*	
Group	Mean	SD	Mean	SD	Mean	SD	Mean	SD
Grade 1								
Boys								
Girls								
Combined								
Grade 6								
Boys								
Girls								
Combined								
Combined Grades								
Boys								
Girls								
Total								

TABLE E1.2
2 X 2 X 2 ANALYSIS OF VARIANCE FOR MEAN RT SCORES

Source of Variation	df	Sum of Squares	Mean Squares	F	p
Between Grades	1				
Between Tasks	1				
Between Sexes	1				
Grade X Task	1				
Grade X Sex	1				
Sex X Task	1				
Grade X Sex X Task	1				
Within Group Error	–				
Total (N – 1)					

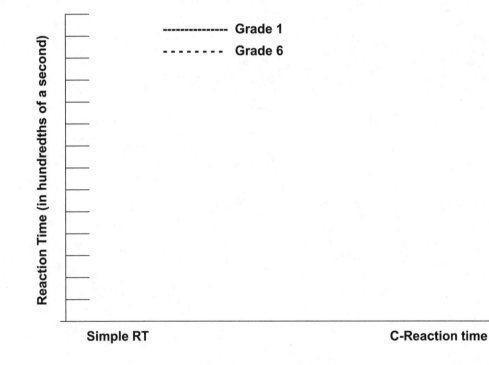

Fig. E1.2. Simple and C-reaction time in children in two grades.

F

Cognitive Development

Background

Look up the word "cognition" in a dictionary and you will find the Latin derivation: cognoscere—to become acquainted with, know, from co- + gnoscere—to come to know. In other words, the act or process of knowing. People who study cognitive development are trying to understand the development of children's changing knowledge of the world, and its maintenance and variability across the lifespan.

The concept of cognition is broad and integrative. It includes perception, learning, memory, language, thinking, intelligence, reasoning, creativity. There is increasing recognition of its interface with biology, environment and experience, personality, socialization, emotions, etc. Research emphases have broadened to include development over the lifespan, neural models, ecological models, cultural influences, context, and genetic/behavioral interactions. Traditional theories have expanded to include dynamic system theories. This is clearly reflected in the recent slew of books and articles, as illustrated in the following list, and includes increased attention to individual and group differences—gender, race, culture.

Biology, neurosciences:
   Gazzaniga, 1992, 2000; Johnson, 1998; Kosslyn and Anderson, 1992; Richards, 1998.

Social cognition:
   Flavell and Miller, 1998; Moskowitz, 2001; Resnick, Higgins, and Levine, 1993; Vygotsky, 1934.

Emotion:
   Eich, Kihlstrom, Bower, Forgas, Niedenthal, 2000; Mackie and Hamilton, 1993; Nelson, 1993.

Culture:
   Geary, 1995.

Family influences:
   Perez-Granados and Callanan, 1997; Zajonc, 2001.

Evolution:
   Geary, 1995.

Ecological approach:
   Gibson and Pick, 2000.

Environmental effects:
   Sternberg and Grigorenko, 2001.

Context:
   Light and Butterworth, 1993; Wozniak and Fischer, 1993.

Executive control:
   Case, 1991; Case and Okamoto, 1996.

As Bourne (1992) pointed out, interest in mental experience dates back to Wundt and Ebbinghaus, late 19th century. Empirical studies of cognition, however, largely faded in the following decades. Indeed, I still remember wryly that when I proposed, in 1950, modifying Heidbreder's sequence of concept attainment (objects, forms, numbers) to include levels of abstractness, my department was worried that a project on cognition was too risky for a dissertation! Modern research on cognitive psychology picked up momentum in the middle and late 1950s; new journals and research centers proliferated; and empirical and theoretical publications now are pervasive.

Any standard child psychology textbook presents an overview of theories of cognitive development. Hetherington and Parke (1999), for example, focus on Piaget's theory, the information processing approach, the neo-Piagetian approach, and Vygotsky's socio-cultural theory. Cole and Cole (1993) and others added a strong focus on biological accounts of mental development and the importance of cultural context.

Piaget's Theory

Piaget, a natural scientist who worked at Binet's laboratory and observed his own children, evolved a theory of *qualitative* changes in the organization or *structures* of children's thinking. These cognitive structures (schemata) are initially based on the infant's physical actions and they change gradually to internal mental activities (operations). Scott Miller, later in this manual, presents a clear summary of Piaget's theory.

The Piagetian theory of qualitatively different *stages* in intellectual development contrasted strongly with the dominant American behaviorism—which emphasized universal principles of learning and was not concerned with age differences. So not until behaviorism began to wane and Flavell (1963) published an English summary of Piaget's theory (few American psychologists could read French), did Piaget's theory become a force in American psychology. And force it was! Despite the recent criticisms and modifications of his theory, Piaget's work has been recognized as monumental, innovative, and influential in the widespread rise of cognitive psychology.

Information Processing Approach

Kail and Wicks-Nelson (1993) describe this approach as likening "the mind to a computer consisting of 'mental hardware' and 'software.' The hardware consists of sensory memory, short-term store, and long-term store; the software consists of strategies used to transfer information between the hardware components (p. 236)." A schematic summary of the major components in an information-processing model plus executive control appears in Fig. F1. The sensory registers include the ionic (visual), echoic (auditory) and haptic (touch). The short-term memory store is short indeed, with limited capacity. (Have you looked up a phone number, dialed it, gotten a busy signal, and immediately needed to look it up again?) The long-term store is limitless and probably permanent.

Humans are believed capable, early on, of processes like recognition, visual scanning of the environment, analysis of perceptual events into features, learning, and integration of the senses. Children have limited information-processing capacities because of their insufficient or uneven attention, limited memory, and limited strategies. The mechanisms whereby improved efficiency and speed are attained include self-modification (similar to Piaget's assimilation and accommodation), automatization (when conscious processes become automatic, as in reading and driving), and proficiency at encoding information (Cole & Cole, 1993).

While most adherents to this approach hold that thinking is information-processing, and their focus is on change mechanisms and their role in development, and the use of careful task analysis (Hetherington & Parke, 1999), they disagree about the continuity/discontinuity issue. Some believe development is continuous and incremental; others believe that gradual changes in one part of the cognitive system can lead to discontinuous stage-type changes—a neo-Piagetian view (Cole & Cole, 1993).

The Neo-Piagetian and Alternative Approaches

Some Neo-Piagetians try to integrate Piagetian notions with information-processing, in order to account for the uneven levels of performance observed in individual children.

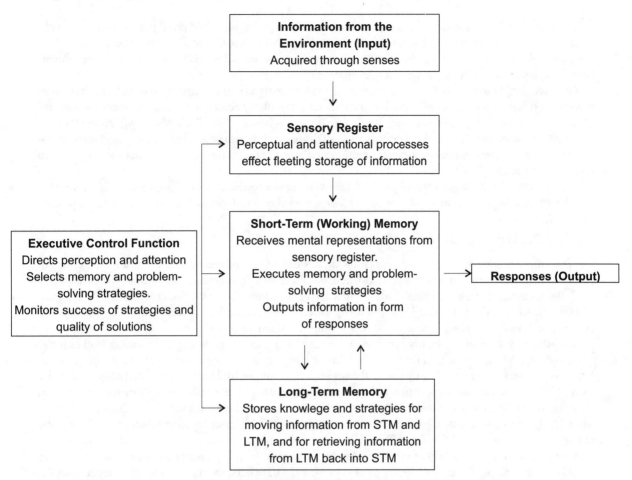

Fig. F.1. Modified information processing model with executive control function. "The store model of information processing represents the way information flows through the cognitive system and is stored, for a brief or longer period, retrieved from storage, and produced in responses to the external world," (p. 368). (Source based on Atkinson & Shifrin, 1968.).
Note: From *Child psychology: A contemporary viewpoint* (p. 368) by R. D. Parke and E. M. Hetherington, 1999, New York: McGraw-Hill College. Copyright © 1999 by McGraw-Hill Companies. Reprinted with permission.

Some psychologists retain the stage concept, but claim there is no generalized global competence. Instead, knowledge proceeds in stages *within* narrow spheres of activity, called *domains* (e.g., music, language, mathematics). Each domain has its own content and logic. A child can be advanced in some domains, average in others, and slow in still others.

Case (1992) and Case and Okamoto (1996), attempting to synthesize Piaget and information processing theories, agree that development occurs in stages, but disagree about the basic cognitive functions. For Piaget, these are assimilation and accommodation. For Case, they are the ability to set goals, solve problems, explore, observe, and imitate. In his theory, the formation and combination of *executive control structure*—mental blueprints or plans for solving problems—are important. (See Fig. F1.) With development, children become more efficient due to the streamlining of these executive control structures and due to biological maturation. Each of Case's stages is characterized by an increasingly sophisticated set of executive control structures.

Biological Approach

Cole and Cole (1993) focus on bio-social-behavioral shifts that occur during development, suggesting that some of the limitations and unevenness in young children's mental performance may "result ... from variations in the rate of maturation of different parts of the nervous system" (p. 335). The growth of the brain (90% by age 6), the pace and location of myelination, the increasing neural connections in the brain—all further cognitive development.

The concept of *mental modules* (Fodor, 1983) has been used to explain child prodigies in music and math. Modules are innate, domain-specific mental faculties, which do not directly interact with other modules. You can be autistic and a numbers whiz; you can be a math prodigy and tone-deaf. By themselves, however, modularity theories cannot fully explain mental development.

The interdisciplinary field of cognitive neuroscience has emerged strongly in the last decade, and attention is being paid to the neural basis of cognitive phenomena, particularly perception, attention, memory, and language (Gazzaniga, 1992, 2000; Johnson, 1998; Kosslyn & Anderson, 1992; Richards, 1998). Attempts have been made to understand how cortical development of the brain and brain structure relate to visual and perceptual capacities, face recognition by infants, attention, and memory (in the limbic system), and language (Broca and Wernicke areas of the brain).

Recent molecular biological techniques and the evolving neuroscience view that plasticity is an inherent property of some brain structures will eventually influence psychological researchers of cognitive development.

Cultural Context Approach

The preceding theories include environmental influences directly or indirectly, but do not emphasize the social/cultural factors in cognitive development to the extent that Lev Vygotsky and cultural-context theorists do.

Cultural-context theorists emphasize the child's active constructive role (as does Piaget) and the parents' and specific societies' role in selecting and shaping the environment for the children. The focus is on specific domains of behavior, defined here as context or setting (Cole & Cole, 1993).

As children go through their daily activities, whether it's a trip to the candy store, or washing clothes in the river, they build up a generalized representation of the event; this representation is called a *script* (Nelson, 1981). A personal example: I grew up during the Great Depression, and did not eat in a formal restaurant until I dated. I had no script for this experience. I did not know whether to precede or follow my date when the maitre d' led us to a table; I was overwhelmed by the array of silverware and the huge menu, which included many items I had never seen or tasted. I did not function well in this unfamiliar setting. Shared scripts enable people in a specific social group to function effectively and meaningfully.

Vygotsky, who is well thought of in Europe, has begun to be influential in America, decades after his death in 1934 (Hetherington & Parke, 1999, Vygotsky, 1934, 1978). He believed that children developed spirally, not incrementally, in a social-historical context. The early interactions with parents and other people more mature than the child slowly become internalized. Knowledge is a social creation, in which the culture in which the child develops and the language play key roles. Like Piaget, Vygotsky was a stage theorist who thought of developmental changes as abrupt shifts.

Interested in the child's potential for intellectual growth, he proposed the *zone of proximal development*. This is the difference between what a child is presently capable of, and what he/she can accomplish when instructed by an adult or more capable peer. Most parents intuitively know that children can carry out tasks with help that they can't initially do alone, and that by reducing and adjusting the provided help over time, they foster the children's competence. Teachers use the concept of zone of proximal development similarly in an instructional process called *scaffolding*.

As more and more researchers recognize the importance of social contexts and cultural variations on cognition, Vygotsky's influence will continue to spread. Even undergraduate textbooks now emphasize the changing child in a changing world and focus on the social contexts within which children develop (e.g., Zigler & Stevenson, 1993).

New Directions

Wellman and Gelman (1992) point out that cognitive development was reviewed twice during the 1980s in the *Annual Review of Psychology*, once on stages of cognitive development, and once on mechanisms of cognitive change. Other cognitive themes which they believe deserve recognition include infant cognitive capacities, instruction, emergent literacy, cognition in the elderly, and cross-cultural study. They devote their review to two topics they consider revolutionary in cognition: contemporary concern with *domains* of cognition and with *naive* theories.

While Piaget's stages were thought to apply across widely varying content areas (and therefore be content independent and domain general), and even some information-processing views were concerned with general processes or architectures, Wellman and Gelman focus instead on domain-*specific* cognitive development. They are interested in the specific bodies of knowledge acquired by young children which underlie later conceptual acquisitions: foundational understandings of naive physics, psychology, and biology. They point to such "early acquisition of foundational theories of core domains ..." (p.371) as a central mechanism of cognitive development.

Siegler and Munakata (1993) listed two beliefs allegedly shared by cognitive development researchers: to understand cognitive development, one must understand how *change* occurs, and current understanding of this is inadequate. They propose an evolutionary framework that emphasizes the processes of *variation* (of thoughts, strategies, concepts) and of *selection*, and they downplay the long emphasis on one-on-one relations between age and way of thinking. They believe that there is a need to study changes while they are occurring, difficult as such methodology is. Three change issues that need to be researched, in their view, are "the ways in which variability [of thoughts] is generated, the ways in which the generation of variability is constrained, and the ways in which people increasingly come to rely on some ways of thinking about the world ... " (p. 11).

The development of cognition in children, particularly the child's theory of mind, has intrigued a growing number of researchers. Experiment 3: False belief in Children's Theory of Mind is preceded by an extensive background section, and continues our discussion of cognitive development.

Your Class Experiments

Over the years, our lab students have run dozens of Piagetian projects: conservation of area, number, volume; classification; moral judgment; egocentrism. Included here is my modification of the Three Mountain Task, to introduce you to the literature and controversy on egocentric perspective-taking. Be sure to read Scott Miller's essay on Piaget's theory; it is clear and comprehensive.

Attention and memory, old topics in psychology, have been rejuvenated by the interest of information-processing adherents. There are several attention tasks here from which to choose: a modification of the classic Stroop test of interference proneness, and the newer Picture-word semantic interference task. The former studies resistance to distraction, and the latter introduces issues of reading ability and processing of words and pictures. It highlights the issue of automaticity. Our memory task involves memory of a random list of words versus memory of those same words categorically organized.

The experiment on children's interpretation of the word *Big* illustrates the interplay of language, cognition, and context. John Coley did this research as a graduate student and I was intrigued. Susan Gelman contributed an essay on cognition and language.

Selected Bibliography

Atkinson, R. C., & Shiffrin, R. M. (1968). Human memory: A proposed system and its control processes. In K.W. Spence & J. Spence (Eds.), *Advances in the psychology of learning and motivation: Research and theory* (*Vol. 2*). New York: Academic.

Bartsch, K., & Wellman, H. M. (1995). *Children talk about the mind. New York*, NY: Oxford University Press.

Bourne, L. E. Jr. (1992). Cognitive psychology: A brief overview. *Psychological Science Agenda*, APA, 5(5), 5, 20.

Case, R. (1992). Neo-Piagetian theories of child development. In R. J. Sternberg & C. A. Berg (Eds.), *Intellectual development* (pp. 161–196), New York: Cambridge University Press.

Case, R., & Okamoto, Y. (Eds.). (1996). The role of central conceptual structures in the development of children's thought. *Monographs of the Society for Research in Child Development, 61*, Serial No. 246, Nos 1 & 2.

Chen, Z., & Zeigler, R. (2000). Across the great divide: Bridging the gap between understanding of toddlers' and other children's thinking. *Monographs for Research in Child Development, 65* (Serial No. 261).

Cole, M., & Cole, S. (1993). *The development of children* (2nd ed.). New York: Freeman/Scientific American Books.

Damon, W. (Ed.-in-Chief). (1998). *Handbook of child psychology* (5th ed.). New York: Wiley.

Eich, E., Kihlstrom, J. F., Bower, G. H., Forgas, J. P., & Niedenthal, P. M. (2000). *Cognition and emotion.* New York: Oxford University Press.

Finke, R. A., Ward, T. B., & Smith, S. M. (1992). *Creative cognition: Theory, research, and applications.* Cambridge, MA: MIT Press, Bradford.

Flavell, J. H. (1963). *The developmental psychology of Jean Piaget.* Princeton, NJ: Van Nostrand.

Flavell, J. H.,& Miller, P. H. (1998). Social cognition. In W. Damon (Gen. Ed.), D. Kuhn, & R. S. Siegler (Vol. Eds.), *Handbook of child psychology: Vol. 2, Cognition, perception, and language* (pp. 851–898). New York: Wiley.

Flavell, J. H.,& Miller, P. H., & Miller, S. A. (1993). *Cognitive development* (3rd ed.). Englewood Cliffs, NJ: Prentice Hall.

Fletcher, G. (1995). *The scientific credibility of folk psychology*. Mahwah, NJ: Lawrence Erlbaum Associates.

Fodor, J. (1983). *The modularity of mind*. Cambridge, MA: MIT Press.

Gazzaniga, M. S. (1992). *Nature's mind: The biological roots of thinking, emotions, sexuality, language and intelligence*. New York: Basic Books.

Gazzaniga, M. S. (Ed.). (2000). *The new cognitive neurosciences,* (2nd ed.). Cambridge, MA: MIT Press/A Bradford Book.

Geary, D. C. (1995). Reflections on evolution and culture in children's cognition. *American Psychologist, 50*, 24–37.

Gibson, E. J., & Pick, A. D. (2000). *An ecological approach to perceptual learning and development*. New York:Oxford University Press.

Hetherington, E.M., & Parke, R.D. (1999). *Child psychology: A contemporary viewpoint* (5th ed.). New York: McGraw-Hill.

Heyes, C., & Huber, L. (Eds.). (2000). *The evolution of cognition*. Cambridge, MA: MIT Press/A Bradford Book.

Johnson, M. H. (1998). The neural basis of cognitive development. In W. Damon (Ed.-in-chief), D. Kuhn & R. Siegler (Vol. Eds.), *Handbook of child psychology: Vol. 2. Cognition, perception, and language* (5th ed., pp. 1–49). New York: Wiley.

Kail, R.V., & Wicks-Nelson, R. (1992). *Developmental psychology* (5th ed.). Englewood Cliffs, NJ: Prentice Hall.

Kimura, D. (2000). *Sex and cognition*. Cambridge, MA: MIT Press/A Bradford Book.

Klahr, D., & MacWhinney, B. (1998). Information processing. In W. Damon (Editor in Chief), D. Kuhn & R. Siegler (Vol. Eds.), *Handbook of child psychology: Vol. 2. Cognition, perception & language* (5th ed., pp. 631–678). New York: Wiley.

Kosslyn, S. M. & Andersen, R. R. (Eds.). (1992). *Frontiers in cognitive neuroscience*, Cambridge, MA: MIT Press, Bradford.

Light, P., & Butterworth, G. (Eds.). (1993). *Context and cognition: Ways of learning and knowing*. Hillside, NJ: Lawrence Erlbaum Associates.

Mackie, D. M., & Hamilton, D. L. (1993). *Affect, cognition, and stereotyping: Interactive processes in group perception*. Orlando, FL: Academic Press.

McClelland, J. L., & Siegler, R. S. (Eds.). (2001). *Mechanisms of cognitive development: Behavioral and neural perspectives*. Mahwah, NJ: Lawrence Erlbaum Associates.

Moskowitz, G. B. (Ed.). (2001). *Cognitive social psychology: The Princeton symposium on the legacy and future of social cognition*. Mahwah, NJ: Lawrence Erlbaum Associates.

Nadelman, L. (1957). Influence of concreteness and accessibility on concept-thinking. *Psychological Reports, Monographs, 3, Monograph Supplement 4*, 189–212.

Nelson, C.A. (Ed.). (1993). *Memory and affect in development: Minnesota symposia on child psychology* (*Vol. 26*). Hillside, NJ: Lawrence Erlbaum Associates.

Nelson, K. (1981). Social cognition in a script framework. In J. H. Flavell & L. Ross (Eds.), *Social cognitive development*. Cambridge, MA: Cambridge University Press.

Perez-Granados, D. R., & Callanan, M. (1997). Conversations with mothers and siblings: Young children's semantic and conceptual development. *Developmental Psychology, 33*(1), 120–134.

Pick, R. L., Jr., van den Broek, P., & Knill, D. C. (Eds.). (1992). *Cognition: Conceptual and methodological issues*. Washington, DC: American Psychological Association.

Resnick, L. B., Higgins, E. T., & Levine, J. M. (1993). Social foundations of cognition. In M. Rosenzweig and L. Porter (Eds.), *Annual Review of Psychology* (*Vol. 44*). Palo Alto, CA: Annual Reviews.

Richards, J. E. (Ed.). (1998). *Cognitive neuroscience of attention: A developmental perspective*. Mahwah, NJ: Lawrence Erlbaum Associates.

Rogoff, B. (1998). Cognition as a collaborative process. In W. Damon (Gen. Ed.), D. Kuhn, & R. S. Siegler (Vol. Eds.), *Handbook of child psychology, Vol. 2. Cognition, perception & language* (pp. 679–744). New York: Wiley.

Sameroff, A. J., & Haith, M. (1996). Interpreting developmental transitions. In A. J. Sameroff & M. M. Haith (Eds.), *The five to seven year shift: The age of reason and responsibility* (pp. 3–15). Chicago, IL: The University of Chicago Press.

Siegler, R. S. (1997). *Children's thinking* (3rd ed.). Englewood Cliffs, NJ: Prentice Hall.

Siegler, R. S., & Munakata, Y. (Winter, 1993). Beyond the immaculate transition: Advances in the understanding of change. *SRCD Newsletter*, 3–11,13.

Sternberg, R. (Ed.). (1998). *The nature of cognition*. Cambridge, MA: MIT Press/ A Bradford Book.

Sternberg, R. J., & Grigorenko, E. L. (Eds.). (2001). *Environmental effects on cognitive abilities*. Mahwah, NJ: Lawrence Erlbaum Associates.

Sternberg, R. J., & Zhang, L. (Eds.). (2001). *Perspectives on thinking, learning, and cognitive styles*. Mahwah, NJ: Lawrence Erlbaum Associates.

Vygotsky, L. S. (1934). *Thought and language*. Cambridge, MA: MIT Press.

Vygotsky, L. S. (1978). *Mind in society*. Cambridge, MA: Harvard University Press.

Wellman, H. M., & Gelman, S. A. (1992). Cognitive development: Foundational theories of core domains. *Annual Review of Psychology, 43*, 337–375.

Wertsch, J. V., del Rio, P., & Alvarez, A. (Eds.). (1995). *Sociocultural studies of mind*. New York: Cambridge University Press.

Wozniak, R., & Fischer, K. W. (Eds.). (1993). *Development in context: Acting and thinking in specific environments*. Hillside, NJ: Lawrence Erlbaum Associates.

Zajonc, R. B. (2001). *The family dynamics of intellectual development. American Psychologist, 56*(6/7), 490–496.

Zigler, E.F., & Stevenson, M.F. (1993). *Children in a changing world: Development and social issues* (2nd ed.). Pacific Grove, CA: Brooks/Cole.

Piagetian Research

Piaget's Theory

—*Scott A. Miller*

"Piaget's theory" is a complex topic, one that Piaget developed across some 50 books and scores of articles and that numerous other workers have added to since. The present chapter provides a brief introduction to this large—and still growing—subject matter. Readers who wish to delve more deeply into the intricacies of Piaget's theory have a number of fuller treatments from which to choose, for example, Flavell (1963), Chapman (1988), and Ginsburg and Opper (1988).

In trying to understand any theory, it is helpful to know something about the theorist—the kinds of training that shaped his or her thinking, the interests that led to the study of psychology. In Piaget's case, it could be argued that such knowledge is essential, for the Piagetian approach to psychology differs in many ways from what we are familiar with in American psychology. This chapter will begin, therefore, with some historical background of Piaget's work. The discussion will then turn to Piaget's notion of stages of development. Piaget claimed that children pass through four intellectual stages as they grow and attempt to make sense of the world around them. Much of what Piaget has to tell us about development is captured in this stage description; thus each of the stages will merit careful attention. Finally, the chapter will conclude with a consideration of some of the issues that are raised by Piaget's work. There are *many* such issues that might be discussed, but the present coverage will focus on three: the accuracy of Piaget's assessments of children's abilities, the validity of the notion of "stage," and the question of how the child moves from one stage, or level of understanding, to another.

Historical Background and Basic Concepts

Jean Piaget was born in Switzerland in 1896, and lived and worked there most of his life until his death in 1980. His early training was primarily in the biological sciences, with a special interest in the study of mollusks. He was a precocious student, publishing his first paper at the age of 10 and some 20 papers before he was 21.

Piaget's interests in biology were quickly supplemented by absorption in a second intellectual discipline: philosophy. The branch of philosophy that especially attracted him was epistemology, or the study of knowledge. Epistemology deals with many of the classic questions of philosophy: Is true knowledge of the world possible? To the extent that knowledge is possible, where does it come from; in particular, is our knowledge inborn or does it derive from experience? Are there different types of knowledge, and if so, what are the types and where do *they* come from?

Quite early in his study of these issues Piaget made two basic decisions. One was that questions of this sort are not purely philosophical matters but are also at least partly empirical; that is, they are questions that should be susceptible to scientific study. Piaget's training in biology was undoubtedly important in his coming to this decision. He has written, in fact, that his early biological studies "functioned ... as instruments of protection against the demon of philosophy" (Piaget, 1952a, p. 239). The second decision was that questions that concern the nature and origin of knowledge are fundamentally *developmental* questions. Just as the biologist studies the growth of the organism, so must the psychologist attempt to study the growth of knowledge. Piaget decided, therefore, that he would devote a few years to the study of thinking in children, after which he would be ready to answer the basic epistemological questions that intrigued him. Although this early goal remained constant, his estimate of the time required proved somewhat off; his research on children's thinking extended for some 60 years.

Piaget's interest in epistemology was thus the impetus for his decision to work with children. More specifically, his epistemological concerns provided much of the content for his work—that is, his conception of exactly what aspects of the child's thought are interesting and important to study. A major goal of this chapter, as well as of the discussion of the experiment that follows, is to convey the kinds of thought processes that Piaget studied. Many psychologists feel that Piaget's work, more than other approaches, succeeded in identifying concepts that are central to our understanding of how children think.

The contribution of Piaget's biological training to his studies of intelligence is less easy to summarize. Essentially, what Piaget takes from biology is the functional aspect of his theory, his conception of human intelligence. Piaget's theorizing is based consistently on the belief that intelligence is a biological phenomenon and as such will show properties that are common to all biological phenomena. Two such properties are stressed: organization and adaptation.

Organization at a biological level is easy enough to understand. Organisms are never random collections of organs, muscles, and other body parts. Rather, they are complicated systems in which the parts interrelate in quite precise ways. Piaget maintains that the same is true of human intelligence. The essence of intelligence does not lie in individually learned responses or isolated pieces of information but in the organized system of cognitive abilities. The work on stages, to be discussed shortly, is an attempt to identify the qualitatively different systems as they develop in the child.

The second biological property—*adaptation*—refers to organisms' adaptations or adjustments to the environment in order to survive. Human intelligence also adapts to the environments with which it is faced. This rather general notion becomes more precise—and more uniquely Piagetian—when two components of the adaptation process are distinguished. Piaget uses the term assimilation to refer to the organism's tendency to alter aspects of the environment to make them fit into its current structures. Perhaps the best synonym for assimilation at a psychological level is "interpretation": The intellectual system interprets new events by fitting them into what it already understands. At the same time, however, the system itself changes as a function of the new experiences with which it must cope. Such alterations of the organism to fit with the environment constitute the second component of the adaptation process, one that Piaget labels *accommodation*. Assimilation and accommodation are complementary processes, and both are involved in all acts of intellectual adaptation.

A specific example (borrowed from Ginsburg & Opper, 1988) may help to clarify these general concepts. Imagine a 4-month-old who is shown a rattle for the first time. What will the baby do? Probably Piaget's most basic point is that what the baby does is by no means random but rather is a function of what he[1] already knows how to do. Thus the baby will certainly look at the rattle; he may be able to reach out and grasp it; should he succeed in grasping it, he may bring it to the mouth; if the rattle reaches the mouth, he will probably suck on it, and so on. The baby will do to the rattle what he already knows how to do, or, in Piaget's terms, he will *assimilate* the rattle to his existing patterns of behavior. At the same time, however, these behaviors must be changed to at least a slight degree as a function of the new challenges posed by the rattle. Thus, in looking at the rattle, the baby must trace a slightly different contour with his eyes than he has ever traced before; when grasping it, he must close his fingers in a slightly different fashion, and so on. In Piaget's terms, he must *accommodate* his behavior patterns to the novel elements of the rattle. Development thus results from countless such instances of assimilation and accommodation. Reality is always understood in terms of the existing cognitive system (assimilation), yet the system is continually changing to adapt to new features of the environment (accommodation).

There are two implications of this assimilation-accommodation framework that are worth noting before we turn to a discussion of the Piagetian stages. The first might be called an epistemological implication. Within this framework it is impossible to talk of a "real world out there," or to assume that people at different points in development experience the world in the same way. Thus, the rattle as an object to shake simply does not exist for the 4-month-old, since the concept of the rattle as noisemaker does not correspond to anything in his prior experience. In contrast, an older child, with his richer cognitive structures, will immediately perceive the rattle as a toy that makes an interesting sound. The second implication of the model might be labeled an educational one. The concepts of assimilation and accommodation imply that cognitive change will always be a slow and gradual process, without large leaps forward in development. This claim follows from the conception of how experience operates. Experiences do not simply happen to the child; rather, they must always be assimilated, which means that they can be effective only if they are not too far beyond the child's current level. We will return to this claim in the concluding section when we discuss the issue of cognitive change.

Let us turn now to a consideration of the Piagetian stages. As noted, there are four stages, and they span the period from birth to adolescence.

---

[1] In this summary, "he" includes she; "she" includes he. To cope with the sexism of the English language, the sex of the child is alternated from section to section, but not from paragraph to paragraph nor sentence to sentence.

The Sensorimotor Stage

The sensorimotor stage is the stage of infancy. It begins at birth and extends until roughly age 2. The term *roughly*, it should be noted, applies to all of the ages that will be mentioned in the following pages. The age norms in a Piagetian description are simple rough guidelines for when things usually happen. The theory makes no claim that abilities emerge at specific ages, which is fortunate, because research reveals that there is in fact wide variability in the speed with which children develop.

Piaget's account of the sensorimotor period is based almost totally upon his study of his own three children's development during the first two to three years of their lives. This is obviously a small and rather biased sample. It should be noted, therefore, that attempts to replicate Piaget's work using larger samples have verified the descriptive accuracy of much of what he claimed. At the same time, recent work has suggested that Piaget's account of infant development requires correction in a number of respects, and some of this work will be discussed in the concluding Issues section.

The picture that Piaget offers of sensorimotor development is both very detailed and very complicated. It is described in three quite lengthy books (Piaget, 1951, 1952, 1954). All that will be attempted here is to highlight some of the major themes that emerge with respect to the nature of infant intelligence. What is the baby's intellectual system like, and how does this system change during the first two years of life?

A first theme to be stressed concerns the importance of the child's own activity. This, in fact, is a leitmotif running throughout Piaget's theory at every stage of development: Children learn about the world to the extent that they act on it. The conception of action during infancy is a broad one that encompasses many different behaviors: looking, sucking, grasping, manipulating, vocalizing, locomoting, and so on. The essential point is that babies are not passive recipients of environmental stimulation; rather, from birth they are actively involved in trying to understand their world.

A further specification of the role of action comes in Piaget's notion of schemes. Piaget uses the term *scheme* to refer to organized patterns of behavior, which the child can apply in a number of different situations. Thus, it is possible to talk of a sucking scheme, a grasping scheme, a kicking scheme, and so on. In each case, there is a complex of skilled behaviors that the child can apply, with suitable modifications, to innumerable different stimuli that the environment presents. This conception is closely tied to the model of assimilation and accommodation. When new experiences are assimilated, they are assimilated *to* schemes; and when accommodation occurs, it is accommodation *of* existing schemes to specific aspects of the environment.

Why does the child act on the world at all? This is the question of cognitive motivation—of what it is that energizes and directs the cognitive system. Piaget's answer to this question represents a departure from traditional drive-based theories of motivation. His position is that the child is an inherently active creature and that intelligence is an inherently active system. There is no need, therefore, to look outside the system of intelligence (e.g., to bodily drives) to explain why intelligence operates. Rather, it is the nature of schemes to be utilized whenever possible. Piaget argued further that the child is most motivated to act on events that are slightly different from those that she has encountered before. Such events are said to create a "disequilibrium" in the cognitive system; further cognitive action then ensues, and equilibrium is restored at a new, more advanced level. As Flavell, Miller, and Miller (1993) point out, the kind of motivational model proposed would seem to be an ideal one for an organism designed to make cognitive progress: an inherently active cognitive system with a basic need to master the world around it. Note that neither biological drives nor external reinforcers play an important role in this mastery.

The two themes discussed so far—the importance of action and the nature of motivation—are not limited to infancy but apply to all of the developmental periods. Let us turn now to some themes that are more specific to the sensorimotor period. Four such themes will be discussed.

Progressive Decentering. A first theme is that of development as a process of *progressive decentering*. According to Piaget, the baby starts life in a state of almost total egocentrism. The term egocentrism does not refer to a selfish concern with one's own wishes. It refers, rather, to a basic inability to distinguish between what is specific to the self—one's own immediate perspective, desires, or behaviors—and what exists separate from the self. A major achievement of the sensorimotor period is then the gradual construction of the distinction between the self and the outer world. The two aspects of this distinction are complementary. The child can understand the world only as she comes to realize the ways in which her own perspective or actions affect (or, in some cases, do not affect) outer reality. At the same time, she can form a conception of herself only as she comes to realize that she is one object in a world of objects that exist and interact largely independent of her.

There are many aspects of the infant's development that illustrate progressive decentering. Undoubtedly the clearest example, however, comes in the formation of the *object concept*. The term refers to the knowledge that objects have a permanent existence that is independent of our immediate perceptual contact with them: that is, that things do not cease to exist simply because we can no longer see, hear, or touch them. It would be hard to imagine a more basic piece of knowledge than this. Piaget's research suggests, however, that for a long time the baby's knowledge of objects is tied to her own immediate actions. Thus, for a baby in the first few months of her life, objects seem to exist only to the extent that she is acting on them. If, for example, a toy with which she is playing is made to disappear, the young baby will make no attempt to search for it but instead will turn immediately to some other activity, behaving as though the toy no longer existed. At a somewhat later age, the baby will begin to search for vanished objects but with a number of interesting limitations. At first, for example, she may search if her own actions have made the toy disappear but not if someone has dropped a handkerchief over it. At a later age, she may be able to handle a single hiding place but become confused if two places are used, searching in the place where she first found the object rather than in the place where she has just seen it disappear. It is only at about 18 to 24 months, according to Piaget, that the infant finally arrives at a full understanding of the permanence of objects.

Formation of Invariants. The object concept can serve as an example not only of decentering but also of our second theme, the formulation of *invariants*. To a good extent we inhabit a world of change. Certainly the stimulation that we receive from the environment is in constant flux, with changes in our sense impressions occurring from moment to moment. Piaget argues that a major task of the intellectual system, at every stage of development, is to figure out what stays the same in the midst of all this change. He maintains, in fact, that rational activity would be impossible unless *some* properties of the world can be understood as remaining constant even though other properties have changed. The object concept is an early and very basic invariant. In this case, what changes is our perceptual contact with the object; what remains the same is the existence of that object. We will encounter other, more advanced invariants when we discuss development during the middle childhood years.

Intentionality. A third important theme of infancy concerns the gradual development of intentionality. A loose (but accurate enough) definition of the term *intentionality* is that it refers to the baby's ability to act intelligently to get the things she wants. Once again, there are marked changes that occur in the first two years of life. The newborn is a creature of inborn reflexes, capable of acting on her world but limited largely to the exercise of wired-in behaviors. As the baby develops, however (i.e., as she assimilates new experiences and accommodates them), the reflexes evolve into intelligent schemes, and the child's ability to affect her environment expands enormously. At first, the baby's control of the environment has an after-the-fact quality; she happens upon a behavior that produces interesting consequences, and then she repeats the behavior again and again. Eventually, however, the baby begins to disentangle the means and the end, and her behavior becomes more clearly intentional. Thus, by about 8 to 12 months, the child can first perceive some desired goal (the end) and only then activate appropriate schemes (the means) by which to achieve the goal. Piaget regards such "truly intentional" behavior as a hallmark of intelligence. There is still one more advance, however. By about 18 months, the baby no longer needs to try out possible means–end schemas overtly; rather, she can think through the possibilities internally and then act immediately in an adaptive fashion. And this brings us to our final theme, the gradual movement towards *representation*.

Representation. We have seen that the sensorimotor child is definitely engaged, from quite early in life, in adaptive and intelligent behavior. What must be stressed, however, is that all of the baby's adaptation to the world must occur overtly. Thus, the sensorimotor schemes, by definition, are systems that eventuate in overt behavior—actually grasping an object, actually moving it from one place to another, and so on. What the baby cannot yet do is to use mental *representation* to think about the object and its movement in the absence of an actual stimulus or an actual behavior. One way to define the sensorimotor stage, in fact, is to say that it is the stage prior to the onset of representational thought. Sensorimotor developments, however, are by no means unrelated to later representational thinking. Rather, the whole sensorimotor period constitutes a kind of extended progression toward the time when the child will be able to do things mentally and not simply overtly. When this time arrives, typically somewhere around 18 to 24 months, the child is no longer totally sensorimotor but has begun the next stage of development.

The Preoperational Stage

The preoperational stage begins at about age 2 and extends until about 6 or 7 years of age. As just noted, the defining characteristic of the transition from sensorimotor to preoperational is the onset of representational ability. Two questions immediately arise. One is what it means to have representational ability. The other is how we know that the child now has it.

The essence of representational functioning lies in the ability to use one thing as a symbol to stand for some other thing, which then becomes the symbolized. Early in the child's representational career, the symbols that he is capable of generating may still be somewhat overt. For example, at 15 months one of Piaget's daughters used the crooking of her finger as a symbol for the protruding feet of her doll. Later symbols may be completely internal, in which case their exact form is no longer determinable. Symbols may be mental images, or words, or some other forms. The important point is that a child who can generate symbols is no longer limited, as was the sensorimotor child, to dealing with the immediate reality in front of him. The grist for his cognitive structures becomes anything that can be symbolically brought to mind—an enormous expansion in the scope of the cognitive system. Furthermore, the child who is skilled at the representational level can not only bring absent objects or events to mind; he can perform *mental actions* on the world. Recall that for Piaget the essence of intelligence always lies in the actions that the child can perform.

How do we know that the 2-year-old has become capable of representational functioning? The answer is that the child begins to show a number of interesting behaviors, none of which were present during infancy and all of which seem to imply that he is now using mental representations. The child begins, for example, to show *deferred imitation*—that is, imitation of behaviors that are not directly in front of him but that occurred some time in the past. Piaget argues that the child can reproduce behaviors from the past only if he has some means of storing those behaviors over time, that is, some representational capacity. A second—and very visible—example comes in the phenomenon of *symbolic play*. The 2-year-old is a great one for pretend play, deliberately using one thing (e.g., a broomstick) to stand for something else (e.g., a horse). The third example is likely to be of greatest interest to parents. This is the time of *language onset*, the first genuinely symbolic use of words as substitutes for the things they designate. The acquisition of language is clearly a major event in the child's cognitive development. For Piaget, however, there is a fourth example of representational functioning that is even more significant. It is, in fact, the example that we have already stressed. Suppose that the child is faced with some problem that he wishes to solve. Whereas the younger child would need to work through possible solutions overtly, the representational child can do the working through in the head, thus engaging in *internal problem solving*. This brings us to the essential point about representational ability. The onset of representations opens the way for a problem-solving system that in speed, flexibility, and power far outstrips anything of which the sensorimotor child is capable.

The preoperational stage thus constitutes an enormous advance over the sensorimotor stage. At the same time, the preoperational child encounters a number of difficulties as he attempts to cope with problems at a representational level. It is because of these difficulties that we have the "pre" in "preoperational:" The child does not yet have the mental operations that allow him to function efficiently at a representational level. We will return shortly to the question of just what these necessary operations are. First, however, let us focus on some of the deficiencies of preoperational thought. Two such deficiencies in particular are worth stressing. Both parallel themes were discussed with respect to development at the sensorimotor level.

First, the preoperational child is often egocentric in his dealings with the world. Again, the term *egocentrism* does not refer to a selfish concern with one's own desires. It refers, rather, to an overdependence on one's own immediate perspective, and a consequent neglect of other perspectives. The young infant demonstrates such egocentrism at the sensorimotor level in his apparent belief that objects exist only when he can see or touch them. The older child's egocentrism is on the plane of representational functioning and is evident in situations that require putting himself in the place of someone else. The preoperational child has a very limited ability to break away from his own point of view and to realize that the other person may have a different perspective—may see, feel, or think differently than he does. Thus, a young child may invite mother to look at a picture yet hold the book so that only he can see it. He may go birthday shopping for his daddy and select a toy truck, confident that everyone must share his love for the toy. Or he may sprinkle his conversations with frequent references to "Johnny," "Billy," and "David," even though his conversational partner has never heard of Johnny, Billy, or David. All these examples illustrate the cognitive egocentrism of the preoperational child.

The second major deficit of preoperational thought is that it is centrated. The term *centrated* subsumes a variety of related aspects of preoperational thinking. It refers most generally to the notion that the child's thinking is perceptually oriented. It is perceptually oriented, moreover, in certain definite ways. The child's thinking tends to focus on immediate perceptual states—how things look at the moment—rather than the transformations that link one state to another. It tends to focus on only certain salient aspects of the perceptual array, ignoring other aspects that may be critical to problem solution. Once the child has focused on a particular aspect of the array, he tends to be inflexible, finding it very difficult to switch attention to other aspects. In short, preoperational thought often "gets stuck"—captured and held by what is most immediately obvious in the perceptual input.

Piaget devised a number of tasks that illustrate the phenomenon of centration. Undoubtedly the best-known example is the conservation problem (Piaget & Inhelder, 1974; Piaget & Szeminska, 1952). A conservation problem begins with two stimuli that are equal on some quantitative dimension (e.g., number, mass, weight). One of the stimuli is then perceptually transformed, and the child is asked whether the quantities are still the same. The test might begin with two rows of six poker chips, lined up in one-to-one correspondence. One of the rows is then spread out, and the conservation question is asked. Perhaps the most dramatic finding from Piaget's entire research career was his demonstration that young children do not understand that quantities are conserved in the face of irrelevant perceptual change. Thus, a 4-year-old who is given the number task just described will typically reply that the longer row now has more. If the child is asked to justify his answer, he finds the explanation obvious: "Because it's longer." What the child is doing is *centrating*: focusing on the perceptually salient dimension of length and ignoring the other relevant dimension, the spacing between the chips.

Note that conservation problems provide another example of the importance of *invariants* in the child's thought. In this case, what the child must come to understand is that certain quantitative attributes of an object remain invariant even though the perceptual appearance has changed. According to Piaget, the understanding of conservation requires certain cognitive operations. These operations are acquired during the next stage of development.

The Concrete-Operational Stage

The stage of concrete operations begins at about 6 or 7 and extends until about 11 or 12 years of age. The most immediately obvious characteristic of the transition to concrete operations is that the child begins to solve a variety of Piagetian tasks that baffled her only a year or two before. She begins, for example, to master the various conservation problems. She does *not* master all of the conservations simultaneously; the acquisition of different forms of conservation is spread out across the concrete-operational years. Some conservations (e.g., number and mass) are relatively easy, emerging by about age 6 in most American samples; others (e.g., weight and distance) are more difficult and may not appear until about 9 or 10.

The conservation problems are just a small subset of the ingenious tasks that Piaget devised to tap cognitive development during the middle childhood years. Although it is impossible to convey the scope of Piaget's research effort here, a few examples of some of the other tasks are given.

One focus of Piaget's research was on the child's ability to form and work with classes (Inhelder & Piaget, 1964). Of particular interest was the child's understanding of class inclusion: the principle that a subclass cannot be larger than the subordinate class that contains it. Once again, Piaget's studies revealed that a seemingly very basic piece of knowledge is not always present but must somehow be developed. Suppose, for example, that the child is shown 20 wooden beads, 17 of which are red and 3 of which are white. She is asked whether there are more red beads or more wooden beads. The preoperational child will confidently assert that there are more red ones. Once she has centrated on the perceptually salient redness, she finds if very difficult to break away from a comparison of subclasses to make use of her knowledge that all of the beads are wooden. In contrast, the concrete-operational child, having mastered the basics of classification, will reply that of course there are more wooden ones She may even be insulted that you have asked her such a silly question.

Piaget was interested in the child's understanding of *relations* as well. One important example of relational reasoning is provided by tasks that require the use of transitive inference (Piaget & Inhelder, 1974; Piaget, Inhelder, & Szeminska, 1960). Suppose one knows, for example, that *A* is greater than *B* and *B* greater than *C* on some quantitative dimension (length and weight have been the dimensions most often studied). It then follows necessarily that *A* must be greater than *C*. This conclusion does not follow for the preoperational child, however. If asked to judge the relation between *A* and *C*, the young child has no systematic basis for response and is likely to fall back upon perceptual comparison or simple guessing. The concrete-operational child, once again, has developed a cognitive system that allows such problems to be solved easily and with certainty.

It should be noted that Piaget's research was not limited to the kinds of logical and physical-world problems described thus far. One of his earliest books (Piaget, 1932) dealt with children's conceptions of morality. A major theme of the work on morality is that a child's thoughts about moral issues are not simply a direct mirroring of what parents and other social agents teach her; they are at least partly a reflection of the child's own level of cognitive development. Piaget maintains, for example, that young children tend to judge the morality of actions in terms of perceptually obvious cues (e.g., the amount of material damage), just as they judge the quantities in a conservation task in terms of what is immediately obvious. It is only later in development that the child can penetrate beyond the surface cues to take into account more subtle information, such as the intentions behind the action.

We can see, therefore, that the concrete-operational child can solve a large number of problems that were beyond the preoperational child. It should be clear by now, however, that Piaget's concern was never simply to catalogue the tasks that the child can or cannot solve. His goal was always to use the child's overt problem-solving behavior as a guide to the underlying cognitive system. During middle childhood this system is said to consist of concrete operations. Let us take the two words in the term *concrete operations* separately, beginning with the notion of operations.

It is helpful in trying to understand *operations* to draw comparisons with the sensorimotor schemes. The operations are, in fact, in many respects quite parallel to the schemes of infancy. First and foremost, the operations are systems of *action*. Thought, for Piaget, is never a matter simply of passively registering or reproducing environmental givens. True understanding requires some transformation of the immediately given, some action on the child's part. Furthermore, the operations are not simply actions but *systems* of action. Just as the sensorimotor schemes come to interrelate in quite definite and complex ways, so do the operations of middle childhood coalesce into a complex, organized totality. The final point of comparison between schemes and operations involves a difference and not a similarity. We have seen that the sensorimotor schemes must always be expressed in overt actions. Concrete operations, in contrast, are systems of *internal* action: the in-the-head problem solving toward which the child has been moving ever since the first dawnings of representation.

This notion of thought-as-internal-action may become clearer if we consider some of the specific tasks that were discussed above. Let us start with classification. Piaget argues that simply to think about an object as a member of a class is an action; classes are cognitive constructions, not environmentally imposed givens. To add together two subclasses to form a superordinate is an action, as is the comparison of subclass and superordinate that yields a correct solution to the class inclusion question. The transitivity problem shows a similar need for mental activity. The *A* versus *C* question can be solved only if the child can logically add the two premises that $A > B$ and $B > C$. Finally, the conservation task requires mental activity to counteract the effects of the misleading perceptual cues. The activity that underlies conservation demonstrates especially clearly a property that Piaget considers a hallmark of operations, that of *reversibility*. The child may arrive at conservation by reasoning that the spread-out chips could be pushed back together—reversibility through negation of the perceptual change. Or the child may reason that the change in length is canceled by the change in density—reversibility through compensation of the opposing changes. Note that in both cases the critical action is an internal one. The operational child does not need to reach out and push the chips back; the pushing back occurs in the head, while the actual chips remain untouched.

What is the meaning of the term *concrete* in concrete operations? Discussion of this question bring us to the major limitation of concrete-operational thought. We have stressed that operational thought is representational thought, that is, not dependent on the actual manipulation of objects. Nevertheless, the concrete-operational child is still very much oriented to immediate reality, still very much occupied with the task of making sense of the concrete data in front of her. The child at this stage of development is quite limited in the ability to move beyond concrete reality to deal with the hypothetical—with the whole world of might-be rather than actually is. This ability to deal with the hypothetical emerges at the next, and final, stage of development.

The Formal-Operational Stage

The stage of formal operations begins at about 11 or 12 years. Once again, the age norms should be regarded as quite rough. Although formal operations are unlikely to develop before about 11, it is clear that some individuals reach this stage at later date and that some never reach it at all. Gifted children may reach it earlier.

As noted above, the distinguishing characteristic of formal-operational thought is the ability to deal with the hypothetical. The younger child can do this to some extent, of course; the kind of reasoning via reversibility described above involves a hypothetical rather than a real change in the material. The concrete-operational child's extensions into the hypothetical are limited, however. One way to characterize the distinction between concrete and formal is to posit a reversal in the relation between reality and possibility. The concrete-operational subject begins always with immediate reality, from which he makes limited extensions into the possible. The formal-operational subject begins with the world of possibility, from which he can then zero in on what happens to be true in the particular case under consideration.

In what sorts of situations might this possible-to-real cognitive orientation be demonstrated? A prototypic situation for the study of formal thought is provided by tasks of scientific reasoning. Piaget's coworker Inhelder devised a number of such tasks, the results of which are reported in a book by Inhelder and Piaget (1958). Although the specific tasks vary, most of them share the following elements. There is a specific outcome that serves as the focus of the experiment, as well as a number of experimental variables that may contribute to the outcome in question. The subject's task is to determine which of the variables, either singly or in combination, produce the indicated outcome. The solution to such problems requires several things. First, of course, the subject must be able to isolate the potentially relevant variables. Second, he must be able to test out the effects of each variable while holding the other variables constant. Third, he must be able to generate all the possible *combinations* of variables and test for the possible effects of each combination. Piaget regards such "combinatorial" reasoning as an especially important element in formal-operational thought. Fourth, the subject must be able to keep track of the tests that he has made and combine their results in a logical fashion.

Let us try a specific example. One of the Inhelder tasks requires the subject to figure out what determines the frequency of oscillation of a simple pendulum. There are a number of potentially relevant variables: the length of the string to which the swinging weight is attached, the amount of the weight, the force with which it is released, and so on. It turns out that the only variable that makes a difference is the length of the string. The point is not that the formal-operational subject knows this fact at the start of the experiment. The point is that he has a cognitive system that will allow him to figure it out. Thus, the formal-operational subject can isolate the potentially relevant variables, test the effects of variations within each while holding the other factors constant (e.g., vary string length without concurrent changes in weight and force), generate the various combinations of variables and test for possible interaction effects, and so on. From these actions, he will learn that the oscillation varies whenever the length varies and only when the length varies; variations in length are both sufficient and necessary to cause variations in oscillation.

The cognitive activities just described may not seem especially remarkable. What should be stressed, therefore, is that this sort of problem solving is well beyond the reach of the concrete-operational child. Concrete-operational children who are faced with the pendulum problem *will* do some intelligent things. They can typically test out certain possible variations in the materials and observe their effects accurately. What they cannot yet do is to generate all the possible combinations and test the effects of each, all the while keeping track of what they have done and what they still need to do. The result that they are almost certain to end up with the wrong answer. They may discover, for example, that a short string with a heavy weight swings quickly and from this fact conclude that both length and weight have an effect—an unwarranted conclusion in the absence of further tests.

Piaget's model of formal-operational thinking is a good deal more precise and more complicated than this brief description indicates (a qualification that applies, in fact, to the description given here of each of the stages). The full model of formal operations can be found in Flavell's (1963) excellent summary, or, of course, in Inhelder and Piaget (1958). For the present simplification, we will be content with reiterating some of the general themes. Formal-operational thought is above all hypothetical-deductive thought. It begins with hypotheses about what might be true (the possible) and works from these to what happens to be true (the real). It is also systematic thought, with a combinatorial power that allows the generation and testing of all the possible hypotheses. It is logical thought, with a complex system of rules for combining the results of various experimental tests to arrive at the only possible conclusion. And—to return to our most pervasive theme—it is a system of action, the culmination of the progressive internalization and complication of intelligent actions that defines the nature of intellectual development for Piaget.

Some Issues

As indicated earlier, our discussion of issues will address three questions: How accurate are Piaget's assessments of what children do and do not know? How valid is the concept of stages of development? And how can we explain movement from one stage or level of understanding to another?

Piaget's characterizations of children's competencies have been controversial ever since the appearance of his first books in the 1920s. Especially controversial have been his claims concerning the deficiencies in young children's thinking—the many and surprising instances in which children fail to understand what seem to be very basic principles about how the world operates. Do 6-month-olds really believe that an object ceases to exist when they can no longer see it? Do 3-year-olds really think that everyone else sees exactly what they see? And do 5-year-olds really believe that the number of objects in a row can be increased by spreading the row out?

A critical examination of Piaget's methods suggests that we should indeed be cautious before accepting such conclusions. Piaget was a remarkably inventive researcher; indeed, no one in the history of the field has devised so many ingenious procedures for exploring how children think. Often, however, Piaget's procedures seem to impose response demands on the child above and beyond the competencies that the task is intended to measure. Because of these extra demands, children may fail the task for the wrong reasons—that is, not because they lack the ability in question, but because they are confused by peripheral features of the problem.

Let us consider this argument with respect to both the sensorimotor and preoperational periods. Piaget's method of studying sensorimotor intelligence rely heavily on the infant's production of active motoric behaviors. This is the case, for example, for the work on object concept; most of what Piaget concludes about infants' knowledge of objects is based on their ability to generate active search behaviors, such as lifting covers, pushing aside screens, or crawling around obstacles. These are behaviors that young babies are not very good at. It seems logically possible that young infants realize that hidden objects still exist but are simply not able or not disposed to organize an effective search routine.

How can we study knowledge of objects without relying on search behaviors? Some recent ingenious studies by Baillargeon (1992) demonstrate one approach. Baillargeon's studies make use of the fact that babies (or any of us, for that matter) tend to respond with interest to new events but lose interest as the events are repeated and become familiar. If, for example, we show an infant a new picture, she is likely to be quite interested at first but attend less and less closely if the picture continues to appear for trial after trial. This decline in attention to a repeated stimulus is referred to as *habituation*. Suppose, once habituation has occurred, that we replace the familiar picture with something new. Now the infant is likely to attend closely again. This renewal of attention when a familiar stimulus is changed is referred to as *dishabituation*. The occurrence of dishabituation is informative, because it tells us that the infant can detect a difference between new and old.

In Baillargeon's research, infants' knowledge of objects is inferred from the changes in objects that they notice and thus dishabituate to. Of particular interest is response to impossible changes—that is, changes that violate the rules of object permanence. In a typical study, infants are first habituated to some recurring event—for example, a toy car that rolls down an inclined ramp, passes behind one end of a screen, and exits at the other end. Initially, this event is quite interesting and infants attend to it closely; eventually, however, looking times drop off, reflecting the fact that the babies are habituating to the familiar event. Following habituation, the infants see a box placed behind a screen. In one experimental condition (labeled the *possible event*) the box is placed behind the tracks on which the car runs; in the other experimental condition (labeled the *impossible event*) the box is placed directly on the tracks. The screen is then set back in place, and the car again makes its journey from one side to the other. Infants show little dishabituation to the possible event; looking times shoot up, however, when the car appears to pass magically through another solid object. Note that the babies cannot see the car and box at the point of their apparent contact; rather, they can be surprised by the impossible event only if they realize that both the car and box continue to exist while out of sight. They can be surprised, in other words, only if they possess some knowledge of the permanence of objects. Through this and similar studies, Baillargeon has shown that such knowledge seems to be present by 3½ or 4 months of age—and thus several months earlier than Piaget believed.

Earlier competence is also the message from much recent research directed to the so-called preoperational child. The preoperational period, you may recall, was characterized by Piaget largely in negative terms; in particular, he emphasized the young child's egocentrism and tendency to centrate on misleading perceptual features. Here, too, later researchers have argued that Piaget's procedures may have led to an underestimation of children's ability. A particular concern has been that the procedures are too verbal—that children may fail a task like conservation because they are confused by the language that is used, not because they really lack the concept. When the verbal demands are lessened or the tasks are otherwise simplified, young children often do perform more impressively than on the original Piagetian measures. They show rudiments of the ability to conserve, for example, well before such knowledge is evident on Piagetian tasks. Similarly, even the "egocentric" 2- or 3-year-old shows some ability to adopt to the point of view of others in very simple situations (Gelman & Baillargeon, 1983).

Having stressed the most positive picture of young children's competence that emerges from recent work, we should add a note of caution. Earlier competence is not necessarily full competence, and the rudimentary skills that infants or toddlers show in simplified situations are seldom equivalent to the mature mastery of the older child. Piaget was correct in his assertion that young children's thinking shows various limitations and that these limitations diminish only gradually with development. But he probably overstated just how strong and long-lasting the limitations are.

We turn next to the notion of stage. We have talked some about each of the four stages posited by Piaget. Thus far, however, there has been little discussion of the concept of *stage* itself. What does it mean to have a stage theory of development? What must be true if the claim of stages is to be valid?

Let us begin with some things that the notion of stage does *not* imply. It does not imply that the stages must emerge at fixed chronological ages. As already stressed, age per se is not important to the stage conception. It does not imply that development results solely from biological unfolding, with no contribution from the environment. As is discussed shortly, Piaget's theory in fact places a heavy emphasis on the environment. Finally, the notion of stage does not imply that there are abrupt jumps in development, with the child moving from totally preoperational one day to totally concrete-operational the next. Stage-to-stage transitions are in fact quite gradual, with considerable overlapping from one stage to the next. A stage description is always and admittedly a kind of idealized abstraction; real development is never so tidy.

What then is implied by the concept of stage? There are at least three criteria. The first is that there must be *qualitative changes* with development and not simply quantitative ones; that is, there must be changes in how the child thinks and not just in how much he knows or how quickly he can do things. The point here is that many developmental changes are essentially quantitative, a matter of getting better at doing something that one has been able to do to some extent all along. For example, short-term memory shows a regular improvement with age across childhood. Clearly, however, it would be pointless to speak of the child moving from a "stage" in which he can remember four things to a "stage" in which he can remember five, for all that is occurring is a quantitative increment in a specific ability. What Piaget insist on is that in addition to such quantitative changes there are also qualitative ones. Thus, he would maintain that the difference between a sensorimotor child and a preoperational child cannot be reduced to quantitative terms. There is a difference in kind between a child who has to act out his adaptation to the world and a child who has developed a representational system that allows him to engage in internal problem solving. This first criterion is really a sort of unwaivable prerequisite: One would not even think about the possibility of stages unless development showed what look like qualitative changes.

The second criterion is that the stages emerge in an *invariant sequence*. Thus, the specific ages may not matter, but the order matters very much. This criterion of invariant sequencing stems from Piaget's belief that each stage builds on the preceding one. Concrete operations, for example, grow out of skills developed during the preoperational period and in turn constitute necessary building blocks for the construction of formal operations. If this conception is correct, then it should be impossible for children ever to skip a stage or develop two stages in the reverse order of that hypothesized. Any violation of the sequence would thus constitute a serious blow to the theory.

The third criterion is that a stage be characterizable in terms of a set of *organized, interrelated structures*. We have talked some about what the structures at each stage look like; let us now focus on Piaget's reasons for seeking such structures. At any point in the child's life it would be possible to compile a long list of the behaviors of which the child is now capable. These behaviors could then be presented as the stage that the child now is in (e.g., "Johnny is at the stage when one can ride a bicycle, count to 100, remember 5 digits"). There would be two problems with such an approach, however. One is that the behaviors would be so disparate, a hodgepodge of skills with no conceivable overall relation. The other is that the account would remain totally descriptive, with no attempt to penetrate beneath the surface to say *why* the child can now do these things. Piaget's attempt was always to penetrate beneath the surface to the underlying system that makes *certain* behaviors (not everything the child can do) possible. It is in this sense that the stage of concrete operations (for example) is a theoretical-explanatory claim and not merely a descriptive summary.

What is the current status of the concept of stage? A brief answer would be, "Very much in dispute." Although virtually everyone agrees that Piaget's work has revealed valuable insights about intellectual development, not everyone agrees that this development is best conceived in terms of stages, whether these stages be Piaget's or some alternative version. Questions can be raised concerning each of the three criteria. Some theorists question whether development is really marked by the major qualitative changes that Piaget claims to have found. They contend that the important changes may be more quantitative in nature, consisting of improvements in such processes as attentional capacity, memory span, information-processing strategies, and so on (see, e.g., Klahr & Wallace, 1976). Others doubt that the sequences of development are really as inviolable as Piaget claims. Although the notion of invariant sequence seems sensible for the major epochs of development (can anyone imaging preoperations coming after formal operations?), the theory also claims a number of more specific, "molecular-level" sequences, the validity of which is less clear. Finally, the criterion of "organized, interrelated structures" has undoubtedly aroused the most debate. The issue here is just how "untidy" development can be and still conform to the expectations of stage theory. We have seen that the various conservation abilities—and we can now add numerous other "concrete-operational" abilities as well—are developed across a span of several years. Can concepts that vary so greatly in difficulty really be ascribed to the same set of operational structures? At the least, Piaget's stage model would seem to be somewhat incomplete, even if it it is not actually incorrect in the assertions that it makes. It should be added, of course, that this charge of incompleteness is one that can be applied to every psychological theory yet devised. For a further discussion of the concept of stage, see Flavell et al. (1993).

The debate about stages concerns the question of how best to characterize the cognitive system at any point in development. There is another basic issue as well, and that is how the child moves from one level of understanding to another. It is to this question of the mechanisms of cognitive change that we turn next.

In discussing the sources of cognitive progress, Piaget typically (e.g., 1964, 1972) lists four factors. The first of these is *biological maturation*, that is, changes attributable to the natural growth of the biological system, independent of any specific experience. Piaget regards maturations as important but by no means sufficient to account for cognitive change. What is also critical are the various experiences that the child encounters as he grows. Certain of these experiences are social in nature and involve a variety of kinds of interaction with a large number of different social agents. The child, for example, clearly learns things from parents and teachers, and he also learns things, usually in much less formal fashion, from interaction with peers. Other experiences involve the nonsocial, physical world. Just as we saw the 4- month-olds learn from their countless encounters with rattles, so individuals throughout life learn from the countless physical objects and events to which they are exposed. These categories of *social experience* and *physical experience* provide the second and third factors of development.

The category of physical experience deserves a somewhat fuller consideration. Piaget distinguishes between two types of physical experience: One he calls simply *physical experience*; the other he labels *logicomathematical experience*. Physical experience (in the restricted sense) refers to cases in which knowledge is derived relatively directly from the object itself. Something like the color or the weight of objects, for example, can be extracted fairly directly from the immediate stimulation. Piaget maintains that experience of this sort is what classical empiricism is concerned with. He also maintains, however, that there is a second, more important, kind of experience: logicomathematical. This type of experience refers to cases in which knowledge is derived less from the object itself than from the actions that are performed upon it. The child may learn about number, for example, by actions of grouping objects together, counting them, rearranging them and counting again, lining the objects up in one-to-one correspondence, adding or subtracting objects, and so on. In this case the knowledge about number is not really contained in the objects themselves; it derives from the various actions that the child performs. Note again the theme that we have encountered so often; the insistence that true understanding derives always from the child's own action.

The fourth factor of development is labeled *equilibration*. A general definition of equilibration is that it is the biological tendency of self-regulation. More specifically, Piaget uses the construct of equilibration to account for several aspects of development. Equilibration is evoked to explain why the knowledge derived from the other factors of development is organized into integrated cognitive structures, rather than remaining separate and individual. Equilibration thus serves the function of *coordination*. Equilibration is also tied to the cognitive system's need to be active, to the ever-present need to resolve states of disequilibrium and restore equilibrium. The construct of the organism as a self-regulating system thus explains the *motivation* for cognitive change. Finally, when action does result in a restoration of equilibrium, the cognitive system typically moves to a higher, more adaptive level than its original starting point. Equilibration thus accounts for the *directionality* of development—for the fact that children are continually constructing more adaptive cognitive structures.

Piaget's discussion of the four factors of development provides a general framework within which to conceptualize cognitive change. It should be obvious, however, that the framework is a very general one indeed. Even in its more specific guises, Piaget's theory does not provide a precise account of exactly how cognitive change comes about. The model of cognitive change is thus subject to the same criticism that was applied to the stage model: that of incompleteness. Even if the model is basically correct, it leaves many details to be filled in. (See Flavell, 1963, 1971, and Flavell et al., 1993, for additional critiques of Piagetian theory.)

Having leveled this charge of incompleteness, let us immediately add some qualifying remarks. First, the problem is again not unique to Piaget. The question of how cognitive change comes about has, in fact, proved an especially intractable one for every theorist of development. Second, Piaget was aware of the gaps in this aspect of his theory, as shown by the fact that some of his last work returned again to issues of cognitive change (Piaget, 1985). Finally, the difficulty in devising a theory of change is at least in part a reflection of the difficulty of doing good research on the issue. The task of measuring the cognitive system at any point in development is difficult enough, but it is simple compared to the task of measuring the process by which the system changes. It might be a useful exercise, in fact, for the reader to attempt to think of research designs from which one could figure out how children master the various cognitive concepts that Piaget has studied. Although various possibilities exist (as exemplified in training studies), all have their problems, and none has yet provided more than tentative evidence.

Inconclusive though the current picture may be, it would be a shame to end the chapter on such a negative note. Piaget's theory does set forth some very important general claims about the nature of intellectual development. In some cases these claims have become fairly widely accepted in the field; in other cases they remain as points of contrast between Piaget's theory and other approaches to the study of intelligence. Let us conclude by reviewing what some of these claims are.

Intelligence for Piaget is always a matter of action upon the world. Children do not acquire concepts like conservation through passive observation, adult teaching, external reinforcers, or the proper use of language. They acquire (or in Piaget's terms, *construct*) such concepts through their own actions, especially through the coordination of actions that Piaget labels logicomathematical experience. Such actions do not need to be spurred on by biological drives or adult-provided inducements. Rather, the child, from birth, has a basic cognitive need to master the world around him. This mastery is by no means instantaneous, however. New experiences can be valuable only to the extent that they can be assimilated by the current cognitive structures. The assimilation-accommodation model thus ensures that cognitive progress will always be slow and gradual. It also ensures, however, that progress *will* be made; the child, in interacting with the world, will construct a progressively more powerful, more adaptive, more highly "equilibrated" cognitive system. In the course of this construction the child moves, within the span of about a dozen years, from the inborn reflexes with which the sensorimotor period began to the scientific problem solving that epitomizes formal operations. And this, considering the magnitude of the achievement, is perhaps not such a "slow" progress after all.

References

Baillargeon, R. (1992). The object concept revisited: New directions in the investigation of infants' physical knowledge. In C. E. Granrud (Ed.), *Visual perception and cognition in infancy*. Hillsdale, NJ: Lawrence Erlbaum Associates.

Chapman, M. (1988). *Constructive evolution: Origins and development of Piaget's thought*. Cambridge: Cambridge University Press.

Flavell, J. H. (1963). *The developmental psychology of Jean Piaget*. Princeton, NJ: Van Nostrand.

Flavell, J. H. (1971). Stage related properties of cognitive development. *Cognitive Psychology, 2*, 421–453.

Flavell, J. H., Miller, P. H., & Miller, S. A. (1993). *Cognitive development* (3rd ed.). Englewood Cliffs, NJ: Prentice Hall.

Gelman, R., & Baillargeon, R. (1983). A review of Piagetian concepts. In J. H. Flavell, E. M. Markman (Eds.), & P. H. Mussen (Series Ed.), *Handbook of child psychology: Vol. 3. Cognitive development* (pp. 167–262). New York: John Wiley.

Ginsburg, H., & Opper, S. (1988). *Piaget's theory of intellectual development* (3rd ed.). Englewood Cliffs, NJ: Prentice-Hall.

Inhelder, B., & Piaget, J. (1958). *The growth of logical thinking from childhood to adolescence*. New York: Basic Books.

Inhelder, B., & Piaget, J. (1964). *The early growth of logic in the child*. New York: Norton.

Klahr, D., & Wallace, J. G. (1976). *Cognitive development: An information-processing view*. Hillsdale, NJ: Lawrence Erlbaum Associates.

Piaget, J. (1932). *The moral judgment of the child*. London: Routledge & Kegan Paul.

Piaget, J. (1951). *Play, dreams, and imitation in childhood*. New York: Norton.

Piaget, J. (1952a). Autobiography. In C. Murchison & E. G. Boring (Eds.), *History of psychology in autobiography* (*Vol. 4*, pp. 237–256). Worcester, MA: Clark University Press.

Piaget, J. (1952b). *The origins of intelligence in children*. New York: Basic Books.

Piaget, J. (1954). *The construction of reality in the child*. New York: Basic Books.

Piaget, J. (1964). Development and learning. *Journal of Research in Science Teaching, 2*, 176–186.

Piaget, J. (1972). Problems of equilibration. In C. F. Nodine, J. M. Gallagher, & R. D. Humphreys (Eds.), *Piaget and Inhelder on equilibration* (pp. 1–20). Philadelphia: The Jean Piaget Society.

Piaget, J. (1975). L'equilibration des structures cognitives. Problem central du developement. *Etudes d'epistemologie genetique* (*Vol. 33*). Paris: PUF.

Piaget, J. (1985). *The equilibration of cognitive structures*. Chicago: University of Chicago Press.

Piaget, J., & Inhelder, B. (1974). *The child's construction of quantities*. London: Routledge & Kegan Paul.

Piaget, J., Inhelder, B., & Szeminska, A. (1960). *The child's conception of geometry*. New York: Basic Books.

Piaget, J. & Szeminska, A. (1952). *The child's conception of number*. New York: Humanities Press.

Experiment 2

Spatial Perspective–Taking: The Three Mountains Task

Part of the genius of Piaget and his co-workers lies in their gradual specification of the complexity and richness of normally developing concepts, and their ingenious ways of observing the relevant phenomena. The concept of space is a vivid example.

Piaget, working towards an understanding of spatial representation, felt it necessary first to study the concepts of speed, movement, and time. Although geometry textbooks present the fundamental ideas of space with euclidean concepts of straight lines, angles, squares, and circles, children presumably first start to build up their notions of space with primitive relationships like proximity and separation, and order and enclosure (Piaget & Inhelder, 1967). Children move from viewing an object in isolation to considering the object in relation to a point of view. This progression reflects the shift from egocentrism to the recognition that other points of view exist and differ from one's own, and to the ability to role-play to take other people's perspectives or points of view.

In the Three Mountains technique, Piaget and Inhelder showed the subject a 1-meter square pasteboard model of green, gray, and brown mountains, then questioned the child in three ways: (a) The child was asked to reconstruct a snapshot, using pieces of shaped cardboard, which could be taken by the child or a wooden faceless doll, of the group of mountains from four positions. (b) The child was shown a collection of six pictures and asked to pick the one most suited to the view seen by the doll in four positions. (c) The child chose a picture and then decided what position the doll would have to occupy to take that snapshot. The child's response was classified as belonging to a particular stage of development (to be described later).

What follows is an adaptation of the Piaget and Inhelder technique, using a new point-scoring system to facilitate age and sex comparisons. We can look for interposition errors (front-to-back, before-behind, top-to-bottom) and right-left errors.

Problem and Hypotheses

According to Piaget's theory, spatial perspective-taking develops slowly and illustrates the kinds of themes and achievements characteristic of the intellectual development of the child: decreasing egocentrism, progressive decentering, the formation of invariant relationships, reversibility, and representational thought.

The three mountains task will be administered to two grades and two sexes.

1. Younger children score lower on the mountains task than older children:
   (a) they make more egocentric choices;
   (b) they make more interposition and right-left errors.

2. Children have more difficulty with right-left relations than with interposition errors.

3. Sex differences?

Method

Subjects

Boys and girls in kindergarten or first grade, and in third or fourth grade

Materials

A simulated mountain scene (Fig. F2.1)

A small bowl or envelope with

   4 pieces of 10-cm square white paper

6 blue triangles, 5 cm tall

6 green triangles, 3.8 cm tall

6 tan triangles, 2.5 cm tall (Fig. F2.2)

6 Prefabricated "snapshots," made of construction paper triangles on white 10-cm square cards
   (Fig. F2.3)

Scotch tape

Mr. Smith, a stick figure about 5 cm tall (Fig. F2.4)

The mountain scene is displayed on a 28 cm X 28 cm cardboard, with predrawn bases for the mountains. The mountains can be made simply from construction paper cones or of styrofoam.

BASE	DIAMETER	VERTICAL HEIGHT
Blue cone	14 cm	15 cm
Green cone	10 cm	10.0 cm
Tan cone	7 cm	6.5 cm

Procedure

The simulated mountain scene is set up prior to the child's arrival; the child is seated at position A.

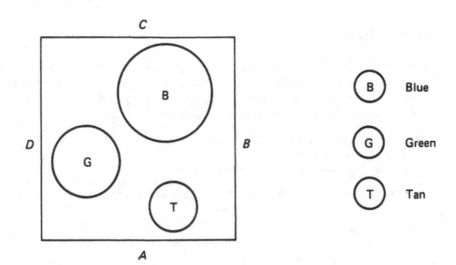

Three kinds of tasks will be performed:

1. Using precut triangular shapes, the child is asked to reconstruct the kind of snapshot that could be taken of the group of mountains from position *A*, then from positions *C*, *B*, and *D*. (Note that the order is not *A*, *B*, *C*, *D*.)

2. From a set of six pictures, the child chooses the one most suited to someone sitting in positions *A*, *C*, *B*, and *D*.

3. The child is handed the pictures one at a time and asked what position a person would have to occupy to take a snapshot similar to it. (Procedure modified from Piaget & Inhelder, 1967.)

Instructions

1. Reconstruction. Seat the child at position *A* and say, **"Let's pretend these are mountains** [wave your hand over the scene], **and let's pretend these are pictures of the mountains."** Hand the child a blue, green, and tan cutout and one of the pieces of white paper.

"Make a snapshot of the scene. Use these cutouts and show me on this little paper how these mountains look to you from your seat."

When the child finishes, put a strip of scotch tape across the cutouts to hold them in place. Immediately label *top* and position *A* on the construction.

Remove the "snapshot" and say, **"Let's pretend this stick figure is a person called Mr. Smith. Mr. Smith is sitting here, opposite you."** [Put Mr. Smith visibly on opposite side of table, facing the mountains.] **"Now take new cutouts and paper and show how the mountains look to Mr. Smith from his seat."** [Don't let the child get up.] **"Make the picture that Mr. Smith would make from his seat."** When the child is finished, again label *top* and position *C* on the paper.

Repeat the process, moving Mr. Smith to positions *B* and *D*, and always labeling the constructions carefully.

2. Picture Choice. Spread the six pictures in random order in a horizontal row immediately in front of the child.

"Pick the one that looks the most like what you see, sitting there." [Note the response (the pictures are lettered on the back). Replace picture, reshuffle, spread out pictures and say] **"Pick the one that looks the most like what Mr. Smith sees from here** [Position *C*]."

Repeat with Mr. Smith at Positions *B* and *D*, reshuffling the pictures quickly each time. Move Mr. Smith to each position conspicuously. Be inconspicuous, however, in noticing the letter on the back of the child's choice.

3. Position Choice. Using pictures *A*, *B*, *C*, *D* only, let the child pick one of the pictures at random and say, **"Now point to one of the pictures–any one, please. . . . Where would Mr. Smith have to be sitting to see this? Where would he be sitting to take a snapshot that looks like this?"** Record the picture and position choices (*A*, *B*, *C*, *D* positions), and have the child pick another picture. Repeat the question, and record the picture choice and the position choice. Continue until all four pictures and corresponding positions are indicated.

Results

Scoring. For Part 1, Reconstruction, each picture that the child constructed for you is scored according to whether the interposition (front-to-back, before-behind, bottom to top) relationships are accurate, whether the left-right relationships are accurate, and whether that construction differs from the *A* view. You may find it easiest to move yourself from position to position, like Mr. Smith, as you score each picture. Look first to see if the overlappings (which mountains are in front of or hide parts of which mountains) are accurate. Score 1 for accuracy, 0 for failure. Score next for the left-to-right relationships on that picture, for example, green, blue, tan for *A*. Go on to picture *C*; score interposition and left-right order. Whether or not these are correct, is the *C* picture *different* from the *A* picture? Score 1 for different, 0 for (egocentric) same. The higher number of points means the more nonegocentric responses. Score *B* and *D* similarly. The total points possible for Reconstruction are 11.

For Part 2, Picture Choice, if the recorded picture choice matches the position, score 1; if mismatched, score 0. The maximum score possible is 4 points.

In Part 3, Position Choice, if the recorded position matched the picture the child was looking at, score 1. If it was mismatched, score 0. The maximum score possible is 4 points.

Total score for the three-part task is a maximum of 19 points.

Enter your child's scores on the Master Data Sheet.

Analysis. Obtain means (and standard deviations) for the mountains task scores, and enter the group data in Table F2.1 on the Group Data Sheet. Run a 2 grade X 2 sex analysis of variance of the total scores, and enter the summary in Table F2.2. State your grade and sex findings. (Optional: Run a 2 grade X 2 sex X 2 scores [repeated measures] anova on the interposition and left-right scores, and enter the summary in Table F2.3. State your findings.)

Alternate Scoring. Read chapter 8 by Piaget and Inhelder (1967) and try to classify your child's stage of development.

STAGE I

Child does not understand the meaning of your questions and cannot be studied systematically.

STAGE II

Child distinguishes hardly or not at all between own viewpoint and that of others:

IIA. The child is confined to reproducing own point of view. Egocentric illusion prevents the child from reversing left–right, before–behind relations. Pictures are constructed from a single point of view, or random choices of doll or position are made, or child chooses own viewpoint A.

IIB. Child does attempt to separate various points of view but fails because of inability to relate the relevant factors in the correct way. The constructions and choices differ from A but are not accurate. The child knows now that one cannot see the same thing from everywhere but still has trouble distinguishing viewpoints.

STAGE III (ABOUT 7–8 TO 11–12 YEARS)

There is a progressive discrimination and coordination of perspectives.

IIIA. "Genuine but incomplete relativity." This is a transitional stage between the egocentric behavior of earlier stages and coordinated perspectives. Perhaps the before-behind relations will be right, but errors may persist in the left-right relations.

IIIB. Complete relativity of perspectives. Child knows only one picture or one position can be accurate for a particular perspective.

Discussion

Was there a significant age difference in the predicted direction on the total score? Account for this in terms of Piagetian theory. How would you account for this in non-Piagetian theory?

Men are alleged to have better visual-spatial abilities than women (Maccoby & Jacklin, 1974). Did you find a significant sex difference in this spatial-perspective task in your two elementary-school-age groups? How do you account for these results?

Looking at the egocentric choices ("Different from *A*?"), were younger children more egocentric than older ones (i.e., were those scores lower in the younger children)? Did they also make more interposition and more left–right errors? Were there more individual differences in the younger or older groups? (Look at the standard deviations.)

Piaget says that left–right errors are more difficult to overcome than interposition errors or egocentric illusions. Does your evidence agree? How can this be explained?

Which of the three parts of the mountains task did the children seem to enjoy most or have most discomfort with? Did you have trouble keeping children in their seats? Did they crane their necks or twist sideways?

Did you have trouble using the stage-scoring system? What are the advantages of our point system over the stage classification? What are the disadvantages? How can we see if the two sets of scores are related?

Notice that we took a task from Piaget's laboratory and changed the scoring to quantitative increments rather than classification of stages. This operationalization of the dependent variable enables one to do parametric statistical analyses of the results and to look at specific kinds of errors made by the child. Does scoring this way necessitate dispensing with a stage interpretation?

The question of early childhood egocentrism and whether it is demonstrated by the mountain task is an issue that has generated a spate of empirical investigations. A number of experimenters (Borke, 1975; Fishbein, Lewis, & Keiffer, 1972; Flavell, Botkin, Fry, Wright, & Jarvis, 1968; Hoy, 1974; Huttenlocher & Presson, 1973) have suggested that perceptual role taking by young children varies with the nature of the task and the type of response required. They claim that children are more successful with discrete, easily differentiated objects, which provide more cues for identification and memory than the mountains do. Children have more difficulty with the response of choosing a picture or constructing a model than they have with other responses like revolving a turntable to show points of view. Perhaps the transition from three-dimensional models to two-dimensional pictures accounts for this response difficulty (Borke, 1975). There is considerable disagreement with the notion that young children are primarily egocentric, and there is considerable emphasis on choosing appropriate tasks.

Another issue concerns the relation of spatial perspective taking to other kinds of perspective or role taking. In other words, is there one general role-taking ability or several? That is, if children are not egocentric on the mountains task, and they do have good coordination of spatial perspectives, are these children also nonegocentric on a more cognitive and/or a more social task? Our students looked for the relation between Flavell's 7/4 task, Piaget and Inhelder's mountains task, and a version of Flavell's blindfold-person task. (We found no correlation in our first graders and a significant high correlation in our upper-elementary schoolchildren.) In the 7/4 task, the child sees seven drawings arranged sequentially and relates the story of a walking boy chased up an apple tree by a dog. Three drawings (with the dog in them) are then removed, and the child's task is to tell the story again, as a new person, Mr. Jones, would perceive the remaining drawings. On a more formal level, several researchers have explored the developmental relations between perceptual, cognitive or conceptual, and affective perspective taking (Kurdek & Rodgon, 1975), or the relation between perspective taking and prosocial behavior (Zahn-Waxler, Radke-Yarrow, & Brady-Smith, 1977), or between perceptual egocentrism and cognitive style (Bowd, 1975). Results were mixed, and the issue continues to interest researchers.

The shift away from an egocentric orientation (which you may have found in your older children compared to your younger ones) may be related to better communication skills and progress in empathic understanding of others (Harter, 1983; Schantz, 1983). Decentering is involved in role taking, which in turn is related to altruistic behaviors (Eisenberg, 1992; Eisenberg & Mussen, 1989). Piagets' theory of the egocentric nature of young children's thinking, its decline, and its relation to many other developing skills, remain viable foci of research.

Flavell (1985) pointed out that even adults show egocentric thinking at times, since "our own points of view are more cognitively 'available' to us than other person's."

Selected Bibliography

Acredola, L. P. (1977). Developmental changes in the ability to coordinate perspectives of a large-scale space. *Developmental Psychology, 13*, 1–8.

Borke, H. (1975). Piaget's mountains revisited: Changes in the egocentric landscape. *Developmental Psychology, 11*(2), 240–243.

Bowd, A. D. (1975). The relationship between perceptual egocentrism and field-dependence in early childhood. *Journal of Genetic Psychology, 127*, 63–69.

Coie, J. D., Costanzo, P. R., & Farnill, D. (1973). Specific transitions in the development of spatial perspective-taking ability. *Developmental Psychology, 9*, 167–177.

Eisenberg, N. (1992). *The caring child*. Cambridge, MA: Harvard University Press.

Eisenberg, N., & Mussen, P. H. (1989). *The roots of prosocial behavior in children*. New York: Cambridge University Press.

Fishbein, H. D., Lewis, S., & Keiffer, K. (1972). Children's understanding of spatial relations: Coordination of perspectives. *Developmental Psychology, 7*, 21–33.

Flavell, J. H. (1985). *Cognitive Development* (2nd ed.). Englewood Cliffs, NJ: Prentice Hall.

Flavell, J. H., Botkin, P. T., Fry, C. L., Wright, J. W., & Jarvis, P. E. (1968). *The development of role-taking and communication skills in children*. New York: Wiley.

Flavell, J., Miller, P., & Miller, S. (1993). *Cognitive development* (3rd ed.). Englewood Cliffs, NJ: Prentice-Hall.

Harter, S. (1983). Developmental perspectives on the self-system. In E. M. Hetherington (Ed.), *Handbook of child psychology: Socialization, personality and social development* (*Vol. 4*). New York: Wiley.

Hoy, F. A. (1974). Predicting another's visual perspective: A unitary skill? *Developmental Psychology, 10*, 462.

Huttenlocher, J., & Presson, C. (1973). Mental rotation and the perspective problem. *Cognitive Psychology, 4*, 277–299.

Kurdek, L. A., & Rodgon, M. (1975). Perceptual, cognitive, and affective perspective taking in kindergarten through sixth-grade children. *Developmental Psychology, 11*, 643–650.

Liben, L. S. (1978). Performance on Piagetian spatial tasks as a function of sex, field dependence, and training. *Merrill-Palmer Quarterly, 24*, 97–110.

Maccoby, E. E., & Jacklin, C. N. (1974). *The psychology of sex differences*. Stanford: Stanford University Press.

Piaget, J., & Inhelder, B. (1967). *The child's conception of space* (Chap. 8). New York: Norton. (First published in France, 1948, under the title *La Representation de L'Espace chez L'Enfant*.)

Piché, G. L., Michlin, M. L., Rubin, D. L., & Johnson, F. L. (1975). Relationships between fourth-graders' performances on selected role-taking tasks and referential communication accuracy tasks. *Child Development, 45*, 965–969.

Rubin, K. H. (1973). Egocentrism in childhood: A unitary construct? *Child Development, 44*, 102–110.

Rubin, K. H., Attewall, P. W., Tierney, M. C., & Tumolo, P. (1973). Development of spatial egocentrism and conservation across the life span. *Developmental Psychology, 9* (3), 432.

Selman, R. L. (1971). Taking another's perspective: Role taking development in early childhood. *Child Development, 42*, 1721–1734.

Shantz, C. V. (1983). Social Cognition. In J. H. Flavell & E. M Markman (Eds.), *Handbook of child psychology: Cognitive development* (*Vol. 3*). New York: Wiley.

Shantz, C. V., & Watson, J. S. (1971). Spatial abilities and spatial egocentrism in the young child. *Child Development, 42*, 171–181.

Zahn-Waxler, C., Radke-Yarrow, M., & Brady-Smith, J. (1977). Perspective taking and prosocial behavior. *Developmental Psychology, 13*, 87–88.

Individual Data Sheet

Title: Mountain Task _____

E: _____   Day and Date: _____   S–Sex: *M or F*   Grade: _____

S: _____   Birthdate: _____   CA: _____

Time Begun: _____   Time Ended: _____   Elapsed Time: _____   Room: _____

1. RECONSTRUCTION
(Staple the four snapshots to data sheet. Don't forget to label each with position—A, B, C, D—on back.)

POSITION	FRONT TO BACK?	LEFT-RIGHT?	DIFFERENT FROM A?	SCORE
A			X	____
C				____
B				____
D	_____	_____	_____	____
	+	+	=	☐

2. PICTURE CHOICE (6 PICTURES)

POSITION	CHILD'S PICTURE CHOICE	SCORE 0 OR 1
A	____	____
C	____	____
B	____	____
D	____	____
		☐

3. POSITION CHOICE (4 PICTURES)

PICTURE	POSITION	SCORE 0 OR 1
A	____	____
C	____	____
B	____	____
D	____	____
		☐

Total Score ☐

Piaget Stage =

GROUP DATA SHEET

Title:_____

E:_____   **Day and Time:** _____

Hypothesis:

Method and Procedure: (as described in text with following modifications, if any)

Group Results and Analysis:

TABLE F2.1
MEAN THREE MOUNTAINS TASK SCORES FOR TWO GRADES

Group	Reconstruction (11 points)			Picture Choice (4 points)	Position Choice (4 points)	Total (19 points)
	Interposition	L-R	Nonegocentric			
Grade _____						
Boys						
Girls						
Combined						
Grade _____						
Boys						
Girls						
Combined						
Combined Grades						
Boys						
Girls						
Total						

TABLE F2.2

2 X 2 ANALYSIS OF VARIANCE OF TOTAL SCORES ON THREE MOUNTAINS TASK

Source	Sum of Squares	df	Mean Square	F	p
Between Grades		1			
Between Sexes		1			
Grade X Sex		1			
Within Group		___			

TABLE F2.3

2 X 2 X 2 ANALYSIS OF VARIANCE OF INTERPOSITION AND LEFT-RIGHT SCORES, REPEATED MEASUREMENT

Source	Sum of Squares	df	Mean Square	F	p
Between Grades		1			
Between Sexes		1			
Grade X Sex		1			
Within Group					
Between Scores (Int; L-R)		1			
Grade X Scores		1			
Sex X Scores		1			
Grade X Sex X Scores		1			
Error					

This page is intentionally blank.

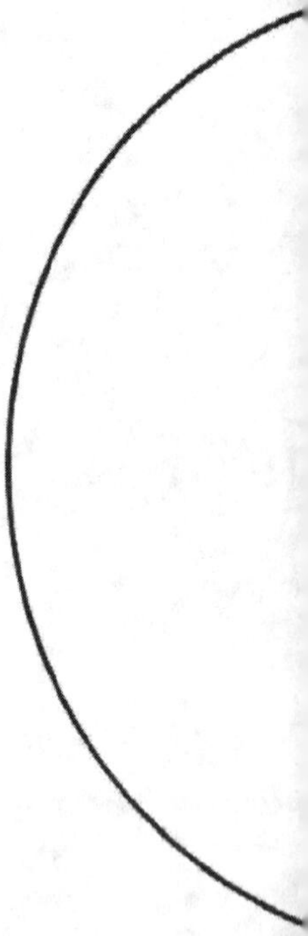

Fig. F2.1. Field for mountains.

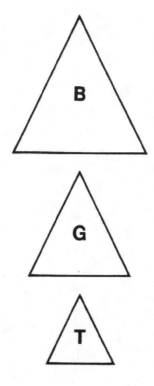

Fig. F2.2. Templates for cutouts of mountains.

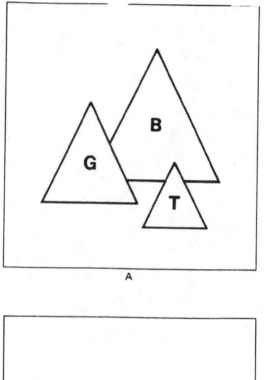

A

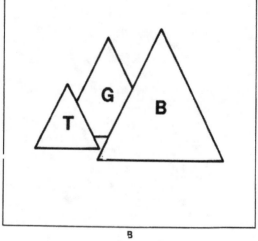

B

Fig. F2.3. Picture choices, Part II, Three Mountains Task.

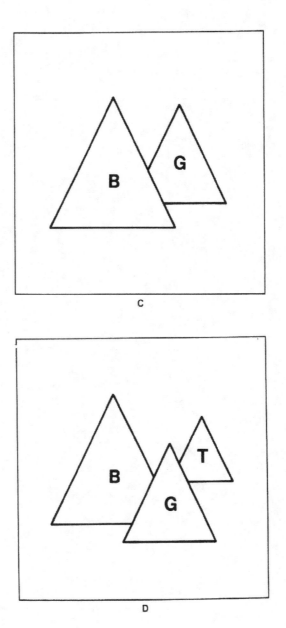

C

D

Fig. F2.3. (Continued)

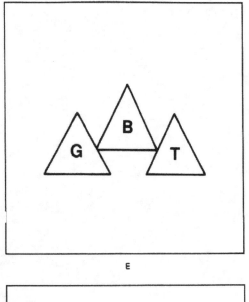

E

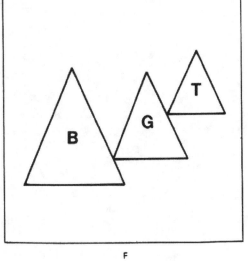

F

Fig. F2.3. (Continued)

Figure F2.4. Mr. Smith.

Theory of Mind: False Belief

Background

A burgeoning area of interest and investigation in the last two and a half decades is the development of a theory of mind, particularly in young children. Theory of mind refers to an ability to impute mental states to oneself and others (Wimmer & Perner, 1983). This ability is considered fundamental to an understanding of the social world, an understanding that own and others' actions are the products of internal mental states like beliefs and desires.

Understanding of mind is not a brand new interest; it has many historical strands. Piaget's notions of *egocentrism*, with which you are familiar, suggested that very young children see the world from their own perspective and have difficulty seeing others' perspectives. Although investigators now believe that young children are not as totally egocentric as Piaget thought, they do agree with Piaget that perspective-taking abilities and related psychological knowledge show increases with age. In the 1970s, research on *metacognitive development* became extensive, (cognition about cognition), mainly focusing on memory or comprehension tasks and how older children and adolescents understand these problem-solving strategies. Research on whether chimpanzees have a theory of mind (Premack & Woodruff, 1978) evoked philosophical and psychological interest and the era of theory of mind investigations began in earnest (Flavell, 2000).

A systematic and comprehensive treatment of the development of the child's understanding of mind was offered by Wellman (1990). The two-year old has a simple desire psychology. Initially, children's desires cause their overt actions. Two-year-olds understand simple desires but not beliefs. They do not understand that they or others have mental representations of the world. They do soon understand a fundamental distinction between mental activities and physical objects. Beliefs come later than desires. Beliefs are thoughts that something is true; they provide mental explanations for actions. By three years of age, children's psychology includes beliefs, and joins beliefs with desires in causal reasoning about actions. Bartsch and Wellman (1995) extended that progression of *desire, desire-belief*, to *belief-desire*, to an *active interpretive theory of mind*.

The favorite investigative tool with preschoolers is the false-belief task, one version of which will be described and utilized in the next experiment. An example of a false-belief task is the "unexpected change" task (Wimmer & Perner, 1983): A child and mother put chocolate in cupboard X. The child goes out, and mother uses some chocolate and puts the remainder in cupboard Y. When child returns, where does the child expect to find the chocolate? The answer by 4- and 5-year-olds is cupboard X; the answer by 3-year-olds is often cupboard Y.

What are some of the many factors affecting understanding of mental states?

Increased information-processing abilities (Fodor, 1992)

Stepwise increase in central-processing ability (Case, 1978)

3-year-old preference to construe behavior in terms of desire, rather than reasoning according to belief (Bartsch & Wellman, 1995)

Basic representing ability (Apperly & Robinson, 1998)

Working memory (Keenan, 1998)

Mental age, not chronological age (Bradmetz, 1998)

Language, certain linguistic structures (deVilliers & deVilliers, 2000)

Understanding of homonymy (Doherty, 2000)

Parenting style (Ruffman, Perner, & Parkin, 1999)

Talk about emotional states (Dunn, 2000; Dunn, Brown, Slomkowski, Tesla, & Youngblade, 1991)

Family size, number of siblings (Perner, Ruffman, & Leekam, 1994; Dunn, Brown, Slomkowski, Tesla, & Youngblade, 1991)

Conceptual deficit (Perner, Leekam, & Wimmer, 1987)

Executive function: planning, response inhibition, cognitive flexibility (Carlson, Moses, & Hix, 1998; Frye, Zelaso, & Palfai, 1995; Russell, 1996)

Cultural variations (Lillard, 1998; Wellman, 1998)

Even a quick scanning of the above list evokes the nature–nurture issue again. It is, however, not necessary to be a nativist OR a constructivist; it is not necessary to see biology and experience in conflict. Rather, it seems likely that neurological maturation in concert with a variety of experiences contribute to a developing understanding of mental states in self and others.

Wellman, Cross, and Watson (2001), in their meta-analysis of research on theory of mind development, looked at some task manipulations that were intended to eliminate or reduce task limitations. These included "framing the task in terms of explicit deception or trickery, involving the child in actively making the key transformations, highlighting the salience of the protagonist's mental state, and reducing the salience of the contrasting real-world state of affairs" (p. 672). Although these manipulations do help young children to perform better, the important point is that they do not improve from below chance to above-chance performance, and they fail to change the developmental trajectory (the basic developmental pattern of performance across the years).

The age range in studies of understanding of mental processes is wider than the preschoolers that have been heavily investigated. It extends down to infancy for a careful look at their abilities and dispositions that may aid in learning about people versus objects (Poulin-Dubois, 1999), intentionality of actions (Woodward, 1998), and some nonegocentric reasoning (Repacholi & Gopnik, 1997).

Research also extends upward to older children (Fabricius & Schwanenflugel, 1994; Flavell, Green, & Flavell, 1995; Pillow & Henrichon, 1996). Older children have a better understanding of conflicting emotions, an understanding that the mind is an active interpretive, constructive processor, a better realization that biases may influence behavior, and a beginning understanding of conscious and unconscious states.

In addition to age, research on the understanding of mind has extended to *autistic* children who generally lack social interaction skills (Baron-Cohen, 1995; Wellman, Baron-Cohen, Gomez, Swettenham, & Toye, in review). Not surprisingly, they fared poorly on false-belief tasks. Another population, *deaf* children, has been studied. Those with deaf parents skillful in sign language do better on false-belief tasks than deaf children with hearing parents who do not sign well (Peterson & Siegal, 1997). Miller (2000) argued that considering pre-existing differences in belief also extends the range of beliefs examined and shows different rates of developmental change for each form of understanding (false-belief, origins of knowledge, ambiguity, communication, etc.).

There is disagreement about what the tasks used to measure understanding of mind (e.g., false-belief, appearance-reality tasks) really do measure; there is insufficient knowledge about the developmental changes that are involved in increased understanding of mental states; there is much more we need to know about how mental representations affect children's social, emotional, and cognitive behaviors; there is a need to discover what is universal in the theory of mind and what is affected by cultural differences. In short, theory of mind research has not peaked, and we can look forward to hundreds more articles and books.

Selected Bibliography

Apperly, I. A., & Robinson, E. J. (1998). Children's mental representation of referential relations. *Cognition, 67*(3), 287–309.

Astington, J. W. (2001). The future of Theory-of- Mind research: Understanding motivational states, the role of language, and real-world consequences. *Child Development, 72*(3), 685–687.

Astington, J.W., Harris, P. L., & Olson, D. R. (Eds.). (1988). *Developing theories of mind.* New York: Cambridge University Press.

Baron-Cohen, S. (1995). *Mind blindness: An essay on autism and theory of mind.* Cambridge, MA: MIT Press.

Baron-Cohen, S., & Ring, H. (1994). A model of the mind reading system: Neuropsychological and neurobiological perspectives. In C. Lewis & P. Mitchell (Eds.), *Children's early understanding of mind: Origins and development.* Hillsdale, NJ: Lawrence Erlbaum Associates.

Bartsch, K. (1996). Between desires and beliefs: Young children's action predictions. *Child Development, 67,* 1671–1685.

Bartsch, K., & Wellman, H. M. (1989). Young children's attribution of action to beliefs and desires. *Child Development, 60,* 946–964.

Bartsch, K., & Wellman, H. M. (1995). *Children talk about the mind.* New York: Oxford University Press.

Bradmetz, J. (1998). Acquisition of a theory of mind and intellectual development in the child aged 3 to 5. *Current Psychology of Cognition, 17*(1), 95–113. (Abstract).

Bretherton, I., & Beeghly, M. (1982). Talking about internal states: The acquisition of an explicit theory of mind. *Developmental Psychology, 18*(6), 906–921.

Cadinu, M. R., & Kiesner, J. (2000). Children's development of a theory of mind. *European Journal of Psychology of Education, 15*(2), 93–111.

Carruthers, P., & Smith, P.K. (1996). *Theories of theories of mind.* Cambridge, UK: Cambridge University Press.

Carlson, S. M., & Moses, L. J. (2001). Individual differences in inhibitory control and children's theory of mind. *Child Development, 72,* 1032–1053.

Carlson, S. M., Moses, L. J., & Hix, H. R. (1998). The role of inhibitory processes in young children's difficulties with deception and false belief. *Child Development, 69,* 672–691.

Case, R. (1978). Intellectual development from birth to adulthood: A neo-Piagetian interpretation. In R. S. Siegler (Ed.), *Children's thinking: What develops?* Hillsdale, NJ: Lawrence Erlbaum Associates.

Case, R. (1989, April). *A neo-Piagetian analysis of the child's understanding of other people, and the internal conditions which motivate this behavior.* Paper presented at the biennial meeting of the Society for Research in Child Development, Kansas City, MO.

Chen, Z., & Siegler, R. S. (2000). Across the great divide: Bridging the gap between understanding of toddlers' and older children's thinking. *Monographs of the Society for Research in Child Development, 65*(2), (Serial No. 261).

de Villiers, J. G., & de Villiers, P. A. (2000). Linguistic determinism and the understanding of false beliefs. In *Children's reasoning and the mind* (pp. 191–228). Hove, England: Psychology Press/Taylor & Francis.

Doherty, M. J. (2000). Children's understanding of homonymy: Metalinguistic awareness and false belief. *Journal of Child Language, 27*(2), 367–392.

Dunn, J. (1994). Changing minds and changing relationships. In C. Lewis & P. Mitchell (Eds.), *Children's early understanding of minds: Origins and development.* Hillsdale, NJ: Lawrence Erlbaum Associates.

Dunn, J. (Ed.). (1999). Relationships and children's understanding of mind (Special issue). *Social Development, 8*(2).

Dunn, J. (2000). Mind-reading, emotion understanding, and relationships. *International Journal of Behavioral Development, 24*(2), 142–144.

Dunn, J., Brown, J., Slomkowski, C., Tesla, C., & Youngblade, L. (1991). Young children's understanding of other people's feelings and beliefs: Individual differences and their antecedents. *Child Development, 62,* 1352–1366.

Fabricius, W. V., & Schwanenflugel, P. J. (1994). The older child's theory of mind. In A. Demetriou & A. Eflides (Eds.), *Intelligence, mind, and reasoning: Structure and development* (pp. 111–132). Amsterdam: Elsevier.

Fabricius, W. V., & Imbens-Bailey, A. L. (2000). False belief about false beliefs. In P. Mitchell & K. Riggs (Eds), *Children's reasoning and the mind* (pp. 167–180). Hove, UK: Psychology Press.

Fivush, R. (1994). Constructing narrative, emotion, and self in parent–child conversations about the past. In U. Neisser & R. Fivush (Eds.), *The remembering self: Construction and accuracy in the life narrative* (pp. 136–157). New York: Cambridge University Press.

Flavell, J. H. (1993). The development of children's understanding of false belief and the appearance-reality distinction. *International Journal of Psychology, 28,* 595–604.

Flavell, J. H. (2000). Development of children's knowledge about the mental world. *International Journal of Behavioral Development, 24*(1), 15–23.

Flavell, J. H., Flavell, E. R., & Green, F. (1983). Development of the appearance-reality distinction. *Cognitive Psychology, 15,* 95–120.

Flavell, J. H., Green, F. L., & Flavell, E. R. (1995). The development of children's knowledge about attentional focus. *Developmental Psychology, 31,* 706–712.

Fodor, J. A. (1992). A theory of the child's theory of mind. *Cognition, 44,* 283–296.

Frye, D., Zelazo, P. D., & Palfai, T. (1995). Theory of mind and rule-based reasoning. *Cognitive Development, 10,* 483–527.

Frye, D., & Ziv, M. (2001, April). *Children's theory of mind: The need to study a broader cultural base.* Poster presented at the meeting of the Society for Research in Child Development, Minneapolis, MN.

Gopnik, A., & Wellman, H. (1994). The theory theory. In L. Hirschfeld & S. Gelman, (Eds.), *Mapping the mind: Domain specificity in cognition and culture,* (pp. 257–293). Cambridge, England: Cambridge University Press.

Harris, P., Johnson, C., Hutton, D., Andrews, G., & Cooke, T. (1989). Young children's theory of mind and emotion. *Cognition and Emotion, 3*, 379–400.

Hughes, C. (1998). Executive function in preschoolers: Links with theory of mind and verbal ability. *British Journal of Development Psychology, 16*, 233–253.

Jenkins, J. M., & Astington, J. W. (1996). Cognitive factors and family structure associated with theory of mind development in young children. *Developmental Psychology, 32*, 70–78.

Karpf, J. C., & Murray, L. (2001, April). *The impact of early mother-infant imitation on pre-theory of mind abilities at 12 and 18 months.* Poster presented at the meeting of the Society for Research in Child Development, Minneapolis, MN.

Keenan, T. (1998). Memory span as a predictor of false belief understanding. *New Zealand Journal of Psychology, 27*(2), 36–43. (Abstract).

Lagattuta, K. H., & Wellman, H. M. (2001). Thinking about the past: Early knowledge about links between prior experience, thinking, and emotion. *Child Development, 72*(1), 82–102.

Lewis, C., & Mitchell, P. (Eds.). (1994). *Children's early understanding of mind: Origins and development.* Hove, England: Lawrence Erlbaum Associates.

Lewis, C., & Osbourne, A. (1990). Three-year-olds' problems with false belief: Conceptual deficit or linguistic artifact? *Child Development, 61*, 1514–1519.

Lillard, A. (1998). Ethno-psychologies: Cultural variations in theories of mind. *Psychological Bulletin, 123*, 3–32.

Miller, S. A. (2000). Children's understanding of preexisting differences in knowledge and belief. *Developmental Review, 20*(2), 227–282.

Mitchell, P., & Lacohee, H. (1991). Children's early understanding of false belief. *Cognition, 39*, 107–127.

Moore, C. (2001, April). *Theory of mind and social competence in the preschool years.* Paper presented at the meeting of the Society for Research in Child Development, Minneapolis, MN.

Nelson, K. (2000). Memory and belief in development. In D. L. Schacter & E. Scarry (Eds.), *Memory, brain, and belief* (pp. 259–289). Cambridge, MA: Harvard University Press.

Notaro, P. C., Gelman, S. A., & Zimmerman, M. A. (2001). Children's understanding of psychogenic bodily reactions. *Child Development, 72*(2), 444–459.

Perner, J. (1989). Is "thinking" belief? Reply to Wellman and Bartsch. *Cognition, 33*, 315–319.

Perner, J., Leekam, S. R., & Wimmer, H. (1987). Three-year-olds' difficulty with false belief: The case for a conceptual deficit. *British Journal of Developmental Psychology, 5*, 125–137.

Perner, J., Ruffman, T., & Leekam, S.R. (1994). Theory of mind is contagious: You catch it from your sibs. *Child Development, 65*, 1228–1238.

Peterson, C. C. (2002). Drawing insight from pictures: The development of concepts of false drawing and false belief in children with deafness, normal hearing, and autism. *Child Development, 73*(5), 1442–1459.

Peterson, C. C., & Siegal, M. (1997). Psychological, physical, and biological thinking in normal, autistic, and deaf children. In H. M. Wellman & K. Inagaki (Eds.), *The emergence of core domains of thought: Children's reasoning about physical, psychological, and biological phenomena.* (*New Directions for Child Development*), (No. 75, pp. 55–70). San Francisco, CA: Jossey-Bass.

Pillow, B. H., & Henrichon, A. J. (1996). There's more to the picture than meets the eye. Young children's difficulty understanding biased interpretations. *Child Development, 67*, 803–819.

Poulin-Dubois, D. (1999). Infants' distinction between animate and inanimate objects: The origins of naive psychology. In P. Rochat (Ed.), *Early social cognition* (pp. 257–280). Mahwah, NJ: Lawrence Erlbaum Associates.

Premack, D., & Woodruff, G. (1978). Does the chimpanzee have a theory of mind? *Behavioral and Brain Sciences, 1*, 515–526.

Repacholi, B. M., & Gopnik, A. (1997). Early reasoning about desires: Evidence from 14- and 18- month olds. *Developmental Psychology, 33*, 12–21.

Ruffman, T., Perner, J., Naito, M., Parkin, L., & Clements, W. A. (1998). Older (but not younger) siblings facilitate false belief understanding. *Developmental Psychology, 34*, 161–174.

Ruffman, T., Perner, J., & Parkin, L. (1999). How parenting style affects false belief understanding. *Social Development, 8*(3), 395–411.

Russell, J. (1996). *Agency: Its role in mental development.* Hove, UK: Lawrence Erlbaum Associates.

Siegal, M., & Beattie, K. (1991). Where to look first for children's knowledge of false beliefs. *Cognition, 38*, 1–12.

Shimmon, K. (2001, April). *A longitudinal study of executive function and theory of mind in preschoolers.* Poster presented at the meeting of the Society for Research in Child Development, Minneapolis, MN.

Swettenham, J., Baron-Cohen, S., Gomez, J. C., & Walsh, S. (1996). What's inside a person's head? Conceiving of the mind as a camera helps children with autism develop an alternative theory of mind. *Cognitive Neuropsychiatry, 1*, 73–88.

Taylor, M., & Carlson, S. (1997). The relation between individual differences in fantasy and theory of mind. *Child Development, 68*, 436–455.

Tomasello, M., Kruger, A. C., & Ratner, H. H. (1993). Cultural learning. *Behavioral and Brain Sciences, 16*, 495–552.

Watson, A. C., Nixon, C. L., Wilson, A., & Capage, L. (1999). Social interaction skills and theory of mind in young children. *Developmental Psychology, 35*(2), 386–391.

Wellman, H. M. (1990). *The child's theory of mind*. Boston: MIT Press.

Wellman, H. M. (1998). Culture, variation, and levels of analysis in folk psychologies: Comment on Lillard. *Psychological Bulletin, 123*(1), 33–36.

Wellman, H., Baron-Cohen, S., Gomez, J. C., Swettenham, J., & Toye, E. *Using thought-bubbles helps children with autism acquire an alternative to a theory of mind*. (Manuscript submitted for publication).

Wellman, H. M., Cross, D., & Watson, J. (2001). Meta-analysis of theory-of-mind development: The truth about false-belief. *Child Development, 72*(3), 655–684.

Wellman, H. M., Hollander, M., & Schult, C. A. (1996). Young children's understanding of thought bubbles and of thoughts. *Child Development, 67*, 768–788.

Wimmer, H., & Perner, J. (1983). Beliefs about beliefs: Representation and constraining function of wrong beliefs in young children's understanding of deception. *Cognition, 13*, 103–128.

Woodward, A. L. (1998). Infants selectively encode the goal object of an actor's reach. *Cognition, 69*, 1–34.

Zelazo, P. D., & Muller, U. (in preparation). *Executive function*. Mahwah, NJ: Lawrence Erlbaum Associates.

Experiment 3

False Belief in Children's Theory of Mind

As seen in the previous section, the developmental course of children's understanding of mind is one of the most widely researched and discussed issues in developmental psychology. In preschoolers, the most widely used test paradigm is the False Belief test (FB).

There are varied versions of the False Belief task. Some involve change of location from one container or place to another; some involve change of contents (identity of the object in container). The questions asked of the child subject also varies; e.g., where will Sam look, where does he think it is, where will he say it is. The protagonist (who did not observe the change in location or identity) can be a real person, or a puppet or doll, or a pretend character, or a videotaped person.

The aim of the False Belief task is to help chart the course of a child's understanding of mental processes.

Problem and Hypotheses

Some differences in children's theory of mind between younger and older preschoolers and between boys and girls will be assessed with a False Belief task.

1. Older preschoolers will obtain (higher–correct) (lower) (same) scores on the FB task as younger preschoolers.

2. Girls obtain (higher) (lower) (equal) scores on the FB task as boys.

3. There (will) (will not) be an interaction of sex and age on the FB task.

Method

Participants

Twenty or more preschoolers: 5 boys and 5 girls, three-years-old; 5 boys and 5 girls, upper four-years or lower five-years-old.

Materials

A container that is familiar to preschoolers, like a Johnson and Johnson Band-Aid box.
A small toy or short pencil or candy kiss that will fit in the above package.
Individual data sheet with places for age, sex, and responses.

Procedure

The experimenter seats the child in front of a table, introduces self and asks the child's name. Some neutral chatting is acceptable.

"Let me show you something." [E puts Band-Aid box in front of the child.] **"What is this?"** [Record response. In the unlikely event that the child does not answer correctly, say **"This is a Band-Aid box."**]

"What is in this box?" [Record response to Question 1. Then hand the box to the child and say:] **"Let's open the box and look inside."** [Record child's expression and reaction.]

"Wow; that's not a Band-Aid; it's a (toy, pencil, candy)."

"Now, let's pretend your friend comes into this room. Here she (he) is! What does she (he) think is in this box?" [Record response to Question 2.]

"Thank you for helping me." [Escort child back to his (her) group.]

Results

Scoring. The correct answer to the first question "What is in this box?" is Band-Aids. The correct answer to the second question "What does your friend think is in this box" is also Band-Aid.

Data Analysis. Record the information from the child's individual data sheet to the Master Data Sheet (provided by the instructor), for the age and sex of your subject.

When the individual results are collated, look at the Group Data Sheet, Table F3.1. Fill in Fig. F3.1, bar graph, for Question 2.

Using the Group Data raw scores for correct answers to question 2, run chi squares for age differences, and sex differences. (See Table F3.2, a and b.) To look at a possible interaction between sex and age, fill in the number of children answering correctly in Table F3.2c. Chi squares with 1 degree of freedom must be equal to or greater than 6.635 to be significant at the .01 level, and 3.841 to be significant at the .05 level. These significances enable you to reject the null hypotheses that your two variables are not related.

If the expected cell frequencies are below 5 in your tables, an alternative statistic should be used: The Fisher Exact Test. This even eliminates the need for computation!

Instead of using the number of children answering correctly, with chi square statistics, you can use the percentages from Table F3.1. Find the significance of the difference between the two percentages for age groups, and for the two sexes, respectively. If the number of children in each group are initially very unequal, using the number of correct answers can be very misleading, and percentages or proportions need to be used.

State your findings.

Discussion

Did all your subjects recognize the Band-Aid box?

Relate your findings to each of your hypotheses. Did your older group have more children answering correctly than your younger group? Was the difference statistically significant? Did your finding re: age differences concur with the research literature on false belief?

Did you find a significant difference between the sexes, that is, were girls more correct than the boys? Did your findings agree with the false-belief literature?

Did one sex show a greater increase in correct answers with age than the other sex? In other words, was there an interaction between age and sex, or did both sexes improve similarly with age?

What are some of the explanations for the results on false belief tasks? Do your findings specifically lend support to any of the explanations or theories offered in the literature?

Would you expect different results if you tested very bright children or tested retarded children? Children from a different culture or language? Children from one- or two-parent families? Children with many or few siblings? Why or why not?

There are many variants of the False Belief task. Would you expect different age or sex results if you used a different version of the task?

Do you consider this False Belief task an adequate measure of the development of understanding of mental processes? Discuss. Can you think of other ways to investigate theory of mind issues?

Selected Bibliography

Carlson, S. M. & Moses, L. J. (2001). Individual differences in inhibitory control and children's theory of mind. *Child Development, 72*(4), 1032–1053.

Fabricius, W. V., & Imbens-Bailey, A. L. (2000). False belief about false beliefs. In P. Mitchell & K. Riggs (Eds), *Children's reasoning and the mind* (pp. 167-180). Hove, UK: Psychology Press.

Flavell, J. H. (1993). The development of children's understanding of false belief and the appearance-reality distinction. *International Journal of Psychology, 28*, 595–604.

Flavell, J. H. (2000). Development of children's knowledge about the mental world. *International Journal of Behavioral Development, 24*(1), 15–23.

Keenan, T. (1998). Memory span as a predictor of false belief understanding. *New Zealand Journal of Psychology, 27*(2), 36–43. (Abstract).

Lewis, C., & Osbourne, A. (1990). Three-year-olds' problems with false belief: Conceptual deficit or linguistic artifact? *Child Development, 61*, 1514–1519.

Mitchell, P., & Lacohee, H. (1991). Children's early understanding of false belief. *Cognition, 39*, 107–127.

Moses, L. J. (2001). Executive accounts of theory-of-mind development. *Child Development, 72*(3), 688–690.

Perner, J., Leekam, S. R., & Wimmer, H. (1987). Three-year-olds' difficulty with false belief: The case for a conceptual deficit. *British Journal of Developmental Psychology, 5*, 125–137.

Perner, J., Ruffman, T., & Leekam, S.R. (1994). Theory of mind is contagious: You catch it from your sibs. *Child Development, 65*, 1228–1238.

Ruffman, T., Perner, J., Naito, M., Parking, L., & Clements, W. A. (1998). Older (but not younger) siblings facilitate false belief understanding. *Developmental Psychology, 34*, 161–174.

Siegal, M., & Beattie, K. (1991). Where to look first for children's knowledge of false beliefs. *Cognition, 38*, 1–12.

Tardif, T., Fung, K., Wellman, H., Liu, D., & Fang, F. (2001, April). *Preschoolers understanding of knowing how, knowing that, and false belief.* Poster presented at the meeting of the Society for Research in Child Development, Minneapolis, MN.

Wellman, H. M., Cross, D., & Watson, J. (2001). Meta-analysis of theory of mind development: The truth about false-belief. *Child Development, 72*(3), 655–684.

See, also, the bibliography at the previous Background section.

INDIVIDUAL DATA SHEET

Title: FB

E:_____ Day and Date:_____ Sex:_____

S:_____ Birthdate:_____ CA:_____

Time Begun:_____ Time Ended:_____ Elapsed Time:_____

FB task

	Child's Response	Score	
Q1		Correct-	No-
		Band-Aid	Other
Q2		Correct-	No-
		Band-Aid	Other

Comments:

GROUP DATA SHEET

Title: *False Belief in Children's Theory of Mind*

Hypothesis:

Method and Procedure: (as described in text with following modifications, if any)

Group Results and Analysis:

TABLE F3.1
FALSE BELIEF SCORES AS A FUNCTION OF AGE AND SEX

Group	Q1 Correct R		Q2 Correct R	
	#	%	#	%
3 year-olds, *n* =				
Boys				
Girls				
Total				
4-5 year-olds, *n* =				
Boys				
Girls				
Total				
Boys *n* =				
Girls *n* =				
Total *n* =				

TABLE F3.2

CHI SQUARES OR FISHER EXACT TESTS FOR AGE AND SEX DIFFERENCES IN CORRECT RESPONSES ON THE FALSE- BELIEF TASK

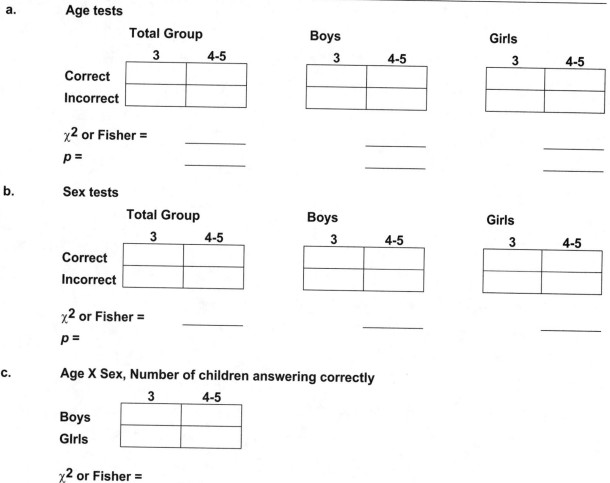

a. **Age tests**

	Total Group		Boys		Girls	
	3	**4-5**	**3**	**4-5**	**3**	**4-5**
Correct						
Incorrect						

χ^2 or Fisher = _____ _____ _____

p = _____ _____ _____

b. **Sex tests**

	Total Group		Boys		Girls	
	3	**4-5**	**3**	**4-5**	**3**	**4-5**
Correct						
Incorrect						

χ^2 or Fisher = _____ _____ _____

p =

c. **Age X Sex, Number of children answering correctly**

	3	**4-5**
Boys		
GIrls		

χ^2 or Fisher = _____

p = _____

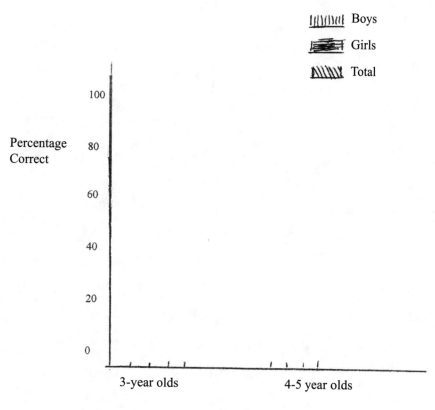

Fig F3.1.   Percent children giving correct answer, by age and sex.

Attention and Memory

Background

The study of attention has again become a prime topic of investigation, judging by the frequency of presentations at recent national or regional psychology conventions and the number of publications. As Lewis (1971) pointed out long ago, "The study of attention, like much investigation in psychology, is not new, and often recurs as a theme." Preyer and Darwin's infant observations in the late 1800s and William James' distinction between two kinds of attention—passive immediate sensorial attention, in which the organism is forced to attend regardless of its intention, and associational or voluntary attending, in which the relation of the stimulation to the organism's ongoing functions is crucial—attest to an early recognition of the importance of the topic. Attention, considered a basic process during the early years of experimental psychology, attracted much experimental effort and theoretical speculation. With the rise of behaviorism in the twentieth century, with its commitment to observable responses, and with the revolt against the use of explanatory concepts that could be inferred only from the behavior they were to explain, the concept of attention became unpopular (Reese & Lipsitt, 1970). Fantz' work in the late 1950s on infant pattern vision and form perception, and work on the orienting reflex begun by Pavlov, are often credited with being the impetus for the current surge of interest in attention and related problems. There appears now to be a general recognition that attention or attention-like concepts (ranging from the orientation reaction through the role of attention in discrimination learning and transfer to exploratory behavior) are necessary for an understanding of the basic cognitive functions in children and their individual differences. Researchers have investigated variables like intensity, complexity, or number of stimuli; others have emphasized surprise, familiarity, incongruity, or discrepancy from a familiar pattern.

Definitions of attention vary; however, for a general definition, we might turn again to Lewis (1971): Attention is "the process by which an organism *directs* his sensory and elaboratory (cognitive) systems" (p. 173, italics added). Operational definitions have included receptor orientation; decreases in various ongoing activities like moving, talking, sucking, vocalizing; changes in the functioning of the autonomic nervous system like decrease in heart rate, alteration of breathing pattern, increase in electrical conductivity of the skin; and changes in cortical activity.

Some of the investigations of development of attention in infancy appear to have been set in a broad context, in the hope of establishing some of the antecedents and correlates of intellectual development and growth of mental structure. There was considerable use of a matching–mismatching model of attending (Kagan & Lewis, 1965; McCall & Kagan, 1967; Sokolov, 1963), which says that attention is elicited when there is a mismatch between internal representation and external event, and attention is inhibited when there is a match. A frequently used measure of attention in these infancy studies has been response decrement or habituation—the decrease in response strength as a function of repeated stimulation. In practice, response decrement is usually measured as a decrease in the amount of fixation time toward a repeated visual signal and has been shown to be positively correlated with the age of the infant (up to 3 years), mother–infant interaction, socioeconomic status, and so on. Lewis (who has been moving away from the match–mismatch model) believes that response decrement, which he considered a measure of internal representation formation, "is a sensitive predictor of individual differences in a wide range of cognitive tasks and reflects efficient CNS (central nervous system) functioning" (1971, p. 205).

An argument can be made for a multiple-response approach to the study of attention. Wilson and Lewis (1971) believed that a multivariate approach is necessary and that a single response measure is inadequate and superficial, first because a response changes its meaning over age; and second because the process of attending in infants involves at least two types of response—the initial orienting responses and subsequent affectual responses.

Still other models and measures, perhaps somewhat distant verbally from the scheme (internal representation) notions and the response decrement measures, and somewhat closer to the learning and mediation notions, have been employed by psychologists interested in the development of attention postinfancy. Experiments on selective attention involve a central-incidental memory task (CIT), developed by Hagen (1967), in which the child is told which material is relevant to remember. It is interesting to note how specific findings or difficulties of interpretation led to one study after another; and how the intial model (Broadbent's information processing and selective filters) has been partially supplanted.

The capacity of the growing child to attend to relevant environmental events is obviously critical for success in school, and educational psychologists are understandably interested in theory and research on arousal and maintenance of attention and related individual differences. There are still many gaps in our developmental information about attentional processes, and there are several laboratories actively exploring the basic and applied facets of attention. The APA Science Directorate (1994) visited some of these research centers and reported on their timely and exciting projects. Attention remains a complex process.

The venerable Stroop test is still used in studies of attention, vulnerability to distraction, and interference proneness (See Experiment 4). Using the same logic as the Stroop test, Rosinski's Picture-Word Interference Task adds the issue of semantic processing to the attention test (Experiment 5). The free recall and clustering project (Experiment 6) is a test of memory and introduces you to some of the variables that influence it.

Memory is one of the oldest and longest-lived topics in psychology. Experimental psychologists, developmental psychologists, and neurological scientists all avidly pursue different facets of memory.

The fifth edition of the *Handbook of Child Psychology* (Damon, 1998) includes in Volume 2, chapters on infant cognition (Haith & Benson) and memory (Schneider & Bjorklund).

Selected Bibliography

American Psychological Association. (1994). Attention. *The APA Monitor, 25*(1), 16–19.

Balaban, M. T., Snidman, N., & Kagan, J. (1997). Attention, emotion, and reactivity in infancy and early childhood. In P. S. Lang, R. F. Simons, & M. T. Balaban (Eds.), *Attention and orienting: Sensory and motivational processes* (pp. 369–391). Mahwah, NJ: Lawrence Erlbaum Associates.

Hagen, J. W. (1967). The effect of distraction on selective attention. *Child Development, 38*, 685–694.

Haith, M. M., & Benson, J. B. (1998). Infant cognition. In W. Damon (Ed.-in-Chief), D. Kuhn & R. Siegler (Vol. Eds.), *Handbook of child psychology: Vol. 2. Cognition, perception & language* (5th ed, pp. 199–254). New York: Wiley.

Kagan, J., & Lewis, M. (1965). Studies of attention in the human infant. *Merrill-Palmer Quarterly, 11*, 95–127.

Lewis, M. (1971). Individual differences in the measurement of early cognitive growth. In J. Hellmuth (Ed.), *Exceptional infant. Studies in abnormalities (Vol. 2)*. New York: Brunner/Mazel.

McCall, R. B., & Kagan, J. (1967). Stimulus-schema discrepancy and attention in the infant. *Journal of Experimental Child Psychology, 5*, 381–390.

Pashler, H. E. (1997). *The psychology of attention*. Cambridge, MA: MIT Press. A Bradford Book.

Posner, M. I. (1992). Attention as a cognitive and neural system. *Current Directions in Psychological Science, 1*(1), 11–14.

Reese, H. W., & Lipsitt, L. P. (1970). *Experimental child psychology*. New York: Academic Press.

Ruff, H. A., & Rothbart, M. K. (1996). *Attention in early development: Themes and variations*. New York: Oxford University Press.

Schneider, W., & Bjorklund, D. F. (1998). Memory. In W. Damon (Ed.-in-Chief), D. Kuhn & R. Siegler (Vol. Eds.), *Handbook of child psychology: Vol. 2. Cognition, perception & language* (5th ed., pp. 467–522). New York: Wiley.

Sokolov, Y. N. (1963). *Perception and the conditioned reflex* (S. W. Waydenfeld, Trans.). New York: Macmillan.

Wilson, C. D., & Lewis, M. (1971, April). *A developmental study of attention: A multivariate approach*. Paper presented at the Eastern Psychological Association meeting, New York.

Experiment 4

Age and Sex Differences in Interference Proneness

Keith Stanovich

Psychologists have recently become increasingly interested in the concept of attention and its related phenomena. Developmental psychologists have shared in this renewed interest and have carried out coherent research programs investigating the development of attentional mechanisms (see an earlier effort by Hagen & Kail, 1975). In addition, researchers have investigated the possibility that attentional deficits might be a contributing factor to the cognitive handicaps of certain subgroups of children. Thus, Zeaman and House (1963), conceptualizing attention as the ability to focus on a particular dimension, have looked into possible attentional deficits in mentally retarded individuals. Hallahan (1975), broadly defining selective attention as the ability to resist various types of distraction, has studied its relationship to learning disabilities. Inhibition as measured by the Stroop test, has been studied in children 8-15 years old, with attention deficit hyperactivity disorder (Gaultney, Kipp, Weinstein, & McNeill, 1999). The Stroop test has also been studied in the performance of clinically depressed children and adolescents (Doost, Taghavi, Yule, & Daigleish, 1997), and in children and adolescents with Post Traumatic Stress Disorder (Moradi, Taghavi, Doost, Yule, & Dalgleish, 1999). The relation of reading proficiency to Stroop scores has been investigated by Cox, Chee, Chase, and Baumgardner (1997). It is reassuring to know that this old Stroop measure showed excellent reliability in children 4.4–12.3 years old, when tested three times at six-month intervals (Neyens, & Aldenkamp, 1997). In short, developmental psychologists have recognized the importance and applicability of the concept of attention to many of the theoretical and practical problems in the field of child psychology.

One stumbling block to the adequate use of the concept of attention has been its multifaceted nature and the concomitant inability of investigators to interpret different attentional phenomena in a common way. What is needed is a coherent taxonomy of different attentional mechanisms and a specification of their roles in various experimental tasks. An attempt at such a conceptualization was made by Treisman (1969). She focused on one central property of attention: Its selectivity—people can focus only on one, or few, things at a time. Other information must be filtered out.

But why is attention selective? Why do some things have to be filtered out? Information processing theorists have hypothesized that the reason that attentional mechanisms developed was to protect a limited capacity central processor from overload. Thus, the concept of attention has, through the history of cognitive psychology, been closely linked with the notion of *limited capacity* (Allport, 1989; Duncan, 1980; Halford, Mayberry, & Bain, 1986, Hirst & Kalmar, 1987, Kahneman, 1973; Posner & Snyder, 1975; Treisman, 1988). The flip side of the notion of limited capacity is the concept of *automaticity*. Automatic mental processes are processes that can execute without drawing much of a person's cognitive capacity. They are processes that can execute while attention is directed elsewhere. Such processes are very useful, because in many cognitive tasks several component processes must be coordinated in a short period of time. As LaBerge and Samuels (1974) argued, "If each component process requires attention, performance of the complex skill will be impossible, because the capacity of attention will be exceeded. But if enough of the components and their coordinations can be processed automatically, then the loads on attention will be within tolerable limits and the skill can be successfully performed" (p. 293).

Experimental psychologists have developed many different tasks to measure aspects of automaticity (Allport, 1989; McLeod, 1978; Paap & Ogden, 1981; Stanovich, 1990; Zbrodoff & Logan, 1986). One group of tasks is designed to indicate whether a process can execute while attention is directed elsewhere. These tasks are often termed interference tasks. One of the most well-known is called the Stroop Color-Word Test (Stroop, 1935). In fact, it has been called the "gold standard" of attentional measures (see MacLeod, 1992).

In their review of the literature, Jensen and Rohwer (1966) traced the origins of the Stroop test back to Wundt's first psychological laboratory, where there was an interest in comparing the time it takes to name colors with the time it takes to read the corresponding color words. Interest in this problem led Stroop (for whom the test is named) to introduce his color-word interference test into American psychology in 1935. Stroop's stimulus materials consisted of three types of cards. On card W, the subject must read a series of color names. On card C, the subject names the colors of a series of color patches. The interference card, CW, contains a series of incongruously colored color names; for example, the word *blue* is printed in yellow ink. The subject is required to name the ink color of each word. On each card, the dependent variable is the time it takes to read a series of items. The basic findings, subsequently replicated in dozens of studies (Dyer, 1973; Jensen & Rohwer, 1966; MacLeod, 1991, 1992), are that word reading is faster than color naming, and that performance on the interference card is significantly slowed relative to card C where the subject is also naming colors.

The simplest verbal explanation for the interference exhibited on card CW has been one of *response conflict* (Dyer, 1973; Jensen & Rohwer, 1966; Kahneman, 1973). Specifically, the perceptual system fails to gate out the irrelevant stimulus attribute (form) that contacts memory at approximately the same time as the relevant attribute (color). Both attributes elicit responses that are appropriate to the task (color names) but the responses are in conflict. The subject must suppress the response elicited by the word and emit the response corresponding to the color. The process of selecting the appropriate response and suppressing the inappropriate response takes time and delays the output of the correct response. This accounts for the delay on card CW relative to card C. Cognitive psychologists have gone beyond this simple verbal explanation and have implemented computer models of performance on the task. Although these are beyond our scope here, the reader is referred to a paper by Cohen, Dunbar, and McClelland (1990) in which one of the more sophisticated theories is implemented as parallel distributed processing computer model.

The Stroop task has had many different theoretical interpretations within the literature in developmental psychology. Two processes that have been of interest to developmental psychologists have been the children's ability to resist distraction and to suppress inappropriate responses. Because the Stroop phenomenon is believed to reflect response conflict, the task became of interest to developmental psychologists and to researchers interested in individual differences (see Ellis, Woodley-Zanthos, Dulaney, & Palmer, 1989). Schiller (1966) examined Stroop test performance in age groups ranging from first graders to adults. First graders named the color patches on card C faster than they read the words designating the colors on card W. However, second graders read words faster than they named colors, as did third, fifth, eighth graders, and first-year college students. The time difference in favor of word reading remained relatively constant across all age groups from second graders to adults. Interference, measured by the derived score CW/C, was minimal in first graders, maximal in second and third graders, and then declined gradually. A similar decline in interference proneness after the second grade was observed in other studies (see Comalli, Wapner, & Werner, 1962; Ehri & Wilce, 1979; Guttentag & Haith, 1978, 1980; MacLeod, 1991; Stanovich, Cunningham, & West, 1981; West & Stanovich, 1978, 1979).

Schiller (1966) attributed this decline in interference proneness with age to the increasing differentiation of the two response tendencies. When the responses are highly differentiated, the correct response can be produced with greater ease even when it is the weaker of the two. The relative lack of interference observed in the performance of the first graders presumably was due to inadequate establishment of the reading response and subsequent absence of response conflict in this age group. Although Schiller's analysis of children's Stroop test performance accounts well for his results, alternative theoretical accounts exist in the literature (see Cohen, et al., 1990; Dunbar & MacLeod, 1984; Jensen & Rohwer, 1966; La Heij, 1988; MacLeod, 1991). An adequate explanation of the age trend in interference proneness would be a valuable addition to psychological theory.

Problem and Hypotheses

The proneness of children to respond to irrelevant stimuli or to be distracted from the task at hand are problems that, owing to their theoretical and practical implications, have provoked interest. Both issues relate to the broadly defined area of selective attention. A task with a firm empirical and theoretical base in the selective attention literature is the Stroop Color-Word Test. The basic phenomenon is one of interference in naming the ink color of words when the words themselves are different color names. The interference comes about when the color of the word and its referent are incongruous (i.e., the word *blue* is printed in red ink). Naming the colors on such a card is delayed relative to naming the colors on a card where the items are a series of colored Xs or color patches with no incongruities. The relative slowness on the interference card of the Stroop test is believed to be due to conflict in the subject's response selection process. The development of interference proneness will be investigated using a form of the Stroop Color-Word Test on boys and girls of three grades.

1. Interference proneness is maximal in the (first), (third), (fifth) grade.

2. Interference proneness is minimal in the (first), (third), (fifth) grade.

3. In general, word reading is (faster), (slower) than color naming.

4. The slowness or fastness of word reading relative to color naming (does), (does not) change with age.

5. Word reading speed is (positively), (negatively) related to interference proneness.

6. Color naming speed is (positively), (negatively) related to interference proneness.

7. Do the relationships in hypotheses 5 and 6 change with age?

8. Sex differences?

Method

Subjects

Boys and girls in the first, third, and fifth grades

Materials

1 48-item word card (W)

1 48-item color card (C)

1 48-item color-word interference card (CW)

3 12-item practice cards (PW, PC, PCW)

1 Card rest stand

1 Stopwatch

1 Individual Data Sheet

The form of the Stroop Color-Word Test used here was first introduced into the literature by Kamlet and Egeth (1969). The three practice and three test cards can be made from white cardboard. The three small practice cards (PW, PC, and PCW) measure 4½ in. X 8 in. (11.4 cm X 20.3 cm), and the three large test cards (W, C, and CW) measure 9 in. X 16 in. (22.9 cm X 40.6 cm). The individual items are constructed by using a Dymo Labelmaker (Dymo Industries Inc., 1 Embarcadero Center, San Francisco, California, 94111) to emboss either Xs or color words on plastic label tapes. Each color word or series of Xs is embossed on an individual color strip measuring 1½ in. X 1½ in. (1.3 cm X 3.8 cm), which is then stuck on the white cardboard. The resulting stimuli are white letters on a colored background. The 48 items on the large test cards are arrayed in 6 rows and 8 columns. The 12 items on the practice cards are arrayed in 3 rows and 4 columns.

The individual items for cards PW and W are the words *red*, *green*, *blue*, and *yellow* embossed on black plastic tape. The four words appear equally often on the cards, and no two consecutive words are the same (i.e., there are no response repetitions). Within these two constraints the items appear randomly. See the Individual Data Sheet, card W, for the word sequence.

The individual items for cards PC and C are red-, green-, blue-, and yellow-colored strips with Xs embossed on them. The number of Xs on each colored strip corresponds to the number of letters in one of the three color names that is not the name of the color of the strip. Thus, a blue strip will have either three, five, or six Xs embossed on it (corresponding to the words *red*, *green*, and *yellow*). There are 12 different combinations of colored strips and Xs. Each combination appears equally often on the card with the additional constraint that no two consecutive strips are the same color. Within these constraints the items appear randomly. The arrangement of items on card C differs from that on card W. See the Individual Data Sheet, card C, for the color-strip sequence.

The individual items for cards PCW and CW are colored strips on which are embossed incongruous color words. Thus, no word is printed on the color that it names. Each color-word combination appears equally often with the additional constraint that no consecutive strips are the same color. The item arrangement on card CW differs from that on cards C and W. See the Individual Data Sheet, card CW, for the color-strip sequence.

Additional apparatus includes a card rest stand on which the cards can be placed perpendicular to the subject's line of sight. This allows performance to be assessed without the subject or experimenter having to hold the card. The correct response sequence for each test card is displayed on the Individual Data Sheet enabling the experimenter to monitor the child's progress while sitting behind the supported test card.

Procedure

The child is first shown the small practice card for words (PW). This is placed on the card rest perpendicular to the child's line of sight. E tells the subject, **"Here is a small card with three rows of words on it. The words are *green*, *blue*, *yellow*, and *red*."** [E points to each word.] **"Can you read the words *green*, *blue*, *yellow*, and *red*?"** [Wait for the child to do so.] **"Try to read the words as *fast* as you can. When you finish one line, continue on to the next until you finish the card. Read from left to right."** [E indicates direction of reading by running a finger across the three rows in the appropriate direction.] **"Start reading when I say 'Go.'"**

The practice card is not timed. The experimenter must make sure that the child has mastered the practice card before going on to card W. In other words, the experimenter should make sure that the child is reading from left to right, and going smoothly to the next row down the card. During administration of the practice card, any pointing responses or handling of the card by the child should be discouraged. Administer as many trials of the practice card as needed to obtain relatively smooth performance. Help as needed. Errorless performance on the Stroop test is not required. Therefore, occasional errors (less than 1 or 2 per line) are ignored. When performance on the practice card seems adequate, proceed to card W. (If the child cannot read the words, skip card W and continue with practice card PC.)

E says, **"Now you are going to read a big card with the same words on it. Read it from left to right just like you read the little card. Try to read as quickly as you can and I will see how *fast* you can go. Ready?"** Card W is placed on the card rest. Timing begins with the first response, not when the card is exposed. Timing ends with the last response. Regardless of the response time, the child's performance is praised. Time is recorded, to the nearest one-half second, on the Individual Data Sheet, in addition to any relevant observations.

After completion of card W, the experimenter shows the small practice card for color naming, PC. E tells the subject, **"Here is a card with rows of colored strips on it. The colors are red, green, blue, and yellow.** [Point as you name.] **Each of the colored strips has Xs on it. Your job is just to name the colors of the strips as *fast* as you can. Name the strips from left to right, and when you finish one line, continue on to the next like this** [E indicates direction of naming by running a finger across the rows in the appropriate direction]. **Start naming when I say 'Go.'"** As with the previous practice card, card PC may be administered more than once if the child's performance is not adequate on the first trial. When performance on the practice card is adequate, go on to card C.

E says, **"Now you are going to name the colors on a big card. Name the colors from left to right just like you named the colors on the little card. Try to name them as *fast* as you can, and I will see how *fast* you can go. Ready?"** Card C is placed on the card rest. Timing and procedure are the same as for card W.

The experimenter next places the small practice card PCW on the card rest and says, **"Here is another card with colored strips on it. The strips have words on them. The words are *red, green, yellow,* and *blue.* Don't read the words aloud. Your job is to *name the colors of the strips* as *fast* as you can."** Additional verbal instructions are given, if necessary, to make it clear that the child is to name the colors and not read the words. Additional trials of practice can be given if the practice card elicits excess laughing or giggling from the child.

Card CW is administered in the same manner as cards C and W. E says, **"Now you are going to name the colors on a big card, just like you did on the little card. Name the colors of the strips from left to right as quickly as you can, and I will see how *fast* you can go. Ready? Go."**

In addition to recording time scores on the Individual Data Sheet, the experimenter should also circle any errors heard while following responses through the sequence. Qualitative notes should be taken on the child's behavior, especially on card CW. For example, is the child showing strain by squirming, twitching, or limb jerking? Is the child giggling or laughing at card CW? Is the child giving contaminated responses ("breen," "gred") or inappropriate responses ("orange")? Such behavioral manifestations of interference are common aspects of Stroop test performance.

Results

Scoring. The basic measures of the Stroop test are the three time scores: W, C, and CW. As many as 16 derived scores have been used at some time by various investigators (Jensen & Rohwer, 1966). Jensen (1965) intercorrelated and factor analyzed these derived scores from an experiment with an N of 436. Three factors accounted for 99% of the variance in all of the scores: a speed factor, a color difficulty factor, and an interference factor. The interference factor, with which we are primarily concerned, was most purely measured by the derived score CW-C. Schiller (1966), in his developmental study, used CW/C as a measure of interference. Although Jensen (1965) found this derived score to be a somewhat less pure measure of interference, we have found correlations of over .80 between CW-C and CW/C. Therefore, in order to obtain results comparable to Schiller's, it is suggested that analyses be carried out on both derived interference scores. It is important to keep in mind that the CW time score by itself is not a pure measure of interference.

Data Analysis. Record the individual data on the Master Data Sheets. Compute the measures of central tendency (means) for Table F4.1 on the Group Data Sheet. The data can be analyzed by running a two-way analysis of variance (3 grades X 2 sexes) on the raw W scores, the raw C scores, the raw CW scores, and the two derived interference measures, CW-C and CW/C (Table F4.2). In addition, if the ANOVA results warrant it, a more fine-grained analysis of age trends is accomplished by running Scheffé tests on all five measures comparing grades one and three, and grades three and five. These comparisons are especially interesting owing to the nonmonotonic relationship between age and interference proneness observed by Schiller (1966).

If, in addition to interference proneness, the relative difficulty of word reading and color naming is of interest, a two-way analysis of variance on the derived score C-W can be run.

Obtain Pearson *r* correlations between W, C, CW, CW?C, CW/C for the whole sample, for all boys, for all girls, for each individual grade, and for the six grade-sex subgroups (Table F4.3).

State your findings for each score with regard to the main effects—age and sex—and the interactions.

Discussion

Relate your data to your first two hypotheses. Do the means for the two derived interference measures, CW/C and CW-C, show the predicted age differences? Do the results of the analysis of variance and comparison tests indicate that the differences are statistically significant? Is there general agreement between your results and Schiller's?

Look at the mean scores for cards W and C. Do you find support for hypothesis 3? Do the results of the analysis of variance on the derived score C–W support your hypothesis 4? In general, is the relationship between word reading speed and color naming speed across age groups similar to that observed by Schiller?

Examine the relationship of word reading and color naming speed to interference proneness by looking at the correlations between C, W, and the interference measures for the whole sample. Do you find support for hypotheses 5 and 6? Look at the same correlations broken down by age for evidence relating to hypothesis 7. Schiller did not use sex as a variable in any of his analyses. Did you obtain any sex differences at the .05 level of statistical significance? What are your general conclusions regarding the developmental changes in interference proneness?

You might want to think about some factors that are peculiar to the Stroop test and how they are related to a variety of issues of interest to psychologists. For instance, performance on card CW indicates that an irrelevant verbal stimulus interferes with the processing of a nonverbal stimulus. How strongly, then, is the Stroop test tapping the reading process? Recent theories of reading (LaBerge & Samuels, 1974; Perfetti, 1985; Perfetti & McCutchen, 1987; Stanovich, 1986) stress the necessity of developing "automatic" processes in order to become a fluent reader. That is, with practice certain letter or word identification processes become "automatized" so that they occur without having attention allocated to them. The automatization of increasingly larger units of material is what differentiates the fluent reader from the beginner. When lower level identification operations are automatized, central processing capacity can be used at higher semantic levels where material is integrated. Consider the possibility that performance on card CW of the Stroop test is related to the idea of automatic processing, since the incongruous color words are identified even though the subject is focusing on the colors as instructed.

Schiller (1966) found word reading to be faster than color naming after the first grade. Is this what you found? If so, what accounts for this result? Do you think it is due to differential practice? If so, wouldn't you predict that the difference between C and W would become greater with age? Schiller found this not to be the case. Can you think of any other explanations, aside from differential practice, why reading is faster than naming? Do any developmental predictions follow from your above speculations?

From these and other considerations, investigators have believed the Stroop Color-Word Test to be tapping some basic and broad cognitive processes (Jensen & Rohwer, 1966) as well as automatized linguistic processes (e.g., Stanovich et al., 1981). An understanding of the development of these psychological processes is of fundamental importance. It is clear that developmental investigations will play a role in future explanations of Stroop test performance.

Selected Bibliography

Allport, A. (1989). Visual attention. In M. I. Posner (Ed.), *Foundations of cognitive science* (pp. 631–682). Cambridge, MA: MIT Press.

Band, G. P. H., van der Molen, M. W., Overtoom, C. E., & Verbaten, M. N. (2000). The ability to activate and inhibit speeded responses: Separate developmental trends. *Journal of Experimental Child Psychology, 75*(4), 263–290.

Cohen, J. D., Dunbar, K., & McClelland, J. L. (1990). On the control of automatic processes: Parallel distributed processing account of the Stroop effect. *Psychological Review, 97*, 332–361.

*Comalli, P. E., Wapner, S., & Werner, M. (1962). Interference effects of Stroop color-word test in childhood, adulthood, and aging. *Journal of Geriatric Psychology, 100*, 47–53.

Cox, C. S., Chee, E., Chase, G. A., Baumgardner, T. L., Schuerholz, L. J., Reader, M. J., Mohr, J., & Denckla, M. B. (1997). Reading proficiency affects the construct validity of the Stroop Test interference score. *Clinical Neuropsychologist, 11*(2), 105–110.

Dash, J., & Dash, A. S. (1982). Cognitive developmental studies of the Stroop phenomena: Cross-sectional and longitudinal data. *Indian Psychologist, 1*(1), 24–33.

Doost, H. T. N., Taghavi, M. R., Yule, W., Daigleish, T. (1997). The performance of clinically depressed children and adolescents on the modified Stroop paradigm. *Personality and Individual Differences, 23*(5), 753–759.

Dunbar, K., & MacLeod, C. M. (1984). A horse race of a different color: Stroop interference patterns with transformed words. *Journal of Experimental Psychology: Human Perception and Performance, 10*, 622–639.

Duncan, J. (1980). The locus of interference in the perception of simultaneous stimuli. *Psychological Review, 87*, 272–300.

Dyer, F. N. (1973). The Stroop phenomenon and its use in the study of perceptual, cognitive, and response processes. *Memory and Cognition, 1*, 106–120.

Ehri, L. C., & Wilce, L. S. (1979). Does word training increase or decrease interference in a Stroop task? *Journal of Experimental Child Psychology, 27*, 352–364.

Ellis, N. R., Woodley-Zanthos, P., Dulaney, C., & Palmer, R. (1989). Automatic-effortful processing and cognitive inertia in persons with mental retardation. *American Journal of Mental Retardation, 93*, 412–423.

Gaultney, J. F., Kipp, K., Weinstein, J., McNeill, J. (1999). Inhibition and mental effort in attention deficit hyperactivity disorder. *Journal of Developmental and Physical Disabilities, 11*(2), 105–114.

Guttentag, R. E., & Haith, M. M. (1978). Automatic processing as a function of age and reading ability. *Child Development, 49*, 707–716.

Guttentag, R. E., & Haith, M. M. (1980). A longitudinal study of word processing by first-grade children. *Journal of Educational Psychology, 72*, 701–705.

Hagen, J. W., & Kail, R. V. (1975). The role of attention in perceptual and cognitive development. In W. M. Cruickshank & D. P. Hallahan (Eds.), *Perceptual and learning disabilities in children* (*Vol. 2*, pp. 165–194). Syracuse, NY: Syracuse University Press.

Halford, G. S., Mayberry, M. T., & Bain, J. D. (1986). Capacity limitations in children's reasoning: A dual-task approach. *Child Development, 57*, 616–627.

Hallahan, D. P. (1975). Distractibility in the learning disabled child. In W. M. Cruickshank & D. P. Hallahan (Eds.), *Perceptual and learning disabilities in children* (*Vol. 2*, pp. 195–220). Syracuse, NY: Syracuse University Press.

Hirst, W., & Kalmar, D. (1987). Characterizing attentional resources. *Journal of Experimental Psychology: General, 116*, 68–81.

Jensen, A. R. (1965). Scoring the Stroop test. *Acta Psychologica, 24*, 398–408.

Jensen, A. R., & Rohwer, W. D., Jr. (1966). The Stroop color-word test: A review. *Acta Psychologica, 25*, 36–93.

Kahneman, D. (1973). *Attention and effort.* Englewood Cliffs, N. J.: Prentice-Hall.

Kamlet, A. S., & Egeth, H. E. (1969). Note on construction of Stroop-type stimuli. *Perceptual and Motor Skills, 29*, 914.

*La Berge, D., & Samuels, S. J. (1974). Toward a theory of automatic information processing in reading. *Cognitive Psychology, 6*, 293–323.

La Heij, W. (1988). Components of Stroop-like interference in picture naming. *Memory & Cognition, 16*, 400–410.

McLeod, P. (1978). Does probe RT measure central processing demand? *Quarterly Journal of Experimental Psychology, 30*, 83–89.

MacLeod, C. M., & MacDonald, P. A. (2000). Interdimensional interference in the Stroop effect: Uncovering the cognitive and neural anatomy of attention. *Trends in Cognitive Science, 4*(10), 383–391.

*MacLeod, C. M. (1991). Half a century of research on the Stroop effect: An integrative review. *Psychological Bulletin, 109*, 163–203.

*MacLeod, C. M. (1992). The Stroop task: The "gold standard" of attentional measures. *Journal of Experimental Psychology: General, 121*, 12–14.

Moradi, A. R., Taghavi, M. R., Heshat Doost, H. T., Yule, W., Dalgleish, T. (1999). Performance of children and adolescents with PTSD on the Stroop colour-naming task. *Psychological Medicine, 29*(2), 415–419.

Neyens, L. G. J., & Aldenkamp, A. P. (1997). Stability of cognitive measures in children of average ability. *Child Neuropsychology, 3*(3), 161–170.

Paap, K. R., & Ogden, W. C. (1981). Letter encoding is an obligatory but capacity-demanding operation. *Journal of Experimental Psychology: Human Perception and Performance, 7*, 518–527.

Perfetti, C. A. (1985). *Reading Ability.* New York: Oxford University Press.

Perfetti, C. A., & McCutchen, D. (1987). Schooled language competence: Linguistic abilities in reading and writing. In S. Rosenberg (Ed.), *Advances in applied psycholinguistics* (*Vol. 2*, pp. 105–141). Cambridge: Cambridge University Press.

Posner, M. I., & Snyder, C. R. R. (1975). Facilitation and inhibition in the processing of signals. In P. Rabbitt & S. Dornic (Eds.), *Attention and performance* (*Vol. 5*, pp. 669–682). London: Academic Press.

Ruff, H. A., & Rothbart, M. K. (1996). *Attention in early development.* New York: Oxford University Press.

*Schiller, P. H. (1966). Developmental study of color-word interference. *Journal of Experimental Psychology, 72*, 105–108.

Stanovich, K. E. (1986). Matthew effects in reading: Some consequences of individual differences in the acquisition of literacy. *Reading Research Quarterly, 21*, 360–407.

Stanovich, K. E. (1990). Concepts in developmental theories of reading skill: Cognitive resources, automaticity, and modularity. *Developmental Review, 10*, 72–100.

Stanovich, K. E., Cunningham, A. E., & West, R. F. (1981). A longitudinal study of the development of automatic recognition skills in first graders. *Journal of Reading Behavior, 13*, 57–74.

*Stroop, J. R. (1935). Studies of interference in serial verbal reactions. *Journal of Experimental Psychology, 18*, 643–662. Reprinted (1992) in the *Journal of Experimental Psychology: General, 121*(1), 15–23.

Treisman, A. M. (1969). Strategies and models of selective attention. *Psychological Review, 76*, 282–299.

Treisman, A. M. (1988). Features and objects: The fourteenth Bartlett Memorial Lecture. *Quarterly Journal of Experimental Psychology, 40A*, 201–237.

West, R. F., & Stanovich, K. E. (1978). Automatic contextual facilitation in readers of three ages. *Child Development, 49*, 717–727.

West, R. F., & Stanovich, K. E. (1979). The development of automatic word recognition skills. *Journal of Reading Behavior, 11*, 211–219.

Zbrodoff, N. J., & Logan, G. D. (1986). On the autonomy of mental processes: A case study of arithmetic. *Journal of Experimental Psychology: General, 115*, 118–130.

Zeaman, D., & House, B. J. (1963). The role of attention in retardate discrimination learning. In N. R. Ellis (Ed.), *Handbook of mental deficiency*. New York: McGraw-Hill.

INDIVIDUAL DATA SHEET

Title: - . (Interference Proneness)_____

E: _____ **Day and Date:**_____ **S–Sex:** *M or F* **Grade:**_____

S:_____ **Birthdate:**_____ **CA:**_____

Time Begun:_____ **Time Ended:**_____ **Elapsed Time:**_____ **Room:**_____

	Response Sequences	Time Scores	Notes
Card W	Y R G Y R B R G		
	Y R B G B G R G		
	B Y R B Y B G Y		
	B R Y R B Y B Y		
	G B G B R G R Y		
	G Y R G Y G R B	_____	
Card C	G Y R B G B G R		
	Y R G Y R G Y B		
	R B Y B G B R Y		
	G Y R Y B R G Y		
	R G Y R G Y B G		
	B Y B G R B R B	_____	
Card CW	R B Y G Y B G R		
	Y G R Y B R G R		
	B G B Y B G R Y		
	B R G Y G R Y G		
	Y R G R B G B G		
	Y B Y B R Y R B	_____	

Derived Scores:

CW–C _____

CW/C _____

GROUP DATA SHEET

Title: *Interference Proneness*

E:_____   Day and Date:_____

Hypothesis:

Method and Procedure: (as described in text with following modifications, if any)

Group Results and Analysis:

TABLE F4.1
SUMMARY OF MEASURES OF CENTRAL TENDENCY FOR STROOP TEST SCORES

Group	Scores				
	W	C	CW	CW–C	CW/C
Grade 1					
Boys					
Girls					
Combined					
Grade 3					
Boys					
Girls					
Combined					
Grade 5					
Boys					
Girls					
Combined					
Combined Grades					
Boys					
Girls					
Total					

TABLE F4.2
3 X 2 ANALYSIS OF VARIANCE FOR STROOP TEST SCORES

Source of Variation	df	W		C		CW		CW–C		CW/C	
		MS	F	MS	F	MS	F	MS	F	MS	F
Between Grades	2										
Between Sexes	1										
Grade X Sex	2										
Within Group (Error)	$N - 6 =$										
Total ($N = 1$)											

TABLE F4.3
PEARSON CORRELATION MATRIX FOR TOTAL GROUP

	W	C	CW	CW–C	CW/C
W					
C					
CW					
CW–C					
CW/C					

PEARSON CORRELATION MATRIX FOR ALL BOYS AND GIRLS

	W	C	CW	CW–C	CW/C
W					
C					
CW					
CW–C					
CW/C					

Note: Correlations for boys appear below and to the left of the diagonal. Correlations for girls appear above and to the right.

PEARSON CORRELATION MATRIX FOR FIRST GRADE BOYS AND GIRLS

	W	C	CW	CW–C	CW/C
W					
C					
CW					
CW–C					
CW/C					

PEARSON CORRELATION MATRIX FOR THIRD GRADE BOYS AND GIRLS

	W	C	CW	CW–C	CW/C
W					
C					
CW					
CW–C					
CW/C					

PEARSON CORRELATION MATRIX FOR FIFTH GRADE BOYS AND GIRLS

	W	C	CW	CW–C	CW/C
W					
C					
CW					
CW–C					
CW/C					

Note: Correlations for boys appear below and to the left of the diagonal. Correlations for girls appear above and to the right.

Experiment 5

Semantic Processing in a Picture–Word Interference Task

In the preceding experiment, sex and age differences in the ability to resist distraction or interference were investigated via the Stroop Color-Word Test. With the Stroop, the task of labeling colors that had incongruent color words on them (i.e., a red strip with the word *blue* on it) clearly took longer than labeling colors without such words. There are several theoretical explanations (input competition, response competition), but what struck many experimenters was the child's seeming inability to ignore the words, even when it was to the child's benefit to do so.

Rosinski, Golinkoff, and Kukish (1975) used a picture–word interference task to assess the processing of the semantic content (the meaning) of words and pictures. The subject's task was either to read the words or label the pictures when pictures and words were superimposed. The degree of congruence between the paired picture and word (i.e., picture of a hen with word *hen*, picture of a hen with word *pig*) was varied, to determine whether the time to perform the task was longer when the *meaning* of the pictures and words did not agree.

Recent studies of reading indicate that the development of reading may proceed through increasing levels of complexity. Beginning readers many use a decoding process to translate graphemes into auditory representations (Gibson & Levin, 1975); average or skilled readers may be able to access directly the meaning of a word without an intervening decoding process or articulatory stage (Kolers, 1970; Rosinski et al., 1975). The point at which the semantic content of a word is automatically processed is, therefore, of great interest to researchers. LaBerge and Samuel's (1974) theory of automatic information processing has been very influential.

We shall attempt to replicate a portion of the Rosinski, Golinkoff, and Kukish (1975) study, using their materials with permission, with

3 grades (second, sixth, adult)

2 tasks (label picture, read words)

2 congruence levels (100%, 0%).

The questions being asked are

Are there age differences in the time scores on this picture-word interference task?

Which task is more difficult (i.e., takes longer): labeling pictures or reading words?

What is the effect of decreasing congruence between words and pictures?

What interactions exist among the three variables (grades, tasks, congruence levels)?

Hypotheses

1. Word reading requires (less) (more) (equal) response time than picture labeling.

2. Response times for either task (are faster) (are slower) at higher ages.

3. For either task, response times are (greater) (smaller) when there is no congruence between the words and pictures than when there is congruence.

4. When words and pictures are incongruent, interference is (greater) (smaller) for picture labeling when words are distracter items than for word reading when pictures are distracter items.

5. Other interactions?

6. Sex differences?

Method

Subjects

Boys and girls from second grade, sixth grade, and college level. The second graders should be of average (or better) reading ability.

Materials

4 stimulus sheets (Figure F5.2)

Stopwatch

Individual Data Sheet

The stimulus sheets are made of 8.5 in. × 11 in. (21.6 cm × 28 cm) paper divided into 20 cells of equal size. The sheets can be mounted on cardboard and laminated with clear contact paper. The picture warmup card has 20 line drawings of common animals or objects. The word warmup card has words naming the same (absent) animals or objects. In one experimental condition, 100% congruence, a word matching the drawing is superimposed. In another experimental condition, 0% congruence, the drawing and its superimposed word do not match. Rosinski et al. (1975) randomly paired their incongruent words and drawings with the constraint that semantic categories were not crossed, that is, an animal drawing was given an animal name, not an object name.

Procedure

The general procedure is the same as in the Rosinski et al. (1975) experiment, except that (a) multiexperimenters are used; and (b) there are two rather than three levels of congruence between words and pictures.

Because each child works with both levels of congruence, 100% or 0%, in counterbalanced order, a repeated measures analysis of variance for this factor is required. Your instructor will tell you whether to use the 0–100%, or 100–0% congruence sequence.

Half the subjects in each age–sex group are told to read the words; half are told to label the pictures. Children are tested individually. For any one child, only three of the four cards accompanying this chapter are used.

Procedure, Pictures Group

Warm-up Task. Place page that contains only drawings before the child and say, **"Here's a page with pictures on it. Please name them for me."** [Correct the labels gently, e.g.,] **"Let's call that a hen [instead of chicken]."**

Test Tasks. **"Now I'll give you another sheet with pictures on it. Just name the pictures again for me. There will be some words, too, but you should ignore the words. Just name the pictures, and this time do it as fast as you can. OK. Just name the *pictures* as *fast* as you can. Ready?"** [Place sheet with 0% or 100% congruence flat in front of subject.] **"Go!"** [Start timing; stop with last response. Record to nearest .1 second. Note errors on data sheet.]

"**Here's another sheet with pictures on it.**" [Repeat the above instructions for the test task. Place the second experimental sheet, and time the performance.]

Procedure, Words Group

Warm-up Tasks. Place page that contains only words before the child, and say, "**Here's a page with words on it. Please read the words for me.**"

Test Tasks. "**Now I'll give you another sheet with words on it. Just read the words again for me. There will be some pictures, too, but you should ignore the pictures. Just read the words, and this time do it as fast as you can. OK. Just read the *words* as *fast* as you can. Ready?**" [Place the sheet with 0% or 100% congruence flat in front of subject.] "**Go!**" [Start time; stop with last response. Record to nearest .1 second. Note errors on data sheet.]

"**Here's another sheet with words on it.**" [Repeat the above instructions for the word-test task. Place the sheet, and time the performance.]

Results

Scoring. Each child has two time scores: the number of seconds to do the 0% congruence card and the number of seconds to do the 100% congruence card. Find the difference between these two scores; we will call that the difference score.

Data Analysis. Record the scores from the Individual Data Sheets to the Master Group Data Sheet for the condition (pictures, words), grade, and sex of your subjects.

Find the mean, medians, and *SD*s for each group, and enter these in Table F5.1 of the Group Data Sheet. Use the mean scores to fill in Fig. F5.1, to illustrate the times for three grade levels of picture-labeling and word-reading tasks as a function of stimulus congruence. You may wish to use two graphs, one for picture-labeling and one for word-reading.

Using the 0% and 100% time scores, run a 2 tasks (pictures vs. words) X 3 grade levels X 2 congruence levels analysis of variance, with repeated measures on the last factor, and enter the summary in Table F5.2. State the significant main effects and interactions found.

(Optional). Using the difference in time between the 0% and 100% congruence condition for each subject, perform a two-way analysis of variance for the three grades and two tasks. Enter the summary in Table F5.3. State the significance and direction of processing interference by grade.

*F*s that are significant and have more than one degree of freedom in the numerator of the *F* ratio should be followed with *post hoc* tests (like Scheffé, Newman-Keuls, simple effects) to determine exactly where the significant differences occur. For example, a significant *F* for age effects would tell you that there were significant differences between the grades but would not itself tell you whether each grade differed from each other grade; the second grade could differ significantly from the sixth and adult, and the latter two may not significantly differ.

To help in the evaluation and discussion, you may wish to summarize your results in Table F5.4.

Discussion

Relate your findings explicitly to each of your hypotheses or expectations, and to the Rosinski et al. (1975) findings. Evaluate and interpret your findings.

For your age subjects, was word reading always faster than picture labeling, even at the youngest age group? How do your results relate to the suggestion that the meaning of pictures is more readily accessible than the meaning of words to very young children?

How do you account for the grade effect? As Rosinski et al. (1975) pointed out, differences in time scores between younger and older children may result from differences in response execution (younger children taking longer to respond), label availability, scan rate, reading speed, and so on. These are not themselves measures of interference between picture and word processing!

To pursue the age difference differently, the difference in time between the 0% and 100% tasks was analyzed. A significant age F (Table F5.3) would show that there was more processing interference at one age than another. Discuss this. Notice that this analysis eliminates the repeated measures approach of Table F5.2.

Your expectation that 100% congruence would result in faster processing than 0% congruence was undoubtedly confirmed (hypothesis 3). Look at your task X congruence F and post hoc tests to see whether hypothesis 4 is confirmed.

The grade X task interaction F helps you evaluate the age-related effects of picture-labeling versus word-reading. Rosinski and Gibson disagree here. How do you interpret your findings?

What do the other interaction findings add to your interpretation? Fig. F5.1 is helpful in this regard. Table F5.4 gives you a summary view of similarities and differences between your results, those of a similar laboratory class, and published results. Rosinski et al. (1975) used the .01 probability level for significance. If your class used the .05 level (as ours did), notice the effect on your conclusions.

Since the Rosinski et al. (1975) study did a preliminary analysis that revealed no effect of sex, their data for boys and girls were pooled. Did you notice that the anovas (Tables F5.2 and F5.3) do not permit you to speak to expectation 6?

This experiment used average and above-average readers. What do you think would happen with below-average readers? Golinkoff and Rosinski (1976) have worked with third and fifth grade skilled and less skilled comprehenders. Briggs and Underwood (1982) studied good and poor readers among university students and 10–12 year olds. Walker and Poteet (1989) studied semantic processing in learning-disabled and non-learning-disabled 4th and 5th graders.

The picture–word interference test and its variations have been widely used, not only with good and bad readers, and LD and non-LD subjects, as mentioned, but also with retarded and nonretarded adolescents (McFarland & Sandy, 1982), and with bilinguals and second-language learners (Goodman et al., 1985), and with wide age ranges. How do these results relate to your age findings and/or to La Berge and Samuel's model of automatic word processing in reading? What does Guttentag's finding that there is more interference from incongruous within-category printed words than cross-category words suggest about our data?

What other experiments can you devise to investigate semantic processing?

Like several experiments in this section, this research combines methodological aspects of a traditional behaviorist approach with the current accepted view of the child as an active processor of information. Reading specialists and researchers in developmental psycholinguistics share this interest in the relation of semantic aspects of language to cognitive processes. Stage theorists might be especially interested in the results of the grade X task interaction, or grade X congruence-level interaction. Why?

Selected Bibliography

Briggs, P., & Underwood, G. (1982). Phonological coding in good and poor readers. *Journal of Experimental Child Psychology, 34*(1), 93–112.

Brooks, P. J., & MacWhinney, B. (2000). Phonological priming in children's picture naming. *Journal of Child Language, 27*(2), 335–366.

Dyer, F. N. (1973). The Stroop phenomenon and its use in the study of perceptual, cognitive, and response processes. *Memory and Cognition, 1*, 106–120.

*Ehri, L. C. (1976). Do words really interfere in naming pictures? *Child Development, 47*, 502–505.

Ehri, L. C., & Wilce, L. S. (1979). Does word training increase or decrease interference in a Stroop task? *Journal of Experimental Child Psychology, 27*(2), 352–364.

Fraisse, P. (1969). Why is naming longer than reading? *Acta Psychologica, 30*, 96–103.

Gibson, E. J. (1991). *An odyssey in learning and perception.* Cambridge, MA: MIT Press.

Gibson, E. J., & Levin, H. (1975). *The psychology of reading.* Cambridge, MA: M.I.T. Press.

Golinkoff, R. M., & Rosinski, R. R. (1976). Decoding, semantic processing, and reading comprehension skill. *Child Development, 47*, 252–258.

Goodman, G. S., Haith, M., Guttentag, R. E., & Rao, S. (1985). Automatic processing of word meaning: Intralingual and interlingual interference. *Child Development, 56*(1), 103–118.

Guttentag, R. E. (1984). Semantic memory organization in second graders and adults. *Journal of General Psychology, 110*(1), 81–86.

*Guttentag, R. E., & Haith, M. M. (1978). Automatic processing as a function of age and reading ability. *Child Development, 49*, 707–716.

Klein, G. S. (1964). Semantic power measured through the interference of words with color naming. *American Journal of Psychology, 77*, 576–588.

Kolers, P. A. (1970). Three stages of reading. In H. Levin & J.P. Williams (Eds.), *Basic studies in reading* (pp. 90–118). New York: Basic Books.

LaBerge, D., & Samuels, S. J. (1974). Toward a theory of automatic information processing in reading. *Cognitive Psychology, 6*, 293–323.

McFarland, C. E., & Sandy, J. T. (1982). Automatic and conscious processing in retarded and nonretarded adolescents. *Journal of Experimental Child Psychology, 33*(1), 20–38.

Perfetti, C. A., & Hogaboam, T. (1975). The relationship between single word decoding and reading comprehension skill. *Journal of Educational Psychology, 67*, 461–469.

Posner, M. I., & Snyder, C. R. R. (1975). Attention and cognitive control. In R. L. Solso (Ed.), *Information processing and cognition: The Loyola Symposium* (pp. 55–85). Hillsdale, NJ: Lawrence Erlbaum Associates. (This is a theoretical article, which is difficult reading, but valuable in understanding the theoretical arguments behind attention and automatic processing.)

Roe, K., Jahn-Samilo, J., Juarez, L, Mickel, N., Royer, I., & Bates, E. (2000). Contextual effects on word production: A lifespan study. *Memory and cognition, 28*(5), 756–765.

*Rosinski, R. R. (1977). Picture-word interference is semantically based. *Child Development, 48*, 643–647.

*Rosinski, R. R., Golinkoff, R. M., & Kukish, K. S. (1975). Automatic semantic processing in a picture-word interference task. *Child Development, 46*, 247–253.

Schiller, P. H. (1966). Developmental study of color-word interference. *Journal of Experimental Psychology, 72*(1), 105–108.

*Stanovich, K. E., Cunningham, A. E., & West, R. F. (1981). A longitudinal study of the development of automatic recognition skills in first graders. *Journal of Reading Behavior, Vol. XIII*(1), 57–74.

Walker, S. C., & Poteet, J. A. (1989). Influencing memory performance in learning disabled students through semantic processing. *Learning Disabilities Research, 5*(1), 25–32.

Weiner, M., & Cromer, W. (1967). Reading and reading difficulty: A conceptual analysis. *Harvard Educational Review, 37*, 620–643.

West, R. F., & Stanovich, K. E. (1979). The development of automatic word recognition skills. *Journal of Reading Behavior, Vol. XI*(3), 211–219.

Willows, D. M. (1974). Reading between the lines: Selective attention in good and poor readers. *Child Development, 45*, 408–415.

INDIVIDUAL DATA SHEET

Group/Condition: <u>P/W</u> Sequence: 100%_____ 0%_____

Title: <u>Picture-Word Interference Test</u>

E: _____   Day and Date:_____   S–Sex: *M or F* Grade:____

S:_____   Birthdate:_____   CA:_____

Time Begun:_____   Time Ended:_____   Elapsed Time:_____   Room:_____

100 Percent Congruence

COW	POT	DOG	HAT
FROG	SEAL	KEY	FISH
SHOE	BEAR	BOAT	PIG
DUCK	GUN	LOCK	CAT
SOCK	CUP	HEN	FLAG

Time _____ sec.

0 Percent Congruence

Picture:	COW	POT	DOG	HAT
Word:	HEN	FLAG	CAT	CUP
Picture:	FROG	SEAL	KEY	FISH
Word:	BEAR	PIG	SOCK	DUCK
Picture:	SHOE	BEAR	BOAT	PIG
Word:	LOCK	FISH	GUN	SEAL
Picture:	DUCK	GUN	LOCK	CAT
Word	FROG	BOAT	SHOE	DOG
Picture:	SOCK	CUP	HEN	FLAG
Word:	KEY	HAT	COW	POT

Time: _____ sec.

Difference: _____ sec.
(0%-100%)

Observations:

GROUP DATA SHEET

Title: *Semantic Processing in a Picture-Word Interference Test*

E:_____   Day and Date:_____

Hypothesis:

Method and Procedure: (as described in text with following modifications, if any)

Group Results and Analysis:

TABLE F5.1
SUMMARY OF MEASURES OF CENTRAL TENDENCY AND VARIABILITY FOR TIME SCORES
(IN SECONDS)

Group	*Pictures*			*Words*			*Combined Mean*		
	Mean	Median	SD	Mean	Median	SD	Mean	Median	SD
2nd grade									
100 percent									
0 percent									
Combined									
Difference score									
6th grade									
100 percent									
0 percent									
Combined									
Difference score									
Adult									
100 percent									
0 percent									
Combined									
Difference score									
Combined Ages									
100 percent									
0 percent									
Combined									
Difference Score									

TABLE F5.2
2 X 3 X 2 REPEATED MEASURES ANALYSIS OF VARIANCE OF TIME SCORES

Source	Sum of Squares	df	Mean Square	F	p
Between Tasks (T) (pictures vs. words)		1			
Between Ages (A)		2			
T X A		2			
Within Group (Error)					
Total		N - 1			
Between Congruence Levels (C)		1			
T X C		1			
A X C		2			
T X A C		2			
Within Group (Error)					
Total		N			
Grand Sum		2 N - 1			

TABLE F5.3
TWO-WAY ANALYSIS OF VARIANCE OF DIFFERENCE IN TIME SCORES BETWEEN 100% AND 0% CONGRUENCE TESTS, FOR THREE AGES AND TWO TASKS

Source	Sum of Squares	df	Mean Square	F	p
Between Ages		2			
Between Tasks (pictures vs. words)		1			
Ages X Tasks		2			
Within Group (Error)					
Total		N - 1			

TABLE F5.4

COMPARISON OF RESULTS FROM SEVERAL PICTURE–WORD INTERFERENCE STUDIES

Analysis of Variance Effect of	Rosinski et al. 1975 Study	Nadelman laboratory* 1975 Study	Your Replication
Task	$F(1,66) = 183.8, p < .01$	$F(1,54) = 6.55, p < .05$	
Age	$F(2,66) = 141.13, p < .01$	$F(2,54) = 18.84, p < .01$	
Congruence	$F(2,132) = 102.36, p < .01$	$F(1,54) = 108.36, p < .01$	
Task X Age	$F(2,66) = 12.05, p < .01$	$F(2,54) = 1.57, p > .05$	
Task X Congruence	$F(2,132) = 49.83, p < .01$	$F(1,54) = 17.48, p < .01$	
Age X Congruence	$F(4,132) = 20.98, p < .01$	$F(2,54) = 19.88, p < .01$	
Task X Age X Congruence	$F(4,132) = 6.59, p < .01$	$F(2,54) = .62, p > .05$	

*Your effects may be different than ours, since we crossed semantic categories in the 0 percent condition, putting an object name on an animal in the 1975 study. See Rosinski (1977) for a study of crossed and noncrossed semantic categories, and Guttentag (1984).

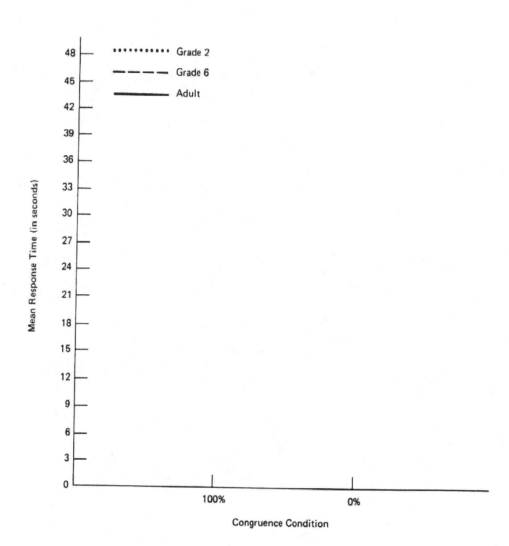

Fig. F5.1. Mean time scores for three grade levels of picture labeling and word reading tasks as a function of stimulus congruence.

Hen	Flag	Cat	Cup
Bear	Pig	Sock	Duck
Lock	Fish	Gun	Seal
Frog	Boat	Shoe	Dog
Key	Hat	Cow	Pot

Fig. F5.2. Stimulus Cards.

Fig. F5.2. (Continued)

Fig. F5.2. (Continued)

Fig. F5.2. (Continued)

Experiment 6

The Influence
of Category–Blocked
and Random Presentation
on Free Recall and Clustering

Although the study of memory is one of the oldest and most respectable areas in psychology, and the study of organization in recall is no newcomer, truly developmental studies of mnemonic skills are of relatively recent vintage (Cole, Frankel, & Sharp, 1971; Reese & Lipsitt, 1970). By 1970, Reese and Lipsitt were still able to comment disparagingly that "child psychologists have merely dabbled now and then in the area [of verbal learning and behavior] and the methodological naiveté of dabblers has often been painfully evident" (p. 221). In the last three and a half decades more studies (and more sophisticated studies) have been appearing in *Child Development*, *Developmental Psychology*, and *Journal of Experimental Child Psychology*, and the high level of interest at conventions indicates a continuing stream of articles. Indeed, the interest and output are now so high that a new journal, *Memory*, was begun in 1993. The new *Handbook of Child Psychology* includes an article on memory by Schneider and Bjorklund (1998).

Studies of the behavioral and neuroanatomical composition of memory systems and subsystems have burgeoned as a consequence of two technical developments working synergistically: sophisticated computers and modern brain scanning techniques (Schachter & Tulving, 1994). In the last decade, about 20 categories have been identified that the brain uses to organize knowledge: fruits/vegetables, plants, animals, body parts, colors, numbers, letters, nouns, verbs, proper names, faces, facial expressions, several emotions, and several features of sound (New York Times, May 30, 1995, pp.B5–6). Another exciting finding is that aspects of a specific memory are processed in different areas of the brain. Brain scanning techniques, although productive, have not been generally used with normal children, however.

Experiments with children have varied in their use of single or repeated trials; in their use of pictures, words, or objects as stimuli; in their use of differing indices to compute clustering scores; in their sophistication and control over the frequency, meaning, or association value of the stimulus items or the categories; and in the amount of time allowed for presentation and recall, respectively. It is no surprise to learn, therefore, that some of the conceptualizations of the memory process in children, and some of the empirical findings, are still in debate.

The basic conceptualization, however, appears relatively noncontroversial. The memory process involves several stages:

initial *acquisition* of information

storage of this information, and

retrieval or recall or utilization of the stored information.

Although Gestalt psychologists, psychoanalysts, and experimental psychologists apparently agreed on these distinctions for many decades, it was long afterward that the separation of the memory processes into these stages began to be reflected in the research and theorizing of psychologists. Tulving and Pearlstone (1966) were able to separate the storage and retrieval stages by holding the conditions of acquisition and storage constant, and varying the retrieval conditions at the time of recall.

There are other empirical findings, like older children performing a free recall verbal learning task better than younger children, that are typically (but not invariably) reported, but there is not yet agreement on the explanation. Current theories to account for an age difference include notions of mediational deficiency; inadequacy in rehearsal and planning strategies; an immature nervous system; a less rich associative network to verbal stimuli, that is, stimulus-meaningfulness (Richman, Nida, & Pittman, 1976). Most theorists agree now that stimulus information is transformed and/or organized by the individual, and the individual is in turn transformed by this interaction. The interest lies in mapping the developmental changes in this process and in specifying which variables are affecting mnemonic skills. In other words, why and under what conditions does memory improve in the free recall situation with age? The following experiment focuses on the effect on the child's recall of varying the organization of the stimuli presented.

Problem

One facet of memory research that is attracting the interest of developmental psychologists and that is hypothesized to play a role in the development of mnemonic skills is the type and degree of organization used in encoding information and in retrieving it from memory. To differentiate these stages, researchers have studied organization in the presentation of the test items and organization in the recall of those items by the subject. Commonly, the type of organization studied has been semantic organization of words or objects or pictures.

The kinds of data produced by free recall tasks include measures of the amount of recall per trial and over trials, and measures of organization. The latter includes measures of subjective organization, which reflect the child's ability to "impose" organization on a list of unrelated items, and associative or category clustering, which reflects the child's ability to "perceive" existing organization. Bousfield (1953) used the term clustering for the tendency to recall items in groups or clusters of semantically related words.

A typical experimental design involves the use of test items that can be grouped into categories of semantically related items, like furniture, parts of body, or fruit. Half the children receive these items in a random presentation; half receive the same items already organized into blocks, that is, all examples of fruit, followed by all examples of furniture, and so on. By using more than one age group and more than one sex, the data can provide some answers to the following questions.

Questions and Hypotheses

1. Does blocked presentation of semantically related items facilitate amount of recall more than random presentation?
   Hypothesis:

2. Does blocked presentation of semantically related items facilitate clustering of recall more than random presentation?

3. Do older children recall more than younger children?

4. Do older children cluster their responses more than younger children?

5. Is there an interaction between age and presentation condition in amount of recall? That is, do older children benefit differently than younger children from the presentation condition?

6. Is there an interaction between age and presentation condition in clustering of recall?

7. Sex differences?

8. Is amount of recall related to amount of clustering of recall?

Method

Subjects

Boys and girls from second and sixth grade

Materials

23 pictures (3 practice and 20 test items)

Data sheet

The pictures were drawn from similar items used in experiments by Moely (Moely, Olson, Halwes, & Flavell, 1969; Moely & Jeffrey, 1974; Moely & Shapiro, 1971) and Kobasigawa (1974), and Kobasigawa and Middleton (1972). They represent four instances each of five common categories (food, toys, furniture, vehicles, body parts). They are black and white line drawings, mounted on 3 X 3 in. (7.62 cm X 7.62 cm) cards. See Fig. F6.1 at the end of the Experiment.

Procedure

Half the children in each grade-sex group are presented the pictures in block order; half are presented the pictures in random order. The experimenter presents one item at a time, pronouncing its verbal label; the child repeats the label immediately and then has one more second of viewing time before the next item is presented. After the 20 items have been presented, the child recalls aloud as many as possible.

The random order list has the constraint that no two stimulus items from the same category appear next to each other. Several different randomized orders of stimulus lists are used. See Table F6.1.

The block order list always has items from the same category presented serially, but both the order of categories and the order of items within a category are randomized. See Table F6.2.

The verbal instructions that follow are adapted from Cole, Frankel, and Sharp (1971). Note, however, that our experimenter provides the verbal label for the picture; there is a brief practice; and there is only one trial. These are important differences!

Instructions. Paste or recopy the assigned list with the specific presentation order on the left column of your Individual Data Sheet, and arrange your pictures in a pile in the corresponding order. Then collect your subject.

The child is seated at a table opposite the experimenter. The experimenter says, "[Subject's name], **I'm interested in how well people remember what they see. I have a group of 20 pictures that I am going to show you one at a time. I will name each thing as I show it to you, and you repeat the name right away aloud. After I show you all of the pictures, I want you to tell me all the ones that you remember, okay? Let's practice first with these three.**"

Practice. Present one of the three practice cards, verbally label it, elicit the same label from the child immediately if it is not promptly given by instructing, "Say it." Count "one second" silently to yourself, and place the next item covering the first. Repeat. After the three are shown, say, **"Tell me which pictures you saw,"** and note responses. Draw a line on your data sheet.

Test. "That was good. Now I'm going to show you a lot more." Show and label the 20 as above, waiting one silent second after the child has named each picture before showing the next. Remove all pictures and say, **"Now tell me all of these that you remember."**

Write the child's answers in the exact order he or she says them. Give the child time to think, and then encourage with phrases like **"Can you remember some more? What others did you see?"** Praise the performance when the child is finished. Use abbreviations or initial letters, if necessary, when jotting down the child's answers, but try not to slow the child down to accommodate your writing speed. Certainly do not permit conversation or digressions in the course of this experiment. If the child repeats an item twice or more and asks if he or she has already said that, just say softly and quickly, **"That's OK; go on."**

Results

Scoring. Carefully count the number of responses given by the child. How many of these were practice items or items *not* among the 20 shown to the child? Note these on your data sheet summary as the number of *intrusions*. (If a child said "lips" instead of "mouth," we scored this as a recall item, not as an intrusion. Your class may decide to be less liberal.)

Often a child will say the same items twice, separated by other items. These appear in your summary as number of *repetitions*.

The total number of responses minus the repetitions and intrusions equal the number recalled. The maximum possible, of course, is 20.

There are five categories of pictures. If a child gives even one instance from that group, score it as a category. From how many categories did the child recite items? Enter that as number of categories. The maximum score is 5.

Below that, enter the actual number of vehicles, furniture, food, toys, and body parts recalled, not counting intrusions and repetitions. These should sum to the number recalled, entered earlier.

The number recalled divided by the number of categories provides the mean per category. The maximum score is 4.

If a child gives two, three, or four items from the same category serially, that is a *run*. Circle each run, and enter the number of runs in the summary.

Count the number of items in each of your circles (runs); add up these numbers and divide by the number of runs. That provides the mean length of run. (Notice that if a run of only one item had been included, the mean length of run would be smaller.)

There are a number of indices that evaluate the extent to which a recall is organized, and these are described by Moely and Jeffrey (1974). The item clustering index (ICI) you are using was developed by Robinson (1966), and it does not assume that organization and recall are independent of one another. It does assume, however, that all items within a given category are available for recall if at least one word from that category is recalled, so it does take into account the number of categories recalled by the child.

$$ICI = \frac{r}{c\,(W_c - 1)}$$

r = the number of category pairs occurring contiguously in recall

c = the number of categories represented in the child's recall

W_c = the number of items per category in the stimulus list (in our experiment, $W_c = 4$)

All these scores provide a huge amount of information for analysis. Our emphasis is on amount recalled and clustering scores, but you may wish to collate and eyeball the other scores.

Data Analysis. Record your subject's scores on the Master Data Sheet (provided by the instructor) for the appropriate subgroup. Compute the means, medians, and standard deviations for the amount recalled and the ICI scores, and enter in Table F6.3 on the Group Data Sheet.

Run a 2 conditions X 2 grades X 2 sexes analysis of variance on the recall and ICI scores, respectively, and enter the summary data in Table F6.4.

Run a Pearson *r* correlation between the recall and clustering scores for all your children. You may wish, also, to run two more *r*s, one for the blocked condition subjects, one for the random condition subjects.

State your results with regard to the main effects (condition, grade, sex) and interactions, giving *p* levels, for recall and clustering scores, respectively. State the relation between recall and clustering scores.

Discussion

Relate your findings to each of your hypotheses or expectations, and to the literature.

Was recall greater with blocked or random presentations? Do you agree with the blocked versus random condition results of Emmerich and Ackerman (1978), Fujishima (1979), Kobasigawa and Orr (1973), Moely and Shapiro (1971) and Sodian, Schneider, and Perlmutter (1986)?

Was clustering of recall greater with blocked or random presentation? Brown, Conover, Flores, and Goodman (1991) found that high clusterers recalled more than low clusterers, but that held whether or not the stimuli were blocked (contiguous) or random.

Your third and fourth hypotheses dealt with age effects on recall and cluster scores, respectively. Did your older children have significantly higher recall and clustering scores than your younger children (ignoring presentation condition)? There is agreement about age differences in recall (Bjorklund & Buchanan, 1989; Frankel & Rollins, 1985; Hasselhorn, 1992; Moely & Shapiro, 1971; Posnansky & Pellegrino, 1975; Todman, 1982), and that even holds for retarded children (Todman & File, 1985). There is less agreement, however, about age differences in cluster scores: Compare your results with those of Bjorklund, 1988; Emmerich and Ackerman, 1978; Hasselhorn, 1992; Hota, 1983; Posnansky and Pellegrino, 1975; Sodian, Schneider, and Perlmutter, 1986; Todman, 1982; Todman and File, 1985.

There is some disagreement in the literature about the grades at which blocked presentation becomes more effective than random presentation (Cole et al., 1971; Kobasigawa & Middleton, 1972; Moely & Shapiro, 1971.) Did your blocked presentation differentially increase recall and clustering as a function of age; that is, was there an interaction between age and presentation condition? Did your results agree with Cole et al. (1971), who did not find that blocked presentation differentially increased the recall of older children?

In accounting for your findings, do not forget the differences in procedure between our experiment and others. Cole et al. (1971), for example, present figures that show performance trial by trial. You would need to compare their *first* trial result to yours.

What effect does a one-trial design have on serial position effects? (Hint: See Cole et al., 1971). Would one expect more or less serial position recall under the blocked or random presentation? Why?

We used a serial presentation of our items. Other studies used simultaneous presentation. What difference might this make?

In addition to naming each item as we did, what do you think would have been the effect of labeling categories, that is, **"I have a group of 20 pictures of parts of the body, toys, fruit ...?"**

We used five categories, with four examples of each. What effect would you anticipate if the number of categories were decreased and examples were increased? or if the number of categories were increased and the number of examples were decreased?

Do you think some categories were more salient or "easy" for the children? How could you look at category differences in our design? Items can differ in their word frequency, and in their "category cohesiveness" or ease of organization. Moely and Jeffrey (1974) have some incisive comments about this that are well worth consideration. Bjorklund and Jacobs (1985) and Frankel and Rollins (1985) were also interested in the effects of differential familiarity of categories; that is, are categories that have high interitem association easier to recall and cluster than categories with low interitem association. To what extent are our materials open to these criticisms? Later in this book, there is a study of the recall of masculine and feminine items that, although in a different context (sex identity), is comparable to the present study in many facets.

Were your recall and clustering scores related as anticipated? (Look at the Pearson *r*.) Inspect Master Data Sheets and see if there were children with high recall scores who had low clustering scores. How does one explain these cases? See Brown et al. (1991).

Following their recall test, Moely and Jeffrey (1974) placed the list items on the table randomly and asked if the child had noticed some that were "kind of alike or go together." The child identified such sets and these sorts were recorded. If you had added this portion to your procedure, and subjected the sorting to ICI scoring, would you expect to obtain higher organization scores for the sorting task than for recall? Why? See Hasselhorn (1992).

Suppose you extended your design to a long-term memory study, and the children were asked to recall the items 48 hours following the presentation. Which presentation would lead to superior delayed recall—block or random? Why?

What other questions could be asked of your voluminous data?

Because of the operational definitions of the stimuli and responses, and the manipulation of the independent variable, you probably have no difficulty in seeing the relation of this study to which paradigm? Its relation to an organismic-developmental framework, as well, is perhaps less obvious. For children to recall items in groups or clusters of semantically related words, especially in the random presentation condition, requires cognitive processing, active structuring, and organizing. There are developmental, as well as individual, differences in this processing. Even back in the 1920s and 1930s, the Gestaltists were emphasizing the "construction" of memory—the way in which the subjects molded, assimilated, changed, or organized the remembered figure or story. Frankel and Moye (1984) examined the relationship between a child's Piagetian developmental level and clustering on a free-recall task. The concrete operational kindergartners displayed greater clustering in recall than the preoperational children. Much of the more recent developmental work on memory quietly weds facets of various approaches.

Selected Bibliography

Best, D. L. (1993). Inducing children to generate mnemonic organizational strategies: An examination of long-term retention and materials. *Developmental Psychology, 29*(2), 324–336.

Bjorklund, D. F. (1985). The role of conceptual knowledge in the development of organization in children's memory. In C. J. Brainerd & M. Pressley (Eds.), *Basic processes in memory development* (pp. 103–142). New York: Springer-Verlag.

Bjorklund, D. (1988). Acquiring a mnemonic: Age and category knowledge effects. *Journal of Experimental Child Psychology, 45*(1), 71–87.

Bjorklund, D. F., & Buchanan, J. (1989). Development and knowledge base differences in the acquisition and extension of a memory strategy. *Journal of Experimental Child Psychology, 48*(3), 451–471.

Bjorklund, D. F., & Jacobs, J. W. (1985). Associative and categorical processes in children's memory: The role of automaticity in the development of organization in free recall. *Journal of Experimental Child Psychology, 39*(3), 599–617.

Bousfield, W. A. (1953). The occurrence of clustering in the recall of randomly arranged associates. *Journal of General Psychology, 49*, 229–240.

Brown, S. C., Conover, J. N., Flores, L. M., & Goodman, K. M. (1991). Clustering and recall: Do high clusterers recall more than low clusterers because of clustering? *Journal of Experimental Psychology: Learning, Memory, & Cognition, 17*(4), 710–721.

*Cole., M., Frankel, F., & Sharp, D. (1971). Development of free recall learning in children. *Developmental Psychology, 4*, 109–123.

Cowan, N. (1995). *Attention and memory: An integrated framework.* New York: Oxford University Press.

Emmerich, H. J., & Ackerman, B. P. (1978). Developmental differences in recall: Encoding or retrieval? *Journal of Experimental Child Psychology, 25*(3), 514–525.

Frankel, M. T., & Moye, E. R. (1984). The effects of cognitive level on clustering in free recall. *Journal of Psychology, 117*(2), 239–243.

Frankel, M. T., & Rollins, H. A. (1985). Associative and categorical hypotheses of organization in the free recall of adults and children. *Journal of Experimental Child Psychology, 40*(2), 304–318.

Fujishima, T. (1979). The effects of stimulus presentation methods and category name on preschool children's recall of categorized items. *Japanese Journal of Psychology, 49*(6), 326–332.

Hagen, J. W., Jongeward, R. H., & Kail, R. V., Jr. (1975). Cognitive perspectives on the development of memory. In H. Reese (Ed.), *Advances in child development and behavior* (Vol. 10, pp. 57–101). New York: Academic Press.

Hasselhorn, M. (1992). Task dependency and the role of category typicality and metamemory in the development of an organizational strategy. *Child Development, 63*(1), 202–214.

Hota, N. (1983). Sex, grade, and SES differences in categorization in a recall task. *Psychological Studies, 28*(1), 48–50.

Kail, R. (1990). *The development of memory in children* (3rd ed.). New York: Freeman.

Kikuno, H. (1990). Examination of categorical clustering measurement in developmental studies of memory. *Japanese Psychological Review, 33*(4), 434–459.

Kobasigawa, A. (1974). Utilization of retrieval cues by children in recall. *Child Development, 45*, 127–134.

*Kobasigawa, A., & Middleton, D. B. (1972). Free recall of categorized items by children at three grade levels. *Child Development, 43*, 1067–1072.

Kobasigawa, A., & Orr, R. R. (1973). Free recall and retrieval speed of categorized items by kindergarten children. *Journal of Experimental Child Psychology, 15*(2), 187–192.

*Moely, B. E., & Jeffrey, W. E. (1974). The effect of organization training on children's free recall of category items. *Child Development, 45*, 135–143.

Moely, B. E., Olso, F. A., Halwes, T. G., & Flavell, J. H. (1969). Production deficiency in young children's clustered recall. *Developmental Psychology, 1*, 26–34.

*Moely, B. E., & Shapiro, S. I. (1971). Free recall and clustering at four age levels: Effects of learning to learn and presentation method. *Developmental Psychology, 4*(3), 490.

Moynahan, E. D. (1973). The development of knowledge concerning the effect of categorization upon free recall. *Child Development, 44*, 238–246.

Nelson, A. (1969). The organization of free recall by young children. *Journal of Experimental Child Psychology, 8*, 284–295.

Plumert, J. M. (1994). Flexibility in children's use of spatial and categorical organizational strategies in recall. *Developmental Psychology, 30*(5), 738–747.

Posnansky, C. J., & Pellegrino, J. W. (1975). Developmental changes in free recall and serial learning of categorically structured lists. *Bulletin of the Psychonomic Society, 5*(5), 361–364.

Rao, N. & Moely, B. E. (1989). Producing memory strategy maintenance and generalization by explicit or implicit training of memory knowledge. *Journal of Experimental Child Psychology, 48*(3), 335–352.

Reese, H. W., & Lipsitt, L. P. (1970). *Experimental child psychology*. New York: Academic Press.

Richman, C. L., Nida, S., & Pittman, L. (1976). Effects of meaningfulness on child free recall learning. *Developmental Psychology, 12*(5), 460–465.

Robinson, J. A. (1966). Category clustering in free recall. *Journal of Psychology, 62*, 279–285.

Schachter, D. L. & Tulving, E. (Eds.). (1994). *Memory systems 1994*. Cambridge, MA: MIT Press/A Bradford Book.

Schneider, W., & Bjorkland, D. F. (1998). Memory. In W. Damon (Ed.-in-Chief), D. Kuhn & R. Siegler (Vol. Eds.), *Handbook of child psychology: Vol. 2. Cognition, perception & language* (5th ed., pp. 467–522). New York: Wiley.

Shapiro, S. I., & Moely, B. E. (1971). Free recall, subjective organization, and learning to learn at three age levels. *Psychonomic Science, 23*, 189–191.

Sodian, B., Schneider, W., & Perlmutter, M. (1986). Recall, clustering, and metamemory in young children. *Journal of Experimental Child Psychology, 41*(3), 395–410.

Todman, J. B. (1982). Sequential consistency and subjective clustering in the multitrial free recall of children. *Acta Psychological, 51*(2), 163–180.

Todman, J. B. & File, P. E. (1985). Output organization in the free recall of mildly retarded children. *Acta Psychologica, 58*(3), 287–291.

Tulving, E., & Pearlstone, Z. (1966). Availability versus accessibility of information in memory for words. *Journal of Verbal Learning and Verbal Behavior, 5*, 381–391.

Yoshimura, E. K., Moely, B. E., & Shapiro, S. I. (1971). The influence of age and presentation order upon children's free recall and learning to learn. *Psychonomic Science, 23*, 261–263.

TABLE F6.1
LISTS FOR RANDOM PRESENTATION CONDITION, RECALL EXPERIMENT

Practice

List 1	List 2	List 3	List 4	List 5	List 6
Mitten	Fork	Mitten	Bell	Fork	Bell
Bell	Mitten	Fork	Mitten	Bell	Fork
Fork	Bell	Bell	Fork	Mitten	Mitten
Ball	Grapes	Foot	Apple	Lamp	Ear
Hand	TV	Bus	Hand	Foot	Swings
Swings	Apple	TV	Banana	Ball	Lamp
Ear	Hand	Banana	Couch	Pear	Ball
Truck	Bus	Doll	Train	Train	Grapes
Apple	Ear	Car	Pear	Ear	Car
Couch	Pear	Hand	TV	Bed	Hand
Doll	Swings	Couch	Mouth	Apple	Drum
Bus	Foot	Swings	Bus	Drum	Foot
TV	Car	Train	Doll	TV	Apple
Train	Banana	Lamp	Truck	Bus	TV
Grapes	Truck	Truck	Ear	Grapes	Train
Bed	Doll	Ear	Grapes	Truck	Bed
Mouth	Bed	Apple	Swings	Banana	Banana
Drum	Ball	Ball	Car	Doll	Truck
Banana	Lamp	Grapes	Bed	Car	Doll
Foot	Train	Mouth	Foot	Hand	Couch
Lamp	Couch	Bed	Drum	Swings	Mouth
Car	Drum	Pear	Lamp	Mouth	Pear
Pear	Mouth	Drum	Bell	Couch	Bus

219

TABLE F6.2
LISTS FOR CATEGORY—BLOCKED PRESENTATION CONDITION, RECALL EXPERIMENT

Practice

List 1	List 2	List 3	List 4	List 5
Fork	Mitten	Mitten	Fork	Bell
Mitten	Bell	Fork	Bell	Mitten
Bell	Fork	Bell	Mitten	Fork
Mouth	Ball	Grapes	Bus	TV
Foot	Swings	Pear	Car	Couch
Ear	Drum	Apple	Train	Lamp
Hand	Doll	Banana	Truck	Bed
Couch	Hand	Car	Swings	Grapes
Lamp	Foot	Train	Doll	Apple
Bed	Ear	Bus	Drum	Banana
TV	Mouth	Truck	Ball	Pear
Bus	Banana	Foot	Couch	Doll
Truck	Grapes	Ear	TV	Swings
Train	Apple	Mouth	Bed	Drum
Car	Pear	Hand	Lamp	Ball
Banana	Couch	Doll	Mouth	Truck
Apple	Bed	Swings	Hand	Train
Grapes	Lamp	Drum	Ear	Bus
Pear	TV	Ball	Foot	Car
Doll	Car	Lamp	Apple	Foot
Ball	Train	TV	Grapes	Hand
Swings	Truck	Couch	Banana	Ear
Drum	Bus	Bed	Pear	Mouth

INDIVIDUAL DATA SHEET

Title: Recall _____   Group/Condition: Blocked or Random

E: _____   Day and Date: _____   S–Sex: _M or F_   Grade: _____

S: _____   Birthdate: _____   CA: _____

Time Begun: _____   Time Ended: _____   Elapsed Time: _____   Room: _____

Presentation Order	Recall	Notes
Practice		
1		
2		
3		
Test		*Summary*
1		No. recalled _____
2		No. intrusions _____
3		No. repetitions _____
4		No. categories _____
5		No. veh. _____
6		furn. _____
7		fd. _____
8		tys. _____
9		b.p. _____
10		Mean per categ. _____
11		No. of runs _____
12		Mean length of run _____
13		ICI _____
14		
15		
16		
17		
18		
19		
20		

GROUP DATA SHEET

Title: *Influence of Category-Blocked and Random Presentation on Free Recall and Clustering*

E:_____   Day and Date:_____

Hypothesis:

Method and Procedure: (as described in text with following modifications, if any)

Group Results and Analysis:

TABLE F6.3
MEASURES OF CENTRAL TENDENCY AND VARIABILITY FOR RECALL SCORES AND ITEM CLUSTERING INDEX SCORES

Group	Amount Recalled			Item Clustering Index		
	Blocked	Random	Combined	Blocked	Random	Combined
Grade_____						
Boys						
Mean						
Median						
SD						
Girls						
Mean						
Median						
SD						
Combined						
Mean						
Median						
SD						

TABLE F6.3 (*Continued*)

Group	Amount Recalled			Item Clustering Index		
	Blocked	Random	Combined	Blocked	Random	Combined
Grade____						
Boys						
Mean						
Median						
SD						
Girls						
Mean						
Median						
SD						
Combined						
Mean						
Median						
SD						
Combined Grades						
Mean						
Median						
SD						
Total Boys						
Mean						
Median						
SD						
Total Girls						
Mean						
Median						
SD						

TABLE F6.4
SUMMARY OF 2 X 2 X 2 ANALYSIS OF VARIANCE FOR RECALL SCORES
AND ITEM CLUSTERING INDEX SCORES

Sources of Variance	df	Recall				Clustering			
		Sum of Squares	Mean Square	F	p	Sum of Squares	Mean Square	F	p
Between Conditions	1								
Between Grades	1								
Between Sexes	1								
Condition X Grade	1								
Condition X Sex	1								
Grade X Sex	1								
Condition X Grade X Sex	1								
Within Group Error									
Total (N - 1)									

Note: $F(1,)$ at 1 percent point = _____
$F(1,)$ at 5 percent point = _____

Fig. F6.1.

Fig. F6.1. (Continued)

Fig. F6.1. (Continued)

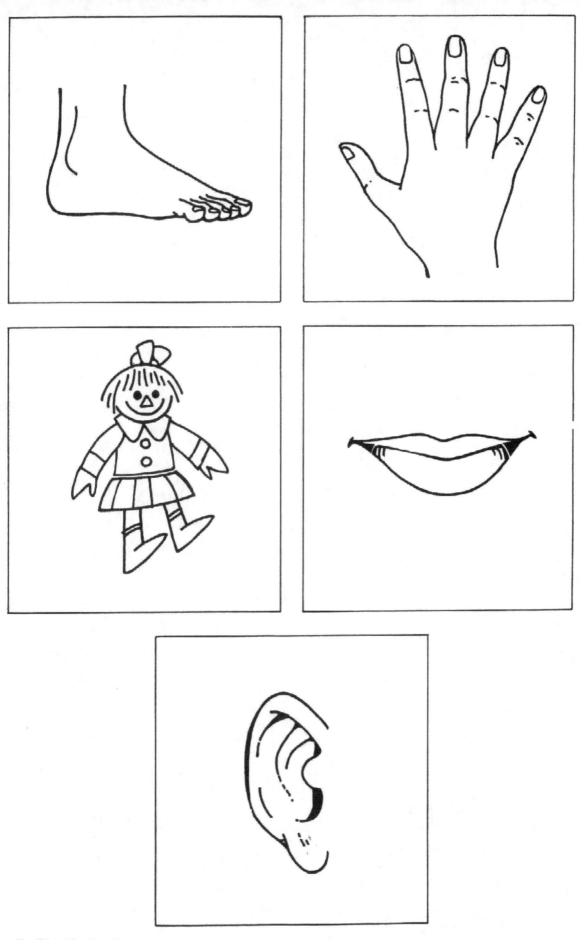

Fig. F6.1. (Continued)

Cognitive Development and Language

Susan A. Gelman

Cognitive Development: Continuities, Discontinuities, and Constancies

Cognitive development involves both continuities and discontinuities. There are striking changes in thought from infancy to adulthood: the amount and complexity of knowledge, the speed and efficiency with which information is encoded, the variety and flexibility of problem-solving strategies, the ability to plan complex sequences of actions, the ability to take on new perspectives, and the tendency to reflect on one's own mental processes. Change itself may be continuous (e.g., gradually increasing amounts of knowledge) or discontinuous (e.g., the acquisition of a new problem-solving insight). Often, it can be controversial how to characterize a particular cognitive change.

In addition to cognitive *change*, there are also important constancies in the mental life of a human throughout that same extended period: even preverbal infants form concepts, remember past events, and appreciate that the world obeys stable physical laws, that objects continue to exist even when out of sight, that causes differ from effects, etc. The endeavor in studying cognitive development is to discover what are normal beginnings, what are normative maturational patterns, and what are the environments, experiences, and conditions that can disrupt or promote such developments.

Early Abilities. One example of research revealing unsuspected early capacities concerns the question of how infants think about objects in their environment: Do they realize that objects (and other people) continue to exist even when they are beyond the infant's view? Years ago, Jean Piaget (1954) discovered that infants don't reach for desirable objects once they are hidden from view. For example, if a 6-month-old child is midreach for a toy, she will withdraw her hand once the toy is covered, and won't even look about for the object. Indeed, numerous studies over the past several decades show that the developmental path of looking for hidden objects is a slow and difficult one, with progress made in only small increments, and errors continuing for nearly two years (reviewed in Harris, 1983). Piaget's observations indicate that a fundamental change is taking place in infancy, in how children search for objects. The challenge is to understand what this behavior reveals about children's underlying thought processes.

Piaget interpreted children's errors to mean that infants don't realize that objects continue to exist when out of sight. For young children, according to Piaget, objects are not constant; they are repeatedly destroyed and recreated. More recently, however, researchers developed new techniques for examining infants' understanding of objects, using tasks that don't require reaching. Various methods measure eye gaze, shifts of attention, heartrate, or rate of sucking. Using these new measures, surprising new findings emerged: Infants as young as 3½ months of age indicate that they know that hidden objects continue to exist. For example, if an object disappears behind a screen, and then the screen is removed, infants gaze longer if no object is revealed than if the object remains. Infants appear to be surprised that the object has disappeared (Baillargeon, 1987). Thus, even young babies think about objects and other people as "permanent"—they keep track of objects and individuals after they have disappeared from view.

Similar kinds of studies reveal that infants have sophisticated perceptual abilities (can detect colors, patterns, depth; Banks & Salapatek, 1983), categorize sounds in linguistically appropriate ways (Eimas, Siqueland, Jusczyk, & Vigorito, 1971), recognize familiar voices (DeCasper & Fifer, 1980), can add small sums (e.g., realizing that if one object is placed with another object, this will result in two objects; Wynn, 1992), can imitate others' facial expressions (Meltzoff & Moore, 1983), appear to have concepts of unity and identity (Spelke, 1985), et cetera. Altogether, these studies reveal that even in early infancy, children are highly aware of their surroundings, are interpreting events around them in largely sensible ways, and are laying the foundations for important skills involving perception, language, and mathematics.

Developmental Changes. Despite these early abilities, there are also fundamental changes that occur with development. It is beyond the scope of this introduction to describe all those changes. Instead we will focus on one important and far-reaching difference between a young child and an adult: Namely, the adult has a detailed, complex, well-organized knowledge base. Recent studies demonstrate that knowledge or expertise can yield dramatic cognitive changes in memory, categorization, and problem-solving. For example, chess experts are particularly skilled at recalling the positions of pieces on a chess board, relative to those unskilled in chess (Chase & Simon, 1973), even though they are no more skilled at recalling non-chess items (such as a list of numbers). Interestingly, this pattern (of superior memory for chess positions by chess experts) holds even when the chess experts are children and the chess novices are adults (Chi, 1978). Expertise can even at times yield what seem like superhuman feats. For example, in one carefully documented study, an undergraduate of nonexceptional intelligence was given intensive practice daily, over more than a year, until he could recall long strings of digits–up to 79 digits in a row (compared to the average of 7 to 9; Ericsson, Chase, & Faloon, 1980).

Expertise also affects problem-solving: Child street vendors who have difficulty solving arithmetic problems in a standard academic context ("How much is 92 + 17?") perform substantially better when the same problem is set within the context of the foods that they sell (adding the cost of two fruits; Carraher, Carraher, & Schliemann, 1985). Categorization, too, is influenced by expertise. Children who are expert about dinosaurs organize that information in qualitatively different ways from children who are not so knowledgeable (Chi & Koeske, 1983).

Recently, there is evidence that children's knowledge about specific content areas is organized into common sense "theories." A common sense theory is not a scientific theory, but rather a well-organized set of beliefs that is resistant to instruction or change. Learning new information about these areas seems to require that children reorganize their understanding, as when a scientist revises a theory (Carey, 1985). That is, children cannot learn new information simply by adding on new facts. Rather, they need to challenge their current, erroneous beliefs. For example, both children and adults hold mistaken beliefs about physical laws regarding gravity and other physical forces (Kaiser, McCloskey, & Proffitt, 1986). Both children and adults typically make erroneous predictions about how objects fall from moving vehicles, or the path of a marble moving through a curved tube. These errors reflect a mistaken, but unstated, set of assumptions about physics that are extremely difficult to overcome. Even a college-level course in introductory physics is typically insufficient to combat the mistaken assumptions.

The "theory" framework has fruitfully begun to be applied to three key domains of children's understanding: physics, mind, and biology (Wellman & Gelman, 1992). We illustrate with research regarding children's theory of mind. A mature understanding of the mind is required for appropriate social interactions, such as making inferences about why people behave as they do, or making predictions about how people will behave in the future. Moral judgments rest on our understanding of others' intent (a mental construct); empathy and perspective-taking are enhanced by sensitive consideration of other's mental and emotional states. Manipulating or deceiving others also requires a theory of mind, because you cannot intentionally deceive someone without realizing that they may be thinking something other than what you are thinking. Thus, understanding of mind is of broad importance.

Recent research indicates that children have the rich beginning of a theory of mind by 2 or 3 years of age, but that important developmental changes are still taking place between 3 and 5 years of age (Astington, Harris, & Olson, 1988; Wellman, 1990). Some of children's early achievements include: the ability to distinguish mental from physical entities (Wellman & Estes, 1986), to distinguish pretense from reality (Leslie, 1987), and to distinguish mental images and dreams from physical representations (e.g., Woolley & Wellman, 1992); the ability to use another person's gaze as a clue to what they are talking about (Baldwin, 1991); a rich understanding of others' wishes and desires (Wellman, 1990). At the same time, however, children make many errors regarding others' beliefs, and have difficulty realizing that information they have is not always shared by others. One of the most striking and well-documented errors that children continue to make concerns their understanding of false belief (e.g., Wimmer & Perner, 1993). Whereas a 5-year-old realizes that people may falsely believe something that is not true, 3- to 4-year olds have tremendous difficulty appreciating the possibility of a false belief. Even when the false belief is made very concrete and obvious, 3year-olds have difficulty understanding it. For example, in one study children see a closed candy box, are asked what is inside, and predict that it has candies inside. They are then shown, to their surprise, that instead it has a pencil inside. The box is closed again, and children are then introduced to a new child who has never seen the box before. They are asked to predict what the new child will say is in the box. Most 3-year-olds will say the new child thinks a pencil is inside; most 4-year-olds will say that the new child thinks candies are inside (Hogrefe, Wimmer, & Perner, 1986). Results from other experiments using different experimental paradigms also provide an increasingly precise specification of the components of children's earliest theory of mind, as well as how it is restructured and transformed so rapidly over the preschool years (Wellman, 1990).

Methodological Issues

As the examples given above illustrate, assessing children's thought processes requires special methodological care, for two reasons: cognition is not directly observable, but only inferred, and young children are behaviorally limited and incapable of being tested by most experimental techniques used with adults (e.g., requiring computer keyboard use, the ability to read, or the ability to interpret verbal instructions). Moreover, children are notorious for their relatively brief attention spans; and even older children often interpret language differently from adults, requiring experimenters to use special skills in developing appropriate verbal or nonverbal techniques. Recent and future research continues on two fronts simultaneously: understanding development, and devising appropriate new techniques for shedding light on children's capacities.

Given these serious methodological issues, any researcher interested in cognition needs to be sensitive to how children use and interpret language. Language is often the tool researchers use to assess children's cognition, ranging from verbal IQ measures to the examiner's question on the Piagetian conservation task: "Which glass has more water?" It is difficult to probe the children's thinking without some use of language, whether it is peripherally, as in the use of verbal instructions, or centrally, when it is the focus of study (for example, when studying how children group words into more abstract categories). Perhaps the most important point to consider is that children and adults do not interpret language in exactly the same way. It is important to consider that children's errors may reflect their differing use of language, rather than fundamental differences in cognition. Thus, from a practical perspective language and cognition are intertwined. The often-difficult challenge for researchers is to figure out if the source of a particular error is linguistic or cognitive. (This was one question in the target study by Coley & Gelman, 1989; see Experiment 7.)

Language and Thought: How are They Related?

In addition to the methodological ties between language and thought, some theorists have proposed deeper links between the two. At least three major positions can be identified, each valid to some extent: (a) Language develops largely independently of non-linguistic thought (Chomsky, 1975). (b) Language and cognition are related, with thought influencing language and the pace of language development (Piaget, 1923). (c) Language and cognition are related, with language influencing thought (Whorf, 1956; see Hill & Mannheim, 1992, for a review). There is some evidence to support each position.

The evidence for the independence of language and thought comes from several sources. For one thing, the pattern of acquisition of language and cognition are quite distinct, in that children master much of the complexities of their native language by age 4 or 5 (Brown, 1973), whereas their cognitive abilities continue to develop in innumerable ways for many years later. Indeed, evidence suggests that children are even more skilled than adults at learning languages (Newport, 1991). Again, this pattern differs from the acquisition of most other cognitive skills, in which adults are better learners than children. Another point is that language appears to unfold in a biologically determined sequence (similar to that of any other maturational unfolding, such as early motor developments—e.g., learning to sit, then crawl, then walk), more than many other cognitive skills (e.g., learning algebra or chemistry). Finally, there are a few intriguing case studies of dissociations between language and cognition, either in children who are cognitively fairly able but linguistically impaired, or in children who are linguistically sophisticated but cognitively impaired (Curtiss, 1982). Again, this suggests that language development and cognitive development can proceed along distinct paths.

Although the evidence described above suggests that language may be special in some ways, apart from other cognitive skills, language and thought do mutually influence one another. One line of research demonstrates that children's level of cognitive development appears to influence aspects of their language development. For example, Gopnik and Meltzoff (1987) have found that specific conceptual milestones (e.g., certain achievements in categorization) precede particular linguistic achievements (e.g., a rapid increase in word-learning). Conversely, recent evidence also suggests that children's language may influence their perspective on a problem or ability to solve it. For example, how an experimenter labels a group of objects on a class-inclusion task affects how well children perform: They are better able to understand the inclusion relation—that all members of a smaller category are part of a larger category—when the objects are labeled as a unified collection (e.g., forest) than when they are labeled as a class of individuals (e.g., trees; Markman & Seibert, 1976). For example, if children are shown three oak trees and two pine trees, they are more correct (a) when told that all five trees are the forest and asked, "Which is more, the oak trees or the forest?" than (b) when told that all five trees are trees and asked, "Which is more, the oak trees or the trees?" Similarly, young children sort objects into different groups, depending on whether the objects are unlabeled by an experimenter, labeled with nouns, or labeled with adjectives (Markman & Hutchinson, 1984; Waxman, 1990). A question that is still open but of great interest is whether languages differ from one another in how they organize experience, thus leading to different patterns of thinking in the speakers of different languages. This controversial notion has received only mixed support to date.

In conclusion, language and cognition develop along somewhat distinct paths. Nonetheless, there are specific and complex relations between language and cognitive development. Moreover, from a practical standpoint, the language an experimenter uses to frame a task can have sizable consequences for a child's performance on a cognitive task. These links are important to consider, for anyone who is interested in the best ways to assess cognitive development.

References

Astington, J. W., Harris, P. L., & Olson, D. R. (1988). *Developing theories of mind*. New York: Cambridge University Press.

Baillargeon, R. (1987). Object permanence in 3.5- and 4.5-month-old infants. *Developmental Psychology, 23*, 655–664.

Baldwin, D. A. (1991). Infants' contribution to the achievement of joint reference. *Child Development, 62*, 875–890.

Banks, M. S., & Salapatek, P. (1983). Infant visual perception. In M. M. Haith & J. J. Campos (Eds.), *Handbook of child psychology: Infancy and developmental psychobiology* (Vol. 2, pp. 435–571). New York: Wiley.

Brown, R. (1973). *A first language*. Cambridge, MA: Harvard University Press.

Carey, S. (1985). *Conceptual change in childhood*. Cambridge, MA: MIT Press.

Carraher, T. N., Carraher, D. W., & Schliemann, A. D. (1985). Mathematics in the streets and in schools. *British Journal of Developmental Psychology, 3*, 21–29.

Chase, W.G., & Simon, H. A. (1988). The mind's eye in chess. In A. Collins & E. E. Smith (Eds.), *Readings in cognitive science* (pp. 461–494). San Mateo, CA: M. Kaufman.

Chi, M. T. H. (1978). Knowledge structures and memory development. In R. S. Siegler (Ed.), *Children's thinking: What develops?* (pp. 73–96). Hillsdale, NJ: Lawrence Erlbaum Associates.

Chi, M. T. H., & Koeske, R. D. (1983). Network representation of a child's dinosaur knowledge. *Developmental Psychology, 19*, 29–39.

Chomsky, N. (1975). *Reflections on language*. New York: Pantheon.

Curtiss, S. (1982). Developmental dissociation of language and cognition. In L. K. Obler & L. Menn (Eds.), *Exceptional language and linguistics* (pp. 285–312). New York: Academic Press.

DeCasper, A. J., & Fifer, W. (1980). Of human bonding: Newborns prefer their mothers' voices. *Science, 208*, 1174–1176.

Eimas, P. D., Siqueland, E. R., Jusczyk, P. W., & Vigorito, J. (1971). Speech perception in infants. *Science, 171*, 303–306.

Ericsson, K. A., Chase, W. G., & Faloon, S. (1980). Acquisition of a memory skill. *Science, 208*, 1181–1182.

Gopnik, A., & Meltzoff, A. (1987). The development of categorization in the second year and its relation to other cognitive and linguistic developments. *Child Development, 58*, 1523–1531.

Harris, P. L. (1983). Infant cognition. In M. M. Haith & J. J. Compos (Eds.), *Handbook of child psychology: Infancy and developmental psychobiology* (Vol. 2, pp. 689–782). New York: Wiley.

Hill, J. H., & Mannheim, B., (1992). Language and world view. *Annual Review of Anthropology, 21*, 381–406.

Hogrefe, G. J., Wimmer, H., & Perner, J. (1986). Ignorance versus false belief: A developmental lag in attribution of epistemic states. *Child Development, 57*, 567–582.

Kaiser, M. K., McCloskey, M., & Proffitt, D. R. (1986). Development of intuitive theories of motion: Curvilinear motion in the absence of external forces. *Developmental Psychology, 22*, 67–71.

Leslie, A. M. (1987). Pretense and representation: The origins of "theory of mind." *Psychological Review, 94*, 412–426.

Markman, E. M., & Hutchinson, J. E. (1984). Children's sensitivity to constraints on word meaning: Taxonomic vs. thematic relations. *Cognitive Psychology, 16*, 1–27.

Meltzoff, A. N., & Moore, M. K. (1983). Newborn infants imitate adult facial gestures. *Child Development, 54*, 702–709.

Newport, E. L. (1991). Contrasting concepts of the critical period for language. In S. Carey & R. Gelman (Eds.), *The epigenesis of mind: Essays on biology and cognition* (pp. 111–130). Hillsdale, NJ: Lawrence Erlbaum Associates.

Piaget, J. (1923). *The language and thought of the child.* London: Routledge and Kegan Paul.

Piaget, J. (1954). *The construction of reality in the child.* New York: Basic Books.

Spelke, E. S. (1985). Perception of unity, persistence, and identity: Thoughts on infants' conceptions of objects. In J. Mehler & R. Fox (Eds.), *Neonate cognition: Beyond the blooming buzzing confusion* (pp. 89–114). Hillsdale, NJ: Lawrence Erlbaum Associates.

Waxman, S. R. (1990). Linguistic biases and the establishment of conceptual hierarchies: Evidence from preschool children. *Cognitive Development, 5*, 123–150.

Wellman, H. M. (1990). *The child's theory of mind.* Cambridge, MA: Bradford Books/MIT Press.

Wellman, H. M., & Estes, D. (1986). Early understanding of mental entities: A reexamination of childhood realism. *Child Development, 57*, 910–923.

Wellman, H. M., & Gelman, S. A. (1992). Cognitive development: Foundational theories of core domains. *Annual Review of Psychology, 43*, 337–375. Palo Alto: Annual Reviews.

Whorf, B. L. (1956). *Language, thought, and reality: Selected writings.* Cambridge, MA: Cambridge Technology Press of MIT.

Wimmer, H., & Perner, J. (1983). Beliefs about beliefs: Representation and constraining function of wrong beliefs in young children's understanding of deception. *Cognition, 13*, 103–128.

Woolley, J. D., & Wellman, H. M. (1992). Children's conception of dreams. *Cognitive Development, 7*, 365–380.

Wynn, K. (1992). Addition and subtraction by human infants. *Nature, 358*, 749–750.

Experiment 7

Children's Interpretation of the Word *Big*

The following project is a modified replication of Coley and Gelman's (1989) experiment on the influence of contextual factors on children's understanding of the word *big*.

Early research on children's language focused on the timing and sequence of attainment of children's language production: from categorical perception to cooing, prelinguistic vocalization, babbling in the first year; holophrases and paired words in the second year; overgeneralization of and use of morphemes, increase of vocabulary size in the third year; correct but noncomplex language, use of negatives and auxiliary verbs in the fourth year; some metalinguistic awareness of language and adult-like complexity in the fifth year (e.g., Gardner, 1980).

Although the four aspects of language interact (*phonology*—the system of sounds, *grammar*—the structure of language, *semantics*—the meaning of words and sentences, and *pragmatics*—the rules governing the use of language in context in real situations), many psychologists are particularly interested in the last two.

In the area of semantic development, researchers report that English-speaking children interpret big as "tall" (Lumsden & Poteat, 1968), and that three to five-year-olds seem to increase, not decrease this incorrect usage (Gathercole, 1982). On the other hand, Ravn and Gelman (1984) looked at whether the children were consistently responding to a particular rule, rather than the number of correct answers. Three-year-olds showed little consistency; five-year-olds consistently used height. (The correct response is to use the *area* rule.)

Why do our preschool children increasingly use big as height? Perhaps the environmental salience of the vertical dimension (Maratsos, 1973, 1974)? Perhaps the many tall objects which the child hears described as big (Carey, 1978; Gathercole, 1982)?

Coley and Gelman (1989) argued against a single interpretation of *big* that holds across contexts. They think *big* has complex meanings which are sensitive to their contexts. Adults rely on area when judging the size of rectangles, and on height when judging human figures (Maloney & Gelman, 1987). So perhaps *object type* may influence the meaning of *big* for children.

Most studies presented stimuli in an upright, vertical position, which may have influenced the salience of height. So, using a horizontal *orientation* may also influence children's interpretation of *big*.

Problem and Hypotheses

Therefore, Coley and Gelman explored the possible influence of object type and object orientation on children's interpretation of *big*. Their object types were representations of people, brownies, rectangles. Their orientations were vertical or horizontal. The children were 3- and 5-year-olds.

Make up hypotheses to answer the following questions:

1. Defining big correctly in terms of overall area, would the 3- or 5-year-olds be more correct?

2. Would children be more correct in the vertical or horizontal *orientation* condition?

3. Would *object-type* (people, brownies, rectangles) affect correctness? If so, which type? Would 3- and 5-year-olds differ on this?

4. When children are categorized as *consistently* using one of three rules (area, height, or salient dimension—see below),
   a) which age group showed more consistency?
   b) which orientation produced more consistency?

5. Other questions?

Method

Subjects

3- and 5-year-olds. Half of each age-sex group are assigned to the vertical orientation condition, half to the horizontal orientation condition.

Material

9 pairs of *brownies*

9 pairs of *people*

17 pairs of *rectangles*

The first pair in each object group (the pretest pair) would be chosen as *big* according to any rule. The rules are the greatest *area* (correct), *height* (the tallest), and *salient dimension* (object with the largest height *or* width). Table F7.1 presents the dimensions of each stimulus pair, and the rules that specific choices demonstrate.

Cut the brownies out of dark brown cork tiles.

Cut the rectangles out of foamcore and then paint or use contact paper to make six red pairs, six blue pairs, and five yellow pairs.

Cut the people out of foamcore and use contact paper and felt-tip markers as indicated in Fig. F7.1. Construct hands of peach-colored contact paper; construct heads of peach-colored cardboard.

Coley and Gelman (1989) followed various constraints in formulating these stimuli. Read their description (pp. 374–375) to learn about the careful detail that stimuli construction often requires.

Identify each item on its back. For example, the 12.5 x 22.5 cm person can be labeled P2-A; the 15 x 9 cm person is P2-B. This will make scoring easier. Also, add arrows on the back indicating the top; this is especially important for the brownies and rectangles.

Procedure

Each child is tested individually, and shown all the stimuli, presented by object type, that is, all pairs of one object, then all pairs of the other object and so on. The pretest pair is always given first in its group. The remaining pairs in that group are presented in a random order, and each item in the pair is shown on the left half the time and on the right half the time. Half the children are given all the stimuli always in vertical orientation; half see them lying down (horizontal orientation). The object types need to be counterbalanced, as follows:

Order 1	Order 2	Order 3
People	Brownies	People
Rectangles	Rectangles	Brownies
Brownies	People	Rectangles
Order 4	**Order 5**	**Order 6**
Rectangles	Rectangles	Brownies
People	Brownies	People
Brownies	People	Rectangles

Arrange your stimuli in their appropriate sequence before going for your child.

TABLE F7.1

STIMULUS DIMENSIONS AND RULE DIFFERENTIATION

Pair	Item A Height x Width	Item B Height x Width	Area	Height	Salient Dimension
Brownies:					
B1.....	6.0 x 6.0	4.0 x 4.0	A	A	A
B2.....	4.0 x 7.5	5.0 x 3.0	A	B	A
B3.....	6.0 x 6.0	9.0 x 2.0	A	B	B
B4.....	10.5 x 2.0	7.0 x 7.0	B	A	A
B5.....	6.0 x 3.5	5.0 x 9.5	B	A	B
B6.....	4.0 x 9.0	6.0 x 3.0	A	B	A
B7.....	5.0 x 5.0	6.0 x 2.0	A	B	B
B8.....	6.5 x 1.5	4.5 x 4.5	B	A	A
B9.....	5.5 x 3.0	4.5 x 7.5	B	A	B
People:					
P1.....	19.0 x 7.5	12.5 x 5.0	A	A	A
P2.....	12.5 x 22.5	15.0 x 9.0	A	B	A
P3.....	12.5 x 20.0	22.5 x 5.5	A	B	B
P4.....	23.0 x 6.5	15.0 x 20.0	B	A	A
P5.....	10.0 x 5.5	7.5 x 15.0	B	A	B
P6.....	12.5 x 25.0	15.0 x 10.0	A	B	A
P7.....	16.0 x 12.5	20.0 x 5.0	A	B	B
P8.....	15.0 x 5.0	12.5 x 12.5	B	A	A
P9.....	12.5 x 7.5	10.0 x 20.0	B	A	B
Rectangles:					
R1.....	12.5 x 10.0	6.0 x 7.5	A	A	A

Note. Measurements (height x width) are in centimeters. Stimulus pairs R2–R9 correspond to stimulus pairs B2–B9; stimulus pairs R10–R17 correspond to stimulus pairs P2–P9.

From "The effects of object orientation and object type on children's interpretation of the word Big," by J. D. Coley and S. A. Gelman, 1989, *Child Development, 60*, p. 374. Copyright © 1989 by *Child Development*. Reprinted with permission.

Using Coley and Gelman's verbatim instructions, say to the child seated across from you at a table, **"We're going to look at some different things, and whenever I show you some things, I want you to look at them and tell me which is the big one, OK? First we're going to look at some brownies** [people, rectangles]**. Do you know what brownies** [people, rectangles] **are?"** After noting the child's answer, show the subject each pair in succession, saying, **"See these brownies [people, rectangles]? Which one is the big one?"** For each subsequent category block, say, **"Now we're going to look at some people** [rectangles, brownies]**, OK?"** (etc.).

On your data sheet, note which object of each pair was chosen as "the big one". As always, note any of the child's comments or behaviors.

Results

Responses to the pretest pairs (B1, P1, R1) are omitted from your statistical analyses. Before doing the following ANOVAs and nonparametric statistics, see if there is a significant sex difference. (If there is, then sex will need to be added as a variable in our analyses).

To answer to your hypotheses, we need to look at correct answers, and at consistent answers, respectively.

Percent Correct

Because there are 8 people pairs, 8 brownie pairs, but 16 rectangles, you need to use the percent of correct answers rather than the raw score. The correct answer is the response based on overall *area*. On the individual data sheet compute this for each child, for each object type, then enter on the master collation sheets. First use a *t* test to see if girls and boys differ significantly. If they don't (as we hope), then run a 2 age x 2 orientation x 3 object-type (brownies, people, rectangles) Repeated Measure ANOVA, and enter your results in Table F7.3. The group means are entered in Table F7.2.

To answer to hypothesis 1, look at the *F* for age. Look at the *F* for orientation and object-type, respectively, to answer to hypotheses 2 and 3. Are there any significant interactions?

Consistent Rule Use

Was the child consistent in using any one of the three rules (area, height, or salient dimension), or not? To determine this, count how many items your child answered according to the height column and then according to the salient dimension column in Table F7.1. You already have the number for the area rule on your Individual Data Sheet. To be consistent, the child has to have answered 23 items out of the total 32, according to one rule. Transfer this information from your Individual Data Sheet to the master collation sheets. From the latter, fill in Table F7.4. Fisher's exact tests can be used to examine the effects of age and orientation on consistent use of a rule. (Fisher exact tests are used instead of Chi Square test when the expected frequency in each cell is below 5). Did more 5-year-olds than 3-year-olds use a rule consistently? Did more children in the vertical orientation condition use a rule consistently than children in the horizontal condition? Which rule was used by more children than were the other rules?

Optional Analyses

Although Coley and Gelman (1989) did not obtain a significant main effect for object-type in their ANOVA for correct (area-based) answers, they ran planned *paired t* tests. These compared the correct answers to the People stimuli (P2-9) and their identically-sized rectangles (R10-17). Similarly, they compared the correct answers to the Brownies stimuli (B2-9) and their identically-sized Rectangles (R2-9). Enter the mean number of area-based answers for these objects, for 3- and 5 year-olds, ignoring orientation, in Table F7.5, and run your *paired t* tests. So, was there more accuracy for people stimuli than for matched rectangles, for 3-year-olds? for 5-year-olds? Was there more accuracy for Brownies than for matched Rectangles for 3-year-olds? for 5-year-olds? Refer again to hypothesis 3.

Discussion

Relate your results to each of your hypotheses, and compare your findings to the literature.

Did more of your 3-year-olds or more of your 5-year-olds define *big* correctly in terms of area? Maratsos (1973) found his 3-year-olds did. Explain how this could happen.

Did the horizontal or vertical orientation evoke more correct answers? Coley and Gelman's (1989) children with the horizontal orientation used the area rule more frequently than the children who were in the vertical presentation group. Which rule did the vertical group use most frequently in their study? In your study? Why?

Were children more correct with people, brownies, or rectangles? Coley and Gelman found their 3-year-olds gave height-based answers (not correct) more frequently for people than rectangles, whereas their 5-year-olds did not. Did you find this? How can this be explained?

How can you tell whether tall and big are synonymous? What would you need to do empirically? How did Coley and Gelman investigate this question?

Did your 5-year-olds show more consistent use of a rule than your 3-year-olds? Which orientation group showed more consistent rule use? Did the people, brownies, or rectangle stimuli produce more consistent rule use? Did these results agree with Coley and Gelman's?

Coley and Gelman (1989) suggested that "developmental changes in children's use of big demonstrate the interplay of cognitive and semantic factors in the process of semantic development (p. 379)." Elaborate on this. How does Piaget's centration notion fit in here (Flavell, 1963; Piaget, 1962)?

Can you suggest future related studies?

Selected Bibliography

Bausano, M. K., & Jeffrey, W. E. (1975). Dimensional salience and judgments of bigness by three-year-old children. *Child Development, 46*, 988–991.

Beals, D. (1987). Sources of support for learning words in conversation: Evidence from mealtimes. *Journal of Child Language, 24*, 673–694.

Bloom, L. (1995). *The transition from infancy to language: Acquiring the power of expression*. New York: Cambridge University Press.

Bloom, L. (2000). *How children learn the meaning of words*. Cambridge, MA: MIT Press.

Carey, S. (1978). The child as word learner. In M. Halle, J. Bresnan, & G. Miller (Eds.), *Linguistic theory and psychological reality*, (pp. 264–293). Cambridge, MA: MIT Press.

*Coley, J. D., & Gelman, S. A. (1989). The effects of object orientation and object type on children's interpretation of the word big. *Child Development, 60*, 372–380.

Ebeling, K. S., & Gelman, S. A. (1994). Children's use of context in interpreting "big" and "little." *Child Development, 65*, 1178–1192.

Flavell, J.H. (1963). *The developmental psychology of Jean Piaget*. New York: Van Nostrand.

Gathercole, V.A. (1982). Decrements in children's responses to big and tall: A reconsideration of the potential cognitive and semantic causes. *Journal of Experimental Child Psychology, 34*, 156–173.

Gardner, H. (1982). *Developmental psychology* (2nd ed.). Boston: Little, Brown & Co.

Gelman, S. A., & Coley, J. D. (1991). Language and categorization: The acquisition of natural kind terms. In S. A. Gelman, & J. P. Byrnes (Eds.), *Perspectives on language and thought: Interrelations in development* (pp. 146–196). New York: Cambridge University Press.

Hoff, E. (in press). *How children use input to acquire a lexicon*. Child Development.

Lumsden, E. A., & Poteat, B. (1968). The salience of the vertical dimension in the concept of bigger in five- and six-year-old children. *Journal of Verbal Learning and Verbal Behavior, 7*, 404–408.

Maloney, L. T., & Gelman, S. A. (1987). Measuring the influence of context: The interpretation of dimensional adjectives. *Language and Cognitive Processes, 2*, 205–215.

Maratsos, M. P. (1973). Decrease in the understanding of the word big in preschool children. *Child Development, 44*, 747–752.

Maratsos, M. P. (1974). When is a high thing the big one? *Developmental Psychology, 10*, 367–375.

McKeown, M. G., & Curtis, M. E. (Eds.). (1987). *The nature of vocabulary acquisition*. Hillsdale, NJ: Lawrence Erlbaum Associates.

Piaget, J. (1962). *Play, dreams, and imitation in childhood*. New York: Norton.

Ravn, K. E., & Gelman, S. A. (1984). Rule usage in children's understanding of big and little. *Child Development, 55*, 2141–2150.

INDIVIDUAL DATA SHEET

Title: *Interpretation of the word* Big

E:_____ Day and Date:_____ S–Sex: *M or F* Grade:____

S:_____ Birthdate:_____ CA:_____

Time Begun:_____ Time Ended:_____ Elapsed Time:_____ Room:_____

Counterbalancing Order:_____ Orientation: *Horizontal or Vertical*

Responses:

Brownies	People	Rectangles
B1 (_____)	P1 (_____)	R1 (_____)
B2 _____	P2 _____	R2 _____
B3 _____	P3 _____	R3 _____
B4 _____	P4 _____	R4 _____
B5 _____	P5 _____	R5 _____
B6 _____	P6 _____	R6 _____
B7 _____	P7 _____	R7 _____
B8 _____	P8 _____	R8 _____
B9 _____	P9 _____	R9 _____
		R10 _____
		R11 _____
		R12 _____
		R13 _____
		R14 _____
		R15 _____
		R16 _____
		R17 _____

Scoring:

Δ Correct (Area response)

			Notes:
Brownies	#	_____	
	a%	_____	
People	#	_____	
	a%	_____	
Rectangles	#	_____	
	b%	_____	
Combined	#	_____	
	c%	_____	

Δ Consistency (using a rule) —> 23

Area (above, combined #)	_____
Height	_____
Salient dimension	_____

[a]Divide by 8, omitting pretest response, B1 or P1.
[b]Divide by 16, omitting pretest response R1.
[c]Divide by 32, omitting pretest responses.

GROUP DATA SHEET

Title: *Children's Interpretation of the Word* Big

E: _____   **Day and Date:** _____

Hypothesis:

Method and Procedure: (as described in text with following modifications, if any)

Group Results and Analysis:

TABLE F7-2
PERCENT CORRECT RESPONSES (AREA) TO "BIG"

Three-Year-Olds	B	P	R	Five-Year-Olds	B	P	R
Boys	_____	_____	_____	Boys	_____	_____	_____
Girls	_____	_____	_____	Girls	_____	_____	_____
Sexes Combined	_____	_____	_____	Sexes Combined	_____	_____	_____
Objects Combined		_____		Objects Combined		_____	

Note: B = Brownies, P = People, R = Rectangles

TABLE F7.3

2 X 2 X 2 REPEATED MEASUREMENT ANALYSIS OF VARIANCE FOR AREA RESPONSES TO *BIG*

Source of variation	Sum of Squares	df	Mean Square F p
Between Subjects			
Between ages (A)		1	
Between orientations (O)		1	
A x O interaction		1	
Within group error		$N-4$	
(Total Between Subjects)		$1(N-1)$	
Between object-types (C)		2	
A x C		2	
O x C		2	
A x O x C		2	
Error		$2N-8$	
Total within subjects		$2N$	
(Total)		$(3N-1)$	

TABLE 7.4

NUMBER OF CHILDREN CONSISTENTLY USING EACH RULE, BY CONDITION

	3-Year-Olds	5-Year-Olds	Total
Area rule:			
Vertical			
Horizontal			
Height rule:			
Vertical			
Horizontal			
Salient-dimension rule:			
Vertical			
Horizontal			
No rule:			
Vertical			
Horizontal			
Total			

Note: Left column labels from Coley and Gelman, 1989.

TABLE F7.5
MEAN NUMBER[a] OF AREA-BASED ANSWERS FOR DIFFERENT OBJECTS

Age	People	People-Rectangles[b]	Brownies	Brownie-Rectangles
3-year olds				
5-year-olds				

Note: [a] Out of a possible 8.

[b] "People-Rectangles" are the plain rectangular stimuli matched to the people stimuli for size.

"Brownie-Rectangles" are the plain rectangular stimuli matched to the brownie stimuli for size.

From Coley and Gelman, 1989.

P1A

P1B

red

blue

black shoes

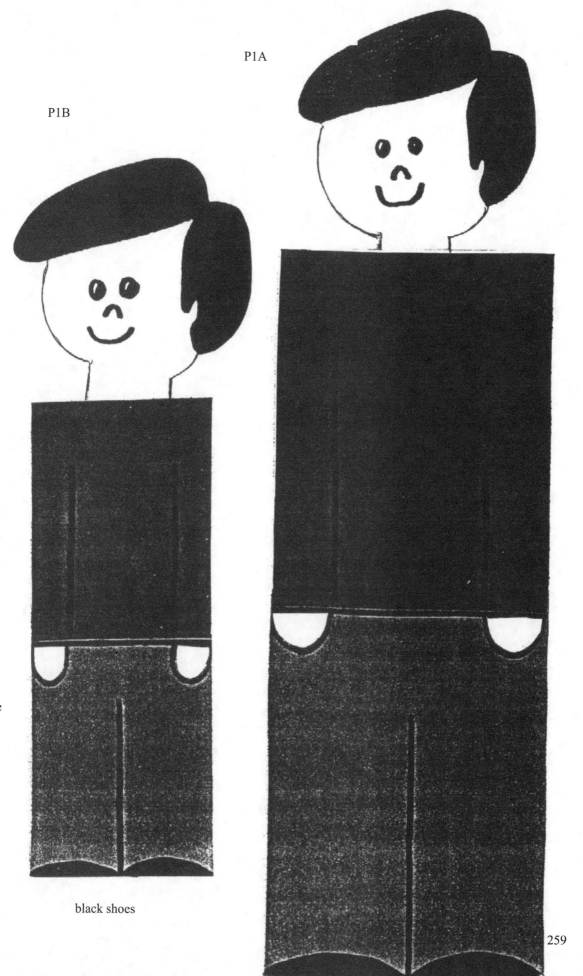

259

P2A

yellow →

blue

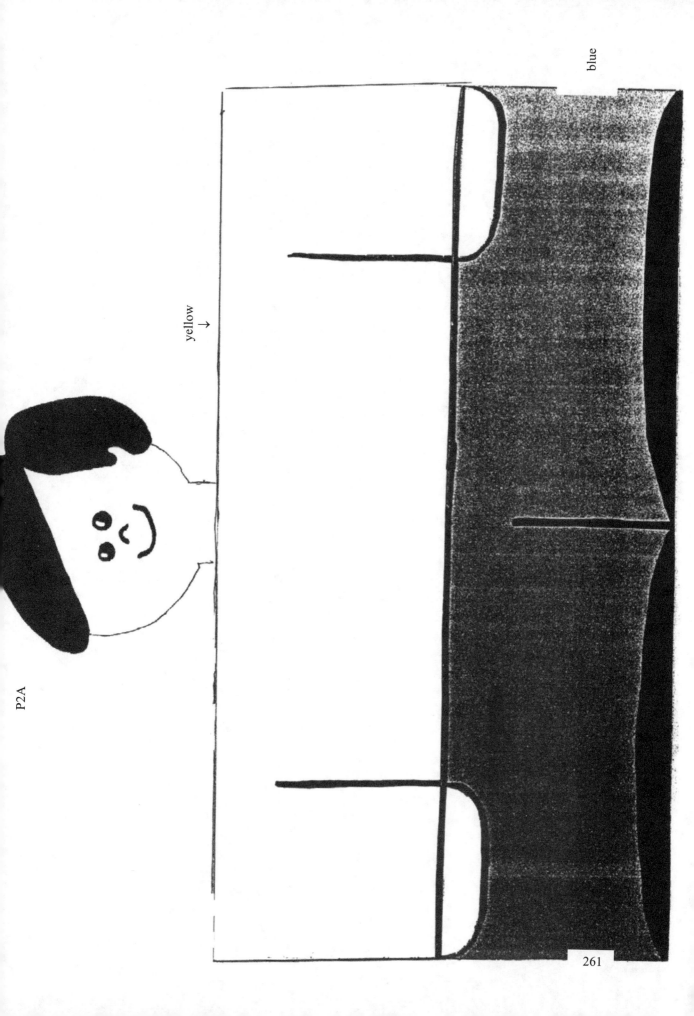

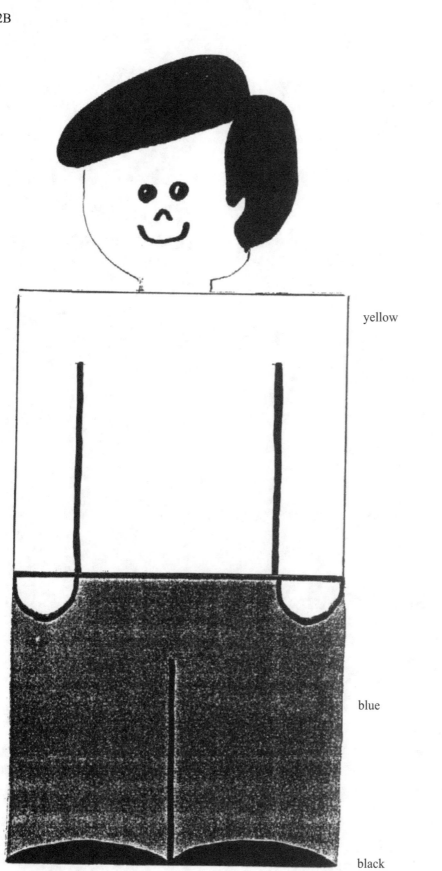

yellow

blue

black

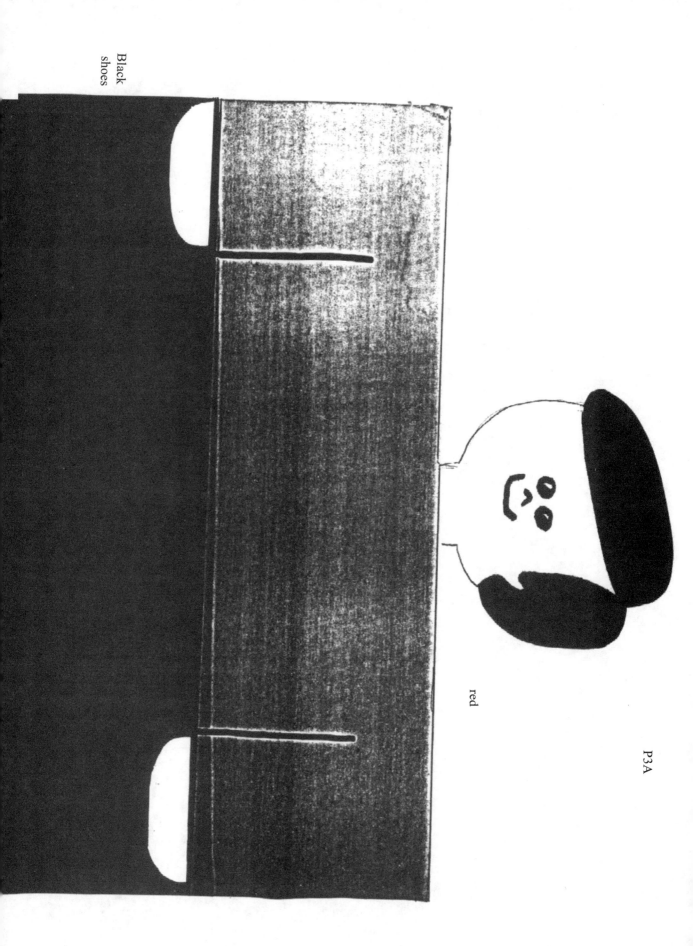

Black
shoes

red

P3A

265

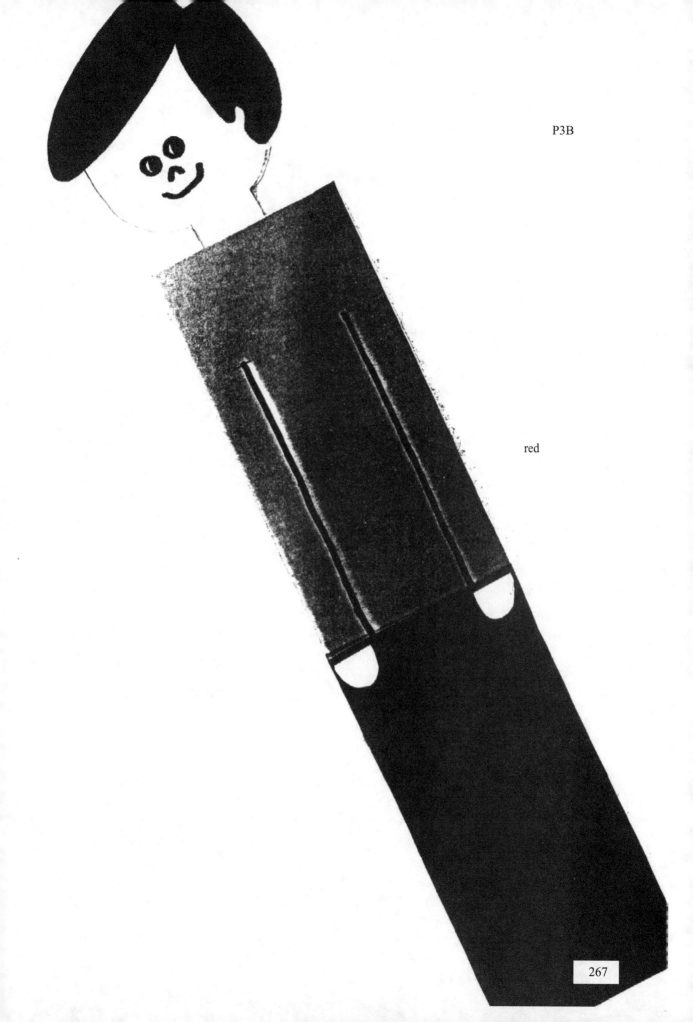

red

P4A

yellow

yellow
↓

P5A

P5B

red

blue

black
shoes

273

yellow

P6A

275

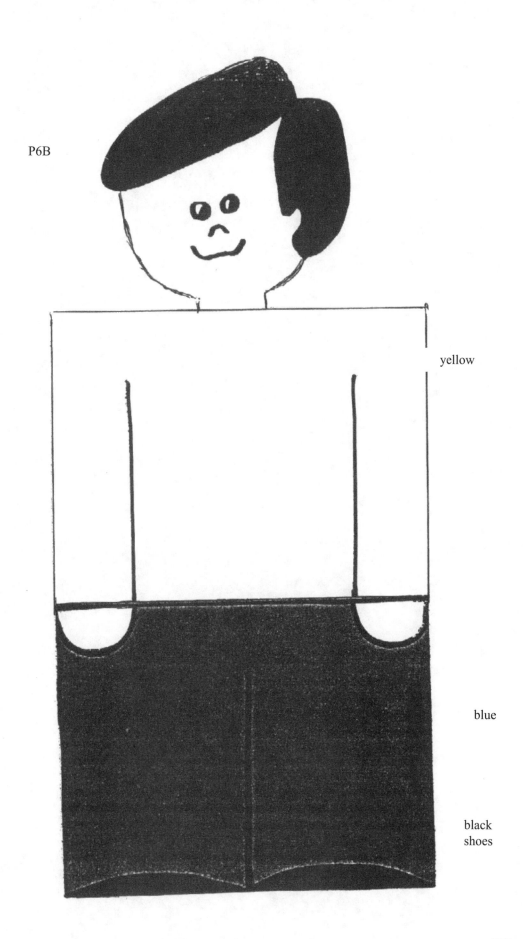

P6B

yellow

blue

black
shoes

P7A

P7B

P9A

red

P9B

red

283

G

The Socialized Child

Although a research manual divided into topics, such as this volume, is necessarily fractionated, the artificiality of such fractionation is most strikingly evident in the consideration of social, emotional, and personality development. If the development of "self" depends to any extent on "significant others," as is widely believed, then surely the child's *perception* of others' reactions to herself or himself is as important as the affect component. Similarly, the development of masculinity or femininity depends on a complex intertwining of genetic contributions, learning by reinforcement, learning by imitation and observation, and cognitive categorization. To play a game with a peer (Experiment 11) involves more than a disposition to cooperate or compete; it may involve understanding of game rules, role-taking ability, ability to infer what one's partner may be thinking and/or feeling, and so on. In short, cognitive and social and emotional development are reciprocally intertwined, and interaction is a life long process. Research and understanding of social behavior involves a merger of cognitive, social, and neurosciences, and is a fast-growing field.

By titling this chapter "The Socialized Child," I do not mean to imply that the child is the passive recipient of socialization forces from the main socializing agents: family, peers, school, media, and community. The title should probably be "The Socialized and Socializing Child"! Psychologists now give at least verbal acceptance to the notion that the child is an active processor of information, an active elicitor of reactions from others, an active contributor to his or her own development because of the child's own individuality and the reciprocal interaction of that individuality with all the experiences available to that child (Shehan, 1999). As indicated earlier, "same" experiences are not the same to different children (nor even to the same child at different times), and "different" experiences may have somewhat similar effects on different children. It should therefore come as no surprise that several decades of early work on child-rearing practices resulted in relatively few generalizations. The increasing recognition of the multiply determined and overdetermined nature of social and personality development may lead, if not to less simplistic experiments, at least to more sophisticated interpretations.

All of the viewpoints or paradigms mentioned earlier are represented in the research literature on social and personality development: traditional S-R theory, social learning theory, information processing theory, (organismic-developmental) stage theory, psychoanalytic theory, and ethological theory. Among the most active researchers were the various social learning theorists, with experiments on the efficacy of positive and negative social reinforcements (punishment), the importance and prevalence of observational learning, the development of role-taking ability. The work on reinforcements is closer to the older S-R viewpoint, with its unidirectional influence process. The observational learning theory, with its emphasis on imitation (where the child's actions resemble those of someone else as a result of direct or symbolic observation), is useful in understanding allegedly nonreinforced behaviors and in recognizing the child's active role. The psychologists interested in social cognition—the cognitive and information-processing abilities that determine the individual's perception of, understanding of, and response to social influences and situations—have researched topics like role taking, empathy, prosocial behavior, and social attitudes (Flavell & Miller, 1998). They have proposed a number of minitheories (e.g., consistency, social judgments, social comparison, attribution) that have relevance to the following experiments.

Many modern psychologists tend to avoid "labeling" themselves, or even to pay much explicit attention to implicit assumptions underlying their work. The process of becoming a good researcher, however, would benefit from a critical look at each experiment, to attempt to identify which issues are and are not addressed, which methodological and theoretical viewpoints or paradigms are reflected, which modifications or extensions would be fruitful, and so on.

Researchers interested in the socialization of the child and the socializing child have extended their foci in many directions. What follows is a partial list with examples of recent publications.

Parents' child rearing
> Holden and Miller (1999); Lytton and Romney (1991)

Nature/Nurture in parenting
> Collins, Maccoby, Steinberg, Hetherington, and Bornstein (2000); Lytton and Romney (1991)

Socialization in the family
> Parke and Buriel (1998)
> See also Experiment 12 about Siblings

Socialization processes
> Bugental and Goodnow (1998)

Social cognition
> Bennett (1993); Flavell and Miller (1998); Kunda (1999)

Social intelligence
> Cantor and Kihlstrom (1987)

Gender/Sex differences
> See Experiments 9 and 10.

Contexts
> Bigelow, Tesson, and Lewko (1996); Collins and Laursen (1998); DeRosier, Cillessen, and Dodge (1994); Eccles, Lord, and Midgley (1991); Forman, Minick, and Stone (1993)

Culture
> Greenfield and Suzuki (1998); Huston and Wright (1998); Kitayama and Markus (1994); Parke (2000); Rubin (1998); Taylor and Wang (1996)

Emotional development
> Dunn (1995); Magai and McFadden (1995); Saarni, Mumme, and Campos (1998)

Identity/Self/Self-esteem
> See Experiment 8.

Evolution
> Simpson and Kenrick (1996)

Social neuropsychology
> Cacioppo et al. (2002)

The above list may seem long but only scratches the surface of the vast body of research and theory on socialization. In a review of Forman et al.'s (1993) book, the comment was made that "psychological functioning is specific to its social context and is dependent on the mastery of culturally defined modes of speaking, thinking, and acting." The complications and constraints implicit in that statement magnify the difficulties for researchers.

Although the following five experiments include areas of contemporary interest, there are many noticeable lacunae, such as direct measurement of parents or teachers; influence of TV and other media; moral development; aggression[1]; empathy. You will probably think of many other topics that merit inclusion. Consider the effects, in the following projects, of changes in the subject variables, that is, of testing retarded or intellectually gifted children; of choosing a different socioeconomic class, race, or culture, of testing children from one-parent rather than intact families.

---

[1]See the observation projects for a study of TV and aggression.

SELECTED BIBLIOGRAPHY

Ashmore, R. D., & Jussim, L. (Eds.). (1997). *Self and identity: Fundamental issues*. New York: Oxford University Press.

Bennett, M. (Ed.). (1993). *The development of social cognition: The child as psychologist*. New York: Guilford.

Bigelow, B. J., Tesson, G., & Lewko, J. H. (1996). *Learning the rules: The anatomy of children's relationships*. New York: Guilford.

Bugental, D. B., & Goodnow, J. J. (1998). Socialization processes. In W. Damon (Editor-in-Chief) & N. Eisenberg (Vol. Ed.), *Handbook of child psychology: Vol. 3. Social, emotional, & personality development* (5th ed., pp. 389–462). New York: Wiley

Cacioppo, J. T., Berntson, G. G., Adolphs, R., Carter, C. S., Davidson, R. J., McClintock, M. K., McEwen, B. S., Meaney, M. J., Schachter, D. L., Sternberg, E. M., Suomi, S. S., & Taylor, S. E. (Eds.). (2002). *Foundations in social neuroscience*. Cambridge, MA: MIT Press.

Cantor, N., & Kihlstrom, J. (1987). *Personality and social intelligence*. Engelwood Cliffs, NJ: Prentice Hall.

Caspi, A., & Bem, D. J. (1990). Personality continuity and change across the life course. In L. Pervin (Ed.), *Handbook of personality: Theory and research* (pp. 549–575). New York: Guilford.

Collins, W. A., & Laursen, B. (Eds.). (1998). *Relationships as developmental contexts: The Minnesota Symposium on Child Psychology, Vol. 30*. Mahwah, NJ: Lawrence Erlbaum Associates.

Collins, W. A., Maccoby, E. E., Steinberg, L., Hetherington, E. M., & Bornstein, M. H. (2000). Contemporary research on parenting: The case for nature and nurture. *American Psychologist, 55*, 218–232.

DeRosier, M. E., Cillessen, A. H. N., Coie, J. D., & Dodge, K. A. (1994). Group social context and children's aggressive behavior. *Child Development, 65*, 1068–1079.

Dunn, J. F. (Ed.). (1995). *Connections between emotion and understanding in development*. (A special issue of *Cognition and Emotion*). Mahwah, NJ: Lawrence Erlbaum Associates.

Eccles, J. S., Lord, S., & Midgley, C. (1991). What are we doing to early adolescents? The impact of educational contexts on early adolescents. *American Journal of Education, 99*, 521–542.

Flavell, J. H., & Miller, P. H. (1998). Social cognition. In W. Damon (Editor-in-Chief), D. Kuhn, & R. S. Siegler (Vol. Eds.), *Handbook of child psychology: Vol. 2. Cognition, perception, and language* (5th ed., pp. 851–898). New York: Wiley.

Forman, E. A., Minick, N., & Stone, C. A. (1993). *Contexts for learning: Sociocultural dynamics in children's development*. New York: Oxford University Press.

Gilbert, D. T., Fiske, S. T., & Lindsey, G. (Eds.). (1998). *The handbook of social psychology* (4th ed., Vols. *1 & 2*).A co-publication of Oxford University Press and McGraw-Hill.

Greenfield, P. M., & Suzuki, L. K. (1998). Culture and human development. In W. Damon (Editor-in-Chief), I. E. Sigel & K. A. Renninger (Vol. Eds.), *Handbook of child psychology: Vol. 4. Child psychology in practice* (5th ed., pp. 1059–1112). New York: Wiley.

Grusec, J. E., & Lytton, H. (1988). *Social development: History, theory and research*. New York: Springer Verlag.

Holden, G. W., & Miller, P. C. (1999). Enduring and different: A meta-analysis of the similarity of parents' child rearing. *Psychological Bulletin, 125*, 223–254.

Huston, A. C., & Wright, J. C. (1998). Mass media and children's development. In W. Damon (Editor-in-Chief), I. E. Sigel, & A. Renninger (Vol. Eds.), *Handbook of child psychology: Vol. 4. Child psychology in practice* (5th ed., pp. 999–1058). New York: Wiley.

Keller, H., & Zach, U. (2002). Gender and birth order as determinants of parental behaviour. *International Journal of Behavioral Development, 26*(2), 177–184.

Kitayama, S., & Markus, H. R. (Eds.). (1994). *Emotion and culture: Empirical studies of mutual influences*. Washington, DC: American Psychological Association.

Kuczynski, L., Bernardini, S., & Harach, L. (1999). Psychology's child meets sociology's child: Agency, power, and influence in parent-child relations. In C. Shehan (Ed.), *Through the eyes of the child: Revisioning children as active agents of family life* (pp. 21–52). New York: JAI.

Kunda, Z. (1999). *Social cognition: Making sense of people*. Cambridge, MA: MIT Press.

Lippa, R. A., (2002). *Gender, nature, and nurture*. Mahwah, NJ: Lawrence Erlbaum Associates.

Lytton, H., & Romney, D. M. (1991). Parents' differential socialization of boys and girls: A meta-analysis. *Psychological Bulletin, 109*, 267–296.

Magai, C., & McFadden, S. (1995). *The role of emotions in social and personality development*. New York: Plenum.

Parke, R. D. (Ed.). (2000). Cultural variation in families. *Journal of Family Psychology, 14*(3).

Parke, R. D., & Buriel, R. (1998). Socialization in the family. In W. Damon (Editor-in-Chief) & N. Eisenberg (Vol. Ed.), *Handbook of child psychology: Vol. 3. Social, emotional, & personality development* (5th ed., pp. 463–552). New York: Wiley.

Rubin, K. H. (Guest editor). (1998). Social and emotional development: A cross-cultural perspective. *Developmental Psychology, 34*(4).

Saarni, C., Mumme, D., & Campos, J. J. (1998). Emotional development. In W. Damon (Editor-in-Chief) & N. Eisenberg (Vol. Ed.), *Handbook of child psychology: Vol. 3. Social, emotional, & personality development* (5th ed., pp. 237–310). New York: Wiley.

Sameroff, A. (1975). Transactional models in early social relations. *Human Development, 18*(1–2), 65–79.

Sameroff, A. J. (1987). The social context of development. In N. Eisenberg (Ed.), *Contemporary topics in developmental psychology* (pp. 273–291). New York: Wiley.

Sameroff, A. J. (1995). General systems theories and developmental psychopathology. In D. Cicchetti & D. Cohen (Eds.), *Manual of developmental psychopathology, Vol. 1*, pp. 659–695. New York: Wiley.

Shehan, C. (Ed.). (1999). *Through the eyes of the child: Revisioning children as active agents of family life.* New York: JAI.

Simpson, J. A., & Kenrick, D. (Eds.). (1996). *Evolutionary social psychology.* Mahwah, NJ: Lawrence Erlbaum Associates.

Sulloway, F. (2000). Birth order, sibling competition, and human behavior. In P. Davies, & H. Holcomb III (Eds.), *The evolution of minds: Psychological and philosophical perspectives.* Boston, MA: Kluwer.

Taylor, R. D., & Wang, M. C. (Eds.). (1996). *Social and emotional adjustment and family relations in ethnic minority families.* Mahwah, NJ: Lawrence Erlbaum Associates.

Self-Concept

Background

Brief History of the Study of Self

Like many other topics in psychology, the origins of the study of self can be traced back at least to early Greek writings. Aristotle made a distinction between physical and nonphysical aspects of the human being, with the latter (although not precisely defined and later taken over by theology as "soul") referring to the essential and unique core of mental functioning. Two thousand years later, Descartes' concept of *I*, as thinker, knower, cognizer, became one direct predecessor of the concept in self in psychology. Philosophers like Berkeley, Hobbes, Hume, James, and Mill added to the tradition from which psychology partly grew, with their interest in the problems of mind/body dualism, and the nature of experiencing oneself. In Wundt's psychology laboratory, a restricted notion of self prevailed, with the self viewed as the person's experiences of one's own body (e.g., awareness of muscle tension), reported via introspection. Around the turn of the 20th century, William James divided self-experience into three categories: (a) the material me—one's body, home, family, and physical objects around oneself; (b) the social me—one's awareness of one's reputation or identity in the eyes of others; and (c) the spiritual me—one's awareness of one's own mental processes, one's thinking and feeling.

James's work was followed by three decades of interest in study of self. Lasting contributions were made by Cooley (1922) and Mead (1934). Cooley believed that one's ideas of self are significantly affected by what one imagines others think of one; and the term *looking-glass* self emphasized the reflection of imagined appraisals of others. Mead was in agreement with the importance of the reflected appraisals of individuals by significant others in their environment, but emphasized the internalization aspect: Children internalize the ideas and attitudes of key people and adopt them as their own.

Contributions by psychoanalysts also reflect widespread concern with self; ego and mechanisms of defense (S. Freud, 1923; A. Freud, 1966), Fromm's (1939) emphasis on the importance of self-love for human happiness, Horney's (1950) concept of self-alienation, Sullivan's (1963) description of the development of self during infancy and the role of the caretaker in this process, Rogers' (1961) emphasis on the maintenance and enhancement of the self as a basic drive (Florida Educational Research and Development Council, 1968; Gergen, 1971).

The advent of behaviorism in the 1920s, with its emphasis on observable fact, led to a decline in the status of a self-theory that emphasized internal activities. In time, however, there was a loosening of the hard-line positivistic strictures on only observing external activities, and studies of the self-concept and self-esteem resurged. Blascovich and Tomaka, by 1991, reported finding over 30,000 separate references since 1967 in more than 1,300 journals, dissertations, and monographs!

One of the best-known and most widely cited recent authorities on the subject of self is Hazel Markus. She originally studied the operation of self-schemas in meaning-making and in organizing individual experience. She distinguished between characteristics that are central to a person's self conception ("schematic" attributes) and those that are more peripheral and labile ("aschematic" attributes). Perhaps best known is her notion of possible selves (desirable and/or undesirable future selves). Her most recent interest is the study of cultural differences in self-concept (1995, Markus & Kitiyama, 1991).

The *ecological* interaction has now become prominent in the self literature, with emphasis on the family context, the environment, socio-economic factors, and cultural differences (Baumeister, 1986; Breakwell, 1992; Douglas, 1994; Gergen, 1991; Giddens, 1991; McGuire, Neiderhiser, Reiss, Hetherington, & Plomin, 1994; Neisser, 1994; Roopnarine & Carter, 1992; Sameroff, 1987; Seidman, Allen, Aber, Mitchell, & Feinman, 1994; Simmons & Blyth, 1987; Rosenberg & Simmons, 1972; Suls, 1993).

Recognition that an understanding of the self concept requires an *interdisciplinary* effort has resulted in recent publications like Bosma, Graafsma, Grotevant, and DeLevita, (1994), and Schore (1994).

Intervention programs have included efforts to understand low self-esteem (Baumeister, 1993), and helping children to develop self-esteem (Galatzer-Levi, & Cohler, 1993; Joseph, 1994).

Many of these researchers have chosen to avoid the global term *self* and deal with *self-esteem*, *self-alienation, body image,* and other specifiable aspects.

Definitions

Here are some older but typical definitions of *self* and *self-esteem*, rephrased to avoid sexist language.

SELF

that organization of qualities that the individual attributes to himself or herself (Kinch, 1963)

the process by which the person conceptualizes (or categorizes) his or her behavior (both the external conduct and the internal states)

the system of concepts available to the person in attempting to define himself or herself (Gergen, 1971).

SELF-ESTEEM

the extent to which the person feels positive about himself or herself (Gergen, 1971)

a personal judgment of worthiness that is expressed in the attitudes the individual holds toward himself or herself (Coopersmith, 1967)

a person's perception of his or her worth (Henderson, Long, & Ziller, 1967b).

Note that the first set of definitions seems to answer the question, Who am I? and the second seems to have an evaluative dimension: How valuable, worthy, and important am I, compared to others?

Development of the Self-Concept and Self-Esteem in Children

Self-awareness develops slowly as the child recognizes the distinction between self and not-self, between his body and the remainder of his visible environment. Only gradually does he learn to recognize and sort out his body parts, name, feelings, and behavior as integral parts of a single me and build a cluster of beliefs about himself. ...The birth of self-awareness very likely occurs when a child begins to make a distinction between his sensations and the conditions which produce them ... Social interaction is the primary medium through which we come to know ourselves. Self-awareness develops as we compare and contrast our physical bodies, skills, attitudes, and achievements to those of other people. (Hamachek, 1971, pp. 11, 28)

These quotations are typical. There seems to be wide agreement about the initial undifferentiation between self and others in the newborn, and about the slow growth of this differentiation—this distinction between self and nonself in the early months. This process is perhaps fostered by the changing interaction with a mother who decreases demand feeding as the months go on and expects more accommodation of the child to the realities of family living. The differentiation between self and not-self certainly seems related to the growth of the object concept, during which the child learns to see herself or himself as an object in space and time, separate from the mother. Bell (1970) related the development of object and person concept to the mother–infant attachment, indicating that differences in the rate of development of person permanence are related to the quality of attachment that baby shows towards mother. The early growth of self is tied by Sullivan (1953) to the emerging concepts of good me/bad me based largely on interactions with the mother, and similarly by Erikson (1963) to the resolution of the trust–mistrust nuclear conflict.

The process of learning and establishing one's self is variously called *imitation, observational learning, or internalization of the behavior of significant others*, and there are more than semantic differences among these terms. All, however, agree on the importance of the family or caretakers in this process. Parsons traces this sequence from the mother–child dyad to the nuclear family system, to peers and school, and media (Baldwin, 1966).

The following picture of development of self comes from standard child psychology texts and references listed at the end.

Preschool Years. Children's understandings of the family's perception of them certainly seem crucial in the ideas children develop about themselves. The pattern of identification with same-sex parent and cross-sex identification with opposite-sex parent is apparently influenced to some extent by the nurturance, affection, competence, and power notions that children have about their respective parents. Sex-typing and conscience development, which appear to be two of the major products of the identification process, are important components of the child's answer to the Who am I? question. Those preschoolers characterized as mature, competent, and independent have parents who are consistent, warm, loving, and secure. Authoritative (not authoritarian) parental control and positive encouragement of a child's independence and strivings for autonomy apparently foster positive qualities.

At about age two, children show a growing sensitivity to adults' standards of good/bad, an awareness of their competence to meet those standards, and an ability to create their own plans and develop autonomy (Cole & Cole, 1993; Kagan, 1981). Stipek, Recchia, and McClintic (1992) suggested that self-evaluation in young children develops in three stages: First, very young children experience joy in their outcome and products, but still lack the cognitive representational skills required for self-evaluation and self-reflection. They still can't usually anticipate others' reactions to their performance. By the age of two, they can anticipate adult reactions and seek positive reactions to successes. In the proposed third stage, they begin to evaluate and react emotionally to their own performance independent of adult reactions. They gradually internalize outsiders' reactions. They are developing a sense of autonomy.

Middle Childhood and Preadolescence. As a result of activities and competitive games with peers, and school evaluation and competition, deliberate and pervasive social comparison becomes important at about eight years of age. Children use these comparative assessments heavily with regard to their physical prowess, their school achievements, their social success, and their psychological state (Damon & Hart, 1988; Ruble & Frey, 1991).

On the basis of work with 10- to 12-year-olds, Coopersmith (1967) emphasized four basic factors in the development of self-esteem: (a) the interaction between parent and child with respect to acceptance, (b) the importance of clear delineation of firm rules and limits of behavior, (c) the necessity of mutual respect and a basically noncoercive relationship, and (d) the relevance of the parents' own self-esteem. Not all of these are essential for the formation of high self-esteem in children, but a combination of some are effective, when combined with a minimum of devaluating conditions like rejection, disrespect, ambiguity.

Adolescence. Adolescents face the problems of feeling "whole" and "separate" and "belonging" all at the same time. The development of identity requires that they perceive themselves as separate from family and peers despite strong ties and needs for them and that they have a feeling of "wholeness" or self-consistency over time. The latter is particularly difficult in view of the tremendous physical changes taking place, which require time to be integrated (Williams & Currie, 2000). The adolescents' means of coping are often to conform in social behavior, appearance, and physical skills to the peer group, and to be adversely affected in what they think of themselves by deviations from idealized norms and stereotypes.

This is a very difficult time, developmentally. The adolescent needs to establish an identity with regard to commitments in occupational choice, religion, political ideology, and sexual orientation (Kroger, 1993; Marcia, 1980; Marcia, Waterman, Matteson, Archer, & Orlofsky, 1993). Cultural attitudes toward gender differentially affect the self-esteem of males and females (Gilligan, 1977, 1982; Jacobs, et al., in press; Simmons & Blyth, 1987). Cultural influences on adolescents' self-image in ten countries were examined by Offer, Ostrov, Howard, and Atkinson (1988), and Markus and Kitayama (1991) looked at contrasting cultures—those that stress an *independent* construal of self and those that stress an *interdependent* construal of self. Chan (2000) compared minority British-Chinese 11–18 year olds to White British and Hong Kong Chinese youngsters.

Harter (1999), an authority on the self system, recently focused her attention on the multiple selves that adolescents create as they achieve greater differentiation. This can lead to opposing characteristics, like being cheerful with peers but depressed with parents or oppositional with teachers.

Interest in the stability or changes of self-esteem is not limited to birth through adolescence. Different portions of the life span have been examined by Byrne (1996), Case (1991), Damon and Hart (1988), Harter (1999), Moore and Lemmon (2001), Newman and Newman (1995), and Pomerantz and Eaton (2000).

Group Differences

Unqualified statements about age, sex, race, and class differences are unrealistic in view of the inconsistent and contradictory data. Differences frequently are not shown to exist. When they do surface, the tendency is for higher scores (better self-esteem or self-concept) for boys over girls, White over Black, middle class over working class, younger over older children. The sex and race differences are especially controversial. Many studies do not report any differences, or sometimes higher scores for Blacks (Rosenberg, 1983; Gray-Little & Hafdahl, 2000), perhaps due to self-protection by members of stigmatized groups, or defensive or self-enhancing biases (Crocker & Major, 1989). Interpretations of differences often borrow from the cognitive theorists the notions of greater maturity, increased realism, and increased perception of differences between ideal self and present self.

Hamacheck (1971) offered an interesting elaboration on possible sex differences, involving two of the major factors in child-rearing: expressions of affection on the one hand and expressions of punishment, control, and authority on the other. It may be that affection and punishment are used in different ways and for different purposes for boys and girls. Girls may be subjected to love-oriented discipline techniques, whereas boys may be subjected to more physical punishment but with more aggression permitted and with more stress on independence and achievement. Socialization practices appear to direct the boy toward the environment but protect the girl from the environment. As a consequence then, girls are (and see themselves as) more obedient, cooperative, and socially adjusted but more anxious, dependent, and sensitive to rejection. Boys are (and see themselves as) independent, confident, self-sufficient, and they have initiative. These sex differences may, of course, be true of the 1960s and 1970s, but close monitoring of these effects during the 1980s and 1990s reveal changes in society that are reflected in parents' child-rearing practices and peer-group relationships. Differential treatment of boys and girls (and men and women) have implications for personality development, social interactions, and clinical issues.

Measures

R. Crandall (in Robinson & Shaver, 1973) reviewed and evaluated 30 measures of self-esteem and related constructs, and included an annotated bibliography of 30 others. (See also Robinson & Shaver, 1991.) Wylie (1961) covered earlier tests, and in her newer volume (1974) reviews methodological considerations and measuring instruments for the self-concept. Walker (1973) limited her handbook to measures for preschool and kindergarten children, and includes 18 tests of self-concept. Blascovich and Tomaka (1991) reviewed five scales developed for use with adolescents and adults, two scales for children, and five scales dealing with narrower or related constructs of self or self-esteem. Byrne (1996) discussed issues and intrumentation in measuring self-concept across the life span. Davis-Kean and Sandler (2001) have performed a meta-analysis of measures of self-esteem for young children.

We call your attention here to several techniques we have used with children in this laboratory course and related research courses:

1. **Engel and Raine's Where Are You Game (1963)** has children in lower elementary school place themselves on a five-rung ladder with regard to seven bipolar dimensions. This is described in detail in Experiment 8.

2. **Thomas Self-Concept Values Test for Children, Ages 3-9 (1967).** Fourteen values were chosen because they appeared to Thomas to be related to the developmental tasks of preschool and primary school children, to the cultural demands of middle-class youngsters, and to the problems young children experience. The value factors are happiness, cleanliness, sociability, sharing, ability, male acceptance, fear of things, fear of people, strength, size, health, attractiveness, material things, and independence. A Polaroid photograph is taken of each child and identified by the child. Then the children report their perceptions of themselves and their perceptions of their mothers', teachers', and peers' perception of them on each of the 14 items: Is Charlie Brown happy or is he sad? Does Charlie Brown's teacher think that Charlie Brown is happy or sad? Does Charlie Brown's mother think that he is happy or sad? Do the other kids in the class think that Charlie Brown is happy or sad? McAdoo (1970) used this scale on young Black children in the north and south, and more recently in the Washington, DC area.

3. **Coopersmith Self-Esteem Inventory (1967).** Based on a 1954 pool of items by Rogers and Dymond, and shortened and reworded for use with children in an upper elementary school, this scale is self-administered in about 10 to 15 minutes, using the briefer version appearing in Robinson and Shaver's handbook (1973). Coopersmith (1975) reduced the original list of items to 25. Although several

kinds of validation (convergent, discriminant, and predictive) are available, we have not found that children of these ages generally like to take this questionnaire. Given the opportunity to comment on specific items, they make incisive comments about the lack of situational context cues and get annoyed at various ambiguities in the phrasing. Care needs to be taken in enlisting serious cooperation.

4. **Who Am I or Who Are You tests.** Nadelman (unpublished) had 240 children, equally divided by sex, socioeconomic status (working vs. professional middle class), and age (5- and 8-year-olds) tell three things about themselves (as the introduction to a large battery of sex-identity and perception-of-parents measures). Bugental and Zelen (1950) and Kuhn and McPartland (1954) had college students answer the question Who Am I? three times and 20 times, respectively, and coded the responses for strength of self-derogation and self-positivity. Gordon (1968) subjected the individual's first 15 answers to a computer analysis, coding each response first into one or more of 30 content categories and then with respect to evaluative weightings, to yield a total self-evaluation score. Most responses fell into two categories: (a) one's membership in various formal and informal groups, and (b) personal or specific attributes of the individual.

This kind of test is quick, flexible, and full of coding possibilities. It can be done verbally with young children and in writing with older ones. There are little validity data published as yet.

5. **Disparity between real self, ideal self, and social self.** We have not yet used this technique with children, but others have; for example, Katz and Zigler (1967) with fifth, eighth, and eleventh graders. The child is asked to go through a questionnaire similar to the Coopersmith one and/or a list of positive and negative adjectives three times: Once for the real self (this is very true of me), once for the ideal self (I would like this to be true of me), once for the social self (people think this is very true of me). The differences between these ratings—the disparity scores—are interpreted differently by different theories. It was common to treat the real-ideal self disparity as a general indicator of maladjustment. A more recent notion is that such disparity is positively related to the individual's level of maturity. It is possible that the more mature person makes greater self-demands and experiences more guilt at not fulfilling them. It is also possible that the more mature person has greater differentiating ability (in the Werner or Piaget sense), that this individual employs more categories and makes finer distinctions within each category, and consequently has greater disparity between self and ideal self ratings (Katz & Zigler, 1967).

6. **Rosenberg and Simmons (1972) Self-esteem Scale (SES) for children.** The original scale of 10 items for adolescents, also used for adults, is the most popular (i.e., most utilized) measure of global self-esteem (Rosenberg, 1965), but is face valid and therefore open to social desirability pressures. The 6-item adaptation for children requires an in-person interview, and is applicable for Black and White children.

7. **Piers-Harris Children's Self-concept Scale (1984).** An 80-item self-report inventory with yes/no answers, designed for 8–18 year-olds, this scale should be read aloud to younger children. It yields a total score and six subscales relevant to self-esteem.

8. **Self-Perception Profile for Children (SPPC), Harter (1985).** Two versions of the 24-item scale exist, one for kindergartners, one for first- and second-graders. The tests look at competence and acceptance in five domains (scholastic competence, social acceptance, athletic competence, physical appearance, and behavioral conduct) plus global self-worth. The third- to eighth-grade version uses pairs of pictures, with positive or negative depiction, respectively. The child decides which is most like him or her, and then whether it is "sort of true" or "really true" for self. Six subscales have six items each, and usually are well accepted by children. Similar scales without pictures are produced for older subjects.

General Comment

An understanding of the development of self-concept and self-esteem requires an understanding of the role of family dynamics in the construction of the child's identity, of the relation between the development of self-concept and the development of cognitive ability, and therefore of the interacting role of *both* socialization and cognition to the development of self. Recent efforts have dealt more explicitly with the emotional and neurobehavioral components of the self construct, and with cultural and ethnic influences. It is important to recognize that parental childrearing styles have different meanings in different cultures, sexes, and ages.

SELECTED BIBLIOGRAPHY

Ashmore, R. D., & Jussim, L. (Eds.). (1997). *Self and identity: Fundamental issues*. New York: Oxford University Press.

Baldwin, A. L. (1966). *Theories of child development*. New York: Wiley (See chap. 18, The family as a social system.)

Banks, J. A., & Grambs, J. D. (Eds.). (1972). *Black self-concept: Implications for education and social science*. New York: McGraw-Hill.

Baumeister, R. F. (1986). *Identity: Cultural change and the struggle for self*. New York: Oxford University Press.

Baumeister, R. F. (Ed.). (1993). *Self-esteem: The puzzle of low self-regard*. New York, NY: Plenum.

Bell, S. M. (1970). The development of the concept of object as related to infant-mother attachment. *Child Development, 41*(2), 291–311.

Blascovich, J., & Tomaka, J. (1991). Measures of self-esteem. In J. P. Robinson and P. R. Shaver, *Measures of personality and social-psychological attitudes*. Orlando, FL: Academic Press.

Bosma, H. A., Graafsma, T. L. G., Grotevant, H. D., & DeLevita, D. J. (Eds.). (1994). *Identity and development: An interdisciplinary approach*. Thousand Oaks, CA: Sage.

Breakwell, G. M. (1992). *Social psychology of identity and the self concept*. Orlando, FL: Academic Press.

Bugental, J., & Zelen, S. (1950). Investigations into the "self-concept," I. The W-A-Y technique. *Journal of Personality, 18*, 483–498.

Byrne, B. M. (1996). *Measuring self-concept across the life span: Issues and instrumentation*. Washington, DC: American Psychological Association.

Carpenter, T. R., & Busse, T. V. (1969). Development of self concept in Negro and white welfare children. *Child Development, 40*(3), 935–940.

Case, R. (1991). Stages in the development of the young child's sense of self. *Developmental Review, 11*, 210–230.

Chan, Y. M. (2000). Self-esteem: A cross-cultural comparison of British-Chinese, White British and Hong Kong Chinese children. *Educational Psychology, 20*(1), 59–74.

Cole, M., & Cole, S. R. (1993). *The development of children* (2nd ed.). New York: Scientific American Books, W. H. Freeman.

Cole, M., Maxwell, S. E., Martin, J. M., Peeke, A. D., Seroczynski, A. D., Tram, J. M., Hoffman, K. B., Ruiz, M. D., Jacquez, F., & Maschman, T. (2001). The development of multiple domains of child and adolescent self-concept: A cohort sequential longitudinal design. *Child Development, 72*(6), 1723–1746.

Cooley, C. H. (1922). *Human nature and the social order*. New York: Scribner.

Coopersmith, S. (1959). A method for determining types of self-esteem. *Journal of Abnormal and Social Psychology, 1*, 87–94.

Coopersmith, S. (1967). *The antecedents of self-esteem*. San Francisco: Freeman and Company.

Coopersmith, S. (1975). *Coopersmith Self-esteem Inventory, technical manual*. Palo Alto, CA:: Consulting Psychologists Press.

Crocker, J., & Major, B. (1989). Social stigma and self-esteem: The self-protective properties of stigma. *Psychological Review, 96*, 608–630.

Culp, R. E., Schadle, S., Robinson, L., & Culp, A. M. (2000). Relationships among parental involvement and young children's perceived self-competence and behavioral problems. *Journal of Child & Family Studies, 9*(1), 27–38.

Damon, W., & Hart, D. (1988). *Self-understanding in childhood and adolescence*. New York: Cambridge University Press.

Davis-Kean, P. E., & Sandler, H. M. (2001). A meta-analysis of measures of self-esteem for young children: A framework for future measures. *Child Development, 72*(3), 887–906.

Douglas, S. D. (1994). *Where the girls are: Growing up female with the mass media*. New York: Times Books.

Engel, M., & Raine, W. J. (1963). A method for the measurement of the self-concept of children in the third grade. *Journal of Genetic Psychology, 102*, 125–137.

Erikson, E. H. (1963). *Childhood and society* (2nd ed.). New York: Norton.

Florida Educational Research and Development Council. (1968). The search for self: Evaluating student self-concepts. *Research Bulletin, 4*(2).

Freud, A. (1966). *The ego and the mechanisms of defense: The writings of Anna Freud* (*Vol. 2*). New York: International Universities Press.

Freud, S. (1923). *The ego and the id*. London: Hogarth.

Fromm, E. (1939). Selfishness and self-love. *Psychiatry, 2*, 507–523.

Funder, D. C., Parke, R. D., Keasey, C. A. T., & Widaman, K. (Eds.). (1993). *Studying lives through time: Personality and development*. Washington, DC: American Psychological Association.

Galatzer-Levi, R. M., & Cohler, B. J. (1993). *The essential other: A developmental psychology of the self.* New York: Basic Books.

Gergen, K. J. (1971). *The concept of self.* New York: Holt, Rinehart, and Winston.

Gergen, K. J. (1991). *The saturated self: Dilemmas of identity in contemporary life.* New York: Basic Books.

Giddens, A. (1991). *Modernity and identity: Self and society in the late modern age.* Stanford, CA: Stanford University Press.

Gilligan, C. (1977). In a different voice: Women's conceptions of self and morality. *Harvard Educational Review, 47,* 481–517.

Gilligan, C. (1982). *In a different voice: Psychological theory and women's development.* Cambridge, MA: Harvard University Press.

Gordon, C. (1968). Self-conceptions: Configurations of content. In C. Gordon & K. J. Gergen (Eds.), *The self in social interaction, (Vol. 1), Classic and contemporary perspectives.* New York: Wiley.

Gray-Little, B., & Hafdahl, A. R. (2000). Factors influencing racial comparisons of self-esteem: A quantitative review. *Psychological Bulletin, 126*(1), 26–54.

Grusec, J. E., & Lytton, H. (1988). *Social development: History, theory and research.* New York: Springer Verlag.

Hamachek, D. E. (1971). *Encounters with the self.* New York: Holt, Rinehart, and Winston.

Harter, S. (1983). Developmental perspectives on the self-system. In M. Hetherington (Ed.), *Carmichael's manual of child psychology: Social and personality development* (pp. 275–385). New York: Wiley.

Harter, S. (1985). *Manual for the Self-Perception Profile for Children* (revision of *The Perceived Competence Scale for Children*). Denver, CO: University of Denver.

Harter, S. (1986). Processes underlying the construction, maintenance, and enhancement of the self-concept in children. In J. Suls & A. G. Greenwald (Eds.), *Psychological perspectives on the self* (Vol. 3, pp. 137–181). Hillsdale, NJ: Lawrence Erlbaum Associates.

Harter, S. (1998). The development of self-representation. In W. Damon (Editor-in-Chief) & N. Eisenberg (Vol. Ed.), *Handbook of child psychology: Vol. 3. Social, emotional, and personality development* (5th ed, pp. 553–617). New York: Wiley.

Harter, S. (2001, paperback; 1999 hardcover). *The construction of the self: A developmental perspective.* New York: Guilford.

Harter, S., & Pike, R. G. (1983). *The Pictorial Scale of Perceived Competence and Acceptance for Young Children.* Denver, CO: University of Denver.

Hattie, J. (1992). *Self-concept.* Hillsdale, NJ: Lawrence Erlbaum Associates.

Henderson, E. H., Long, B. H., & Ziller, R. C. (1967). *Children's self-social constructs test, preschool form.* (Obtainable from Educational Testing Service, Office of Special Tests, 17 Executive Park Drive, NE, Suite 100, Atlanta, Georgia, 30329.)

Horney, K. (1950). *Neurosis and human growth.* New York: Norton.

Jacobs, J. E., Lanza, D., Osgood, W., Eccles, J. S., & Wigfield, A. (2002). Changes in children's self-competence and values: Gender and domain differences across grades one through twelve. *Child Development, 73*(2), 509–527.

Joseph, J. M. (1994). *The resilient child: Preparing today's youth for tomorrow's world.* New York: Plenum Publishing.

Kagan, J. (1981). *The second year.* Cambridge, MA: Harvard University Press.

Katz, P., & Zigler, E. (1967). Self-image disparity: A developmental approach. *Journal of Personality and Social Psychology, 5,* 186–195. Also in I. J. Gordon (Ed.), (1971), *Readings in research in developmental psychology.* Glenview, IL: Scott, Foresman, pp. 341–351.

Kernis, M. H., Brown, A. C., & Brody, G. H. (2000). Fragile self-esteem in children and its associations with perceived patterns of parent-child communication. *Journal of Personality, 68*(2), 225–252.

Kinch, J. W. (1963). A formalized theory of the self-concept. *American Journal of Sociology, 68,* 481.

Kroger, J. (Ed.). (1993). *Discussions on ego identity.* Hillsdale, NJ: Lawrence Erlbaum Associates.

Kuhn, M. H., & McPartland, T. S. (1954). An empirical investigation of self-attitudes. *American Sociological Review, 19,* 68–76.

Lipsitt, L. P. (1958). A self concept scale for children and its relationship to the children's form of the manifest anxiety scale. *Child Development, 29,* 463–472.

Long, B. H., Henderson, E. H., & Ziller, R. C. (1967a). *Children's self-social constructs test, primary form.* (Obtainable from Educational Testing Service, Office of Special Tests, 17 Executive Park Drive, NE, Suite 100, Atlanta, Georgia, 30329.)

Long, B. H., Henderson, E. H., & Ziller, R. C. (1967b). Developmental changes in the self-concept during middle childhood. *Merrill-Palmer Quarterly, 13,* 201–215.

Long, B. H., Henderson, E. H., & Ziller, R. C. (1967c). *Manual for the self-social symbols task and the children's self-social constructs test.* (Obtainable from Educational Testing Service, Office of Special Tests, 17 Executive Park Drive, NE, Suite 100, Atlanta, Georgia, 30329.)

Marcia, J. E. (1980). Identity in adolescence. In J. Adelson (Ed.), *Handbook of adolescent psychology* (pp. 159–187). New York: Wiley.

Marcia, J. E., Waterman, A. S., Matteson, D. R., Archer, S. L., & Orlofsky, J. L. (1993). *Ego identity: A handbook for psychosocial research.* New York: Springer-Verlag.

Markus, H. (1977). Self-schemata and processing information about the self. *Journal of Personality and Social Psychology, 35*(2), 63–78.

Markus, H. R. (1995). The sociocultural self. *Newsletter, International Society for the Study of Behavioral Development*, No. 1, Serial No. 27, 10–11.

Markus, H. R., & Kitayama, S. (1991). Culture and the self: Implications for cognition, emotion, and motivation. *Psychological Review, 98*, 224–253.

McAdoo, H. (1970). *Racial attitudes and self concepts of black preschool children.* Doctoral Dissertation, University of Michigan.

McGuire, S., Neiderhiser, J. N., Reiss, D., Hetherington, E. M., & Plomin, R. (1994). Genetic and environmental influences on perceptions of self-worth and competence in adolescence: A study of twins, full siblings, and step siblings. *Child Development, 65*(3), 785–799.

Mead, G. H. (1934). *Mind, self, and society.* Chicago: University of Chicago Press.

Moore, C., & Lemmon, K. (Eds.). (2001). *The self in time: Developmental perspectives.* Mahwah, NJ: Lawrence Erlbaum Associates.

Neisser, U. (Ed.). (1994). *The perceived self: Ecological and interpersonal sources of self knowledge.* New York, NY: Cambridge University Press.

Newman, B. M., & Newman, P. R. (1995). *Development through life: A psychosocial approach.* Pacific Grove, CA: Brooks/Cole.

Offer, D., Ostrov, E., Howard, K. I., & Atkinson, R. (1988). *The teenage world: Adolescents self-image in ten countries.* New York: Plenum Press.

Oosterwegal, A., & Oppenheimer, L. (1993). *The self-system: Developmental changes between and within self-concepts.* Hillsdale, NJ: Lawrence Erlbaum Associates.

Parker, S. T., Mitchell, R. W., & Boccia, M. L. (Eds.). (1994). *Self-awareness in animals and humans: Developmental perspectives.* New York: Cambridge University Press.

Piers, E. V. (1984). *Piers-Harris Children's Self-Concept Scale: Revised Manual.* Los Angeles, CA: Western Psychological Services.

Pomerantz, E. M., & Eaton, M. M. (2000). Developmental differences in children's conceptions of parental control: "They love me, but they make me feel incompetent." *Merrill-Palmer Quarterly, 46*(1), 140–167.

Robinson, J. P., & Shaver, P. R. (1973). *Measures of social psychological attitudes* (Rev. ed.). Ann Arbor, MI: Survey Research Center, Institute for Social Research.

Robinson, J. P., & Shaver, P. R. (1991). *Measures of personality and social-psychological attitudes.* Orlando, FL: Academic Press.

Rogers, C. (1961). *On becoming a person.* Boston: Houghton Mifflin.

Roopnarine, J. L., & Carter, D. B. (Eds.). (1992). *Parent-child socialization in diverse cultures.* Norwood, NJ: Ablex.

Rosenberg, M. (1965). *Society and the adolescent self-image.* Princeton, NJ: Princeton University Press.

Rosenberg, M. (1983). Self-esteem research: A phenomenological corrective. In *Advancing the art of inquiry in school desegregation research.* Santa Monica, CA: System Development Corporation.

Rosenberg, M., & Simmons, R. G. (1972). *Black and white self-esteem: The urban school child.* Washington, DC: American Sociological Association.

Ruble, D. N., & Frey, K. S. (1991). Changing patterns of comparative behavior as skills are acquired: A functional model of self-evaluation. In J. Suls & T. H. Wells (Eds.), *Social comparison: Contemporary theory and research* (pp. 79–113). Hillsdale, NJ: Lawrence Erlbaum Associates.

Sameroff, A. J. (1987). The social context of development. In N. Eisenberg (Ed.), *Contemporary topics in developmental psychology* (pp. 273–291). New York: Wiley.

Schore, A. N. (1994). *Affect regulation and the origin of the self: The neurobiology of emotional development.* Hillsdale, NJ: Lawrence Erlbaum Associates.

Seidman, E., Allen, L., Aber, J. L., Mitchell, C., & Feinman, J. (1994). The impact of school transitions in early adolescence on the self-system and perceived social context of poor urban youth. *Child Development, 65*, 507–522.

Simmons, R. G., & Blyth, D. A. (1987). *Moving into adolescence: The impact of pubertal change in school context.* New York: A. de Gruyter.

Stipeck, D., Recchia, S., & McClintic, S. (1992). Self-evaluation in young children. *Monographs of the Society for Research in Child Development, 57*(1, Serial No. 226).

Sullivan, H .S. (1953). *The interpersonal theory of psychiatry.* New York: Norton.

Suls, J. (Ed.). (1993). *Psychological perspectives on the self, (Vol. 4): The self in social perspective.* Hillsdale, NJ: Lawrence Erlbaum Associates.

Taylor, R. D., & Wang, M. C. (Eds.). (1996). *Social and emotional adjustment and family relations in ethnic minority families.* Mahwah, NJ: Lawrence Erlbaum Associates.

Tesser, A., Felson, R. B., & Suls, J. M. (Eds.). (2000). *Psychological perspectives on self and identity.* Washington, DC: American Psychological Association.

Tesser, A., Stapel, D. A., & Wood, J. V. (Eds.). (2002). *Self and motivation: Emerging psychological perspectives.* Washington, DC: American Psychological Association.

Thomas, W. L. (1967). *The Thomas Self-Concept Values Test for Children, Ages 3–9.* (Obtainable from Educational Testing Service Company, P. O. Box 1882, Grand Rapids, Michigan 48501.)

Thorne, A., & Michaelieu, Q. (1996). Situating adolescent gender and self-esteem with personal memories. *Child Development, 67,* 1374–1390.

Walker, D. K. (1973). *Socioemotional measures for preschool and kindergarten children: A handbook.* San Francisco: Jossey-Bass.

Watson, G. S., & Gross, A. M. (2000). Familial determinants. In M. Herson & R. T. Ammerman (Eds.), *Advanced abnormal child psychology* (2nd ed., pp. 81–99). Mahwah, NJ: Lawrence Erlbaum Associates.

Williams, J. M., & Currie, C. (2000). Self-esteem and physical development in early adolescence: Pubertal timing and body image. *Journal of Early Adolescence: Special issue: Self-esteem in early adolescence, 20*(2), 129–149.

Wylie, R. (1961). *The self-concept: A critical survey of pertinent literature.* Lincoln: University of Nebraska Press.

Wylie, R. (1974). *The self-concept: A review of methodological considerations and measuring instruments* (Rev. ed.). Lincoln: University of Nebraska Press.

Ziller, R. C., Long, B. H., & Henderson, E. H. (1966). *Self-social symbols tasks, adolescent form.* (Obtainable from Educational Testing Service, Office of Special Tests, 17 Executive Park, NE, Suite 100, Atlanta, Georgia 30329.)

Experiment 8

Age and Sex Differences in Self-Esteem

Problem and Hypotheses

The differences in self-esteem between boys and girls, and between early- and middle-elementary school-aged children, will be assessed with the Where Are You Game (Engel & Raine, 1963).

1. Younger children obtain (higher) (lower) (equal) scores on this self-esteem measure compared to older children.

2. Boys obtain (higher) (lower) (equal) scores on this self-esteem measure compared to girls.

3. Scale differences? (Read the test description first.)

   Do you expect the seven scales to differ in the positiveness of the self-esteem scores obtained by the whole group of children?
   Do you predict boys will be higher than girls on specific scales? Which ones?
   Do you predict girls will be higher than boys on specific scales? Which ones?
   Do you expect certain scales to have higher correlations with the total self-esteem scores than others? Which ones?

Method

Subjects

Boys and girls in the first grade and in the fourth grade, of the same race and of homogeneous socio-economic class.

Materials

Where Are You Game (Engel & Raine, 1963, slightly modified)

Individual Data Sheet

Crayons or thick pens

The Where Are You Game requires a child to rate himself or herself on seven bipolar dimension that the constructors thought important in the child's self-concept:

A. seeing oneself as intellectually gifted versus seeing oneself as lacking in such capacities;

B. seeing oneself as happy as opposed to considering oneself unhappy;

C. considering oneself well liked by peers versus seeing oneself as unpopular;

    D. seeing oneself as brave as opposed to considering oneself easily frightened;

    E. conceiving of oneself as physically attractive or unattractive;

    F. considering oneself strong or weak physically;

    G. seeing oneself as doing what one should versus seeing oneself as being disobedient.

For each of the seven dimensions, there is a page with five lines, vertically arranged, representing the five-point rating scale. Next to the top and bottom line, there are stick figures (Fig. G8.1 at the end of the experiment).

Procedure

The experimenter seats the child in front of a table and presents the crayons and the rating sheet, saying, **"Today we'll look at these pictures together. Here is a sheet of paper with some lines on it and two boys."** ["Girls" and "she" should be substituted throughout when testing females.] **"Let me tell you about these boys. Here** [point] **is the boy who is very smart. He learns easily and remembers well, and is a good thinker. Now let's look at the other boy** [point]. **This boy is not very smart. He finds it hard to learn and remember, and he is not a good thinker."** [Permit the child to comment, change drawings, explore the situation briefly.]

    "Now I'll tell you about the other lines in between. When I finish, you'll take your crayon and decide where you are between these two boys, and make a mark on one of these five lines. If you put your check mark here [point to appropriate line], **that means you think you are like him** [point to smart boy]— **smart and a good learner, a good rememberer, a good thinker. If you put your check mark here** [point to appropriate line], **that means that you think you are like him** [point to other boy]— **not very smart, a poor learner, not very good at remembering and thinking. But you can put your mark anywhere in between, on these three lines, too** [point to each], **depending on where you are."** [Expand on the other three lines. Try to ascertain whether the child has understood the five-point rating scale and your instruction. Have him place his check mark as he wishes, and allow him to make changes in his decision if he wishes to.]

    "Now I would like you to tell me how come you decided to put your mark on that line." [Record the child's response verbatim on the Individual Data Sheet.]

    Remove the rating sheet from sight; supply the next one, and repeat the same procedure for each of the seven dimensions, with appropriate changes in the wording, as follows:

    A. [As given above.]

    B. **"Here is a boy who is very happy. He's always smiling and laughing and full of fun ... This boy is not very happy; in fact, he's mostly sad and serious. He doesn't smile and laugh like the other one."**

    C. **"Here is a boy who has a lot of friends. He is well liked and popular ... This boy has very few friends. He is not well liked. He is not very popular."**

    D. **"Here is a boy who is very brave. He's hard to frighten and is very courageous ... This boy is not very brave. He gets frightened easily and is not very courageous."**

    E. **"Here is a boy (girl) who is very handsome (pretty). He is very attractive and good looking ... This boy (girl) is not very handsome (pretty). He is not very attractive and not very good looking."**

    F. **"Here is a boy who is very strong. He is sturdy; he is not physically weak ... This boy is not very strong. He is weak physically; he is not sturdy."**

    G. **"Here is a boy who does as he is told. He minds well and is very obedient ... Here is a boy who is very disobedient. He does not mind; he does not do as he's told."**

    The scales are presented in the given order, with the inquiry following each rating. The positive and negative poles are counterbalanced so that for *each* child, 3 (or 4) of the positive dimensions are associated with the top line, 4 (or 3) of the negative dimensions are associated with the bottom line. This can most easily be accomplished by having each experimenter given the appropriate instruction in advance for each child; for example, "A-Top positive" would mean "smart boy on top rung, dumb one bottom." The experimenter would then know that scale B would be top-negative; scale C, top-positive; and so on, *alternately*. An equal number of experimenters would be started "A-Top negative." It is, therefore, crucial that each experimenter label *each* rating sheet, preferably on the back, and in advance, with the scale letter or name, and a + for positive on the top or bottom as appropriate.

Note that on the Individual Data Sheet, the name of the experiment and the name of each scale are abbreviated to limit the subjects to the information directly given them.

Results

Scoring. The five lines permit a 1–5 rating, with 5 points being the most positive (most smart, happy, popular, etc.), and 1 point the least positive. Be very careful, because with the counterbalancing, the 5-point line is sometimes the top, sometimes the bottom. With seven scales, the minimum positiveness rating any child could get would be 7; the maximum, 35 points. Translate the child's rating, as indicated by the check mark on each sheet, to the appropriate number and enter it on the Individual Data Sheet. Find the child's total self-esteem score by adding the seven number ratings, compute the mean scale score, and find the median scale score.

Data Analysis. Record the information from the child's Individual Data Sheet on the Master Data Sheets (provided by the instructor) for the grade and sex of your subjects.

Find the mean and median measures for each age-sex group and enter them on Table G8.1 on the Group Data Sheet provided.

Engel and Raine (1963) used analysis of variance to test for significance of the differences between children and between scales. Should you decide to run a 2 X 2 analysis of variance for age and sex differences, use the columns from the master tables headed *Total Self-Esteem Score*, and summarize the computations in Table G8.2.

Carpenter and Busse (1969), however, noted that their data were highly skewed (piling up toward the more positive end of the self-esteem scale), and that the assumptions underlying the analysis of variance could, therefore, not be met. They used instead a series of Mann-Whitney U tests. The U test is one of the most powerful of the nonparametric tests, and a very useful alternative to parametric measures when you're worried about meeting the assumptions underlying the latter. The null hypothesis of this test is that your groups have the same distribution. See a statistics text which includes nonparametric tests for detailed description and procedure. If you use this test, fill in the summary Table G8.3.

Another alternative would be to use a somewhat less powerful but simpler nonparametric measure, the median test, whose null hypothesis is that your groups are from populations with the same median. Read about chi-square tests in your statistics book for the description and steps to follow. If you use this test, fill in the Table G8.4. The size of the sample determines whether you use chi-square or Fisher tests to analyze data split at the median.

Sometimes, the skewness of the data and the heterogeneity of variance in groups can be handled by transformations of the scores, using square root, logarithmic, or reciprocal transformations. This may make the application of analysis of variance appropriate.

If the class has some time to explore statistics, it is interesting to use all three techniques (analysis of variance, Mann-Whitney U tests, median tests), with each one third of the class using the assigned one. Are your respective conclusions about the significance of your data the same?

To see the relations among the scales, and how closely each relates to the total self-esteem score, Pearson correlations may be run. Use Table G8.5.

It is possible and profitable to compare the choice of extreme ratings of self-esteem in each grade, either by counting the *number of children* choosing lines 1 and 5, or by counting the *number of 1s and 5s ratings* on the Master Data Sheet for each group. (Again, be careful of the top/bottom counterbalancing.) Enter the latter frequencies in Table G8.6.

State Your Findings. Do the means in Table G8.1 show the predicted age differences, and is this effect statistically significant (Tables G8.2, G8.3, or G8.4)? Is there a statistically significant sex difference, and in what direction? Did your children tend to use only the top and bottom lines, and was this most noticeable for younger children? Were there more individual differences in scores in the younger or older groups? in boys or girls?

Discussion

Relate your data to the first hypothesis about age effects. How do your results compare with the Carpenter and Busse (1969) data? Two cautions are in order when comparing your data to those of Carpenter and Busse:

1. Use the means for the appropriate race.

2. Their scale is the reverse of ours: In theirs, the lower mean scores indicate the more positive self-concept. Use the following conversion:

Engel and Raine	Scale	1	2	3	4	5
	Total	7	14	12	28	35
Carpenter and Busse	Total	35	28	21	14	7
	Scale	5	4	3	2	1
		Low			High	
		Self-Esteem			Self-Esteem	

You will find Gray-Little and Hafdahl's (2000) analysis of racial comparisons of self-esteem worthwhile.

It is interesting to note that in working with educable mentally handicapped children, chronologically aged 8 to 9 years and 12 to 13 years, we found Where Are You Game scores of 32.47 and 28.97, respectively (*F* for age significant at .01). Shiffler, Lynch-Sauer, and Nadelman (1977) found no significant grade differences in a first- through sixth-grade sample in open classrooms, using a different measure—a modified Davidson and Lang Adjective Checklist.

Is your hypothesis about sex differences confirmed by your data? Relate your results to the Carpenter and Busse (1969) finding of higher self-concept in boys (much more noticeable in their Black than their White children); and the Nadelman and Wallace finding of no significant sex difference in first-grade children. (The latter experiment used Wallace's variation of the Engel and Raine measure). In a series of studies to examine the development of self-evaluation in children aged 1–5 years, Stipek, Recchia, and McClintic (1992) found few sex differences in reaction to success or failure on their tasks. Simmons and Blyth (1987) studied older subjects undergoing pubertal changes and found the effects of early maturation were more negative for girls than boys on a variety of measures. Why do you think you found (or did not find) a sex difference in self-esteem?

While Engel and Raine (1963) found that the seven scales did not differ significantly in the positiveness ratings they elicited, they did find that the children's responses to some of them were related. Compare your correlation matrices with theirs. (Be careful not to confuse their correlational and factor analysis results. The latter will merit careful reading, however.)

Many of the questions posed at the outset in your third group of hypotheses can only be answered tentatively, eyeballing the results, because you have not performed the requisite tests of significance. Think what further statistical analyses would be needed and what trends are suggested by your data.

Considering the age effects in this study (Table G8.1 and associated significance tests), and the frequency of extreme ratings in the various subgroups (Table G8.6), speculate about what a measure like the Where Are You Game seems to tell us about cognitive maturity and differentiation.

Suppose, instead of the cross-sectional study you just performed, you did a longitudinal one, using the same group of children in their first and fourth grades. Suppose Betty, who scored 32 in the first grade and was sixth highest in self-esteem, now scores 28 in fourth grade and is still sixth highest (since the class generally scored lower). Would you say she had dropped in self-esteem? Discuss the theoretical and practical implications of this.

The Master Data Sheets are well worth careful perusal. For example, we found in our laboratory section that seven of the nine second-grade boys gave themselves the highest rating (5) for bravery (Scale D). This was far more extreme than the same-age girls, or the older boys and girls. Can you spot such patterns? Speculate on their implications.

Are you comfortable with the Where Are You Game as a self-esteem measure? Because they found at least five significant factors as a result of their Principal Components Factor Analysis after a Quartimax rotation, Engel and Raine (1963) believed it "appropriate to consider the seven scales as representing seven different components of the self-concept," and "the sum of the seven ratings as a measure of a rather global self-concept" (p. 131). How does this measure fit in with the real, ideal, and social self-disparities discussed by Katz and Zigler (1967)? Can you suggest changes in the administration of the Where Are You Game that might clarify and elaborate on its use?

The children's reasons for rating themselves as they did on each scale were used in an interesting fashion by Engel and Raine (1963) to define operationally what they labeled as the "sources" of the self-ratings. The verbalizations were sorted into five categories, which were conceptualized as lying on a continuum reflecting "inner" to "outer" judgmental basis. The child on the "outer" pole actively compares himself or herself to others and relies heavily on their judgments. Engel and Raine were then able to make some hypotheses and to test them statistically. They found, for example, that children who rated themselves high in obedience (scale G) did indeed tend to rely on the judgments of others. In our exercise, we are not using the inquiry data systematically, but we wish to give you practice in collecting verbatim data, and to give you some intuitive feel for the kind of information elicited by such techniques, as well as to provide additional material for class discussion and criticism.

You may be surprised to discover that Engel and Raine's subjects were 29 third graders, and Carpenter and Busse's 80 welfare children broke down to 10 in each age–sex–race group. Why do we bring this to your attention?

Notice that we called this a study in self-esteem, while Engel and Raine are using the Where Are You Game as a measure of self-concept. What is your reaction?

To which issues in development does research on the self-concept and self-esteem relate? Why would social-learning theorists be interested in this topic? Sociologists? Stage theorists? Ego-psychoanalysts? Where do their viewpoints converge? Diverge?

Aside from theoretical and empirical considerations, self-concept and self-esteem have practical applications for educators and policy makers. There is recurrent interest in affective education, and deliberate efforts are made by Head Start and open classroom personnel (among others) to foster the self-esteem of children. Research efforts to investigate the relationship between self-concept and classroom behavior, although demonstrating the link (e.g., Shiffler, Lynch-Sauer, & Nadelman, 1977), have not yet fully clarified the sequence or causality relationship. That is, do children high in self-esteem behave in certain ways in school because of their high self-esteem; and/or do they act in certain ways, get reinforced for these actions, and therefore develop high self-esteem? Is there a feedback loop constantly operating in which self-concept affects and is affected by the individual's experience in the social environment?

Selected Bibliography

*Carpenter, T. R., & Busse, T. V. (1969). Development of self concept in Negro and white welfare children. *Child Development, 40*(3), 935–939.

Davidson, H. H., & Lang, G. (1960). Children's perceptions of their teacher's feelings toward them related to self-perception, school achievement and behavior. *Journal of Experimental Education, 29*, 107–118.

*Engel, M., & Raine, W. J. (1963). A method for the measurement of the self-concept of children in the third grade. *Journal of Genetic Psychology, 102*, 125–137.

Gray-Little, B., & Hafdahl, A. R. (2000). Factors influencing racial comparisons of self-esteem: A quantitative analylsis. *Psychological Bulletin, 126*(1), 26–54.

Katz, P., & Zigler, E. (1967). Self-image disparity: A developmental approach. *Journal of Personality and Social Psychology, 5*, 186–195.

Nadelman, L., & Wallace, E. E. (Unpublished manuscript). *The relationship of self-concept, conceptual tempo and intelligence to reading achievement of first-graders.*

Rosenberg, M., & Simmons, R. G. (1972). *Black and white self-esteem: The urban school child.* Washington, DC: American Sociological Association.

Schiffler, N., Lynch-Sauer, J., & Nadelman, L. (1977). Relationship between self-concept and classroom behavior in two informal elementary classrooms. *Journal of Educational Psychology, 69* (4), 349–359.

Siegel, S. (1956). *Nonparametric statistics for the behavioral sciences.* New York: McGraw-Hill.

Simmons, R. G., & Blyth, D. A. (1987). *Moving into adolescence: The impact of pubertal changes in school context.* New York: A. de Gruyter.

Stipek, D., Recchia, S., & McClintic, S. (1992). Self-evaluation in young children. *Monographs of the Society for Research in Child Development, 57* (1, Serial No. 226).

Wylie, R. C. (1974). *The self-concept: A review of methodological considerations and measuring instruments* (Rev. ed.). Lincoln, Nebraska: University of Nebraska Press.

Also see the bibliography in the preceding background essay.

INDIVIDUAL DATA SHEET

Title: S-E _____

E: _____ Day and Date: _____ S–Sex: *M or F* Grade: _____

S: _____ Birthdate: _____ CA: _____

Time Begun: _____ Time Ended: _____ Elapsed Time: _____ Room: _____

WHERE ARE YOU GAME

Scale	Child's Rating	Inquiry and Notes
A (sma)		
B (hap)		
C (pop)		
D (bra)		
E (att)		
F (str)		
G (obe)		
Total		
Mean		
Median		

GROUP DATA SHEET

Title: *Age and Sex Differences in Self-Esteem*

E:_____   **Day and Date:**_____

Hypothesis:

Method and Procedure: (as described in text with following modifications, if any)

Group Results and Analysis:

TABLE G8.1
MEANS FOR THE WHERE ARE YOU GAME (ENGEL AND RAINE SELF-ESTEEM TEST)

Group	N	A Smart	B Happy	C Popular	D Brave	E Attractive	F Strong	G Obedient	Total Self-esteem	Mean Scale	Median Total
Grade_____ Boys Girls											
Grade_____ Boys Girls											
Boys Girls											
Total											

Note. Ratings for each scale range from 1–5.

Total self-esteem scores range from 7–35. These are used in most of the analyses that follow.

Mean scale score for each group = Total mean score divided by 7.

The last column is the median, rather than the mean. Total self-esteem score. These are needed in the Median test, Table G8.4.

TABLE G8.2

SUMMARY OF A 2 X 2 ANALYSIS OF VARIANCE FOR SELF-ESTEEM SCORES

Source of Variation	Sum of Squares	df	Mean Square	F	p
Between Ages					
Between Sexes					
Age X Sex					
Error					
Total					

Note: F at 1 percent point = _____; F at 5 percent point = _____ .

TABLE G8.3

SUMMARY OF MANN-WHITNEY U-TESTS OF AGE AND SEX DIFFERENCES IN SELF-ESTEEM

Sex Differences			*Age Differences*		
Group	U	p	Group	U	p
Total Children			Total Children		
Younger Group			Boys		
Older Group			Girls		

TABLE G8.4
MEDIAN TESTS FOR AGE AND SEX DIFFERENCES IN SELF-ESTEEM SCORES

A. General form for data

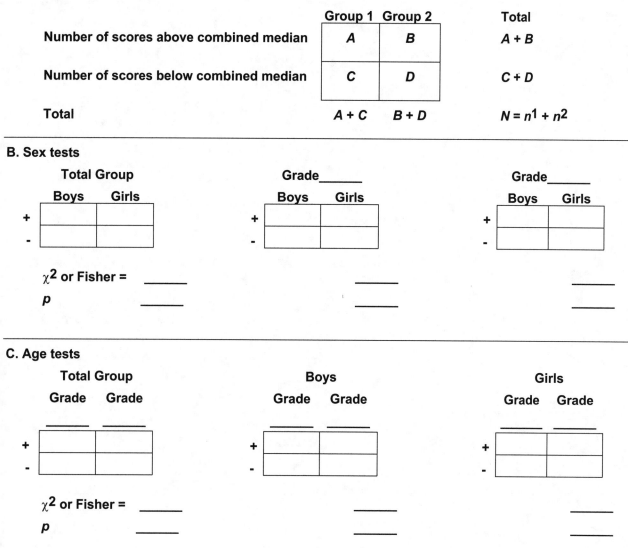

	Group 1	Group 2	Total
Number of scores above combined median	A	B	A + B
Number of scores below combined median	C	D	C + D
Total	A + C	B + D	N = n_1 + n_2

B. Sex tests

Total Group

	Boys	Girls
+		
-		

χ^2 or Fisher = _____

p _____

Grade_____

	Boys	Girls
+		
-		

_____

_____

Grade_____

	Boys	Girls
+		
-		

_____

_____

C. Age tests

Total Group

	Grade	Grade
+		
-		

χ^2 or Fisher = _____

p _____

Boys

	Grade	Grade
+		
-		

_____

_____

Girls

	Grade	Grade
+		
-		

_____

_____

TABLE G8.5
CORRELATION MATRICES

	A	B	C	D	E	F	G	Total
A	1.00							
B		1.00		a. ALL BOYS				
C			1.00					
D				1.00				
E					1.00			
F						1.00		
G							1.00	
Total								1.00

$n =$; $df =$
*r at .05 level   =
**r at .01 level   =

	A	B	C	D	E	F	G	Total
A								
B				b. ALL GIRLS				
C								
D								
E								
F								
G								
Total								

$n =$; $df =$
*r at .05 level   =
**r at .01 level   =

	A	B	C	D	E	F	G	Total
A	1.00							
B		1.00		c. GRADE_____				
C			1.00					
D				1.00				
E					1.00			
F						1.00		
G							1.00	
Total								1.00

$n =$; $df =$
*r at .05 level   =
**r at .01 level   =

	A	B	C	D	E	F	G	Total
A								
B				d. GRADE_____				
C								
D								
E								
F								
G								
Total								

$n =$; $df =$
*r at .05 level   =
**r at .01 level   =

TABLE G8.6

FREQUENCY OF EXTREME RATINGS ON SELF-ESTEEM TEST

Group	Number of 1s	Number of 5s	Percentage (1)	Percentage (5)
Total Sample				
Grade_____				
Boys				
Girls				
Grade_____				
Boys				
Girls				
Boys				
Girls				

Note: The children rated themselves on seven scales, so the highest possible frequency is 7 X the number of subjects in each group.

If the number of children in each of the four groups is not equal, change the frequencies entered in the first two columns to percentages of responses.

Fig. G8.1.

Fig. G8.1. (Continued)

Sex Identity

"Who am I?" This question of *identity* or *self* interests laypersons as much as it does professionals. An aspect of self (only one, but an important one!) is an individual's *masculinity* or *femininity*; that is, one's sex or gender identity. (This is not the same as whether one is biologically a male or female.) Psychoanalysts and psychodynamically oriented theorists have long been concerned with this issue; it is only since the 1950s, however, that American experimental psychologists and sociologists have awakened to its researchability.

The novice first encountering the huge amount of empirical work that has piled up in less than 50 years might find it difficult to make sense of the findings, because this research is characterized by difficulties and differences in the definitions of the basic concepts, by a variety of theories underlying the experiments, and by a variety of instruments and population samples. A brief summary of some of the concepts and theories follows.

Definitions of Concepts

The term *identification*, as loosely used in these studies, sometimes refers to process, sometimes to content.[1] There have been attempts to make the following distinctions among sex-role identification, sex-role adoption, sex-role preference, sex-role discrimination, and parental versus sex-role identification:

Sex-role identification: actual incorporation or internalization by the child of the role considered appropriate to a given sex and the unconscious reactions characteristic of that role.

Sex-role preference: desire to adopt the behavior associated with one sex or another; perception of such behavior as preferable or more desirable.

Sex-role adoption: overt behaviors characteristic of a given sex (not as frequently researched, since much of this behavior may be expediency, e.g., girls are in slacks).

Sex-role discrimination: knowing which behaviors are characteristic of males and of females in one's culture.

Parental identification: internalization of characterisitics or attributes of one's own parent and unconscious reactions similar to those of that parent.

Miller and Swanson's (1960) global definition of sex identity is a convenient one: *the total pattern of sex-linked characteristics that mark a person as masculine or feminine, both to himself or herself and to others*. The concepts defined above would be different aspects of this total pattern. Nowadays, the phrase "sex identity" more often appears as "sex-typing" or "gender role development" and is recognized as complex and multiply-determined.

Theories of Identity

The theories stem from psychoanalysts, psychologists stressing learning theory and information processing, psychologists stressing cognitive development, and sociologists interested in family structure and role theories. These notions, as interpreted or used by experimenters are not always clearly separate or separable. Sex identity was occasionally treated as solely an aspect of identification with the same-sex parent, or more loosely, identification with the same-sex parent was assumed to be operationally identical with strongly sex-typed preferences. (Both assumptions were unwarranted.)

Defensive identification or identification with the aggressor: After discriminating a world of objects separate from the self, and being motivated by oedipal situation hostilities and anxieties of the phallic stage, the child identifies with the same-sex parent (or model) to alleviate anxiety over anticipated counteraggression or domination by a threatening model.

---

[1] Identification as a *process* refers to the actions or operations performed by an individual, leading to a condition of similarity or sameness. Identification as *content* refers to the condition or state or goal; for example, "I am female, like my mother."

Anaclitic identification: a presexual dependency relationship; anxiety over the anticipated loss of love (presumably a major motive for the girl's identification with her mother). This is often used loosely and interchangeably with developmental identification.

Developmental identification: The child imitates or reproduces the behavior of a model in order to "reproduce bits of the beloved and longed-for parent"—responses that have acquired secondary reward value through association with a nurturant and affectionate model.

Power theory: Children identify with models who control the resources, who have the power to reinforce and to punish them.

Sex-role differentiation theory: Both sexes identify with the father in differentiated role relationships—the father's attitude toward boys being instrumental and toward girls being expressive. This follows the earlier identification of both boys and girls with an expressive mother. Expressiveness is characterized by a primary orientation to positive and negative emotional reactions and relationships between people (generally seen as the mother's job in America). An instrumental role player is actively trying to secure a favorable relation between the system (i.e., the family) and its environment. (Daddy brings home the bacon in the form of a paycheck.) For Parsons (1955) and others, identification would be the internalization of a reciprocal role relationship that is functional at a particular time in the child's development. The amount of the child's interaction with the identificand would then be important; that is, how salient is that parent?

Love reciprocity theory: the mechanism appropriate to expressive learning—the child is motivated by the positive desire to get love by giving love.

The above theories of identification, although stemming from different broad paradigms (psychoanalytic theory, behaviorist reinforcement theory, social learning theory, family-system role theory) and differing somewhat in their explanations for the motivation to identify, all assume that identification (with parent or relevant model) *precedes* sex-role identity. In other words, the child's sex identity is a *product* of identification with the same-sex parent. In contrast cognitive-developmental theorists like Kohlberg (1966) believe that the reversed sequence occurs. First, children learn their sexual identity (that is, they categorize themselves as boy or girl), and their identifications with same-sex parents are derivative. The importance of observational learning of social roles is not played down by the cognitive developmentalists, but they stress the child's active cognitive organization of these social-role experiences, and the child's need to preserve a stable and positive self-image. Kohlberg (1966) contrasted the two viewpoints thus:

> The social-learning syllogism is: "I want rewards, I am rewarded for doing boy things, therefore I want to be a boy." In contrast, a cognitive theory assumes this sequence: "I am a boy, therefore I want to do boy things", therefore the opportunity to do boy things (and to gain approval for doing them) is rewarding. (p. 89).

Kohlberg's (1966) cognitive-developmental analysis is "based on the Piagetian conception of cognitive growth as a process in which basic changes, or qualitative differences, in modes of thinking lead to transformed perceptions of the self and the social world." (p. 147)

When I started doing research with my students in the 1950s on sex-role knowledge and recall and preference, and giving speeches, I focused on socialization theories. Rather quickly, I added biology and cognitive development. It was, therefore, interesting to read Jacklin's (1989) summary that gender is or has been a primary focus of research in three areas—measurement of intellectual abilities, biology and behavior, and socialization processes. Mathematical and spatial ability have been a focus of the intellectual abilities research (Benbow & Stanley, 1983; Casey, Nuttall, Pezaris & Benbow, 1995; Eccles & Jacobs, 1986; Lynn & Peterson, 1985). Biology and behavior researchers have recognized the greater male vulnerability as fetus, child, and adult, and the pursuit of sex-hormones and brain and behavior linkages has become an exciting research area (Becker, Breedlove, & Crews, 1992; Geschwind & Galaburda, 1987). Socialization proponents have combined social learning theory with the information processing strategies and the cognitive maturity notions from cognitive development theory to arrive at gender schema theory. Gender schema is defined as a set of constructed ideas that help an individual organize information about male and female characteristics which may guide his/her perceptions, actions and beliefs (Archer & Lloyd, 1982; Bem, 1981; Liben & Signorella, 1987).

Although these theories differ in their emphases, they are not totally incompatible. They should, rather, be viewed as complementary and we should recognize that cognitive, biological, and social-environmental factors all interact and contribute to sex-role development (Serbin, Powlishta, & Gulko, 1993).

Instruments

The measurement techniques used in the study of sex identity vary greatly and have included actual toys, pictures, projective doll-play interviews, Franck's projective line drawings, personality inventories, games inventories or check lists, semantic differential tests, interviews, and so on.

One major issue raised by the use of certain instruments has been related to the ambiguity of the concepts of masculinity and femininity. Are these the bipolar opposites of *one* dimension? That is, does being "less masculine" necessarily mean one is "more feminine"? Or are masculinity and femininity more properly treated as independent dimensions?

Bem (1974, 1975) argued strongly for the conception of masculinity and femininity as two independent dimensions. This conception enables a person to be *both* masculine and feminine, that is, androgynous. She developed the Bem Sex Role Inventory (BSRI), which characterizes a person as masculine, feminine, and androgynous as a function of the difference between the person's feminine and masculine scores. The inventory consists of 20 masculine characteristics, 20 feminine characteristics, and 20 sex-neutral characteristics mixed together. The subject indicates on a 1 to 7 scale how true each characteristic is of himself or herself, with 1 as "never true" and 7 as "always true."

Another issue relevant to the measurement techniques has to do with the broadness of sex-role stereotypes. Many instruments (including the ones in this volume) investigate sex-role stereotypes. They tap young children's knowledge and preference for what men and women, girls and boys do. Another aspect, however, concerns sex-*trait* stereotypes: the psychological characteristics associated with men and women, like aggressiveness or emotionality. This has been studied in adults or in older children who can read and understand the directions for adjective checklists or rating scales, and more recently in younger children. Stereotypes about traits probably develop later than the knowledge of roles appropriate to each sex.

For specific instruments used in various countries and ethnic groups, see Beere (1990). Although each empirical study describes the specific instrument used, some tests appear frequently in the literature. For a variety of past measures, see Bem (1974); Franck (1948), Franck and Rosen (1949); Gough (1957); Gouze and Nadelman (1980); Lipsitz (2000); Nadelman (1974, 1976); Spence, Helmreich, and Stapp (1974).

Theoretical Issues

In addition to the issue of dimensionality, a major theoretical question has been, for whom is the process of establishing appropriate sex identification more difficult—the boy or the girl? Theorists who answer "the girl" have recourse to notions of penis envy, masculine protest, the girl's need to shift the final love object from a female to a male, the lesser value of the female role in society, ambiguity and ambivalence toward that role, and so on. Theorists who answer "the boy" point to his need to shift from early identification with the mother to identification with the father, lesser contact with a male model, and the greater abstractness of the identification process.

Lynn (1962, 1969) presented an interesting theoretical formulation based on the postulate that males tend to identify with a cultural stereotype of the masculine role, whereas females tend to identify with aspects of their own mother's specific role. He believed there are not only basic sex differences in the nature of sex-role identification and parental identification, but that there are basic sex differences in the *process* of achieving such identifications. He used Woodworth and Schlosberg's differentiation of two kinds of learning tasks into the *problem* and the *lesson*, and considers that the task for the female is parallel to the lesson, whereas the task for the boy is parallel to the problem. The little girl acquires a learning method that primarily involves a personal relationship and imitation, rather than restructuring the field and abstracting principles. The little boy acquires a learning method that primarily involves finding the goal, restructuring the field, and abstracting the principles. This would then have implications for future sex differences in many areas, including problem-solving behavior.

The major theoretical issue of the relation between a child's identification with same-sex parent and establishment of the child's sex identity (i.e., which comes first?) was discussed earlier. Despite the large number of studies of gender self-labeling, constancy of gender identity, the relation of cognitive development to sex-role attitudes, family and cultural determinants of sex-role development, and so on, the issue remains controversial.

Much research has been involved with parental socialization of children, especially differential treatment of boys and girls. Recent examples include Bumpus, Crouter and McHale (2001), Eccles, Jacobs, Harold, Yoon, Abreton, and Freedman-Doan (1993), Leaper, Anderson, and Sanders (1998), Lytton (1991).

The nature–nurture issue, although present, is somewhat muted by the recognition that genetic and experiential influences reciprocally interact. Attention is paid to genetic differences, to prenatal hormonal factors and their possible influences on the central and autonomic nervous system and subsequent behaviors, but most psychologists focus their research efforts on socialization influences on sex identity, and/or cognitive aspects.

The experimental recognition of the importance of the *cross-sex* parent, and of the role of the *siblings* and *peers*, is belated but crucial. The importance of the father to the girl's femininity, and perhaps of the mother to the boy's masculinity, and of the peer examples and pressures to appropriate sex typing were relatively untilled fields of empirical investigation initially (Johnson, 1963) but soon became popular research topics (Biller, 1971; Gerson, 1993; Gervai, Turner, & Hinde, 1995; Gustafson, 1994; Lamb, 1976; Lynn, 1974; Maccoby & Jacklin, 1974; Seigel, 1987; Starrels, 1994).

"Sugar and spice and puppy-dog tails." "Equality of the sexes: Orwell style." These were titles I used for my speeches, which obviously pointed to sex differences. "The exaggeration of differences which we call *alpha bias*, can be seen in approaches that focus on the contrasting experiences of men and women. The minimizing of differences, *beta bias*, can be seen in approaches that stress the similarity or equality of men and women" (Hare-Mustin & Maracek, 1988, p. 455). Alpha examples would include Brown and Gilligan (1992) and Gilligan (1982). Beta examples include the early systems approaches to family therapy, which focused on age differences more than class, race, or gender; Hyde and Linn's research (1988) showing less sex difference in verbal-ability scores recently than formerly believed, and Feingold's (1988) review of cognitive gender differences. Recent research on sex differences and similarities include Geary (1998), Geary, Saults, Liu, and Heard (2000), Halpern (2000), Kimura (2000), and Worell (2001).

Implications

Research, especially this kind, has consequences. It alerts teachers and education administrators to the short-changing of girls in our schools (AAUW, 1991; Sadker & Sadker, 1994) and the differences in interaction between teachers and their girl/boy students. It calls for more attention to father (and sib) interaction with male and female children (Gerson, 1993). It points to the need for research and recognition of cultural and ethnic differences, and nonconventional family life styles (Weisner & Wilson-Mitchell, 1990). It draws attention to the economic implications—the differences in status between males and females and the consequent differences between them in power (Kalbfleisch & Cody, 1995; Lockheed, 1993). The complexity of sex-role development shouts its need for interdisciplinary research. The media are not without fault, and need to be more careful in their use of sex stereotypes (Douglas, 1994).

Problem

The two experiments that follow are adapted from Nadelman's research (1970, 1974) on some aspects of sex identity in 100 London and 240 American children of the working and middle classes, as related to their perception of their parents. It seemed to her likely that different processes in the establishment and maintenance of sex identity may be found for the two *sexes*; different processes may be more relevant at different *ages* or stages; and different processes may be more common in different *socioeconomic classes*. It also seemed likely that a battery of measures would be more productive than the choice of a single dependent variable like "preference." For class purposes, we will limit our experiment to age and sex variables, and to two measures of her battery.

The specific purpose, then, is to investigate age and sex differences on several measures believed to tap various aspects of sex identity. Experiment 9 investigates age and sex differences in *recall* of masculine and feminine material; Experiment 10 investigates age and sex differences in *preferences* for masculine and feminine material.

Selected Bibliography

American Association of University Women. (1991). *Shortchanging girls, shortchanging America*. Washington, DC: Author.

Archer, J., & Lloyd, B. B. (2002). *Sex and gender* (2nd Ed.). New York: Cambridge University Press.

Beall, A. E., & Sternberg, R. J. (Eds.). (1993). *The psychology of gender*. New York: Guilford Publications.

Becker, J. B., Breedlove, S. M., & Crews, D. (Eds.). (1992). *Behavioral endocrinology*. Cambridge, MA: MIT Press.

Beere, C. A. (1990). *Gender roles: A handbook of tests and measures*. New York: Greenwood.

Bem, S. L. (1974). The measurement of psychological androgyny. *Journal of Consulting and Clinical Psychology, 42*, 155–162.

Bem, S. L. (1975). Sex-role adaptability: One consequence of psychological androgyny. *Journal of Personality and Social Psychology, 31*, 634–643.

Bem, S. L. (1981). Gender schema theory: A cognitive account of sex-typing. *Psychological Review, 88*, 354–364.

Benbow, C. P., & Stanley, J. C. (1983). Sex differences in mathematical reasoning ability: More facts. *Science, 222*, 1029–1031.

Biller, H. B. (1971). *Father, child, and sex role: Paternal determinants of personality development*. Lexington, MA: Heath Lexington.

Block, J. H. (1973). Conceptions of sex-role: Some cross-cultural and longitudinal perspectives. *American Psychologist, 23*, 512–526.

Block, J. H. (1976). Issues, problems, and pitfalls in assessing sex differences: A critical review of *The Psychology of Sex Differences*. *Merrill-Palmer Quarterly, 22*, 283–308.

Bornstein, R. F., & Masling, J. M. (Eds.). (2002). *The psychodynamics of gender and gender role*. Washington, DC: American Psychological Association.

Breedlove, S. M. (1994). Sexual differentiation of the human nervous system. In M. Rosenzweig and L. Porter (Eds.), *Annual Review of Psychology* (*Vol. 45*, pp. 389–418). Palo Alto, CA: Annual Reviews.

Brown, L. M., & Gilligan, C. (1992). *Meeting at the crossroads: Women's psychology and girls' development*. Cambridge, MA: Harvard University Press.

Bumpus, M. F., Crouter, A. C., & McHale, S. M. (2001). Parental autonomy granting during adolescence: Exploring gender differences in context. *Developmental Psychology, 37*(2), 163–173.

Buss, D. M. (1995). Psychological sex differences: Origins through sexual selection. *American Psychologist, 50*(3), 164–168.

Casey, M. B., Nuttall, R., Pezaris, E., & Benbow, C. P. (1995). The influence of spatial ability on gender differences in mathematics college entrance test scores across diverse samples. *Developmental Psychology, 31*(4), 697–705.

Denmark, F. L. (1994). Engendering psychology. *American Psychologist, 49*(4), 329–334.

Douglas, S. D. (1994). *Where the girls are: Growing up female with the mass media*. NY: Times Books.

Eagly, A. H. (1995). The science and politics of comparing women and men. *American Psychologist, 50*(3), 145–158.

Eccles, J. S., & Jacobs, J. E. (1986). Social forces shape math attitudes and performance. *Signs, 11*, 367–389.

Eccles, J. S., Jacobs, J., Harold, R., Yoon, K. S., Abreton, A., & Freedman-Doan, C. (1993). Parents' and gender-role socialization during the middle childhood and adolescent years. In S. Oskamp & M. Constanzo (Eds.), *Gender issues in contemporary society* (pp. 59–83). Newbury Park, CA: Sage.

Eckes, T., Trautner, H. M. (Eds.). (2000). *The developmental social psychology of gender*. Mahwah, NJ: Lawrence Erlbaum Associates.

Fagot, B. I. (1978). The influence of sex of child on parental reactions to toddler children. *Child Development, 49*, 459–465.

Feingold, A. (1988). Cognitive gender differences are disappearing. *American Psychologist, 43*, 95–103.

Franck, K. (1948). *Franck drawing completion test: A preliminary manual*. Melbourne: Australian Council for Educational Research.

Franck, K., & Rosen, E. (1949). A projective-test of masculinity-femininity. *Journal of Consulting Psychology, 13*, 247–256.

Gallas, K. (1997). *Sometimes I can be anything: Power, gender, and identity in a primary classroom*. Williston, VT: Teachers College Press.

Gaulin, S. J. C. (1993). How and why sex differences evolve, with spatial ability as a paradigm example. In M. Haug, R. E. Whalen, C. Aron, & K. L. Olsen (Eds.), *The development of sex differences and similarities in behaviour* (pp. 111–130). London, England: Kluwer Academic.

Geary, D. C. (1998). *Male, Female: The evolution of human sex differences*. Washington, DC: APA Books.

Geary, D. C., Saults, S. J., Liu, F., & Hoard, M. K. (2000). Sex differences in spatial cognition, computational fluency, and arithmetical reasoning. *Journal of Experimental Child Psychology, 77*(4), 337–353.

Gerson, K. (1993). *No man's land: Men's changing commitments to family and work*. New York: Basic Books.

Gervai, J., Turner, P. J., & Hinde, R. A. (1995). Gender-related behaviour, attitudes, and personality in parents of young children in England and Hungary. *International Journal of Behavioral Development, 18*(1), 105–126.

Geschwind, N., & Galaburda, A. M. (1987). *Cerebral lateralization: Biological mechanisms, associations, and pathology*. Cambridge, MA: MIT Press.

Gilligan, C. (1982). *In a different voice: Psychological theory and women's development*. Cambridge, MA: Harvard University Press.

Golombok, S., & Fivush, R. (1994). *Gender development*. New York, NY: Cambridge University Press.

Goodenough, E. W. (1957). Interest in persons as an aspect of sex difference in the early years. *Genetic Psychology Monographs, 55*, 287–323.

Gough, H. G. (1957). *Manual for California Psychological Inventory*. Palo Alto, CA: Consulting Psychologists Press.

Gouze, K. R., & Nadelman, L. (1980). Constancy of gender identity for self and others in children between the ages of three and seven. *Child Development, 51*, 275–278.

Gustafson, S. B. (1994). Female underachievement and overachievement: Parental contributions and long-term consequences. *International Journal of Behavioral Development, 17*(3), 469–484.

Hall, M., & Keith, R. A. (1964). Sex-role preference among children of upper and lower social class. *Journal of Social Psychology, 62*, 101–110.

Halpern, D. F. (1992). *Sex differences in cognitive abilities* (2nd Ed.). Hillsdale, NJ: Lawrence Erlbaum Associates.

Halpern, D. (2000). *Sex differences in cognitive abilities* (3rd Ed.). Mahwah, NJ: Lawrence Erlbaum Associates.

Hare-Mustin, R. T. (1987). The problem of gender in family therapy theory. *Family Process, 26*, 15–27.

Hartley, R. E. (1964). A developmental view of female sex-role definition and identification. *Merrill-Palmer Quarterly, 10*, 3–16.

Hartley, R. E., & Hardesty, F. P. (1964). Children's perceptions of sex roles in childhood. *Journal of Genetic Psychology, 105*, 43–51.

Hyde, J. S., & Linn, M. C. (1988). Are there sex differences in verbal abilities? A meta-analysis. *Psychological Bulletin, 104*(1), 53–69.

Hyde, J. S., & Plant, E. A. (1995). Magnitude of psychological gender differences: Another side to the story. *American Psychologist, 50* (3), 159–161.

Intons-Peterson, M. J. (1989). *Children's concept of gender*. Norwood, NJ: Ablex.

*Jacklin, C. N. (1989). Female and male: Issues of gender. *American Psychologist, 44*(2), 127–133.

Journal of Experimental Child Psychology (2000), 77(4). Special issue on sex and gender in development.

Kalbfleisch, P. J., & Cody, M. J. (Eds.). (1995). *Gender, power, and communication in human relationships*. Hillsdale, NJ: Lawrence Erlbaum Associates.

Kaschak, E. (1993). *Engendered lives: A new psychology of women's experience*. New York: Basic Books.

Katz, P. A., & Ksansnak, K. R. (1994). Developmental aspects of gender role flexibility and traditionality in middle childhood and adolescence. *Developmental Psychology, 30*(2), 272–282.

Kimura, D. (2000). *Sex and cognition*. Cambridge, MA: MIT Press.

Kohlberg, L. (1966). A cognitive-developmental analysis of children's sex-role concepts and attitudes. In E. E. Maccoby (Ed.), *The development of sex differences* (pp. 82–173). Stanford, CA: Stanford University Press.

Labouvie-Vief, G. (1994). *Psyche and Eros: Mind and gender in the life course*. New York: Cambridge University Press.

Lamb, M. E. (Ed.). (1976). *The role of the father in child development*. New York: Wiley.

Lamb, M. E., & Urberg, K. A. (1978). The development of gender role and gender identity. In M. E. Lamb (Ed.), *Social and personality development* (pp. 178–199). New York: Rinehart and Winston.

Leaper, C., Anderson, K. J., & Sanders, P. (1998). Moderators of gender effects on parents talk to their children: A meta-analysis. *Developmental Psychology, 34*(1), 3–27.

Levy, G. D. (Ed.). (1993). An integrated collection on early gender-role development. *Developmental Review, 13*(2).

Liben, L. S., & Signorella, M. L. (Eds). (1987). *Children's gender schemata*. San Francisco: Jossey-Bass.

Linn, M. C., & Peterson, A. C. (1985). Emergence and characterization of sex differences in spatial ability: A meta-analysis. *Child Development, 56*, 1479–1498.

Lippa, R. A. (2002). *Gender, nature, and nurture*. Mahwah, NJ: Lawrence Erlbaum Associates.

Lipsitz, A. (2000). Research methods with a smile: A gender difference exercise that teaches methodology. *Teaching of Psychology, 27*, 111–113.

Lockheed, M. E. (1993). The development of sex typing: Implications for economic development. In L. A. Serbin, K. K. Powlishta, & J. Gulko, The development of sex typing in middle childhood. *Monographs of the Society for Research in Child Development, 58* (2, Serial No. 232), 86–92.

Lynn, D. B. (1969). *Parental and sex role identification: A theoretical formulation.* Berkeley, CA: McCutchan.

Lynn, D. B. (1974). *The father: His role in child development.* Monterey, CA:Brooks/Cole.

Lytton, H., & Romney, D. M. (1991). Parents' differential socialization of boys and girls: A meta-analysis. *Psychological Bulletin, 109,* 267–296.

Maccoby, E. E. (1990). Gender and relationships: A developmental account. *American Psychologist, 45*(4), 513–520.

Maccoby, E. E. (1998). *The two sexes: Growing up apart, coming together.* Cambridge, MA: Belknap Press/Harvard University Press.

Maccoby, E. E., & Jacklin, C. N. (1974). *The psychology of sex differences.* Stanford, CA: Stanford University Press.

Markovits, H., Benenson, J., & Dolenszky, E. (2001). Evidence that children and adolescents have internal models of peer interactions that are gender differentiated. *Child Development 72*(3), 879–886.

Martin, C. L., Eisenbud, L., & Rose, H. (1995). Children's gender based reasoning about toys. *Child Development, 66*(5), 1453–1471.

Miller, D. R., & Swanson, G. E. (1960). *Inner conflict and defense.* New York: Holt, Rinehart and Winston.

Minuchin, P. (1965). Sex-role concepts and sex typing in childhood as a function of school and home environments. *Child Development, 36,* 1033–1048.

Mischel, W. (1970). Sex-typing and socialization. In P. H. Mussen (Ed.), *Carmichael's manual of child psychology* (3rd Ed., *Vol. 2,* pp. 3–72). New York: Wiley.

Nadelman, L. (1970). Sex identity in London children: Memory, knowledge, and preference tests. *Human Development, 13,* 28–42.

Nadelman, L. (1974). Sex identity in American children: Memory, knowledge, and preference tests. *Developmental Psychology, 10,* 413–417.

Nadelman, L. (1976). Perception of parents by London five-year-olds. In D. McGuigan (Ed.), *New research on women and sex roles* (pp. 269–271). Ann Arbor, MI: Center for Continuing Education of Women.

Neto, F. (1997). Gender stereotyping in Portuguese children living in Portugal and abroad: Effects of migration, age, and gender. *International Journal of Behavioral Development, 20*(2), 219–229.

Parsons, T. (1955). Family structure and the socialization of the child. In T. Parsons & R. F. Bales (Eds.), *Family, socialization, and the interaction process* (pp. 35–131). Glencoe, IL: Free Press.

Power, T. G., McGrath, M. P., Hughes, S. O., & Manire, S. H. (1994). Compliance and self-assertion: Young children's responses to mothers versus fathers. *Developmental Psychology, 30*(6), 980–989.

Powlishta, K. K., Serbin, L. A., Doyle, A-B. D., & White, D. R. (1994). Gender, ethnic, and body type biases: The generality of prejudice in childhood. *Developmental Psychology, 30*(4), 526–536.

Rabban, M. (1950). Sex-role identification in young children in two diverse social groups. *Genetic Psychology Monographs, 42,* 81–158.

Rosenberg, B. G., & Sutton-Smith, B. (1972). *Sex and identity.* New York: Holt, Rinehart and Winston.

Ruble, D. N., & Martin, C. L. (1998). Gender development. In W. Damon (Editor-in-Chief), and N. Eisenberg (Volume Editor), *Handbook of Child Psychology: Vol. 3. Social, emotional and personality development* (5th ed., pp. 933–1016). New York: Wiley.

Saario, T., Jacklin, C., & Tittle, C. (1973). Sex role stereotyping in the public schools. *Harvard Educational Review, 43,* 386–416.

Sadker, M. P., & Sadker, D. M. (1994). *Failing at fairness: How America's schools cheat girls.* New York: Scribners.

*Serbin, L. A., Powlishta, K. K., & Gulko, J. (1993). The development of sex typing in middle childhood. *Monographs of the Society for Research in Child Development, 58* (2, Serial No. 232).

Sheldon, A. (Ed.). (1996). *Constituting gender through talk in childhood: Conversations in parent-child, peer, and sibling relationships.* (A special issue of *Research on Learning and Social Interaction*). Mahwah, NJ: Lawrence Erlbaum Associates.

Siegel, M. (1987). Are sons and daughters treated more differently by fathers than mothers? *Developmental Review, 7,* 183–209.

Signorella, M. L., Bigler, R. S., & Liben, L. S. (1993). Developmental differences in children's gender schemata about others: A meta-analytic review. *Developmental Review, 13,* 147–183.

Spence, J. T, & Buckner, C. (1995). Masculinity and femininity: Defining the undefinable. In P. Kalbfleisch & M. J. Cody, *Gender, power, and communication in human relationships* (pp. 105–138). Hillsdale, NJ: Lawrence Erlbaum Associates.

Spence, J. T., Helmreich, R., & Stapp, J. (1974). The Personal Attributes Questionnaire: A measure of sex role stereo-types and masculinity-feminity. *JSAS Catalog of Selected Documents in Psychology, 4*, 43.

Starrels, M. E. (1994). Gender differences in parent-child relations. *Journal of Family Issues, 15*, 148–165.

Taylor, M. G. (1996). The development of children's beliefs about social and biological aspects of gender differences. *Child Development, 67*(4), 1555–1571.

Trachtenberg, S., & Viken, R. J. (1994). Aggressive boys in the classroom: Biased attributions or shared perceptions? *Child Development, 65*, 829–835.

Unger, R. K. (Ed.). (2001). *Handbook of the psychology of women and gender*. New York: Wiley.

Weisner, T.S., & Wilson-Mitchell, J. E. (1990). Nonconventional family life-styles and sex typing in six-year-olds. *Child Development, 61*(6), 1915–1933.

Williams, C., & Bybee, J. (1994). What do children feel guilty about? Developmental and gender differences. *Developmental Psychology, 30*(5), 617–623.

Williams, J. E., Bennett, S. M., & Best, D. L. (1975). Awareness and expression of sex stereotypes in young children. *Developmental Psychology, 11*(5), 635–642.

Worell, J. (Ed.). (2001). *Encyclopedia of women and gender: Sex similarities and differences and the impact of society on gender*. San Diego, CA: Academic Press.

Experiment 9

Differential Recall of Sex-Typed Material

Problem and Hypotheses

If children are shown drawings of objects or activities that adults in our society consider masculine or feminine, will there be any differences in their immediate recall of these items?

Although there was little in the psychological journals (but much in the psychoanalytic journals) on the subject of sex identity in the early 1950s, several students sparked and shared my interest in the above and related questions (Doris Heller at New York University; Jane Beebe and Eda Small, Nita Dressler and Pat Dionne, Carolyn Bryan and Catherine Clark at Mount Holyoke College). These pioneer projects were the forerunners of the present experiment, and were acknowledged in more detail earlier (Nadelman, 1970).

If masculinity and femininity are indeed pervasive and salient dimensions, then their influence should be discernible in cognitive measures as well as social or personality ones. The "good girl"—"good boy," "just like mommy"—"just like daddy" socialization techniques of sex typing inform as well as evaluate (Hartley, 1964). Much research effort over decades has been expended on parental socialization of children with regard to sex-typing and gender schema, with recent emphases on fathers, siblings, teachers, and peers (e. g., Parke & Buriel, 1998; Pomerantz & Ruble, 1998; and see previous bibliography on sex-role identity). The media, too, is believed to have influence on gender-role knowledge and stereotypes (Dietz, 1998; Douglas, 1994). Furthermore, given the alleged sexual revolution and women's liberation movement, investigations of cognitive measures affected by sex-typing practices need to be repeated at long intervals to see if the different historical contexts affect the findings (Minton, Solomon, Stokes, Charash, & Kendzior, 1999). The fact that differential recall of sex-typed items was found in a 1968 sample of American children (Nadelman, 1974) does not necessarily mean that the same findings prevail in 1978 or 1988 or 1998. Hypotheses for this study are as follows:

1. Older children recall (more) (fewer) (the same number of) items than (as) younger children.

2. Boys recall (more) (fewer) (the same number of) items than (as) girls.

3. Masculine items are recalled (more than) (less than) (equal to) feminine items.

*4. Sex by sex of item interaction: Children remember (same-) (opposite-) sex items more than (opposite-) (same-) sex items.

Method

Subjects

At least two grades of boys and girls in early elementary school are preferred; for example, first and third, or kindergarten and second.

Materials

20 Nadelman M-F drawings (see list, Table G9.1, items numbered 1–20 and items in Fig. G9.1). Cut out each drawing. Label and number appropriately on its back. You may prefer first to paste them on stiffer paper or index cards.

Procedure

E uses only cards numbered 1–20, well shuffled and combined.

E: **"Let's look at these now, OK? Just look and listen quietly while I put them down. This is xxx, xxx."** [E labels each picture twice aloud, very clearly.]

Place the cards on the table directly in front of the child, one at a time, in rapid sequence—3 seconds viewing time, 1 second changing time. Card changing can be accomplished efficiently by removing the card with one hand while simultaneously laying the next one out with the other hand. Total time = (20 X 3 seconds) + (20 X 1 seconds) = c. 80 seconds. Practice with a stopwatch!

E, immediately after last card is removed: **"The game is for you to tell me what I showed you."**

Permissable prods include: **"Think of some more." "Tell me as many as you can." "What else did you see, what did I show you?"**

List the child's answers, verbatim, on right side of the Individual Data Sheet, under "*Verbatim Recall Items.*"

Results

Scoring. Look at the recall answers, in conjunction with Table G9.1. Indicate by plus signs in the numbered columns on the Individual Data Sheet which specific items the child remembered.

Now look at the summary at the bottom of the columns. How many masculine items (odd-numbered) did the child recall? how many feminine (even-numbered)? Enter and total.

Transfer the summary information for your subject(s) to the Master Data Sheet, provided by the instructor.

Analysis. For each sex-age group of children, compute (from the Master Data Sheet) the mean number of masculine items recalled, mean number of feminine items recalled, and mean number of total items recalled. Enter in Table G9.2.

Because both a masculine and a feminine recall score are present for each child, an analysis of variance is needed that looks between subjects for age and sex differences, and within subjects for differences between masculine and feminine items. See Table G9-3 for a 2 (age) X 2 (sex) X 2 (sex of item, within groups) ANOVA.

Look at the means in Table G9.2 together with the *F*s in Table G9.3, and state your findings. The *F* for age indicates whether one grade recalled more items *totally* than the other grade. The *F* for sex indicates whether one sex recalled more items totally than the other sex. The age X sex interaction indicates whether the sex differences in total recall differed with age or the age differences were differentially related to sex. None of the above three *F*s says anything about the different kinds of items. The *F* for sex of items indicates whether there was a significant difference in recall of masculine versus feminine items in your total sample of children. The age X sex of item *F* indicates whether masculine and/or feminine items were differentially remembered at each age. The sex of subject X sex of item *F* indicates whether masculine and/or feminine items were differentially remembered by boys and/or girls. This is an important *F*, and graphing these four means will help you to understand your findings. If an interaction *F* is significant, it is customary to analyze the data further by comparing pairs of means (using Scheffé or other tests). State your findings.

Discussion

Relate your results to each hypothesis. Which hypotheses are supported? How do your results relate to the results on American children (Nadelman, 1974) or English children (Nadelman, 1970)? What could account for similar results? Different results? Is Bauer's (1993) research relevant to this project?

Does differential recall of sex-typed items tap sex identity? What might it reflect instead?

Would different results be expected with different samples? For example, suppose you tested children in a feminist nursery? In an orphanage? In one-parent day-care centers? In a different socioeconomic class?

An optional related exercise for the class is an item analysis. For *each* of the 20 items, do a frequency count of how many boys and girls, respectively, recalled each item. Which items showed the greatest sex difference in recall? Which showed the least? If you administer the preference measure, in the next experiment, you may wish to investigate the relation between recall and preference.

The items you used in this project were last revised in 1968. Are there any that you believe are now improperly sex typed? How would you revalidate the items? The prototype for the 40 items was established in the early 1950s by adult questionnaires in the Mount Holyoke College and Amherst College area of Massachusetts. The 20 items used for the recall test had adult agreement on the sex typing of well over 90%. The items were revised in London in 1966 by Tavistock Clinic psychiatrists and psychologists and by school headmistresses and headmasters. They were revised in Ann Arbor, Dearborn, and Detroit by psychologists and educators in 1968.

You may wish to substitute other items for the cigar one (or even for the pipe). Why is that suggestion being made? Should we continue using the thimble item?

We redid the selective attention task (Central/Incidental Recall), substituting masculine–feminine items for the household objects Hagen originally used as incidental items. What do you think happened and why? In half the children, we first aroused the masculine–feminine coding by having them sort other masculine-feminine items into piles in front of Susie and Tommie paper dolls. What would you expect the effect of this arousal would be on the subsequent recall task?

Kail and Levine (1976), intrigued by the investigations of differential recall of masculine and feminine items (Nadelman, 1970, 1974), decided to look at the masculine-feminine attribute of encoding in a proactive inhibition (PI) release paradigm. The "release from proactive inhibition" task (Wickens, 1972) involves presentation of several words to be remembered, a brief distracting task, and a recall test. If the words share a common attribute, recall over successive trials usually declines owing to proactive inhibition buildup: What has been learned earlier interferes with present learning and recall. If, however, the words on a later trial are different (i.e., from a different conceptual class or category), recall may improve, indicating that these new words are encoded differently in memory than the earlier ones. Working with 7- and 10-year-olds, Kail and Levine found a significant improvement in recall following such a masculine–feminine category shift for younger and older boys, and for younger girls, compared to a control group that received all-masculine or all-feminine words. (See the preference experiment that follows for discussion of another aspect of their study.) Their work supported Nadelman's contention that masculinity–femininity categories were salient attributes for children, discernible in cognitive measures.

Suppose your subjects had initially been invited to "draw a picture of a person." On the basis of your results with the differential recall test, would you expect more boys or more girls to draw own sex first? Would you expect the children with the most differentiated recall (i.e., the highest proportion of masculine items to total recall or the highest proportion of feminine items to total recall) to draw male and female figures, respectively, more than children with less differentiated recall? Why?

Review the methodological and theoretical issues described in the introduction, "Sex Identity." Which are pertinent to this experiment?

This project was intended to demonstrate the integration of the individual, that is, how cognitive and social development interact and meld. Comment on this.

Selected Bibliography

*Bauer, P. J. (1993). Memory for gender-consistent and gender-inconsistent event sequences by 25-month-old children. *Child Development, 64*, 285–297.

Bryan, J. W., & Luria, Z. (1978). Sex-role learning: A test of the selective attention hypothesis. *Child Development, 49*, 12–23.

Dietz, T. L. (1998). An examination of violence and gender role portrayals in video games: Implications for gender socialization and aggressive behavior. *Sex Roles, 38*(5-6), 425–442.

Hartley, R. E. (1964). A developmental view of female sex-role definition and identification. *Merrill-Palmer Quarterly, 10*, 3–16.

*Kail, R. V., Jr., & Levine, L. E. (1976). Encoding processes and sex-role preferences. *Journal of Experimental Child Psychology, 21*, 256–263.

Koblinsky, S. G., Cruse, D. F., & Sugawara, A. I. (1978). Sex role stereotypes and children's memory for story content. *Child Development, 49,* 452–458.

Leinbach, M. D., Hort, B. E., & Fagot, B. I. (1997). Bears are for boys: Metaphorical associations in young children's gender stereotypes. *Cognitive Development, 12*(1), 107–130.

Lowe, K. (1998). Gender maps. In N. Yelland (Ed.), *Gender in early childhood*, (pp. 206–222). New York: Routledge.

Martin, C. L. (1993). New directions for investigating children's gender knowledge. *Developmental Review, 13,* 184–204.

Martin, C. L., Eisenbud, L., & Rose, H. (1996). Children's gender-based reasoning about toys. *Child Development, 66*(5), 1453–1471.

Nadelman, L. (1970). Sex identity in London children: Memory, knowledge, and preference tests. *Human Development, 13,* 28–42.

*Nadelman, L. (1974). Sex identity in American children: Memory, knowledge, and preference tests. *Developmental Psychology, 10,* 413–417.

Sandnabba, N. K., & Ahlberg, C. (1999). Parents' attitudes and expectations about children's cross-gender behavior. *Sex Roles, 40*(3–4), 249–263.

Wickens, D. D. (1972). Characteristics of word encoding. In A. W. Melton & E. Martin (Eds.), *Coding processes in human memory* (pp. 191–215). Washington, DC: Winston and Sons.

See also the preceding bibliography.

TABLE G9.1

MASCULINE AND FEMININE ITEMS USED IN RECALL, KNOWLEDGE, AND PREFERENCE TESTS

1. Owning a train set	2. Wheeling a baby buggy
3. Playing football	4. Dressing a dolly
5. Boxing	6. Giving a tea party
7. Smoking a pipe	8. Wearing high-heeled shoes
9. Smoking a cigar	10. Using perfume
11. Fighting fires	12. Using lipstick
13. Laying bricks	14. Dusting furniture
15. Repairing a car	16. Using a sewing machine
17. Driving a motorcycle	18. Ironing
19. Working a crane	20. Wearing earrings and necklaces
21. Building model airplanes	22. Having pigtails or braids
23. Playing baseball	24. Wearing a skirt
25. Using a dump truck	26. Going to the beauty parlor
27. Owning a tool set	28. Wearing a petticoat or slip
29. Fixing a faucet	30. Using a thimble
31. Driving a truck	32. Washing clothes
33. Being a zoo keeper	34. Bathing the baby
35. Chopping wood	36. Baking cupcakes
37. Hunting tigers	38. Cleaning the house
39. Building a house	40. Playing skipping-rope

INDIVIDUAL DATA SHEET

Title: Differential Recall _____

E: _____ Day and Date: _____ S–Sex: _M or F_ Grade: _____

S: _____ Birthdate: _____ CA: _____

Time Begun: _____ Time Ended: _____ Elapsed Time: _____ Room: _____

RECALL

A. Enter the subject's verbatim responses in a column, in the space provided.

B. Compare responses to Table G9-1; put a + mark in column m or f next to the number of each item recalled.

m	f	Verbatim Recall Items
1. ____	2. ____	
3. ____	4. ____	
5. ____	6. ____	
7. ____	8. ____	
9. ____	10. ____	
11. ____	12. ____	
13. ____	14. ____	
15. ____	16. ____	
17. ____	18. ____	
19. ____	20. ____	

Sum   m [   ]   f [   ]

Combined Total   [   ]

GROUP DATA SHEET

Title: *Sex identity: Differential Recall*

E: _____   Day and Date: _____

Hypothesis:

Method and Procedure: (as described in text with following modifications, if any)

Group Results and Analysis:

TABLE G9-2
MEANS OF MASCULINE AND FEMININE ITEMS RECALLED

Group	N	Items m	f	t
Grade				
Boys	_____			
Girls	_____			
Combined	_____			
Grade				
Boys	_____			
Girls	_____			
Combined	_____			
Grade				
Boys	_____			
Girls	_____			
Combined	_____			
Grade				
Boys	_____			
Girls	_____			
Combined	_____			
Boys	_____			
Girls	_____			
Total	_____			

TABLE G9-3
A 2 X 2 X 2 REPEATED MEASUREMENT ANALYSIS OF VARIANCE OF RECALL SCORES

Source of Variation	Sum of Squares	df	Mean Square	F	p
Between Subjects					
Between Ages		1			
Between Sexes		1			
A X Sex		1			
Within Group Error	_____	___			
Total Between Subjects		$N-1$			
Between Sex of Item (SI)		1			
Age X SI		1			
Sex X SI		1			
Age X Sex X SI		1			
Pooled Subjects X SI (Error)	_____	___			
Total Within Subjects		N			
Total		$2N-1$			

Fig G9.1.   Feminine and masculine items, 1–20.

Fig G9.1. (Continued)

Fig G9.1. (Continued)

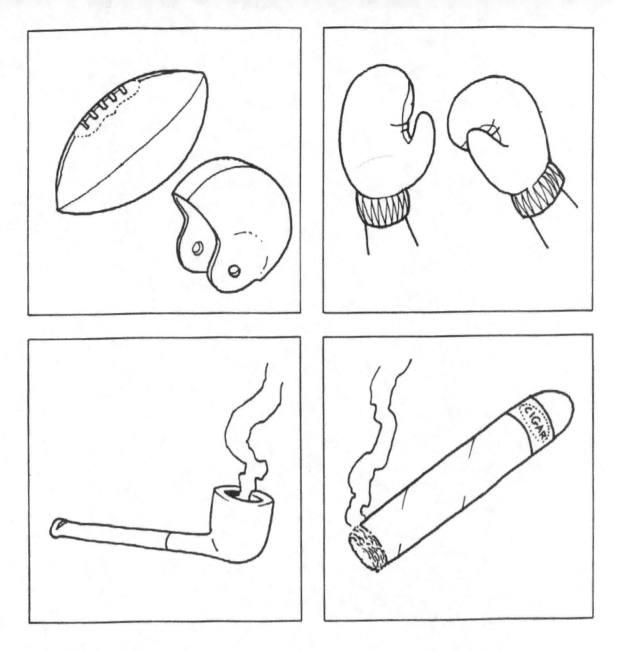

Fig G9.1. (Continued)

Experiment 10
Preference for Sex-Typed Material

Problem and Hypotheses

When shown drawings of objects or activities that adults in our society consider masculine or feminine, and asked to express preferences, will children show age and/or sex differences in their preferences for these items?

In older surveys (Fortune Survey, 1946; Gallup, 1955; Terman, 1938), men and women were asked whether they had ever wished to belong to the opposite sex. Less than 5% of the men and as much as 31% of the women reported having consciously wanted to be of the opposite sex. These figures have become larger and closer, but with larger proportions of women than men still desiring opposite-sex identity.

Studies of preference with children have frequently used toy preference (Rabban, 1950; Brooks & Lewis, 1974), picture preference (It Scale–Brown, 1957; DeLucia, 1963; SERLI–Serbin, Powlishta, & Gulko, 1993), games preference (Sutton-Smith, Rosenberg, & Morgan, 1963), or toy or doll choice (Bryan, Handlon, & Nadelman, 1957; Kaminski, 1973; Lynn, 1959). Beere (1990) discussed instruments used in various countries and ethnic groups. Beyond infancy these results are generally congruent with the findings on adults in that more girls prefer the masculine sex-role items and activities than boys prefer the feminine role ones.

What is the developmental course of these preferences? Rabban (1950) found no significant differences among 3-year-old children, but beyond that, boys were more sex-typed than girls in his sample of 30 months to 8½-year-olds. Brown (1957) found girls showing a predominant preference for the feminine role only by the fifth grade. Nadelman (1974) found both 5- and 8-year-olds same-sex typed in their preferences, with increasing stereotypy in the older boys and in working-class girls. Serbin et al. (1993) found that preferences for sex-typed activities and occupations and for same-sex peers were generally strong throughout the elementary grades.

In your sample of two grades and two sexes, the hypotheses are as follows:

1. Children prefer same-sex over opposite-sex items.

2. This preference for same-sex items is stronger in older children.

3. The increasing preference for same-sex items with age is stronger in (boys) (girls).

4. Over the total sample, masculine items are preferred (more than) (less than) (equally to) feminine items.

Method

Subjects

At least two grades of boys and girls in early elementary school are preferred; for example, first and third, or kindergarten and second.

Materials

40 drawings(20 masculine and 20 feminine. The same cards are used as in the Recall experiment, plus 20 more (Table G9.1 and Fig. G10.1). The first 20 pictures are found in Experiment 9; the second 20, here. Mount on in-

dex cards; number and label on back. Be careful that the number and label match exactly with those in Table G9.1. Use all 40 drawings. Use the Individual Data Sheet supplied.

Procedure

The experimenter shuffles all 20 odd-numbered cards into a randomly ordered masculine (m) pile in his or her lap while chatting casually with the child. The experimenter then shuffles all 20 even-numbered cards into a randomly ordered feminine (f) pile, and places them on top of the masculine pile. (This should be done before getting the child, if the Recall experiment is not being run.)

E: **"Now watch!"** [E takes 4 m cards from the bottom of the pile and 4 f cards from the top of the pile and spreads the 8 cards randomly in front of the child in three rows consisting of 3, 3, and 2 cards, *naming* them once as the cards are laid down.]

E: **"Pick the one you like best."** [E takes the card chosen by the child, notes its number on the Individual Data Sheet in the A1 slot, and puts it aside.]

E: **"Pick the one you like next best."** [E notes this as A2. E repeats the phrase twice more. The four choices are noted in A1-4 sequence; the first-chosen card is saved; the other 3 cards are piled elsewhere. The 4 unchosen cards are piled with the latter.]

The procedure is repeated with 8 new cards, using line B on the data sheet, and so on, making 5 groups of 8 cards, with the child choosing 4 of each 8.

The experimenter then spreads the 5 *first choices* (A1, B1, C1, D1, E1) and says, **"These were the ones you liked the best. Pick the one you like the best of these."** The choice is noted in the *Best* slot, by the number on its back.

Results

Scoring. Look at the first column of five preference scores on the Individual Data Sheet (all the first choices), and count how many were masculine (odd number), how many feminine (even number). Indicate this in the *Summary* on the bottom of the Individual Data Sheet in the column labeled *Choice 1*.

Look at the second column, count as described, and enter in column 2 in the *Summary*, and so on.

Ratio m/t—the number of masculine preferences over 20, expressed as a decimal to two places. Ratios approaching 1.0 indicate strong masculine preferences. Ratios approaching 0 indicate strong feminine preferences.

Ratio m/5—the number of masculine preferences in the 5 *first choices* over 5, also expressed as a decimal.

Enter your subject's data from the *Summary* to the Master Data Sheet, provided by your instructor.

Analysis. For each sex-age group of children, compute the mean m/5 ratio, here called the *Preference "5"* *Scores*. Do the same for the m/20 ratio—the *Preference "20" Scores*. Enter these in Table G10.1.

A simple two-way analysis of variance for age and sex of child can be run, using the m/5 ratios. The same analysis can be performed for the m/20 ratios. See Table G10.2.

State your findings with regard to differences in the preference ratios as a function of *age*, ignoring the sex of the children. Remember that a higher mean preference ratio over .50 indicates a stronger preference for masculine items and activities.

State your findings with regard to *sex*: Do boys and girls significantly differ in their preference scores? This *F* relates to your first hypothesis.

The interaction *F* for *age X sex effects* indicates whether the preference scores change similarly for boys and girls with age, or change differentially. Making a graph of the (four) means related to the interaction *F* helps clarify the findings and relates to hypotheses 2 and 3. If the interaction *F* is significant, Scheffé tests may be run to compare pairs of means.

What is the mean preference score for the total sample? Is it above .50 (masculine)? Is it below .50 (feminine)? Is the difference between the obtained mean and .50 significant? This relates to hypothesis 4.

Discussion

Relate your results to the hypotheses. Which were significantly supported?

Did your preference data agree with Brown's? Nadelman's? Rabban's? More recent research? (Aubry, Ruble, & Silverman, 1999; Turner, Gervai, & Hinde, 1993; Weinraub, Clemons, Sokoloff, Ethridge, Gracely, & Myers, 1984).

Did your Preference "5" and Preference "20" scores act similarly? Which showed less sex-typing rigidity (i.e., moved closer to .50)? Why?

Look back to your data on recall, if Experiment 9 was performed. Is there any relation between preference and differential recall? How could these data be handled statistically to demonstrate these relations? In the preceding experiment on differential recall of masculine and feminine items, we noted that Kail and Levine (1976) found supporting evidence that children encoded the masculine–feminine attribute of items in memory. Kail and Levine used a release from proactive inhibition memory task (see the description in the discussion section of Experiment 9) and followed this with our preference task. Those children who showed very sex-typed preferences apparently encoded the masculine–feminine dimension (as shown by their performance on the proactive inhibition release task); the older girls who did not prefer feminine items over masculine ones did *not* appear to encode along a masculine–feminine dimension in the memory task! What then would you expect from your data?

As an optional class exercise, consider an item analysis. For each of the 40 items, count how many Grade x boys, Grade x girls, Grade y girls, Grade y boys, respectively, preferred each item. Use just the "best" choice, or the five first-choices for each child. Which items are heavily chosen by both girls and boys? Which items are chosen only or mainly by one sex?

While a score closer to .50 than to 0 or 1 means less same-sex-typed preference for girls and boys, respectively, on the measure used in this project, the child is forced to some extent to choose *between* masculine and feminine items. In Bem's inventory (1974), no such polarity is necessary. How could our 40 pictures be adapted to Bem's method? Signorella, Bigler, and Liben (1993) reviewed the impact that forced and nonforced choice methodologies have had on the measurement and conceptualization of developmental differences in young children's gender schemas. This is a good illustration of how one's choice of measurement can heavily affect results.

If your subjects had been invited to draw a picture of a person, prior to taking the preference test, would you expect more boys or girls to draw their own sex first? Would you expect the girls and boys whose preference scores were most extremely sex typed (closest to 0 or to 1) to draw females and males, respectively? Comment on this in relation to the distinction and overlap between "preference" and "identification." (Reread the introduction, "Sex Identity.")

What changes in your results might be anticipated by changing samples? For example, suppose you tested children in a feminist nursery? In an orphanage? In one-parent day-care centers? In low versus high socioeconomic classes? In a retarded group? With differing numbers of younger or older brothers or sisters? Discuss in terms of the social learning, cognitive-development, and psychoanalytic viewpoints.

Cultural differences in gender-typing interest researchers in cross-cultural studies. For example, Turner, Gervai, & Hinde (1993) examined 4- to 4½-year-olds in Cambridge and Budapest and found girls less stereotyped than boys in their toy preference and Budapest children significantly more masculine and less feminine on behavioral measures. Think of several cultures and speculate on probable differences in sex-typing as a function of their family structure and dynamics, religion, schooling.

Would you expect college women to have more masculine preferences than noncollege women? Explain.

Which of the methodological and theoretical issues discussed in the introduction ("Sex Identity") are pertinent to the preference test used? Which ones are not spoken to by this measure and design?

By early elementary school, children's *knowledge of sex roles* (as distinguished from psychological *traits*) is quite sophisticated. Their *preference* for these roles may vary as a function of age and other characteristics of the sample. Variables that are not measured in the present design and that probably do have measurable effects are cohort group and time of testing. Five-year-olds in 1955 and 5-year-olds in 1980 or 1995 may differ in their preference scores (particularly girls); (see Minton, Solomon, Stokes, Charash, & Kendzior, 1999). How and why?

Selected Bibliography

Albers, S. M. (1998). The effect of gender-typed clothing on children's social judgments. *Child Study Journal, 28*(2), 137–159.

Aubry, S., Ruble, D. N., & Silverman, L. B. (1999). The role of gender knowledge in children's gender typed preferences. In L. Balter & C. S. Tamis-LeMonda (Eds.), *Child Psychology: A handbook of contemporary issues* (pp. 363–390). Philadelphia, PA: Psychology Press/Taylor & Francis.

Beere, C. A. (1990). *Gender roles: A handbook of tests and measures.* New York: Greenwood.

Bem, S. L. (1974). The measurement of psychological androgyny. *Journal of Consulting and Clinical Psychology, 42*, 155–162.

Boyatzis, C. J., & Eades, J. (1999). Gender differences in preschoolers and kindergartners' artistic production and preference. *Sex Roles, 41*(7-8), 627–638.

Brooks, J., & Lewis, M. (1974). Attachment behavior in thirteen-month-old, opposite-sex twins. *Child Development, 45*, 243–247.

Brown, D. G. (1956). Sex-role preference in young children. *Psychological Monographs, 70*(14, Whole No. 421).

Brown, D. G. (1957). Masculinity-femininity development in children. *Journal of Consulting Psychology, 21*, 197–202.

Bryan, C., Handlon, B., & Nadelman, L. (1957, April). *The influence of a single sex labeling of toys upon the play behavior of younger and older boys and girls.* Paper presented at the meetings of the Eastern Psychological Association, New York City.

Caldera, Y. M., Huston, A. C., & O'Brien, M. (1989). Social interaction and play patterns of parents and toddlers with feminine, masculine, and neutral toys. *Child Development, 60*, 70–76.

Connor, J. M., & Serbin, L. A. (1977). Behaviorally-based masculine and feminine activity scales for preschoolers: Correlates with other classroom behaviors and cognitive tests. *Child Development, 48*, 1411–1416.

DeLucia, L. A. (1963). The toy preference test: A measure of sex-role identification. *Child Development, 34*, 107–117.

Fortune Survey. (1946). *Fortune*, August.

Gallup, G. (1955). *Gallup Poll.* Princeton, NJ: Audience Research, June.

Hartup, W. W., & Moore, S. G. (1963). Avoidance of inappropriate sex-typing by young children. *Journal of Consulting Psychology, 27*, 467–473.

*Kail, R. V., & Levine, L. E. (1976). Encoding processes and sex-role preferences. *Journal of Experimental Child Psychology, 21*, 256–263.

Kaminski, L. R. (1973). *Looming effects on stranger anxiety and toy preferences in one-year-old infant.* Unpublished master's thesis, Stanford University (Abstract in Maccoby and Jacklin, 1974).

Lynn, D. (1959). *The Structured Doll Play Test.* Burlingame, CA: Test Developments.

Lynn, D. (1969). *Parental and sex role identification: A theoretical formulation.* Berkeley, CA: McCutchan. See chap. 8, Preference, adoption, identification.

Maccoby, E. E., & Jacklin, C. N. (1974). *The psychology of sex differences.* Stanford, CA: Stanford University Press. See chap. 8, Sex typing and the role of modeling.

Martin, C. L., Eisenbud, L., & Rose, H. (1995). Children's gender-based reasoning about toys. *Child Development, 66*(5), 1453–1471.

Miller, L. & Budd, J. (1999). The development of occupational sex-role stereotypes, occupational preferences and academic subject preferences in children at ages 8, 12, and 16. *Educational Psychology, 19*(1), 17–35.

Minton, J., Solomon, L. Z., Stokes, M., Charash, M., & Kendzior, J. (1999). Attitudes toward being female viewed over time. *Journal of Social Behavior and Personality, 14*(2), 207–220.

*Nadelman, L. (1970). Sex identity in London children: Memory, knowledge, and preference tests. *Human Development, 18*, 28–42.

*Nadelman, L. (1974). Sex identity in American children: Memory, knowledge, and preference tests. *Developmental Psychology, 10*, 413–417.

Rabban, M. (1950). Sex-role identification in young children in two diverse social groups. *Genetic Psychology Monographs, 42*, 81–158.

Sandnabba, N. K., & Ahlberg, C. (1999). Parents' attitudes and expectations about children's cross-gender behavior. *Sex Roles, 40*(3–4), 249–263.

Serbin, L. A., Poulin-Dubois, D., Colbume, K. A., Sen, M. G., Eichstedt, J. A. (2001). Gender stereotyping in infancy: Visual preferences for and knowledge of gender-stereotyped toys in the second year. *International Journal of Behavioral Development, 25*(1), 7–15.

Serbin, L. A., Powlishta, K. K., & Gulko, J. (1993). The development of sex typing in middle childhood. *Monographs of the Society for Research in Child Development, 58*(2, Serial No. 232).

Signorella, M. L., Bigler, R. S., & Liben, L. S. (1993). Developmental differences in children's gender schemata about others: A meta-analytic review. *Developmental Review, 13*, 147–183.

Sutton-Smith, B., Rosenberg, B. G., & Morgan, E. F. (1963). Development of sex differences in play choices during pre-adolescence. *Child Development, 34*, 119–126.

Terman, L. M. (1938). *Psychological factors in marital happiness*. New York: McGraw-Hill.

Terman, L. M., & Miles, C. C. (1936). *Sex and personality*. New York: McGraw-Hill.

Turner, P. J., Gervai, J., & Hinde, R. A. (1993). Gender-typing in young children: Preferences, behavior, and cultural differences. *British Journal of Developmental Psychology, 11*, 323–342.

Vaughter, R. M., Sadh, D., & Vozzola, E. (1994). Sex similarities and differences in types of play in games and sports. *Psychology of Women Quarterly, 18*, 85–104.

Volling, B. L., & Belsky, J. (1992). The contribution of mother-child and father-child relationships to the quality of sibling interaction: A longitudinal study. *Child Development, 63*, 1209–1222.

Weinraub, M., Clemens, P. L., Sokoloff, A., Ethridge, T., Gracely, E., & Myers, B. (1984). The development of sex-role stereotypes in the third year: Relationships to gender labeling, gender identity, sex-typed toy preference, and family characteristics. *Child Development, 61*, 1915–1933.

See also the preceding bibliographies.

INDIVIDUAL DATA SHEET

Title: *Differential Preference (m/f)*l _____

E: _____ Day and Date: _____ S–Sex: *M or F* Grade: _____

S: _____ Birthdate: _____ CA: _____

Time Begun: _____ Time Ended: _____ Elapsed Time: _____ Room: _____

Write the number of the child's response card, in rows:

A. 1. _____   2. _____   3. _____   4. _____
B. 1. _____   2. _____   3. _____   4. _____
C. 1. _____   2. _____   3. _____   4. _____
D. 1. _____   2. _____   3. _____   4. _____
E. 1. _____   2. _____   3. _____   4. _____

Best:

SUMMARY:

	Choice 1	Choice 2	Choice 3	Choice 4	Total
No. m	_____	m _____	m _____	m _____	m _____
No. f	_____	f _____	f _____	f _____	f _____
	(5)	(5)	(5)	(5)	$t = 20$

Ratio m/5 = _____

Ratio m/t _____

Ratio f/t _____

GROUP DATA SHEET

Title: *Sex Identity, Preference for Sex-Typed Material*

E:_____   **Date:**_____

Hypothesis:

Method and Procedure: (as described in text with following modifications, if any)

Group Results and Analysis:

TABLE G10.1
MEANS OF PREFERENCE RATIO SCORES, BY SEX AND GRADE

Group	N	Preference "5" (m/5)	Preference "20" (m/20)
Grade_____			
Boys			
Girls			
Combined			
Grade_____			
Boys			
Girls			
Combined			
Grade_____			
Boys			
Girls			
Combined			
Boys			
Girls			
Total			

357

TABLE G10.2

SUMMARY OF TWO-WAY ANALYSES OF VARIANCE FOR PREFERENCE SCORES

Sources of Variation	I. Preference "5" Scores					II. Preference "20" Scores				
	SS	*df*	MS	*F*	*p*	SS	*df*	MS	*F*	*p*
Age		1					1			
Sex		1					1			
Age X Sex		1					1			
Error (within)										
Total		*N* - 1					*N* - 1			

Fig. G10.1. Feminine and masculine items, 21–40.

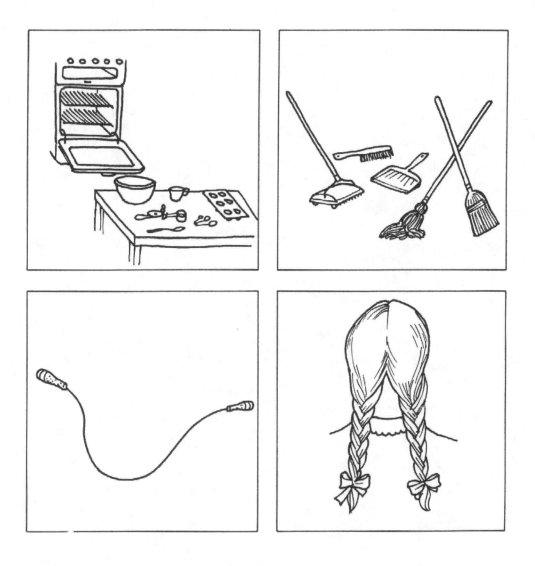

Fig. G10.1. (*Continued*)

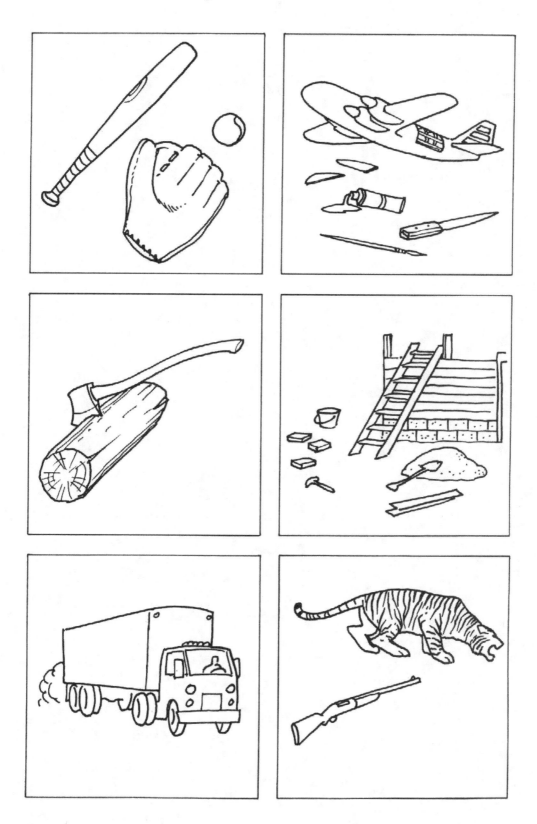

Fig. G10.1. (*Continued*)

Fig. G10.1. (*Continued*)

Cooperation/Competition

Background

In the 1920s and 1930s, cooperative and competitive behaviors were of sufficient interest to psychologists and anthropologists to be included in a popular experimental psychology text (Crafts, Schneirla, Robinson, & Gilbert, 1938) and to be the subject of a commissioned survey of primitive societies by the Social Science Research Council (Mead, [1937] 1961).

A cooperative situation was defined (Crafts et al., 1938) as one that stimulates an individual to *strive with* the other members of the group for a goal object that is to be shared equally among all of them. A competitive situation is one that stimulates the individual to *strive against* other individuals in the group for a goal object of which the individual hopes to be the sole, or a principal, possessor. In group competition, where one cooperates with one's group in competition against other groups, the rewards accrue to the group as a whole.

The early studies (e.g., Leuba, 1930; Maller, 1929) investigated whether cooperative situations or competitive situations were more effective as motives (incentives) to work and effort. Some child psychologists (Berne, 1930; Parten, 1932) used naturalistic observations to study the development of cooperation and social interaction. With the rise of Skinnerian thinking, the effect of reinforcement and various training regimes as influencing cooperation became the focus of investigation (e.g., Azrin & Lindsley, 1956; Mithaug & Burgess, 1968). By and large, while cultural and social influences were frequently investigated then (Kagan & Madsen, 1971; Madsen, 1971; Madsen & Shapira, 1970), personality characteristics that may affect cooperative behavior were not generally studied in laboratory situations. This is no longer true.

Development of Cooperation or Competition. There is no agreement as to whether cooperation or competition increases with age when school children are the subjects. Some studies find younger children more cooperative than older children (de Moja, 1992; Fitzgerald & Frankie, 1982; Stein, 1986), with competition increasing with age (Herndon & Carpenter, 1982). Yet, Handel (1989) found his 10–12-year-olds were more cooperative than the 5–7 or 8–10-year-olds. Several studies find no or little developmental differences (Schmidt, Ollendick, & Stanowicz, 1988; Schwalb & Schwalb, 1985; Sparkes, 1991). Sex X age interactions further complicate the picture: Stockdale, Galejs, and Wolins (1983) found that although their girls remained cooperative over the 4th–6th grades, boys declined in cooperative preferences. Some of these conflicting results may be explained by the differing measures—games, self-reports, with or without a peer partner, observation, parent or teacher ratings, or the differing samples of subjects—different nationalities, SES, special populations.

Sex Differences. On the basis of stereotypes, one expects to find girls more cooperative than boys, and boys more competitive than girls. And indeed, several studies so find (de Moja, 1992, Italy; Knight & Chao, 1989; Rubinstein, Feldman, Rubin, & Noveck, 1987; Schwalb & Schwalb, 1985, Japan; Sparkes, 1991; Stockdale, Galejs, & Wolins, 1983). On the other hand, Pal, Verma, and Vasudeva (1989) found their Indian 12–16-year-old girls more competitive than and as cooperative as boys. The presence of an adult and the nature of the task seem to change the sex relationship: Neither sex dominated in a cooperative task, with or without an adult present; in a competitive task, boys dominated if the adult was absent (Powlisha & Maccoby, 1990). It is encouraging to note, that in most of the studies, both sexes generally respond more positively to cooperative items or situations than to competitive ones.

Learning and Training Interventions. Why do educators advocate cooperative learning? Compared to competitive or individualistic learning, "cooperative learning promotes greater interaction, greater feelings of acceptance, a more dynamic view of classmates and self, greater liking of classmates, more positive expectations, and higher self-esteem and self-acceptance" (Johnson & Johnson, 1983, p. 119).

Preschoolers exposed to cooperative or competitive game conditions reacted as hypothesized: cooperative behavior increased and aggression decreased during cooperative games and subsequent free play periods, and conversely for the competitive games conditions (Bay-Hinitz, Peterson, & Quilitch, 1994). A study of the relative effectiveness and cost-effectiveness of cooperative, competitive, and independent monetary incentive systems with handicapped children indicated that the cooperative condition was a little more effective than the other conditions (Allison, Silverstein, & Galante, 1992). Children (1st–3rd graders) exposed to adult models in films or direct instructions to cooperate did cooperate significantly more than control group children, and this persisted in the older group to a generalization session 7 weeks later (Sagotsky, Wood-Schneider, & Konop, 1981).

Contrary to the above findings, Maori, Pakeha, and Samoan children exposed for 3 weeks to cooperative or competitive learning conditions showed no overall effect of the learning condition on their mathematics achievement scores and other measures (Rzoska & Ward, 1991). Several of these intervention studies used special populations. In addition to the Allison et al. (1992) study mentioned above, handicapped children were also studied by Johnson and Johnson (1983), who demonstrated that cooperative learning experiences promoted more interpersonal attraction between handicapped and nonhandicapped 4th graders. Working with Black and White 6th graders, Johnson and Johnson (1985) found more cross-ethnic social interaction in the intergroup cooperation condition than in the intergroup competition condition. Contrarily, a study with 8–17 year old boys with nonpsychotic psychosocial disorders did not support the hypothesis that a cooperative experience with dice games would enhance subsequent group productivity in a tinker toy task (Nelson & Peterson, 1991).

Variables Related to Cooperation–Competition. In addition to the age and sex variables already discussed, and the cultural differences (to be discussed in the next section), many other relationships have been explored. These include:

interpersonal similarity (Brown, 1984; Dakin & Arrowood, 1981; Segal, 1984)

positive/negative affect (Fry & Preston, 1981)

SES (Knight, 1982; Pal, Verma, & Vasudeva, 1989)

group size (Benenson, Nicholson, White, Roy, & Simpson, 2001)

task type (Powlishta & Maccoby, 1990)

birth order (Knight, 1982; Pal, Verma, & Vasuveda, 1989)

locus of control (Nowicki, 1982; Stockdale et al., 1983)

dominance (Charlesworth & La Freniere, 1983; La Freniere & Charlesworth, 1987)

parental strictness and maternal style (Arap-Maritim, 1984; Kagan & Knight, 1984)

communication (Fitzgerald & Frankie, 1982)

companions' behavior and context (Brady, Newcomb, & Hartup, 1983)

Cross–Cultural Investigations. The 1980s and 1990s saw a burst of interest in examining cooperation–competition in various cultures. Some studies contrasted American children with children from different countries, some compared different ethnic groups within America (Johnson & Johnson, 1985), some omitted American or English comparisons. Although many did find American or English children the more competitive, not all studies did. One study, for example, found Chinese children more competitive (Sparkes, 1991)! Children sampled included those from:

Japan (Schwalb & Schwalb, 1985)

Israel (Rubinstein et al., 1987)

China (Domino, 1992; Li, 1991; Sparkes, 1991)

Greece (Georgas, 1985)

Mizo, India (Srivastava & Lalnunmawii, 1989)

Maori, Paheki, and Samoan children (Rzoska &Ward, 1991)

Papua, New Guinea (Madsen & Lancy, 1981)

Mexico and Mexican-American (Kagan & Knight, 1984; Kagan & Madsen, 1971, 1972; Kagan & Zahn, 1983; Knight, Cota, & Bernal, 1993)

Italy (de Moja, 1992)

Theoretical Issues. Until recently the interest has been more empirical than theoretical. And even the earlier empirical interest waned while cognitive psychology took center field in the 1950s and 1960s! In the last few decades, the interest in prosocial behaviors (helping, sharing, empathy, altruism, cooperation) and in the *interaction* of social and cognitive processes has burgeoned, and the development of "social cognition" (one's understanding of one's own social world) now warrants review chapters and university courses. As Shantz indicated (1975), two theories of mental growth dominated—Werner's and Piaget's. Increasing differentiation, perspectivism, decreasing egocentrism, increasing decentration were all concepts that could be applied to the development of cooperation and competition and other aspects of social cognition.

Shantz adds to these theories *social attribution theory*, which deals with the way in which people answer the question *why* a person behaves as she or he does. Certainly it seems sensible to believe that the way a person behaves in a situation in which one can cooperate or compete depends to some extent on the person's detailed understanding of the situation, of the possible strategies and their effects, of the intentions of the partner; and the person's role-taking abilities and concern for others—in other words, an interaction of cognitive and social abilities and processes.

Knight and his colleagues claimed that the discrepant findings in many cooperation-competition studies were because the cooperative or competitive alternative was confounded with individualistic motivation (Knight, 1981; Knight & Chao, 1991; Knight & Kagan, 1981; Knight et al., 1981). They presented children with distinct cooperative, competitive, and individualistic alternatives, and found that individualistic motivation rather than competition was the strongest social motive among Anglo-American children. This challenged the results of previous cooperation-competition studies. By interpreting results dichotomously (cooperative vs. competitive) and trichotomously (cooperative/individualistic/competitive), Stein (1986) offered partial support for the Knight/Kagan hypothesis that girls were more individualistic than boys. Kagan and Zahn (1983) argued against cultural differences in the strength of individualistic motivation in their Mexican-American, Anglo-American, and Black children; they found age rather than cultural differences in the strength of individualistic motivation.

Another challenge to a simple cooperation–competition dichotomy has been suggested by Tani (1994), namely, that the links between cooperative and aggressive behavior in children's interaction strategies are complex: These behaviors are not mutually exclusive, and often are significantly associated.

The following project uses a familiar folk game to look at cooperative and competitive behavior in boys and girls at two ages.

REFERENCES

See the bibliography at the end of Experiment 11.

Experiment 11

Cooperation and Competition as a Function of Sex of Dyads

When our students in the Experimental Child Psychology course at Mount Holyoke College in the early 1950s investigated cooperation, we used a ribbon track apparatus, in which both children had to push their respective buttons simultaneously to activate the ribbon track. The ribbon carried a single prize on each trial: a Christmas seal or decalcomania. The dependent variables were latency to button push and the children's pattern of allocation of the rewards. The independent variables were, at various times, age of children (nursery and kindergarten), high popular–low popular (measured previously by sociometric techniques), boys–girls.

In the 1970s, when the time seemed ripe for another look at cooperative-competitive patterns of behavior, I asked my laboratory class to choose independent variables of interest and theoretical and practical relevance, and to design an inexpensive task.

Glenda Vogt, then a graduate student in the class, and Lloyd Diehl, an undergraduate, suggested an adaptation of a children's folk game: Scissors–Paper–Rock in a Prisoner's Dilemma paradigm; Babette Kronstadt (the teaching assistant) aided and supervised the subgroup. The independent variable was sex, and the children were assigned to male–male, male–female, and female–female dyads. The experiment you are about to do is a simplified version of this, omitting the mixed-sex dyad, and including an age variable.

Problem and Hypotheses

The anecdote used to illustrate an early version of the Prisoner's Dilemma game had two prisoners charged with the same crime and not allowed to communicate. If both confess, both will be convicted; if neither confesses, neither can be convicted. But if one confesses and the other doesn't, the one who confessed is freed with a reward, and the other gets a stiffer sentence than if both had confessed.

Read the "Method" section below and the background section on developmental changes and sex differences before writing your hypotheses. The questions we want answered by our experiment are:

- What is the modal response pattern in this game by children?

- Do younger and older children differ in their cooperative–competitive patterns?

- Do boys and girls differ in their cooperative–competitive response patterns?

- Is there an interaction of age and sex; that is, do differences between boys and girls in play patterns differ with age?

- (Optional). If data are analyzed in trial blocks of 10, is there a change in response patterns over trial blocks? Do younger and older children play the game differently over trials?

- Do boys and girls play the game differently over trials?

The hypotheses are as follows:

1. The modal (most frequent) response by children in the Scissors–Paper game is (paper–paper) (paper–scissors) (scissors–scissors).

2. The older children are more (cooperative) (competitive) than the younger children.

3. Boys are more (cooperative) (competitive) than girls.

4. There (is) (is not) an interaction of age and sex, indicating _____.

(Optional).

5. (a) There is no charge in response patterns over trial blocks.
   (b) Response patterns become more competitive as the game proceeds.
   (c) Response patterns become more cooperative as the game proceeds.

6. There (is) (is not) an interaction of age and trial blocks, indicating_____.

7. There (is) (is not) an interaction of sex and trial blocks, indicating_____.

Method

Subjects

Same-sex pairs of children from each of two grades; for example:

   5 or more pairs of girls, second grade

   5 or more pairs of boys, second grade

   5 or more pairs of girls, fifth grade

   5 or more pairs of boys, fifth grade

Materials

   2 Point-system cards (Fig. G11.3)

   2 Scoreboards (Fig. G11.4)

   2 Pushpins

   Portable support stand and divider

   Large looseleaf ring of 30 numbered cards

   Experimenter's Pair Data Sheet for scoring

The scoreboard ranges from 370 to –275 points and is illustrated in this chapter. Paste it on very firm thick cardboard or corrugated paper so that the child can use the pushpin without danger. The point-system card (a payoff matrix constructed by Glenda Vogt), also illustrated, shows the points that will be won or lost for each of the four possible combinations of scissor or paper responses. The portable support stand is sturdy wood roughly 9 in. X 36 in. (22.8 cm X .91 m), with braces to support the moving divider (pairs of bookends placed back-to-back slightly apart, at the two ends, work well). The divider or movable screen of heavy corrugated paper between the two children measures about 30 in. X 20 in. (76 cm X 51 cm) and slides along the support stand. The ring of trial number cards is attached at the center top of the screen with double card numbers (1, 1, 2, 2, 3, 3,...) so arranged so that each child will see the appropriate trial number. (See Fig. G11.1).

Procedure

The two children sit facing one another across a table with the support stand between them, and the experimenter sitting to one side between them. The experimenter teaches them the scissors and paper gestures, gives

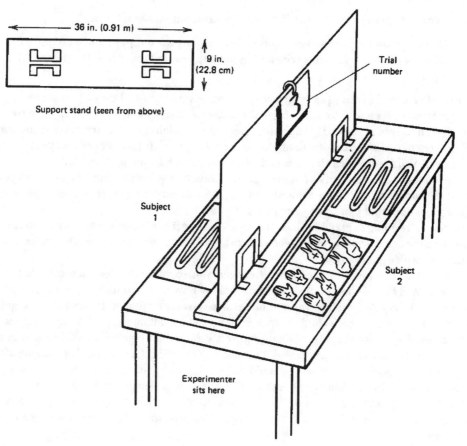

Fig. G11.1. Arrangement for the Scissor–Paper game.

each a point-system card to keep and explains the contingencies, gives each a scoreboard and pushpin and explains its use, gives the pair practice as indicated in playing and scoring, explains the green winning squares and the no-talking rule, puts the screen between the children and demonstrates how it will be slid open and shut. It pays to do all this slowly and carefully, speaking clearly and making sure at each step that the child understands. Then the 30 trials go very quickly and smoothly. The sex of the experimenter should be balanced among the four conditions (second-grade male pairs, second-grade female pairs, etc.) as evenly as possible.

Specific Instructions. **"This is what we're going to be doing today. When I say 'go,' each of you puts out either two fingers** [demonstrate] **or your whole hand** [demonstrate]. **Two fingers means scissors and your whole hand means paper. On each turn you either get some points or lose some points."** [Give each child a card showing the points for each pair of answers.] **"Look at these cards while I explain them to you."** [Explain in random order. The random order is noted on the lines below.]

_____ **"If both of you put out paper, both of you get 5 points."**

_____ **"If both of you put out scissors, both of you lose 5 points."**

_____ **"If one of you puts out paper and the other puts out scissors, the one with the scissors gets 10 points and the one with the paper loses 10 points."**

"Here's how we'll keep score." [Point to score boards.] **"Each of you will start with 100 points [give each child a push-pin], so put your markers on the box marked 100. We're going to play this game 30 times. Each time we play the game, if you win 5 or 10 points you move the marker *up* 5 or 10 points; if you lose 5 or 10 points, you move the marker *down* 5 or 10 points. Okay, let's practice."** [Ask the following questions in random order:]

_____ **"What happens to your score if both of you put out paper?"**[Check their moves.]

_____ **"What happens to your score if both of you put out scissors?"**[Check.]

_____ **"If one person puts out scissors and the other one puts out paper, what happens to the score of the person with scissors? What happens to the score of the person with paper?"**

"If your marker is on a green square [demonstrate] after we play all 30 times, you get an extra prize. Remember, everyone gets one prize when he or she helps us after school, but you can have two prizes if you are on a green square at the end of the game. *Both* of you might get an extra prize or *just one* of you might get an extra prize or *neither* of you might get an extra prize. It just depends on your scores at the *end* of the game. Your score each time depends on what you *and* your partner do.

"After we're all done you can talk about the game as much as you want, but I do *not* want you to talk at all during the game. And also, do not make any signs or do anything to let your partner know what you are going to do or what you want your partner to do.

"Remember we're going to play 30 times. It doesn't matter if you're on a green square before the end of the game; it only counts if you're on a green square at the very end of the game. Do you have any questions about what we're going to do?

"I'm going to put this piece of cardboard between you so you can't see each other's hands until you're both ready. These numbers up here [point] show how many times you've already played the game. Now when I say 'Go,' each of you put out either scissors or paper. Ready? 1, 2, 3, go!"

For the first few trials, state each child's response aloud and the number of points each receives or loses. Make sure each child is moving the pushpin marker correctly. When this is going smoothly, just the number of points lost or gained by each child can be stated. On your Pair Data Sheet, circle the *P* or *S* response (paper or scissors gesture) for each child. Consider the child on your left as S_1, the child on your right as S_2.

After the game, ask, **"Do you think this game would have been easier to play if you could have talked to your partner? What would you have said?"** Note down each child's answers to these questions verbatim on the bottom or back of the data sheet. Take back the point-system cards and the scoring boards and pushpins. Distribute prizes.

Some color is helpful. Color the top and bottom of the winning squares (i.e., +185 through +370) green on each scoreboard. On the point-system matrix card, outline the *You* hand in red and *Your partner* hand in blue. Remind the child that she or he is the red one. Maintain the atmosphere of a game and not an arithmetic classroom.

Results

Scoring. Because you or the children may have erred in addition or subtraction during the trials, recheck the arithmetic for each trial and arrive at the correct final score for each child. Enter the first move (paper or scissor) and the final score for each child in the summary at the bottom of your data sheet. Count the frequency of paper–paper, paper–scissors, scissors–paper, scissors–scissors responses in the 30 trials. (If your class has decided to analyze for the effect of trial blocks, do the same frequency counting for each 10 trials.)

Data Analysis. Transfer the summary data for each pair to the appropriate Master Data Sheet, provided by the instructor. Compute means (and medians, if you wish), and enter group results on Table G11.1 and in the bar graph in Fig. G11.2.

Analysis of these data poses problems because of the dependencies and restrictions: Each child's response may be dependent on the partner's response; each pair of responses may be dependent on the preceding trials; the frequencies add up to a fixed 30. Different researchers resolve these issues differently: Many of the early Prisoner's Dilemma games were described without much statistical analysis. Kronstadt and Vogt (1976) randomly dropped one of the pair of children when analyzing single responses. Nadelman and Shiffler (1977) used multivariate techniques. When using repeated measures analysis of variance on the joint response patterns, they dropped one of the four response patterns to avoid the fixed 30.

If your class is not ready for multivariate techniques and profile analysis, look for grade and sex differences for each dependent variable *separately*, by running a 2 X 2 anova, as summarized in Table G11.2, for each score. (It is possible to combine the PS and SP frequencies for each pair instead of doing separate analyses of these.) If your class decided to include trial blocks in the analysis, do a 2 X 2 X 3 repeated measures analysis instead (2 sexes X 2 grades X 3 trial blocks) with repeated measures on the last variable.

State your findings.

Discussion

Relate your results explicitly to each of your hypotheses or expectations, and to the literature. Evaluate and interpret your findings.

In our laboratory courses, in Kronstandt and Vogt (1976) and Nadelman and Shiffler (1977), the scissors-scissors response was the most frequent (about 50%), and the paper–paper response the least frequent, among a middle-class, mainly White, sample of children. Did your children function similarly? What do you think might happen in an Israeli kibbutz? A Russian residential school? And why? Look at some of the cross-cultural findings on other cooperation-competition games referred to in the Background section to this experiment.

Was there a significant change in response patterns with age, and did it agree with Bryan's (1975) summary that when competition and cooperation are posed as alternative responses to the child the older child will be more likely than the younger one to compete? See the Development section in the Background pages for newer studies on age differences. What effect do you think the laboratory game testing as against naturalistic observation may have? (See Levine & Moeller, 1975.) How do your results compare to the adult studies using a Prisoner's Dilemma matrix (Rapoport & Chammah, 1965a)?

Did you find a significant difference in response patterns between boy pairs and girl pairs? Is there any agreement in the literature on sex differences on which conditions affect boys and girls differentially? Nadelman and Shiffler (1977) did not find different response profiles among their sex pairings. Skotko, Langmeyer, and Lundgren (1973, 1974) and Kronstadt and Vogt (1976) found an interaction of the sex pairing with the sex of the experimenter (and grade) on some scores. Speculate on the relation of your findings to the sex-typing literature and the socialization practices in your community.

We ignored sex of experimenter in the statistical analysis, although this may be an important variable. Speculate on how the sex of the experimenter may be interacting with the sex and age of the child to influence response patterns.

If you analyzed for the effects of trial blocks, did your children become more or less competitive as they played the game? Did the number of mixed responses (*S-P* or *P-S*) decline? Did younger and older children differ more or less as the game progressed? Did boys and girls differ more or less as the game progressed? What have you learned about cognitive development and social processes in your child psychology courses that help you to explain these data?

Assess the Scissors–Paper game as a measure of cooperation–competition. What other kinds of games and situations could one utilize in studying cooperative and competitive responses? What other independent variables interest you and may be fruitful? Relatively little, for example, has been done with personality characteristics; which ones should be tackled first, and why? Do you think cooperation will be a consistent trait or totally vulnerable to situation-specific variables, or what? How do the role-taking investigations relate to the study of cooperation-competition?

More Suggestions for Cooperation-Competition Studies

In addition to the boy pairs and girl pairs, you may wish to try *mixed-sex pairs*, as we did, and as Kronstadt and Vogt (1976) and Nadelman and Shiffler (1977) did. What differences would you expect, on the basis of sex-typing literature?

You paired children from the same grade. What do you think would have resulted from pairing a second grader with a fifth grader, that is, *mixing ages*?

Suppose you had permitted unlimited *communication*. What kind of effect might that have on the progress of the game? Why? (See Fitzgerald & Frankie, 1982.)

Suppose you had permitted a third same-sex child to participate as an onlooker who offers comments, and had explained best strategies in advance to half these onlookers. Do you think such a "trained" onlooker would have affected the play more than an untrained one? Do you think the presence of a third child would affect the game? How about the presence of an adult?

Set has a long history in psychology. If half your children are read stories with a cooperation theme, or shown prosocial TV programs or videotapes, in comparison to the other half who are given similar neutral material, would the play be different between these two groups? (See the training/intervention part in Background.)

How could you *manipulate your payoff matrix* to affect results? (See Allison et al., 1992; Tedeschi, Hiester, & Gahagan, 1969.)

Do you expect a *relation* between performance on the Scissors–Paper game and performance on any of the Madsen circle-matrix games—group reward, limited reward, rivalry?

Suppose you tell your pair of subjects to start their first trial with Paper–Paper. Would you expect that initial cue to increase the cooperative responses? In both sexes? In all ages? (See Brady, Newcomb & Hartup, 1983.)

As you can see, it is easy to spin out endless variations. It is less easy, however, to choose variables (and values of those variables) that relate in a meaningful way to theories that advance our understanding of children's cooperative and competitive behaviors and their relation to other social and cognitive processes.

Selected Bibliography

Allison, D. B., Silverstein, J. M., & Galante, V. (1992). Relative effectiveness and cost-effectiveness of cooperative, competitive, and independent monetary incentive systems. *Journal of Organizational Behavior Management, 13*(1), 85–112.

Arap-Maritim, E. K. (1984). Relation of parental strictness to competitive and cooperative attitudes of primary school children. *Psychological Reports, 54*(3), 864–866.

Axelrod, R. (1984). *The evolution of cooperation.* New York: Basic Books.

Azrin, N. H., & Lindsley, O. R. (1956). The reinforcement of cooperation between children. *Journal of Abnormal and Social Psychology, 52*, 100–102.

Bay-Hinitz, A. K., Peterson, R. F., & Quilitch, H. R. (1994). Cooperative games: A way to modify aggressive and cooperative behaviors in young children. *Journal of Applied Behavior Analysis, 27*(3), 435–446.

Benenson, J. F., Gordon, A. J., & Roy, R. (2000). Children's evaluative appraisals of competition in tetrads versus dyads. *Small Group Research, 31*(6), 635–652.

Benenson, J. F., Nicholson, C., White, A., Roy, R., & Simpson, A. (2001). The influence of group size on children's competitive behavior. *Child Development, 72*(3), 921–928.

Berne, E. V. C. (1930). An experimental investigation of social behavior patterns in young children. *University of Iowa Studies: Studies in Child Welfare, 4*, Nos. 2 & 3.

Bonino, S. (1989, July). *Cooperation and competition: The influence of two different training.* Poster presented at the Tenth Biennial Meetings of the International Society for the Study of Behavioral Development, Jyvaskyla, Finland.

Bonino, S., & Cattelino, E. (1999). The relationship between cognitive abilities and social abilities in childhood: A research on flexibility in thinking and co-operation with peers. *International Journal of Behavioral Development, 23*(1), 19–36.

Bonta, B. D. (1997). Cooperation and competition in peaceful societies. *Psychological Bulletin, 121*(2), 299–320.

Brady, J. E., Newcomb, A. F., & Hartup, W. W. (1983). Context and companion's behavior as determinants of cooperation and competition in school-age children. *Journal of Experimental Child Psychology, 36*(3), 396–412.

Brown, R. J. (1984). The effects of intergroup similarity and cooperative vs. competitive orientation on intergroup discrimination. *British Journal of Social Psychology, 23*(1), 21–33.

Bryan, J. H. (1975). Children's cooperation and helping behaviors. In E. M. Hetherington (Ed.), *Review of child development research* (*Vol. 5*, pp. 127–181). Chicago: University of Chicago Press.

Charlesworth, W. R., & La Freniere, P. (1983). Dominance, friendship, and resource utilization in preschool children's groups. *Ethology & Sociobiology, 4*(3), 175–186.

Cook, H., & Stingle, S. (1974). Cooperative behavior in children. *Psychological Bulletin, 51*, 918–933.

Crafts, L. W., Schneirla, T. C., Robinson, E. E., & Gilbert, R. W. (1938). *Recent experiments in psychology.* New York: McGraw-Hill.

Dakin, S., & Arrowood, A. J. (1981). The social comparison of ability. *Human Relations, 34*(2), 89–109.

de Moja, C. A. (1992). Cooperativeness and competitiveness among pupils in southern Italy. *Psychological Reports, 70*(1), 99–105.

Domino, G. (1992). Cooperation and competition in Chinese and American children. *Journal of Cross-Cultural Psychology, 23*(4), 456–467.

Dorsch, A., & Keane, S. P. (1994). Contextual factors in children's social information processing. *Developmental Psychology, 30*(5), 611–616.

Feldhusen, J. F., Dai, D. Y., & Clinkenbeard, P. R. (2000). Dimensions of competitive and cooperative learning among gifted learners. *Journal for the Education of the Gifted, 28*(3), 328–342.

Fitzgerald, M. A., & Frankie, G. H. (1982). The effects of age and communication on cooperation and competition in children and adolescents. *Journal of Genetic Psychology, 141*(2), 295–296.

Fry, P. S., & Preston, J. (1981). Achievement performance of positive and negative affect subjects and their partner under conditions of cooperation and competition. *British Journal of Social Psychology, 20*(1), 23–29.

Georgas, J. (1985). Cooperative, competitive and individual problem-solving in sixth grade Greek children. *European Journal of Social Psychology, 15*(1), 67–77.

Grenier, M. E. (1985). Gifted children and other siblings. *Gifted Child Quarterly, 29*(4), 164–167.

Handel, S. J. (1989). Children's competitive behavior: A challenging alternative. *Current Psychology, 8*(2), 120–129.

Herndon, B. K., & Carpenter, M. D. (1982). Sex differences in cooperative and competitive attitudes in a Northeastern school. *Psychological Reports, 50*(3), 768–770.

Hughes, L. A. (1991). A conceptual framework for the study of children's gaming. *Play & Culture, 4*(3), 284–301.

Johnson, D. W. (1975). Affective perspective taking and cooperative predisposition. *Developmental Psychology, 11*, 869–870.

Johnson, R. T., & Johnson, D. W. (1985). Relationships between Black and White students in intergroup cooperation and competition. *Journal of Social Psychology, 125*(4), 421–428.

Johnson, D. W., & Johnson, R. T. (1983). The socialization and achievement crisis: Are cooperative learning experiences the solution? *Applied Social Psychology Annual, 4*, 119–164.

Johnson, R. T., & Johnson, D. W. (1983). Effects of cooperative, competitive, and individualistic learning experiences on social development. *Exceptional Children, 49*(4), 323–329.

Kagan, S., & Knight, G. P. (1984). Maternal reinforcement style and cooperation-competition among Anglo-American and Mexican-American children. *Journal of Genetic Psychology, 145*(1), 37–47.

Kagan, S., & Knight, G. (1981). Social motives among Anglo American and Mexican American children: Experimental and projective measures. *Journal of Research in Personality, 15*(1), 93–106.

Kagan, S., & Madsen, M. C. (1971). Cooperation and competition in Mexican, Mexican-American, and Anglo-American children of two ages under four instructional sets. *Developmental Psychology, 5*, 32–39.

Kagan, S., & Zahn, G. L. (1983). Cultural differences in individualism? Just artifact. *Hispanic Journal of Behavioral Sciences, 5*(2), 219–232.

Knight, G. P. (1981). Behavioral and sociometric methods of identifying cooperators, competitors, and individualists: Support for the validity of the social orientation construct. *Developmental Psychology, 17*(4), 430–433.

Knight, G. P. (1982). Cooperative-competitive social orientation: Interactions of birth order with sex and economic class. *Child Development, 53*(3), 664–667.

Knight, G. P., & Chao, Chia-chen. (1991). Cooperative, competitive, and individualistic social values among 8- to 12-year-old siblings, friends, and acquaintances. *Personality and Social Psychology Bulletin, 17*(2), 201–211.

Knight, G. P., & Chao, Chia-chen. (1989). Gender differences in the cooperative, competitive, and individualistic social values of children. *Motivation and Emotion, 13*(2), 125–141.

Knight, G. P., Cota, M. K., & Bernal, M. E. (1993). The socialization of cooperative, competitive, and individualistic preferences among Mexican American children: The mediating role of ethnic identity. *Hispanic Journal of Behavioral Sciences, 15*(3), 291–309.

Knight, G., & Kagan, S. (1981). Apparent sex differences in cooperation-competition: A function of individualism. *Developmental Psychology, 17*(6), 783–790.

Knight, G. P., Kagan, S., & Buriel, R. (1981). Confounding effects of individualism in children's cooperation-competition social motive measure. *Motivation & Emotion, 5*(2), 167–178.

Kronstadt, E. B., & Vogt, G. L. (1976). *The effects of age, sex-group pairing, and sex of experimenter on cooperation in a prisoner's dilemma paradigm.* Unpublished manuscript, University of Michigan Psychology Department (Developmental Program), Ann Arbor.

La Freniere, P. J., & Charlesworth, W. R. (1987). Effects of friendship and dominance status on preschooler's resource utilization in a cooperative/competitive situation. *International Journal of Behavioral Development, 10*(3), 345–358.

Leuba, C. J. (1930). A premininary experiment to quantify an incentive and its effects. *Journal of Abnormal and Social Psychology, 25*, 275–288.

Levine, L. E., & Hoffman, M. L. (1975). Empathy and cooperation in four-year-olds. *Developmental Psychology, 11*(4), 533–534.

Levine, L. E., & Moeller, T. P. (April, 1975). Cooperation: A comparison of observational and experimental measures. *Developmental Reports, No. 64*, University of Michigan Psychology Department, Ann Arbor.

Li, X. (1991). An experimental research study on the effects of goal structure on cooperative and competitive behavior of 6-9 year old children. *Psychological Science (China), 2*(12). (English Abstract).

Lindskold, S., Cullen, P., Gahagan, J., & Tedeschi, J. T. (1970). Developmental aspects of reaction to positive inducement. *Developmental Psychology, 3*, 277–284.

Lougee, M. D., Grueneich, R., & Hartup, W. W. (1977). Social interaction in same- and mixed-age dyads of preschool children. *Child Development, 48*, 1353–1361.

Maccoby, E. E., & Jacklin, C. N. (1974). *The psychology of sex differences*. Stanford, CA: Stanford University Press.

Madsen, M. C. (1971). Developmental and cross-cultural differences in the cooperative and competitive behavior of young children. *Journal of Cross-Cultural Psychology, 2*, 365–371.

Madsen, M. C., & Lancy, D. F. (1981). Cooperative and competitive behavior: Experiments related to ethnic identity and urbanization in Papua, New Guinea. *Journal of Cross-Cultural Psychology, 12*(4), 389–408.

Madsen, M. S., & Shapira, A. (1970). Cooperative and competitive behavior of urban Afro-American, Anglo-American, Mexican-American, and Mexican village children. *Developmental Psychology, 3*, 16–20.

Maller, J. B. (1929). Cooperation and competition, an experimental study of motivation. *Teacher's College Contributions to Education, No. 384*.

Mander, G. (1991). Some thoughts on sibling rivalry and competitiveness. *British Journal of Psychotherapy, 7*(4), 368–379.

Maras, P., Lewis, A., & Simonds, L. (1999). Elephants, donuts, and hamburgers: Young children co-operating to co-operate and co-operating to compete in two primary schools. *Educational Psychology, 19*(3), 245–258.

Mead, M. (Ed.). (1961). *Cooperation and competition among primitive peoples* (Rev. ppbk. ed.). Boston: Beacon Press. (First published 1937 by McGraw-Hill.)

Mithaug, E. D., & Burgess, R. L. (1968). The effects of different reinforcement contingencies in the development of social cooperation. *Journal of Experimental Child Psychology, 6*, 402–426.

Moely, B. E., Skarin, K., & Weil, S. (1979). Sex differences in competition-cooperation behavior of children at two age levels. *Sex Roles, 5*, 329–342.

Nadelman, L., & Shiffler, N. (1977, May). *The influence of sex of dyads on children's cooperation-competition in the Scissors-Paper game*. Paper presented at the meeting of the Midwestern Psychological Association, Chicago.

Nelson, D. L., & Peterson, C. Q. (1991). The effects of competitive vs. cooperative structures on subsequent productivity in boys with psychosocial disorders. *Occupational Therapy Journal of Research, 11*(2), 93–105.

Norem-Hebeisen, A. A., & Johnson, D. W. (1981). The relationship between cooperative, competitive, and individualistic attitudes and differentiated aspects of self-esteem. *Journal of Personality, 49*(4), 415–426.

Nowicki, S. (1982). Competition-cooperation as a mediator of locus of control and achievement. *Journal of Research in Personality, 16*(2), 157–164.

Pal, A., Verma, P., & Vasudeva, P. (1989). Sex and SES differences in competition and cooperation. *Psychological Studies, 34*(3), 160–165.

Parten, M. B. (1932). Social participation among pre-school children. *Journal of Abnormal and Social Psychology, 27*, 243–269.

Parten, M. B. (1933). Social play among preschool children. *Journal of Abnormal and Social Psychology, 28*, 136–147.

Phillips, B. N., & DeVault, M. V. (1957). Evaluation of research on cooperation and competition. *Psychological Reports, 3*, 289–292.

Powlishta, K. K., & Maccoby, E. E. (1990). Resource utilization in mixed-sex dyads: The influence of adult presence and task type. *Sex Roles, 23*(5-6), 223–240.

Rapoport, A., & Chammah, A. M. (1965a). *Prisoner's dilemma: A study in conflict and cooperation*. Ann Arbor: University of Michigan Press.

*Rapoport, A., & Chammah, A. M. (1965b). Sex differences in factors contributing to the level of cooperation in the prisoner's dilemma game. *Journal of Personality and Social Psychology, 2*, 831–838.

Rubinstein, J., Feldman, S. S., Rubin, C., & Noveck, I. (1987). A cross-cultural comparison of children's drawings of same- and mixed-sex peer interactions. *Journal of Cross-Cultural Psychology, 18*(2), 234–250.

Rzoska, K. M., & Ward, C. (1991). The effects of cooperative and competitive learning methods on the mathematics achievement, attitudes toward school, self-concepts and friendship choices of Maori, Pakcha, and Samoan children. *New Zealand Journal of Psychology, 20*(1), 17–24.

Sagotsky, G., Wood-Schneider, M., & Konop, M. (1981). Learning to cooperate: Effects of modeling and direct instruction. *Child Development, 52*(3), 1037–1042.

Schmidt, C. R., Ollendick, T. H., & Stanowicz, L. (1988). Developmental changes in the influence of assigned goals on cooperation and competition. *Developmental Psychology, 24*(4), 574–579.

Schwalb, D. W., & Schwalb, B. J. (1985). Japanese cooperative and competitive attitudes: Age and gender effects. *International Journal of Behavioral Development, 8*(3), 313–328.

Segal, N. L. (1984). Cooperation, competition, and altruism within twin sets: A reappraisal. *Ethology & Sociobiology, 5*(3), 163–177.

Segal, N. L. (1993). Twin, sibling, and adoption methods: Tests of evolutionary hypotheses. *American Psychologist, 48*(9), 943–956.

Sermat, V. (1970). Is game behavior related to behavior in other interpersonal situations? *Journal of Personality and Social Psychology, 6*(1), 92–109.

Shantz, C. U. (1975). The development of social cognition. In E. M. Hetherington, J. W. Hagen, R. Kron, & A. H. Stein (Eds.), *Review of child development research* (*Vol. 5*, pp. 257–323). Chicago: University of Chicago Press.

Skotko, V. P., Langmeyer, D., & Lundgren, D. (1973). Effect of sex of experimenter and sex of subject on defection level in the prisoner's dilemma. *Proceedings of the 81st Annual Convention of the American Psychological Association, 8*, 321–322.

Skotko, V. P., Langmeyer, D., & Lundgren, D. C. (1974). Sex differences as artifact in the prisoner's dilemma game. *Journal of Conflict Resolution, 18*, 707–713.

Sparks, K. K. (1991). Cooperative and competitive behavior in dyadic game-playing: A comparison of Anglo-American and Chinese children. (Special issue: Varieties of early child care research). *Early Child Development and Care, 68*, 37–47.

Stein, W. (1986). Sex and age differences in preschool children's cooperative behavior: Partial support for the Knight/Kagan hypothesis. *Psychological Reports, 58*(3), 915–921.

Srivastava, A. K., & Lalnunmavii. (1989). Cooperative-competitive behaviour and conflict resolution style among Mizo children: A cultural perspective. *Psychology & Developing Societies, 1*(2), 191–205.

Stockdale, D. F., Galejs, I., & Wolins, L. (1983). Cooperative-competitive preferences and behavioral correlates as a function of sex and age of school-age children. *Psychological Reports, 53*(3, Pt 1), 739–750.

Tani, F. (1994, June-July). *Aggression and cooperation in children's interaction strategies*. Poster presented at the XIIIth Biennial Meetings of the International Society for the Study of Behavioral Development, Amsterdam, The Netherlands.

*Tedeschi, J. T., Hiester, D., & Gahagan, J. P. (1969). Matrix values and the behavior of children in the prisoner's dilemma game. *Child Development, 40*, 517–527.

Ware, C. K. (1970). Cooperation and competition in children: A developmental study of behavior in prisoner's dilemma and maximizing differences game (Doctoral dissertation, Yale University). *Dissertations Abstract International, 30*, 3857B–3858B. (University Microfilms No. 70(2826, 95)

Zahn-Waxler, C., Cummings, E. M., & Iiannotti, R. J. (Eds.). (1986). *Altruism and aggression: Biological and social origins*. Cambridge, MA: Cambridge University Press.

PAIR DATA SHEET

Study: C-C **Group:** 2MM 2FF 5MM 5FF

E: _____ **Day & Date:** _____ **Time Start:** _____ **Finish:** _____ **Elapsed:** _____

S1: _____ **S2:** _____

M F **Grade** 2 5 M F 2 5

Birthdate: _____ **CA:** ____ **Birthdate:** _____ **CA:** ____

Trial	S1 Response	S1 Score	S2 Response	S2 Score	Trial	S1 Response	S1 Score	S2 Response	S2 Score
1	P S	_____	P S	_____	16	P S	_____	P S	_____
2	P S	_____	P S	_____	17	P S	_____	P S	_____
3	P S	_____	P S	_____	18	P S	_____	P S	_____
4	P S	_____	P S	_____	19	P S	_____	P S	_____
5	P S	_____	P S	_____	20	P S	_____	P S	_____
6	P S	_____	P S	_____	21	P S	_____	P S	_____
7	P S	_____	P S	_____	22	P S	_____	P S	_____
8	P S	_____	P S	_____	23	P S	_____	P S	_____
9	P S	_____	P S	_____	24	P S	_____	P S	_____
10	P S	_____	P S	_____	25	P S	_____	P S	_____
11	P S	_____	P S	_____	26	P S	_____	P S	_____
12	P S	_____	P S	_____	27	P S	_____	P S	_____
13	P S	_____	P S	_____	28	P S	_____	P S	_____
14	P S	_____	P S	_____	29	P S	_____	P S	_____
15	P S	_____	P S	_____	30	P S		P S	

Final Score [____] [____]

Frequency of responses, in 30 trials

PP ____ PS ____ SP ____ SS ____

Frequency of responses, in trials 1-10

PP ____ PS ____ SP ____ SS ____

Frequency of responses, in trials 11-20

PP ____ PS ____ SP ____ SS ____

Frequency of responses, in trials 21-30

PP ____ PS ____ SP ____ SS ____

First Move: **Final Score:**

S1 ____ S1 ____

S2 ____ S2 ____

GROUP DATA SHEET

Title: Cooperation-Competition _____

E: _____   **Day and Date:** _____

Hypothesis:

Method and Procedure: (as described in text with following modifications, if any)

Group Results and Analysis:

TABLE G11.1
MEAN FREQUENCY OF RESPONSE PATTERNS IN SCISSORS-PAPER GAME FOR SAME-SEX PAIRS IN TWO GRADES

Group	Response Patterns				First Move	
	PP	PS	SP	SS	P	S
Grade _____						
Boy Pairs						
Girl Pairs						
Combined						
Grade _____						
Boy Pairs						
Girl Pairs						
Combined						
Total Sample						
Boy Pairs						
Girl Pairs						
Combined						

TABLE G11.2

SUMMARY 2 X 2 (SEX X GRADE) ANALYSES OF VARIANCE OF THE RESPONSE PATTERNS ON THE SCISSORS-PAPER GAME

Source of Variation	df	Paper-Paper		Paper-Scissors		Scissors-Paper		Scissors-Scissors	
		Mean Square	F	Mean Square	F	Mean Square	F	Mean Square	F
Between Sexes	1								
Between Grades	1								
Grade X Sex	1								
Error N - 4	___								
Total N - 1									

TABLE G11.3

2 X 2 X 2 REPEATED MEASURES ANALYSES OF VARIANCE OF THE RESPONSE PATTERNS ON THE SCISSORS-PAPER GAME WITH TRIAL BLOCKS AS REPEATED MEASURES

Source of Variation	df	Paper-Paper		Paper-Scissors		Scissors-Paper		Scissors-Scissors	
		Mean Square	F	Mean Square	F	Mean Square	F	Mean Square	F
Between Sexes	1								
Between Grades	1								
Grade X Sex	1								
Error N - 4	___								
Total N - 1									
Beteween Trial Blocks	2								
Trials X Sex	2								
Trials X Grade	2								
Trials X Sex X Grade	2								
Error (2 N - 8)	___								
Total (2 N)	___								
(3 N - 1)									

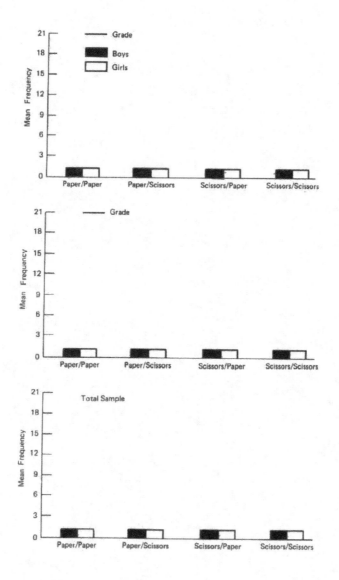

Fig. G11.2. Bar graphs of the mean frequency of different patterns of response for male dyads and female dyads.

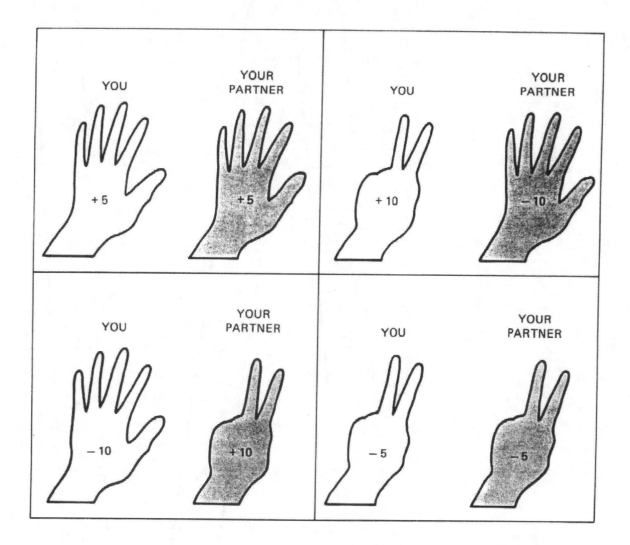

Fig. G11.3.

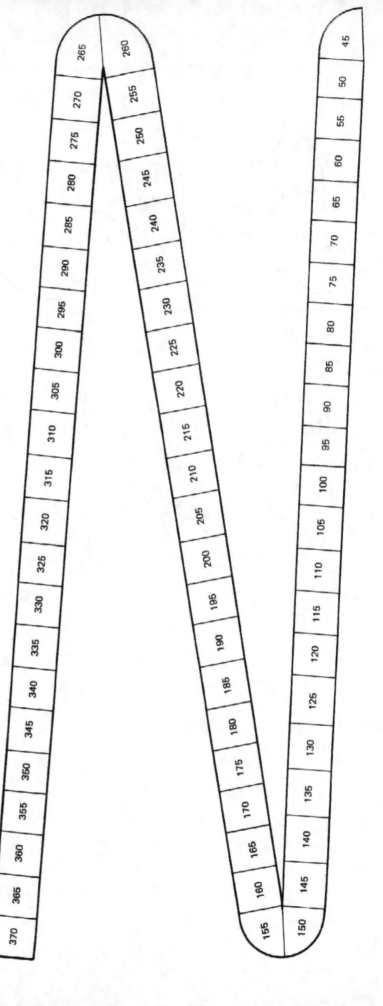

Fig. G11.4.

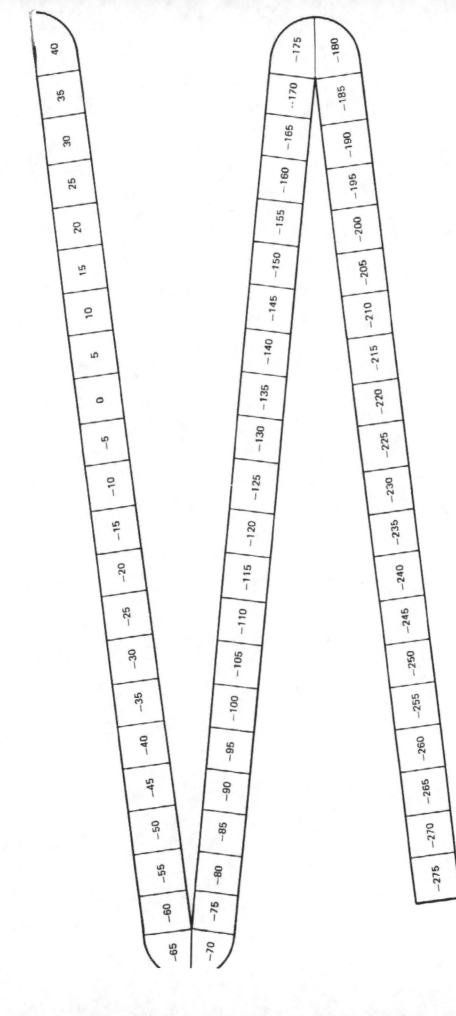

Sibling Relationships

As indicated earlier (Nadelman & Begun, 1982; Wagner, Schubert, & Schubert, 1979), there were more than 2,000 research articles published about sibs by 1979, not including Biblical stories (Cain and Abel, Esau and Jacob, Joseph and his brothers), fairy tales, plays, novels, nor laypersons' publications. The interest in the research literature was focused on sibship variables like number of sibs, ordinal position, age spacing, and the effect of these variables on achievement, intelligence, creativity, personality, and health. There was particular interest in first-borns contrasted with later-borns. Most of these early publications concerned the individual and intrapsychic theories of development.

With the rise of family systems theory and family therapy, and the explicit recognition by social scientists and clinicians that our personalities are influenced by (and reciprocally influence) our relationships, an interest in sibling relationships has surged. More than 2,000 articles about sibs have appeared since 1975. By 1982, Lamb and Sutton-Smith were able to edit a book on sibling relationships that was subtitled "Their Nature and Significance Across the Lifespan," and which demonstrated research covering the birth of a sib through sibling relationships in old age, and included a cross-cultural view, a chapter on nonhuman primates, and the genetic/environmental issue of similarities and differences among siblings. Simultaneously, Dunn and Kendrick (1982) and Bank and Kahn (1982) published their influential books. Cicirelli (1995) updated our knowledge of sibling relationships across the life span.

The importance of the sibling as a socializing agent has finally been recognized, albeit slowly. One usually has a sib longer than a parent or spouse. A family is a complex social system in which all the elements interact, and siblings have direct and indirect influences on family members. Whether as companion, confidante, model, social support, object of social comparison, rival, et cetera, siblings are important contributors to their own, their sibs, and their family's development. The importance of the vertical bond (parents' dominance over children) is challenged by the growing recognition of the importance of the horizontal bond (siblings) (Bedford, 1989; Boer & Dunn, 1992).

Theories

Researchers have approached sibling relationships from various theoretical perspectives, in different disciplines.

Psychodynamic theories emphasize the intense feelings generated by siblings—the feelings of displacement, hostility, rivalry, envy, rage, death wishes. Early articles focused on negative affect like rivalry (e.g., Levy, 1934, 1937).

Sociologists and family therapists, relying on the notion of the family as a dynamic system (a set of elements in interaction), recognize that changing family composition can result in the stimulation of both growth and dysfunction. Certainly the births of children are major modal events in the family life cycle (Carter & McGoldrick, 1980). Although accepting that negative affect can occur, it is important to recognize that being a sibling provides positive opportunities like learning cooperation, sharing, practicing negotiation skills, competing and establishing territoriality, and learning that others have different rights and needs at different times. Siblings may be especially important "in the development of successful modulation of aggressive motivation and expression in the context of enduring relations" (Bryant, 1979, p. 10).

Attachment theory (Ainsworth, 1973), with its early focus on the mother–child affective bond, has moved on to the father and sib (Emde & Harmon, 1982; Stewart, 1983). Early attachments are believed crucial to the ability to form later attachments, and are influential in personality and social development (Bowlby, 1969).

Social psychologists, in addition to social learning theory (Bandura, 1977), with its emphasis on observation, imitation, and modelling, and its newer elaboration (Bandura, 1986) on the interplay of cognitive, behavioral, and environmental factors, can offer notions of group dynamics, territoriality, and personal space to the study of sibling relationships.

Cognitive developmental psychologists have long recognized the importance of cognitive processes to all facets of behavior, including sibling relationships. Children recognize that they have a brother before they realize that their brother has a brother (Phillips, 1969). A developing cognitive maturity affects notions of self and relationships.

Dunn (1983), theorizing about sibling relationships in early childhood, proposed thinking about sibling interaction in terms of "reciprocal" and "complementary" interaction. The former style is probably of more developmental significance than the latter. The reciprocal nature of a relationship is shown in "the familiarity and intimacy of the children, the extent to which they recognize and share each other's interests, and the emotional intensity of their relationship" (p. 788). Differences in age, language ability, caretaking and support, and teaching roles are elements of a complementary interaction. Both types of interaction occur in sibling relationships, and may be as influential in development as the more researched parent/child relationships.

Schachter and her colleagues (1976, 1978, 1982) offer the hypothesis that sibling deidentification is a defense against sibling rivalry. Sibling deidentification refers to the phenomenon of being "different" from one's sibling. In addition, when one sibling in a pair identifies with one parent, the other sibling identifies with the other parent; this is called *split-parent identification*. Schachter's work has relevance to our next experiment.

Sibling Research Areas

In the last two decades, the research emphasis on sibs has switched from effects to process, from preschoolers and young children to lifespan studies, from one shot to longitudinal research, from an emphasis on negative affect to many facets of behavior. What follows is a list of many of the research areas tackled by people interested in sibling relationships, and a sample of the relevant references:

Effect of the newborn on the firstborn
　　(Dunn, Kendrick, & MacNamee, 1981; Legg, Sherick, & Wadland, 1985; McCall, 1984; Nadelman & Begun, 1982; Stewart, Mobley, Van Tuyl, & Salvador, 1987)

Sib relationships at different ages in the lifespan
　　(see chapter authors in Lamb & Sutton-Smith, 1982)

Perception of sibling relationships by the child, by sib, by parent, by others
　　(Bigner, 1984; Furman & Buhrmester, 1985; Jacobson & Nadelman, 1994; Kramer & Baron, 1993; Nadelman, Ray, Hill, & Davis, 1996, Nadelman & Ray, 1997)

Mother's behavior toward sibs
　　(Dunn & Plomin, 1986; Kendrick & Dunn, 1983; Ward, Vaughn, & Robb, 1988)

Sib and peer interaction
　　(Abramovitch, Corter, Pepler, & Stanhope, 1986; Dunn & McGuire, 1992; Santrock, Readdick, & Pollard, 1980; Vandell & Wilson, 1987)

Sib contribution to cognitive development
　　(Azmitia & Hesser, 1993; Stewart, 1983b; Wishart, 1986)

Sib attachment and bonding
　　(Bank & Kahn, 1982; Stewart, 1983a)

Sib caretaking
　　(Stewart & Marvin, 1984; Warschausky, 1988; Weisner, 1982)

Sib cooperation and conflict
　　(Bermann, 1987; Hertzberger & Hall, 1993; Santrock & Minnett, 1981; Stillwell & Dunn, 1985)

Sib similarities and differences
　　(Blanck, Zuckerman, DePaulo, & Rosenthal, 1980; Daniels, 1986; Scarr & Grajek, 1982)

Shared and nonshared environments/Nature–nurture
　　(see above, plus Hetherington, Reiss, & Plomin, 1993; Hoffman, 1991)

Sib temperament
　　(Brody, Stoneman, & Burke, 1987; Schachter & Stone, 1985; Stocker, Dunn, & Plomin, 1989; Stoneman & Brody, 1993)

Sib language and communication
  (Dunn & Kendrick, 1982; Dunn & Shatz, 1989; Phinney, 1986)

Sex effects, dyad composition
  (Holden, 1986; Nadelman & Begun, 1982; Nystul, 1981; Shulman, 1987; Stoneman, Brody, & MacKinnon, 1986)

Disabled, chronically ill, mentally retarded sibs
  (Breslau, 1982; Daniels, Miller, Billings, & Moos, 1986; Ferrari, 1984; Simeonsson & McHale, 1981; Stoneman & Berman, 1992)

Drug use, pregnancy risk among sibs
  (Brook, Whiteman, Gordon, & Brenden, 1983; East & Felice, 1992; Needle, McCubbin, Wilson, Reineck, et al., 1986)

Sibs and only children
  (Chen, Rubin, & Li, in press; Falbo & Polit, 1986; Jiao & Jing, 1986; Rosenberg & Hyde, 1993)

Animal sibs
  (Janus, 1993; Small & Smith, 1981; Suomi, 1982)

Death of a sib
  (Rosen, 1986)

Methods

The methods for examining sibling relationships are familiar to all psychologists. They include observations, interviews, case studies, questionnaires or inventories or ratings, behavioral measures, projective tests, etc. Brief examples follow:

  Observation— Dunn and Kendrick (1982)
    Bryant (1982)
  Interview—Ross and Milgram (1982)
    Holden (1986) and Shulman (1987)
  Sibling questionnaires—Furman and Buhrmester (1985)
    Graham-Bermann and Cutler (1994)
    Nadelman et al. (1996, 1997)
  Parent questionnaires—Nadelman and Begun (1982)
    Kramer and Baron (1992)
    Lanthier and Stocker (1993)
  Behavioral measures—Bermann (1987)
    Aquan-Assee (1993)
  Projective measures—Nadelman and Mac Iver (1983)
    Bermann (1987)
  Global ratings by experimenter—Nadelman and Begun (1982)
  Semantic differential task—Schachter (1976)
    Jacobson and Nadelman (1994)
    Nadelman et al. (1996, 1997)
  Memories—Bank (1992)
    Nadelman (1987)

Although not required for all studies of siblings, a control or comparison group of nonsibs (or "onlies") can often aid interpretations of the data and prevent wrong generalizations about sib behavior. Parents (and researchers), for example, can mistake normal developmental changes for negative sib reactions to the newborn (Nadelman & Mac Iver, 1983). In a doll play task, for example, we discovered that on the second administration, shortly after the second baby was born, the older sib showed fewer positive or neutral responses to the baby doll and slightly more negative ones than on the prebirth visit (Nadelman & Mac Iver,

1987). These data would easily fit a rivalry/distress interpretation, except for the fact that our comparison group of children with no sibs behaved similarly! The appropriate interpretation has to do, therefore, with the situational characteristics of the doll-play task—the increasing permissiveness and comfort.

The presentation that follows introduces the Brother Sister Questionnaire, the instrument that we will use in our next experiment.

Selected Bibliography

Abramovitch, R., Corter, C., Pepler, D. J., & Stanhope, L. (1986). Sibling and peer interaction: A final follow-up and comparison. *Child Development, 57*, 217–229.

Ainsworth, M. D. (1973). The development of infant-mother attachment. In B. Caldwell & H. Riccuiti (Eds.), *Review of child development research* (*Vol. 3*, pp. 1–94). Chicago: University of Chicago Press.

Aquan-Assee, J. (1993, March). *Sibling relationship quality as a predictor of game behavior with siblings during middle childhood*. Presentation at the biennial meeting of the Society for Research in Child Development,New Orleans.

Azmitia, M., & Hesser, J. (1993). Why siblings are important agents of cognitive development: A comparison of siblings and peers. *Child Development, 64*, 430–444.

Bandura, A. (1977). *Social learning theory*. Englewood Cliffs, NJ: Prentice-Hall.

Bandura, A., (1986). *Social foundations of thought and action: A social cognitive theory.* Englewood Cliffs, NJ: Prentice-Hall.

Bank, S. (1992). Remembering and reinterpreting sibling bonds. In F. Boer & J. Dunn (Eds.), *Children's sibling relationships: Developmental and clinical issues* (pp. 139–151). Hillsdale, NJ: Lawrence Erlbaum Associates.

Bank, S. P., & Kahn, M. D. (1982). *The sibling bond*. NY: Basic Books.

Bedford, V. H. (September/October, 1989). Sibling research in historical perspective: The discovery of a forgotten relationship. *American Behavioral Scientist, 33*(1), 6–18.

Bermann, S. A. M. (1987). Siblings in dyads: Cooperation, conflict and self concept. Unpublished doctoral dissertation, University of Michigan, Ann Arbor, MI.

Bigner, J.J. (1974). Second born's discriminations of sibling role concepts. *Developmental Psychology, 10*, 564–573.

Blanck, P. D., Zuckerman, M., DePaulo, M., & Rosenthal, R. (1980). Sibling resemblances in nonverbal skill and style. *Journal of Nonverbal Behavior, 4*, 219–226.

Boer, F., & Dunn, J. (Eds.). (1992). *Children's sibling relationships: Developmental and clinical issues*. Hillsdale, NJ: Lawrence Erlbaum Associates.

Breslau, N. (1982). Siblings of disabled children: Birth order and age-spacing effects. *Journal of Abnormal Child Psychology, 10*, 85–96.

Brody, G. H. (Ed.). (1996). *Sibling relationships: Their causes and consequences*. Norwood, NJ: Ablex.

Brody, G. H., Stoneman, Z., & Burke, M. (1987). Child temperaments, maternal differential behavior, and sibling relationships. *Developmental Psychology, 23*(3), 354–362.

Brody, G. H., Stoneman, Z., & Kelly McCoy, J. (1994). Forecasting sibling relationships in early adolescence from child temperaments and family processes in middle childhood. *Child Development, 65*, 771–784.

Brook, S., Whiteman, M., Gordon, A., & Brenden, C. (1983). Older brother's influence on younger sibling's drug use. *Journal of Psychology, 114*, 83–90.

Bowlby, J. (1969). *Attachment and loss, Vol. 1: Attachment*. New York: Basic Books.

Bryant, B. K. (1979). *Siblings as caretakers*. Paper presented at the meeting of the American Psychological Association, New York City.

Bryant, B. K. (1982). Sibling relationships in middle childhood. In M. Lamb & B. Sutton-Smith (Eds.), *Sibling relationships: Their nature and significance across the life span* (pp. 87–121). Hillsdale, NJ: Lawrence Erlbaum Associates.

Buhrmester, D. (1992). The developmental courses of sibling and peer relationships. In F. Boer & J. Dunn, (Eds.), *Children's sibling relationships: Developmental and clinical issues* (pp. 19–40). Hillsdale, NJ: Lawrence Erlbaum Associates.

Buhrmester, D., & Furman, W. (1990). Perceptions of sibling relationships during middle childhood and adolescence. *Child Development, 61*, 1387–1398.

Burkheimer, E., & Waldron, M. (2000). Nonshared environment: A theoretical, methodological, and quantitative review. *Psychological Bulletin, 126*, 78–108.

Carter, E. A., & McGoldrick, M. (Eds.) (1980). *The family life cycle: A framework for family therapy*. New York: Gardner Press.

Chen, X., Rubin, K. & Li, B. (1994). Only children and sibling children in urban China: A reexamination. *International Journal of Behavioural Development,17*(3), 413–421.

Cicirelli, V. G. (1995). *Sibling relationships across the life span*. New York: Plenum.

Daniels, D. (1986). Differential experiences of siblings in the same family as predicters of adolescent sibling personality differences. *Journal of Personality and Social Psychology, 51*, 339–346.

Daniels, D., Miller, J. III, Billings, A. G., & Moos, R. H. (1986). Psychosocial functioning of siblings of children with rheumatic disease. *Journal of Pediatrics, 109*, 379–383.

Downey, D. B. (2001). Number of siblings and intellectual development: The resource dilution explanation. *American Psychologist, 56*(6/7), 497–504.

Dunn, J. (1983). Sibling relationships in early childhood. *Child Development, 54*, 787–811.

Dunn, J. (1985). *Sisters and brothers*. Cambridge, MA: Harvard University Press.

Dunn, J., & Kendrick, C. (1982). *Siblings: Love, envy, and understanding*. Cambridge, MA: Harvard University Press.

Dunn, J., Kendrick, C., & MacNamee, R. (1981). The reaction of first-born children to the birth of a sibling: Mothers' reports. *Journal of Child Psychology and Psychiatry, 22*, 1–18.

Dunn, J., & McGuire, S. (1992). Sibling and peer relationships in childhood. *Journal of Child Psychology and Psychiatry, 33*(1), 67–105.

Dunn, J., & Plomin, R. (1986). Determinants of maternal behaviour towards 3-year-old siblings. *British Journal of Developmental Psychology, 4*, 127–136.

Dunn, J., & Plomin, R. (1991). Why are siblings so different? The significance of differences in sibling experience within the family. *Family Process, 30*, 271–283.

Dunn, J., & Shatz, M. (1989). Becoming a conversationalist despite (or because of) having an older sibling. *Child Development, 60*, 399–410.

East, P. L., & Felice, M. E. (1992). Pregnancy risk among the younger sisters of pregnant and childbearing adolescents. *Developmental and Behavioral Pediatrics, 13*(2).

Emde, R. N., & Harmon, R. J. (1982). *The development of attachment and affiliative systems*. New York: Plenum.

Falbo, T., & Polit, D. F. (1986). Quantitative review of the only child literature: Research evidence and theory development. *Psychological Bulletin, 100*, 176–189.

Fanos, J. (1996). *Sibling loss*. Mahwah, NJ: Lawrence Erlbaum Associates.

Feinberg, M. E., & Hetherington, E. M. (2000). Sibling differentiation in adolescence: Implications for behavioral genetic theory. *Child Development, 71*(6), 1512–1524.

Ferrari, M. (1984). Chronic illness: Psychosocial effects on siblings–1. Chronically ill boys. *Journal of Child Psychology and Psychiatry, 25*, 459–476.

Furman, W., & Buhrmester, D. (1985a). Children's perceptions of the qualities of sibling relationships. *Child Development, 56*, 448–461.

Furman, W., & Buhrmester, D. (1985b). Children's perceptions of the personal relationships in their social networks. *Developmental Psychology, 21*, 1016–1024.

Garner, P. W., Jones, D. C., & Palmer, D. J. (1994). Social cognitive correlates of preschool children's sibling caregiving behavior. *Developmental Psychology, 30*(6), 905–911.

Graham-Bermann, S. A., & Cutler, S. E. (1994). The Brother-Sister Questionnaire (BSQ): Psychometric assessment and discrimination of well functioning from dysfunctional relationships. *Journal of Family Psychology, 8*(2), 224–238.

Herzberger, S.D., & Hall, J. A. (1993). Consequences of retaliatory aggression against siblings and peers: Urban minority children's expectations. *Child Development, 64*, 1773–1785.

Hetherington, E. M., Henderson, S. H., & Reiss, D. (1999). Adolescent siblings in step-families: Family functioning and adolescent development. *Monographs of the Society for Research in Child Development, 64* (4, Serial No. 259).

Hetherington, E. M., Reiss, D., & Plomin, R. (Eds.). (1994). *The separate social worlds of siblings: The impact of nonshared environment on development*. Hillsdale, NJ: Lawrence Erlbaum Associates.

Hoffman, L. W. (1991). The influence of the family environment on personality: Accounting for sibling differences. *Psychological Bulletin, 110*(2), 187–203.

Holden, C. E. (1986). Being a sister: Constructions of the sibling experience. (Doctoral dissertation, University of Michigan). *Dissertation Abstracts International, 47*(10), 4301B.

Howe, N., Rinaldi, C. M., Jennings, M., & Petrakos, H. (2002). "No! The lambs can stay out because they got cosies": Constructive and destructive sibling conflict, pretend play, and social understanding. *Child Development, 73*(5), 1460–1473.

Jacobson, J. D., & Nadelman, L. (1994). *Young adults' perceptions of the sibling relationship.* Poster presented at the meeting of the International Society of Behavioural Development, Amsterdam, The Netherlands.

Janus, M. (1993, March). *Older sisters make relationships special: Young primates' bonds with siblings and non-siblings.* Poster presented at the biennial meetings of the Society for Research in Child Development, New Orleans.

Jiao, S., & Jing, Q. (1986). Comparative study of behavioral qualities of only children and sibling children. *Child Development, 57,* 357–361.

Kendrick, C., & Dunn, J. (1983). Sibling quarrels and maternal responses. *Developmental Psychology, 19,* 62–70.

Kramer, L., & Baron, L. A. (1993, March). *What parents say about children's sibling relationships (Might surprise you).* Poster presented at the biennial meeting of the Society for Research in Child Development, New Orleans.

Lalumiere, M. L., Quinsey, V. L., & Craig, W. M. (1996). Why children from the same family are so different from one another. A Darwinian note. *Human Nature, 7,* 281–290.

Lamb, M., & Sutton-Smith, B. (Eds.) (1982). *Sibling relationships: Their nature and significance across the lifespan.* Hillsdale, NJ: Lawrence Erlbaum Associates.

Lanthier, R. P., & Stocker, C. (1993, March). *Sibling relationships: Development from childhood to early adulthood.* Poster presented at the biennial meeting of the Society for Research in Child Development, New Orleans.

Legg, C., Sherick, I., & Wadland, W. (1975). Reactions of preschool children to the birth of a sibling. *Child Psychiatry and Human Development, 5,* 5–39.

Levy, D. M. (1934). Rivalry between children of the same family. *Child Study, 11,* 233–261.

Levy, D. M. (1937). Studies in sibling rivalry. *American Orthopsychiatric Association Research Monographs,* (Vol. 2).

McCall, R. B. (1984). Developmental changes in mental performance: The effect of the birth of a sibling. *Child Development, 55,* 1317–1321.

Mekos, D., Hetherington, E. M., & Reiss, D. (1996). Sibling differences in problem behavior and parental treatment in nondivorced and remarried families. *Child Development, 67*(5), 2148–2165.

Nadelman, L. (1987, April). *Earliest memories of siblings.* Poster presented at the meeting of the Society for Research in Child Development, Baltimore, MD.

Nadelman, L., & Begun, A. (1982). The effect of the newborn on the older sibling: Mother's questionnaires. In M.E. Lamb & B. Sutton-Smith (Eds.), *Sibling relationships: Their nature and significance across the lifespan* (pp. 13–37). Hillsdale, NJ: Lawrence Erlbaum Associates.

Nadelman, L., & Mac Iver, D. (1983, April). *The effect of the newborn on the older sibling: Doll play.* Paper presented at the meeting of the Society for Research on Child Development, Detroit, MI.

Nadelman, L., & Mac Iver, D. (1987, July). *Firstborns vs. "onlies": The importance of a control group in sibling research.* Paper presented at the meeting of the International Society for the Study of Behavioural Development, Tokyo.

Nadelman, L., Ray, D., Hill, L, & Davis, L. (1996, August). *Black female young adults' perceptions of sibling relationships.* Poster presented at the meetings of the International Society for the Study of Behavioural Development, Quebec.

Nadelman, L., & Ray, D. (1997, April). *Perceptions of sibling relationships by African-American college students.* Poster presented at the meetings of the Society for Research in Children's Development, Washington, DC.

Needle, R., McCubbin, H., Wilson, M., Reineck, R., et al. (1986). Interpersonal influences in adult drugs use: The role of older siblings, parents, peers. *International Journal of the Addictions, 21*(7), 739–766.

Nystul, S. (1981). Effects of siblings' sex composition on self- concept. *Journal of Psychology, 108,* 133–136.

Perner, J., Ruffman, T., & Leekam, S. R. (1994). Theory of mind is contagious: You catch it from your sibs. *Child Development, 65,* 1228–1238.

Phillips, J. (1969). *The origin of intellect: Piaget's theory.* San Francisco: Freeman.

Phinney, J. S. (1986). The structure of 5-year-olds' verbal quarrels with peers and siblings. *Journal of Genetic Psychology, 147,* 47–60.

Plomin, R., Reiss, D., Hetherington, E. M., & Howe, G. W. (1994). Nature and nurture: Genetic contributions to measures of the family environment. *Developmental Psychology, 30*(1), 32–43.

Rosen, H. (1986). *Unspoken grief: Coping with childhood sibling loss.* Lexington, MA: Lexington Books.

Ross, H. G., & Milgram, J. I. (1982). Important variables in adult sibling relationships: A qualitative study. In M. Lamb & B. Sutton-Smith (Eds.), *Sibling relationships: Their nature and significance across the lifespan* (pp. 225–249). Hillsdale, NJ: Lawrence Erlbaum Associates.

Rust, J., Golombok, M. H., Johnston, K., & Golding, J. (2000). The role of brothers and sisters in the gender development of preschool children. *Journal of Experimental Child Psychology, 77*(4), 292–303.

Santrock, J. W., & Minnett, A. M. (1981, April). *Sibling interaction in cooperative, competitive, and neutral settings: An observational study of sex of sibling, age spacing, and ordinal position.* Paper presented at the meeting of the Society for Research in Child Development, Boston.

Santrock, J. W., Readdick, C. A., & Pollard, L. (1980). Social comparison processes in sibling and peer relations. *Journal of Genetic Psychology, 137*, 91–107.

Scarr, S., & Grajek, S. (1982). Similarities and differences among siblings. In M. Lamb & B. Sutton-Smith (Eds.), *Sibling relationships* (pp. 357–381). Hillsdale, NJ: Lawrence Erlbaum Associates.

Schachter, F. F. (1982). Sibling deidentification and split-parent identification: A family tetrad. In M. Lamb and B. Sutton-Smith (Eds.), *Sibling relationships: Their nature and significance across the lifespan* (pp. 123–151). Hillsdale, NJ: Lawrence Erlbaum Associates.

Schachter, F. F., Gilutz, G., Shore, E., & Adler, M. (1978). Sibling deidentification judged by mothers: Cross-validation and developmental studies. *Child Development, 49*, 543–546.

Schachter, F. F., Shore, E., Feldman-Rotman, S., Marquis, R. E., & Campbell, S. (1976). Sibling deidentification. *Developmental Psychology, 12*, 418–427.

Schachter, F. F., & Stone, R. K. (1985). Difficult sibling, easy sibling, temperament and the within-family environment. *Child Development, 56*, 1335–1344.

Schachter, F. F., & Stone, R. K. (1987). Comparing and contrasting siblings: Defining the self. *Journal of Children in Contemporary Society, 19*, 55–75.

Sheldon, A. (Ed.). (1996). Constituting gender through talk in childhood: Conversations in parent-child, peer, and sibling relationships. A special issue of *Research on Learning and Social Interaction*. Mahwah, NJ: Lawrence Erlbaum Associates.

Shulman, M. E. (1987). *On being a brother: Constructions of the sibling experience*. Unpublished doctoral dissertation, University of Michigan, Ann Arbor.

Simeonsson, R. J., & McHale, S. M. (1981). Review: Research on handicapped children: Sibling relationships. *Child: Care, Health and Development, 7*, 153–171.

Slomkowski, C., Rende, R., Conger, K. J., Simons, R. L., & Conger, R. D. (2001). Sisters, brothers, and delinquency: Evaluating social influence during early and middle adolescence. *Child Development, 72*(1), 271–283.

Small, M. F., & Smith, D. G. (1981). Interactions with infants by full siblings, paternal half-siblings, and nonrelatives in a captive group of rhesus macaques (Macaca mulatta). *American Journal of Primatology, 1*, 91–94.

Stewart, R. B. (1983a). Sibling attachment relationships: Child-infant interactions in the strange situation. *Developmental Psychology, 19*, 192–199.

Stewart, R. B., Jr. (1983b). Sibling interaction: The role of the older child as teacher for the younger. *Merrill-Palmer Quarterly, 29*, 47–68.

Stewart, R., & Marvin, R. S. (1984). Sibling relations: The role of conceptual perspective-taking in the ontogeny of sibling caregiving. *Child Development, 55*, 1322–1332.

Stewart, R. B., Mobley, L. A., VanTuyl, S. S., & Salvador, M. A. (1987). The firstborns adjustment to the birth of a sibling: A longitudinal assessment. *Child Development, 58*, 341–355.

Stillwell, R., & Dunn, J. (1985). Continuities in sibling relationships: Patterns of aggression and friendliness. *Journal of Child Psychology and Psychiatry, 26*, 627–637.

Stocker, C., Dunn, J., & Plomin, R. (1989). Sibling relationships: Links with child temperament, maternal behavior, and family structure. *Child Development, 60*, 715–727.

Stoneman, Z., & Berman, P. W. (Eds.). (1992). *The effects of mental retardation, disability, and illness on sibling relationships*. Baltimore, MD: Brookes Publishing.

Stoneman, Z., & Brody, G. H. (1993). Sibling temperaments, conflict, warmth, and role asymmetry. *Child Development, 64*, 1786–1800.

Stoneman, Z., Brody, G. H., & MacKinnon, C. E. (1986). Same-sex and cross-sex siblings: Activity choices, roles, behavior, and gender stereotypes. *Sex Roles, 15*, 495–511.

Suomi, S. J. (1982). Sibling relationships in nonhuman primates. In M. Lamb & B. Sutton-Smith (Eds.), *Sibling relationships: Their nature and significance across the lifespan* (pp. 329–356). Hillsdale, NJ: Lawrence Erlbaum Associates.

Vandell, D. L., & Wilson, K. S. (1987). Infants' interactions with mother, sibling, and peer: Contrasts and relations between interaction systems. *Child Development, 58*(1), 176–186.

Volling, B. L., & Belsky, J. (1992). The contribution of mother-child and father-child relationships to the quality of sibling interaction: A longitudinal study. *Child Development, 63*, 1209–1222.

Volling, B. L., McElwain, N. L., & Miller, A. L. (2002). Emotion regulation in context: The jealousy complex between young siblings and its relation with child and family characteristics. *Child Development, 73*(2), 581–600.

Wagner, M. E., Schubert, H. J. P., & Schubert, D.S.P. (1979). Sibship-constellation effects on psychosocial development, creativity, and health. In H.W. Reese & L.P. Lipsitt (Eds.), *Advances in child development and behavior* (*Vol.14*, pp. 57–148). New York: Academic Press.

Wan, C., Fan, C., Lin, G., & Jing, Q. (1994). Comparison of personality traits of only and sibling school children in Beijing. *Journal of Genetic Psychology, 155*(4), 377–388.

Ward, M. J., Vaughn, B. E., & Robb, M.D. (1988). Social-emotional adaptation and infant-mother attachment in siblings: Role of the mother in cross-sibling consistency. *Child Development, 59*, 643–651.

Warschausky, J. S. (1988). *Sibling caretaking and its impact on the caretaker's relationships and aspirations in young adulthood*. Unpublished doctoral dissertation, Boston University, Boston, MA.

Weisner, T. S. (1982). Sibling interdependence and child caretaking: A cross-cultural view. In M. Lamb & B. Sutton-Smith (Eds.), *Sibling relationships: Their nature and significance across the lifespan* (pp. 305–327). Hillsdale, NJ: Lawrence Erlbaum Associates.

Wishart, J. G. (1986). Siblings as models in early infant learning. *Child Development, 57*, 1232–1240.

Zukow, P. (Ed.). (1989). *Sibling interaction across cultures*. New York: Springer-Verlag.

Assessing Four Domains of the Childhood Sibling Relationship

Sandra A. Graham-Bermann

The sibling relationship is one of the longest, most enduring relationships, often outlasting the relationship with a spouse or with children (Bank, 1992). Researchers have now explored the salient qualities of normal sibling relationships and have concentrated primarily on birth order studies, sibling cooperation, and the birth of a second child into the family (Boer & Dunn, 1992; Furman & Buhrmester, 1992; Stocker & McHale, 1992). Furthermore, most of the research on sibling relationships has relied on researcher observation and mothers' reports. Little is known about sibling relationships from the perspective of the children themselves. Even less is known about the extent and consequences of dysfunctional sibling relationships, particularly those embued with violence (Graham-Bermann, 2001; Steinmetz, 1981; Weihe, 1990).

This chapter describes two studies designed to assess dysfunctional and healthy sibling relationships during childhood. The studies were undertaken with the help of a team of graduate and undergraduate student research assistants. We were able to evaluate four areas of sibling relationships and assess how abusive and nonabusive sibling dyads can be distinguished using these constructs with a new measure. Along the way it became clear that older siblings and male siblings were more likely to be the bullies, or perpetrators of sibling violence and that younger and female siblings were most at-risk for being victims of sibling violence (Graham-Bermann & Cutler, 1994; Graham-Bermann, Cutler, Litzenberger, & Schwartz, 1994).

One of the difficulties of studying abnormal or dysfunctional sibling relationships has been the lack of previous work in this area. Most developmental researchers have studied only mild levels of children's conflicts such as rivalry between siblings, verbal disagreements, or mild forms of aggression (Buhrmeseter, 1992; Buhrmester & Furman, 1990; Erel, Margolin, & John, 1998). There are a few studies of sibling homicide, but almost no studies of abusive or highly dysfunctional sibling relationships. Therefore, our first task was to define the essential characteristics of both healthy and dysfunctional sibling relationships, then find a way to study these properties. By reviewing the research and theoretical literature, four family systems constructs that have relevance for the sibling relationship were selected as useful to our purposes and are summarized below (Graham-Bermann & Cutler, 1994).

Constructs Pertaining to Sibling Relationships

Researchers who study child development, family systems, and family violence have most often defined well-functioning and abusive relationships either between adult partners or between parents and their children. Yet it is clear from reviewing the literature, that most meaningful family relationships have been described in terms of four qualities: (1) sufficient generational and individual boundaries, (2) some similarities as well as differences between family members, (3) low levels of coercion within the family, and (4) high levels of empathy. It was hypothesized that these characteristics would adequately describe childhood sibling relationships as well.

The concept of *boundary maintenance* within the family was first described by Minuchin and colleagues (Minuchin, Montalvo, Guerney, Rosman, & Schumer, 1967). They argued that boundaries are set up between individuals within the family and also between the family and the outside world both to offer a buffer and to serve as a line of demarcation. Minuchin and colleagues found that families did not function well when the boundaries were either too rigid or too open. In other words, excessively rigid boundaries led to a loss of control whereas overly lax boundaries lead to symbiosis and loss of identity among family members. They found that the healthiest boundaries between family members were those that were semipermeable, flexible, and adaptive (Minuchin, 1974).

Since that time, other psychologists have studied boundary ambiguity in families. They hypothesized that families become distressed when the boundaries and membership of families are unclear (Boss, Doherty,

LaRossa, Schumm, & Steinmetz, 1993). In this model, families function best when the boundaries are clearly agreed on and negotiated. The construct of family boundaries also can be used in studying siblings. In this case, one developmental task would be learning to establish and to respect mutually agreed-on boundaries between the self and the other sibling.

The second family relationship construct is the *differentiation of the self from other people* in the family, a concept first identified by Bowen (1966). In one study, Grotevant and Cooper (1986) described how individuation worked to solidify the teens' identity and aid in the development of their role taking skills. Similarly, Schachter's group wrote about sibling deidentification, a process that describes how separating from a sibling can take the the form of actively assuming an opposing role or identity from the other sibling. In that study, extreme cases of sibling deidentification were associated with whole family dysfunction (Schachter, Shore, Feldman-Rotman, Marquis, & Campbell, 1976).

The differentiation construct can be used to describe the qualities of a healthy and a dysfunctional sibling relationship. For healthy relationships, the task would be to balance the shared or common interests with a sibling with some unique or individual characteristics of each sibling in the dyad. Dysfunctional sibling relationships would be characterized as those with no differentiation in identity or roles among the two siblings in the dyad.

The third element of family relationships is the relative balance and distribution of *power.* Flexible and shared distribution of power between family members marks the healthy relationship (Furman & Burhmester, 1992). We know that abusive relationships are characterized by power imbalances, where the victim may be coerced or threatened into performing acts or doing things against his or her will, for example not defending him or herself, not telling the parents about a problem. Over time, childhood relationships with an imbalanced power structure can result in the solidification of inequitable victim and perpetrator (bully) roles (Graham-Bermann & Cutler, 1994). A number of studies of intimate partner relationships have also identified the power and control imbalances that accompany domestic violence (Jouriles, et al., 2001; Graham-Bermann, 2001). In this case, women who are physically abused are also frequently threatened, coerced, and controlled by their partners. Thus, there is ample evidence that the presence of coercive processes and an unequal distribution of power characterizes dysfuntional relationships.

The repeated use of control and coercion tactics by a sibling are indications that the relationship is unbalanced. When Patterson and colleagues studied physical aggression between siblings they found older children taught patterns of deviant functioning to their younger siblings (Patterson, Dishion, & Bank, 1984). Although Patterson (1986) described the socialization of one aggressive sibling by another, Weihe (1990) provided qualitative accounts of three forms of sibling abuse (physical, emotional, and sexual). Emotionally abusive siblings were those who sought to dominate the brother or sister by any means, most often with insults, name calling, and coercive control. The former study is of mutually aggressive siblings, while the latter study focuses on only victims of sibling abuse. In another study, problems of aggression in the sibling relationship were linked to violence between parents in the same families (McCloskey, Figueredo, & Koss, 1995).

The fourth construct is the ability to *empathize* with another person. Being able to take the other's perspective is considered an essential quality for all healthy relationships, and has been described by most major child developmental theorists, like Erikson (1968) and Piaget (1932). Those who hurt or abuse other people are assumed to have little empathy. For example, abusive and nonabusive parents have been shown to be distinguishable from each other based on their levels of empathy (Newberger & Cook, 1983). Similarly, siblings in high-conflict families were found to have little empathy and to exhibit emotionally abusive behaviors than comparison children raised in families without high levels of violence (Eastin, Graham-Bermann, & Levendosky, in press).

By extension, these four constructs may be used to describe healthy, supportive, and balanced relationships. That is, siblings who are adequately differentiated, able to empathize with one another, respect each other's boundaries, and do not use coercive control tactics, would appear to function at a higher level than siblings who lack these qualities.

The Brother–Sister Questionnaire (BSQ): The 35 items used in the Brother–Sister Questionnaire were selected to reflect the elements of relationships related to family health and violence discussed above, namely, the degree of differentiation, boundary maintenance, empathy, and the relative balance of power and control in the relationship (Graham-Bermann & Cutler, 1994).

Each subject is asked to complete this questionnaire in reference to the relationships between the subject and sibling with whom he or she had the most conflict while growing up. The questions were designed to reflect the subject's assessment of what the relationship was generally like when they were children, that is, across the childhood and teenage years. Using Likert scales, subjects are asked to rate how much each item describes their relationship with their designated sibling, with ratings from one (Not at all true), Two (Not very true), Three (Sometimes true), Four (Often true), to Five (Very much true). The individual items are shown in Table 1.

Study One

The first study of childhood sibling relationships tried to document the validity and reliability of the 35 item Brother–Sister Questionnaire (BSQ). In order to do this, the qualities of four distinct types of highly conflictual sibling relationships were assessed: These four types of relationships were where the subject was (1) the victim of serious conflict, (2) the instigator or perpetrator of the conflict, (3) involved in high levels of

TABLE 1

THE BROTHER–SISTER QUESTIONNAIRE (S. GRAHAM-BERMANN, PH.D., 1993)

There are _____ children in my family of origin (including me).
The OLDEST child is _____ years old. Male or female? (circle one)
The NEXT OLDEST child is _____ years old. Male or female?
The NEXT OLDEST child is _____ years old. Male or female?
The NEXT OLDEST child is _____ years old. Male or female?
The NEXT OLDEST child is _____ years old. Male or female?

Put a star (*) next to your age. Now put a circle around the age of the brother or sister with whom you had the most conflict— either the brother or sister who hassles or bothers you the most, the one YOU hassle or bother the most or just the one you have the most conflict with. Please indicate in the right hand margin whether any brother or sisters are step-siblings, halfsiblings, or adopted siblings.

Read the sentences below about YOU and THAT brother or sister whose age you have circled. Now circle the number from one to five which best describes your relationship living at home together.

	Never True Always True
1. We are very much alike.	1 – 2 – 3 – 4 – 5
2. We do a lot of arguing or fighting.	1 – 2 – 3 – 4 – 5
3. He or she always tries to copy me.	1 – 2 – 3 – 4 – 5
4. I would loan money to him or her.	1 – 2 – 3 – 4 – 5
5. I get to do things before my brother or sister.	1 – 2 – 3 – 4 – 5
6. We like the same sports and games.	1 – 2 – 3 – 4 – 5
7. I care a lot about what he or she does.	1 – 2 – 3 – 4 – 5
8. He or she cares a lot about what I do.	1 – 2 – 3 – 4 – 5
9. We have the same friends.	1 – 2 – 3 – 4 – 5
10. We argue a lot about whose turn it is to do things.	1 – 2 – 3 – 4 – 5
11. We are good at the same school subjects.	1 – 2 – 3 – 4 – 5
12. We like to do the same things.	1 – 2 – 3 – 4 – 5
13. We get in about the same amount of trouble.	1 – 2 – 3 – 4 – 5

14. When she or he feels happy, I do too.	1 – 2 – 3 – 4 – 5
15. We like the same TV shows.	1 – 2 – 3 – 4 – 5
16. He or she takes my things without asking.	1 – 2 – 3 – 4 – 5
17. We spend a lot of time together.	1 – 2 – 3 – 4 – 5
18. We do about the same amount of chores.	1 – 2 – 3 – 4 – 5
19. We are very close to each other.	1 – 2 – 3 – 4 – 5
20. We usually get along very well.	1 – 2 – 3 – 4 – 5
21. I would tell my biggest secret to her or him.	1 – 2 – 3 – 4 – 5
22. He or she feels bad when I feel bad.	1 – 2 – 3 – 4 – 5
23. My brother or sister gets blamed more than me.	1 – 2 – 3 – 4 – 5
24. I felt rejected by my brother or sister.	1 – 2 – 3 – 4 – 5
25. He or she tries to keep me away from my friends.	1 – 2 – 3 – 4 – 5
26. He or she always tries to do what I am doing.	1 – 2 – 3 – 4 – 5
27. She or he always gets into my stuff.	1 – 2 – 3 – 4 – 5
28. We are good friends or buddies.	1 – 2 – 3 – 4 – 5
29. I care a lot about what he or she thinks.	1 – 2 – 3 – 4 – 5
30. He or she cars a lot about what I think.	1 – 2 – 3 – 4 – 5
31. If I get something, he or she always wants it too.	1 – 2 – 3 – 4 – 5
32. She or he always makes a mess of my things.	1 – 2 – 3 – 4 – 5
33. He or she shows me how to do bad things.	1 – 2 – 3 – 4 – 5
34. I feel used or taken advantage of by him or her.	1 – 2 – 3 – 4 – 5
35. He or she takes care of me a lot.	1 – 2 – 3 – 4 – 5

reciprocal conflict, and (4) a comparison group where the subject was in a relationship with moderate or modest (presumed normal) levels of conflict.

Method

Subjects

Two hundred two subjects were selected from a total of 1,685 college students who enrolled in an Introductory Psychology course. They were selected to fit into one of these four categories: Conflict Victims, Conflict Perpetrators, those with Reciprocal Conflict, and a Comparison group of subjects described above. The students were selected into the three high-conflict groups by reporting on a prescreening questionnaire that, compared to other families they knew, they felt the conflict perpetrated by a sibling onto themselves was high (Conflict Victims), they felt the conflict perpetrated by themselves onto a sibling was high (Conflict Perpetrators), or they had been both the bully and the victim of a sibling conflict that was high (Reciprocal Conflict). The fourth group consisted of subjects with a sibling randomly selected from the remaining subject pool, in other words, those with moderate levels of conflict in their relationship with a sibling. There were approximately equal numbers of male and female students in each group.

Measures and Procedures

As part of a larger study on the emotional adjustment of late adolescents with highly conflictual childhood sibling relationships, all subjects were given an amended version of the Straus (1979) Conflict Tactics Scales

(CTS). The CTS is a valid measure of the use of problem solving behaviors, including verbal reasoning, mild violence, and severe violence, among dyads. All subjects were asked to fill out this 15-item form. Subjects indicated what behavior they engaged in and also indicated what behaviors the sibling engaged in during each of two periods during childhood. The levels of reported violence on the CTS paralleled subjects' classification into the four groups: Those who cited high levels of violence by a sibling against themselves on the prescreening measure reported the highest levels of physically aggressive conflict tactics used by their sibling. Similarly, those who reported Perpetrating violence against a sibling reported performing high levels of physically aggressive conflict tactics on their sibling. The Reciprocal group had high levels of physical aggression by both the target subject and the sibling, and the Comparison group had only moderate and/or low levels of violence in their relationship with a sibling. For further description of this study see Graham-Bermann, Cutler, Litzenberger, & Schwartz (1994).

Results

For the first study, principal components analysis of the BSQ items confirmed the coherence of the items in terms of the four sibling relationship domains. The four factors accounted for 48.6% of the total variance. All item loadings on their respective factors were above 0.40. The resulting weighted items matrix is presented in Table 2. The factors were labeled Empathy (that accounts for 22.7% of the variance after rotation), Boundary Maintenance (11.7%), Similarity (9.0%), and Coercion (5.2%).

The four BSQ subscales confirmed by the factor analyses contained items tapping into the following elements of the four sibling relationship domains.

Empathy. This 14-item scale assesses the extent to which the siblings care about one another, would feel bad if the other felt bad, would share secrets, feel close, spend time together, and care for one another The scale items reflect the degree to which the siblings are emotionally connected and tuned in to what the other person is experiencing. Higher scores indicate greater empathy and caring in the relationship.

Boundary Maintenance. The six items in this scale assess the degree to which siblings are able to maintain interpersonal boundaries. This scale suggests the extent to which the two siblings are successful in establishing and respecting firm and reasonable boundaries between them. These parameters include boundaries around both physical property and feeling that one's wishes are understood, in other words respecting the other person's physical and psychological space. It is assumed that during childhood most siblings squabble over boundaries and defining territory vis-à-vis one another. Lower scores reflect a failure to maintain boundaries, perhaps those which are easily or repeatedly violated, whereas higher scores reflect less concern with and greater success in having one's boundaries respected.

Similarity. This nine-item scale examines ways in which the two siblings have common interests and experiences. Items include the degree to which the siblings have shared friends, and like the same sports, hobbies, and school subjects. This scale also assesses the extent to which they have the same experience within the family in terms of doing the same chores and getting in about the same amount of trouble. Higher scores indicate greater similarity in the relationship. Low scores suggest that the siblings are strongly differentiated or deidentified and see themselves as having little in common.

Coercion. This six-item scale assesses elements of power and control of one sibling over the other. It includes questions about exploitative behavior, such as having been introduced to deviant or "bad behavior" by a sibling and feeling used by the sibling. The scale also taps rejection by a sibling and efforts to isolate the sibling by keeping friends away. When the subject indicates being dominated and controlled by a sibling, the coercion score will be higher.

For the most part, these factors were significantly correlated with one another in the expected directions. Empathy was positively correlated with Similarity ($r = .40$, $p < .001$, $N = 202$), Boundary Maintenance ($r = .17$, $p < .001$), and negatively associated with Coercion ($r = -.23$, $p < .001$). Boundary Maintenance was not related to Coercion, but was significantly related to Similarity ($r = .19$, $p < .003$). Cronbach's alpha was used as a proportional measure of estimating the degree to which each factor is reliably similar and consistent. Results

TABLE 2
WEIGHTED FACTOR COEFFICIENTS OF THE BROTHER-SISTER QUESTIONNAIRE

	FACTORS			
BSQ ITEM NUMBER	Empathy	Boundaries	Similarity	Coercion
28	.82			
19	.81			
7	.75			
29	.71			
20	.70			
17	.67			
8	.67			
30	.66			
22	.64			
14	.61			
4	.60			
21	.59			
2*	.57			
35	.49			
27*		.81		
26*		.75		
3*		.71		
32*		.69		
16*		.65		
31*		.63		
12			.67	
18			.59	
6			.57	
9			.56	
1			.53	
13			.49	
10			.46	
15			.45	
11			.44	
33				.76
34				.67
24				.64
5*				.54
23				.45
25				.40

*reverse item for scoring

Note: From "The Brother-Sister Questionnaire (BSQ): Psychmetric assessment and discrimination of well functioning from dysrunctional relationships" by S. A. Graham-Bermann and S. E. Cutler, 1994. *Journal of Family Psychology, 8*(2), p. 224–238. Copyright © by American Psychological Association. Reprinted with permission.

of the reliability analyses for the four factors were as follows: Empathy ($a = .92$), Boundary Maintenance ($a = .85$), Similarity ($a = .73$), and Coercion ($a = .69$). These results indicate moderate reliability and strong internal consistency of these four scales.

Ten-day test–retest reliability on a sample of 25 college students was significant for each of the four factors at the $p < .001$ level: Empathy ($r = .67$), Boundaries ($r = .65$), Similarity ($r = .75$), and Coercion ($r = .66$). The total scale reliability coefficient for the four subscales combined was .91 for all subjects.

A multiple analysis of the variance (MANOVA) of the four BSQ factors by the conflict groups and the comparison group showed that the groups differed (Hotelling's $T^2 = .873$, approx. $F = 14.09$, $p < .001$). Univariate F tests ($df = 3,198$) showed that the four groups differed significantly on all four relationship scales: Empathy ($p < .001$), Boundary Maintenance ($p < .001$), Similarity ($p < .01$), and Coercion ($p < .001$). Results are shown in Table 3.

Interesting patterns in sibling factors among the four groups reveal that there were significant differences between the Comparison group and the Conflict Victim group for all four BSQ factors (Graham-Bermann & Cutler, 1993). Generally, Comparison subjects were higher in Empathy, Boundary Maintenance, and Similarity, but lower in Coercion. The Comparison group reported more Empathy than did the Perpetrators group and greater Boundary Maintenance. Interestingly, the Comparison group did not differ from the Perpetrators in terms of Similarity or Coercion. The Reciprocal violence group reported more Similarity, more Empathy, less Coercion, and weaker Boundaries with their sibling than did those in the Conflict Victims group. Finally, Victims rated less Empathy and Similarity in their relationships than did Perpetrators, and rated the level of Coercion in their relationships as high. Thus this first study served to establish the reliability and validity of the BSQ and to show its utility in distinguishing the relationship qualities of four types of sibling relationships.

TABLE 3
ANOVAS OF SIBLING FACTORS BY RELATIONAHIP CATEGORY FOR STUDY 1

	Relationship Category				
	Conflict Perpetrator ($N = 51$)	Reciprocal Conflict ($N = 51$)	Conflict Victim ($N = 51$)	Comparison Group ($N = 49$)	F value
BSQ Factor:					
Empathy					
M	2.00	1.96	1.68	2.73	20.21***
SD	0.73	0.74	0.63	0.73	
Boundaries					
M	3.08	2.75	3.20	3.64	9.93***
SD	1.00	0.82	0.81	0.76	
Similarity					
M	1.95	2.17	1.73	2.10	4.67***
SD	0.71	0.62	0.58	0.67	
Coercion					
M	0.90	1.16	1.95	0.92	29.01***
SD	0.60	0.62	0.67	0.65	

$**p < .01$, $***p < .001$

Note: From "The Brother–Sister Questionnaire (BSQ): Psychmetric assessment and discrimination of well functioning from dysrunctional relationships" by S. A. Graham-Bermann and S. E. Cutler, 1994. *Journal of Family Psychology, 8*(2), p. 224–238. Copyright © by American Psychological Association. Reprinted with permission.

Study Two

The aims of the second study were first, to correctly classify abusive (or dysfunctional) and nonabusive sibling relationships using the four subscales of the BSQ and, second, to test the relationship between reports of behavior, self perceptions of having been abused, and the BSQ subscales. In this study a second group of students were prescreened by their reports of physical and emotional abuse by a sibling, whereas in Study One, they were prescreened on high levels of conflict with a sibling.

Method

Subjects

In testing the ability of the BSQ to discriminate between abused and comparison subjects it is important to use a second, independent sample of subjects from the sample in the first study which was used to confirm the four proposed relationship subscales. As such, a second group of subjects was selected for this task from a completely different group of individuals than those in the first study. For this study only sibling abuse victims and a comparison group of subjects without excessively high levels of sibling violence were selected.

Fifty six abuse and 42 comparison subjects were selected from a subject pool consisting of 1,183 introductory psychology college students. The abuse group was chosen from students who described their childhood relationship with a sibling as abusive. The comparison group was randomly selected from the rest of those in the subject pool who had at least one sibling. There was an even balance of males and females in each group. Once again, the Conflict Tactics Scale (Straus, 1979) was used to measure levels of violence and to validate the abuse group's status. As expected, those in the abuse group were significantly more likely to have seriously high levels of violence in their relationship that the other sibling perpetrated than did the comparison, or nonabuse, group.

Measures and Procedures

Again, as part of a larger study, all subjects were asked to complete the BSQ (Graham-Bermann, 1993).

Results

As a validity check of the levels of relationship categories that characterize sibling relationships in the Comparison group and in the Abuse/Victims group, the means and standard deviations for the two Study 2 groups are given in Table 4. A MANOVA showed that Comparison subjects differed from Conflict Victims on the four relationship categories (Hotelling's $T^2 = 0.708$, $F(4,93) = 16.46$, $p < .001$). Univariate F-tests showed that the two groups differed significantly on Coercion, Empathy, and Boundaries, and there was a marginally significant difference in Similarity. A comparison of the values in Tables 3 and 4 shows that the Comparison and Conflict Victims groups of Study 2 had quite similar mean values on each relationship category to the same groups of Study 1.

One way of measuring whether and how much all of the BSQ subscales are useful in sorting out those who have been abused from those who haven't is to use the discriminant analysis test. Results of discriminant analysis classified correctly 82.1% of the abused/victim group and 81% of the comparison group, using all four BSQ subscales as predictors. Each factor contributed to the final discriminant function. Using each factor alone also discriminated the two groups at above chance rates: Empathy 68.4%, Boundaries 69.4%, Similarity 60.2%, and Coercion 66.3% of the cases were correctly classified. In this study, all four of the BSQ scales were useful in discriminating dysfunctional from nondysfunctional sibling relationships.

Discussion

Overall, the Brother–Sister Questionnaire, measuring Empathy, Boundary Maintenance, Similarity, and Coercion, differentiates the comparison group from the three types of highly conflictual sibling relationships

TABLE 4

ANOVAS OF SIBLING FACTORS BY RELATIONAHIP CATEGORY FOR STUDY 2

| | Relationship Category | | |
	Conflict Victim (*N* = 56)	Comparison Group (*N* = 42)	*F* value
BSQ Factor:			
Empathy			
M	1.68	2.53	31.36***
SD	0.79	0.67	
Boundaries			
M	3.17	3.90	24.75***
SD	0.77	0.63	
Similarity			
M	1.72	1.97	3.58'
SD	0.68	0.60	
Coercion			
M	1.73	1.14	21.01***
SD	0.70	0.52	

'$p < .1$, ***$p < .001$

Note: From "The Brother–Sister Questionnaire (BSQ): Psychmetric assessment and discrimination of well functioning from dysrunctional relationships" by S. A. Graham-Bermann and S. E. Cutler, 1994. *Journal of Family Psychology, 8*(2), p. 224–238. Copyright © by American Psychological Association. Reprinted with permission.

(first study). This measure was also successful in discriminating abusive from nonabusive relationships (second study), thus providing support and validity for the constructs assessed by these scales. Furthermore, we found patterns of relationship qualities that distinguished subjects in the four conflict groups. High conflict Victims differed from the Comparison group in terms of Similarity, Empathy, Coercion, and Boundary Maintenance.

By extension, these results reflect findings from studies dealing with lower levels of childhood conflict and cooperation, where children who perceive themselves to be similar to a sibling had more cooperative relationships than those who described themselves as having little in common, and children who were rigidly differentiated or deidentified from a sibling had more conflictual relationships than those not so markedly differentiated from the sibling (Graham-Bermann, 1991; Schachter, et al., 1976). Also consonant with the findings reported in the present studies are Buhrmester and Furman's reports that school-age children who feel warm and close to a sibling, who shared power with a sibling (relative to their respective ages) also had less conflict in their relationships than did children not evincing these feelings (Buhrmester, 1992; Buhrmester & Furman, 1990).

Thus, children who were Victims of high conflict sibling relationships were less likely to develop empathy, less likely to feel similar to the sibling, and more likely to feel coerced and invaded by their sibling, relative to those without high levels of such conflict. Those who were active in perpetrating the conflict toward a sibling (either in the Perpetrator or Reciprocal groups) also were less likely to develop empathy for their brother or sister, and less likely to work to respect the other person's personal and territorial boundaries. In addition, Perpetrators did not report high levels of coercive behavior with a sibling, as did those who were in the Victims or in Reciprocal conflict groups.

If the sibling relationship is one paradigm or model for other, homologous relationships, such as those with peers, teammates, roommates, or possibly even spouses, as some researchers have suggested, then we would expect those with a deleterious or abusive sibling relationship to have difficulty establishing and navigating social developmental tasks in these other interpersonal arenas as well (Boer & Dunn, 1992). Barring the protective factor of a positive relationship with another sibling or adult in the family, these subjects in highly conflictual and abusive childhood sibling relationships may be at risk for repeating and replicating the patterns and roles they have acquired with the sibling, in other relationships throughout their lives (Bank, 1992).

References

Bank, S. (1992). Remembering and reinterpreting sibling bonds. In F. Boer, & J. Dunn (Eds.), *Children's sibling relationships: Developmental and clinical issues* (pp. 139–151). Hillsdale, NJ: Lawrence Erlbaum Associates.

Boer, F., & Dunn, J. (1992). *Children's sibling relationships: Developmental and clinical issues*. Hillsdale, NJ: Lawrence Erlbaum Associates.

Boss, P. G. (1993). The reconstruction of family life with alzheimer's disease. In P. G. Boss, W. J. Doherty, R. LaRossa, W.R. Schumm, & S. K. Steinmetz (Eds.), *Sourcebook of family theories and methods: A contextual approach* (pp. 163–166). NY: Plenum Press.

Bowen, M. (1966). The use of family theory in clinical practice. *Comprehensive Psychiatry, 7*, 345–374.

Buhrmester, D. (1992). The developmental courses of sibling and peer relationships. In F. Boer, & J. Dunn (Eds.), *Children's sibling relationships: Developmental and clinical issues* (pp. 19–40). Hillsdale, NJ: Lawrence Erlbaum Associates.

Buhrmester, D., & Furman, W. (1990). Perceptions of sibling relationships during middle childhood and adolescence. *Child Development, 58*, 1101–1113.

Eastin, J., Graham-Bermann, S. A., & Levendosky, A. A. (in press). Observed sibling conflict and psychological maltreatment among children with a range of family violence experiences. *Journal of Emotional Abuse*.

Erikson, E. (1968). *Identity: Youth and crisis*. New York: Norton.

Erel, O., Margolin, G., & John, R. S. (1998). Observed sibling interaction: Links with the marital and mother–child relationship. *Developmental Psychology, 34*(2), 288–298.

Furman, W., & Buhrmester, D. (1985). Children's perceptions of the qualities of sibling relationships. *Child Development, 56*, 448–461.

Furman, W., & Buhrmester, D. (1992). Age and sex differences in perceptions of networks of personal relationships. *Child Development, 63*, 103–115.

Graham-Bermann, S. (1991). Sibling in dyads: Relationships among perceptions and behavior. *Journal of Genetic Psychology, 152*(2), 207–216.

Graham-Bermann, S. A. (2001). Child abuse in the context of domestic violence. In J. E. B. Myers (Ed.), *APSAC Handbook on Child Maltreatment* (2nd Ed., pp. 119–130). Thousand Oaks, CA: Sage.

Graham-Bermann, S.A., & Cutler, S.E. (1994). The Brother–Sister Questionnaire (BSQ): Psychometric assessment and discrimination of well functioning from dysfunctional relationships. *Journal of Family Psychology, 8*(2), 224–238.

Graham-Bermann, S.A., Cutler, S.E., Litzenberger, B., & Schwartz, W. (1994). Perceived sibling violence and emotional adjustment during childhood and adolescence. *Journal of Family Psychology, 8*(1), 85–97.

Graham-Bermann, S. A. & Edelson, J. L. (Eds.). (2001). *Domestic violence in the lives of children: The future of research, intervention, and social policy*. Washington, DC: American Psychological Association Books.

Grotevant, H., & Cooper, C. (1986). Individuation in family relationships: A perspective on individual differences in the development of identity and role-taking skill in adolescence. *Human Development, 29*, 82–100.

McCloskey, L. A., Figueredo, A. J., & Koss, M. P. (1995). The effects of systemic family violence on children's mental health. *Child Development, 66*, 1239–1261.

Minuchin, S. (1974). *Families and family therapy*. Cambridge, MA: Harvard University Press.

Minuchin, S., Montalvo, B., Guerney, B.G., Jr., Rosman, B.L., & Schumer, F. (1967). *Families of the slums: An exploration of their structure and treatment*. New York: Basic Books.

Newberger, C.M., & Cook, S. (1983). Parental awareness and child abuse: A cognitive-developmental analysis of urban and rural samples. *American Journal of Orthopsychiatry, 53*, 512–524.

Patterson, G. R., Dishion, T. J., & Bank, L. (1984). Family interaction: A process model of deviancy training. *Aggressive Behavior, 10*, 253–267.

Piaget, J. (1932). *The moral judgment of the child*. New York: Harcourt, Brace & World.

Schachter, F., Shore, E., Feldman-Rotman, S., Marquis, R., & Campbell, S. (1976). Sibling deidentification. *Developmental Psychology, 12*, 418–429.

Steinmetz, S. K. (1981). A cross-cultural comparison of sibling violence. *International Journal of Family Psychiatry*. 337–351.

Stocker, C., & McHale, S. (1992). The nature and family correlates of preadolescents' perceptions of their sibling relationships. *Journal of Social and Personal Relationships, 9*, 179–195.

Straus, M.A. (1979). Measuring intrafamily conflict and violence: The conflict tactics scale. *Journal of Marriage and the Family, 41*, 75–88.

Weihe, V. (1990). *Sibling abuse: Hidden physical, emotional and sexual trauma*. Lexington, MA: Lexington Books, Inc.

EXPERIMENT 12

Sibling Relationships and Sibling Status: Older or Younger

The importance of sibling relationships to the development of the individual and family over time has been documented in the previous sections. The experiences of a particular child are partially determined by the child's standing in the family constellation (Buhrmester & Furman, 1990). Age and sex are recognized as particularly influential variables in sibling relationships (Bigner, 1974; Hoffman, 1991; Pulakos, 1989). Are you the older or younger sibling? Are you male or female? Is your sib male or female?

In this study, we examine perceived sibling relationships with a focus on three independent (subject) variables: sib status (older or younger of a pair), sex, and sex of sib. Our measuring instrument will be Graham-Bermann's Brother–Sister Questionnaire (BSQ), described in the previous pages. Our dependent variables will be her outcome measure—the four described constructs: Boundary Maintenance, Empathy, Similarity, and Coercion (being coerced).

Questions and Hypotheses

The questions we will ask of the data are:

1. Are sibling relationships described differently by same-age children who are the older or younger sib of a pair?

2. Are sibling relationships described differently by males and females?

3. Are sibling relationships described differently by children who have a same-sex or opposite-sex sib?

4. What are the relations among the four BSQ subscales?

Based on your initial readings, compose your hypotheses as follows:

1. The child who is the older sib will report:
   a. (Stronger or weaker) boundary maintenance than the child who is the younger sib.
   b. (More or less) empathy ...
   c. (More or less) similarity ...
   d. (Being more or less) coerced than the child who is the younger sib.

2. The female subject, compared to the male subject, will report: (adjust and follow the outline above, a–d).

3. The child with the same-sex sib, compared to the child with the opposite-sex sib, will report: (adjust and follow the outline above, a–d).

4. Relations among the four BSQ subscales:
   a. Boundary maintenance scores will correlate (positively, negatively, or not   correlate) with
      1) empathy scores
      2) similarity scores
      3) coercion scores.

      b. Empathy scores will correlate (positively, negatively, or not correlate) with
          1) similarity scores
          2) coercion scores.
      c. Similarity scores will correlate (positively, negatively, or not correlate) with
          1) coercion scores.

Method

Subjects

Choose one large age group, for example—sixth graders. They are usually 11–12 years old. There will be eight dyads: the older male with a younger male sib, or with a younger female sib; the younger male with an older male sib, or with an older female sib. These four groups apply to your female subjects as well.

    Indicate the mean ages, races, general socioeconomic status, geographic location.

Measures

The demographic portion of the Brother–Sister Questionnaire will enable you to determine which of the eight groups your subject is in. Code him or her as follows: O or Y (older or younger), M or F (male or female), m or f (male or female sib). An older boy with a female sib, for example, would be coded as OMf.

    The demographic information also reveals the number of children, and the age spacing between your subject and the sib about whom he or she is answering questions. (Note the changed BSQ instructions; the target sib is the one *closest in age* to your subject).

    The 35 items, when scored and grouped, will provide scores for boundary maintenance, empathy, similarity, and being coerced. (Reread Graham-Bermann's description of these constructs in this manual and in Graham-Bermann & Cutler, 1994).

Procedure

Each child is administered the BSQ individually. (Adult subjects can be tested in groups.) Sit opposite the child, give him or her a pencil, and say, "Today we're going to talk about family. I come from a family of (three) children. How many children are there in your own family, including you?" Finish the demography portion of the questionnaire. Make it clear to the child that names do not appear on the pages (i.e., that the answers are confidential and anonymous).

    Sit back, so that you don't appear to be looking at the child's responses, and read each item aloud clearly, using your own copy. Wait quietly until the child circles a number on her copy and go on to the next item. Note the time begun, ended, and elapsed; thank the child and escort her out; and then jot down comments on her behavior. Did she chatter and elaborate on various items? Did she seem comfortable or reluctant? Did she avoid eye contact? Did she reflect on each response or was she circling numbers very quickly? and so on.

Results

    Scoring. Transfer your child's responses for each item to the subscale items Table G12.1. Be vary careful to reverse the scoring on the eight starred items; that is, a circled 4 changes to 2, a 1 to 5, and so on. Compute the mean for each subscale column.

    Data analysis. Record the means from Table G12.1 to one of the eight Master Data Sheets (provided by your instructor). Be careful to use the correct group sheet that matches your child's code.

    Find the means and standard deviations for the four subscales for each of the eight groups and enter these in Table G12.2.

    Compute a 2 x 2 x 2 analysis of variance for each subscale, using the data from the Master Data Sheets. Use Table G12.3, and repeat for Boundaries, Similarity, Coercion.

Correlate the subscale scores with one another, as in Table G12.4. The correlations below and to the left of the diagonal are from Graham-Bermann and Cutler (1994) data on 202 college students. Enter the correlations from the present study above and to the right of the diagonal. Note your *N*, and asterisk your *R*s accordingly.

State your results with regard to the main effects (sib status, sex, sex of sib) and interactions, giving *F* and *p* levels, for each of the four subscales. State the relations among the four subscales.

Discussion

As usual, relate your data to each of your hypotheses or questions, and to the literature.

Was there a significant difference between the children who were the *older or younger* sibs on any of the four subscales? (Look at the *F* for sib status.) Several studies report the older sib as being more powerful, dominant, coercive (Bigner, 1974; Furman & Buhrmester, 1985; Holden, 1986; Jacobson & Nadelman, 1994; Nadelman, Ray, Hill, & Davis, 1996; Nadelman & Ray, 1997; Shulman, 1987). Remember that on the BSQ, the higher coercion score indicates that the subject feels dominated or controlled by a sibling, that is, being coerced. Pulakos (1989), with college students and 26–84 year-olds, found the younger sib reported being closer to their sib than did the older. A study of Israeli Arab sisters found that the younger ones were viewed as subordinate and submissive (Seginer, 1992).

Was there a significant difference between your *boys and girls* on any of the subscales? (Look at the *F* for sex.) Females have been reported to express more positive feelings and closeness toward sibs than do males (Cicirelli, 1988; Newman, 1991; Pulakos, 1989). Males were higher on power than females (Jacobson & Nadelman, 1994).

Does having a sibling of the *same sex* result in different subscale scores than having a sibling of the *opposite sex*? Note that a significant *F* for sex of sib does not answer to this question; it will tell you only whether having a male versus a female sib makes a difference regardless of the sex of your subject. To talk about same-sex and opposite-sex dyads, you need to look at the *F* and relevant means for sex of subject x sex of sib. Same-sex pairs are reported to feel closer than opposite-sex pairs (Pulakos, 1989), but show more rivalry when the age gap is small (Davis, 1990). Sisters are the closest (Cicirelli, 1977; Gold, 1989); brothers are the most competitive (Cicirelli, 1987). For the first pair of a three-child family, same-sex siblings (college undergraduates) deidentified significantly more often than opposite-sex (Schachter, 1982); that is, they reported less similarity.

Do the relations among the subscales in your children data resemble Graham-Bermann and Cutler's college data?

In general, when comparing your findings to the literature, be careful to notice the ages of the subjects. Relationships among siblings often change with age and changing situations, sometimes becoming more egalitarian, less asymmetrical and less intense with age (Buhrmester & Furman, 1990). For a focus on middle childhood sibs, see Bryant (1982) & Vandell, Minnett & Santrock (1987).

On the basis of this limited experience with the BSQ, what do you like or dislike about it? What changes can you suggest? Would you and how would you use it in future research?

Dunn and McGuire (1992) pointed to the need in sibling research for "more longitudinal data, especially on middle childhood and adolescence, more attention to the possible independent contribution of sibling relationships to adjustment outcome, and more large-scale study of the relation of parental behavior to sibling conflict" (p.95). (See also Dunn, 1992.)

Selected Bibliography

Bigner, J.J. (1974). Second born's discriminations of sibling role concepts. *Developmental Psychology, 10*, 564–573.

Buhrmester, D., & Furman, W. (1990). Perceptions of sibling relationships during middle childhood and adolescence. *Child Development, 61*, 1387–1398.

Cicirelli, V.G. (1977). Relationship of siblings to the elderly person's feelings and concerns. *Journal of Gerontology, 131*, 309–317.

Cicirelli, V.G. (1982). Sibling influence throughout the life-span. In M. Lamb & B. Sutton-Smith (Eds.), *Sibling relationships: Their nature and significance across the lifespan* (pp. 267–284). Hillsdale, NJ: Lawrence Erlbaum Associates.

Davis, G.E. (1990). *Sibling relationships: Rivalry and identification: An empirical assessment of the sibling experience*. Unpublished doctoral dissertation. University of Michigan, Ann Arbor.

Dunn, J. (1992). Sisters and brothers: Current issues in developmental research. In F. Boer & J. Dunn (Eds.), *Children's sibling relationships: Developmental and clinical issues* (pp. 1–17). Hillsdale, NJ: Lawrence Erlbaum Associates.

Gold, D.T. (1989). Generational solidarity: Conceptual antecedents and consequences. *American Behavioral Scientist, 33*(1), 19–32.

Graham-Bermann, S. A., & Cutler, S. E. (1994). The Brother–Sister Questionnaire (BSQ): Psychometric assessment and discrimination of well-functioning from dysfunctional relationships. *Journal of Family Psychology, 8*(2), 224–238..

Hoffman, L.W. (1991). The influence of the family environment on personality: Accounting for sibling differences. *Psychological Bulletin, 110*(2), 187–203.

Holden, C.E. (1986). Being a sister: Constructions of the sibling experience. (Doctoral dissertation, University of Michigan). *Dissertation Abstracts International*, 47(10), 4301B.

Jacobson, J.D., & Nadelman, L. (1994). *Young adults' perceptions of the sibling relationship*. Poster presented at the meeting of the International Society of Behavioural Development, Amsterdam, The Netherlands.

Nadelman, L., & Ray, D. (1997, April). *Perceptions of sibling relationships by African-American college students*. Poster presented at the meetings of the Society for Research in Children's Development, Washington, DC.

Nadelman, L., Ray, D., Hill, L., & Davis, L. (1996). *Black female young adults' perceptions of sibling relationships*. Poster presented at the meetings of the International Society for the Study of Behavioral Development, Quebec.

Newman, J. (1991). College students: Relationships with siblings. *Journal of Youth and Adolescence, 20*(6), 629–644.

Pulakos, J. (1989). Brothers and sisters: Nature and importance of the adult bond. *Journal of Psychology, 121*(5), 521–522.

Schachter, F.F. (1982). Sibling deidentification and split-parent identification: A family tetrad. In M. Lamb and B. Sutton-Smith (Eds.), *Sibling relationships: Their nature and significance across the lifespan* (pp. 123–151). Hillsdale, NJ: Lawrence Erlbaum Associates.

Seginer, R. (1992). Sibling relationships in early adolescence: A study of Israeli Arab sisters. *Journal of Early Adolescence, 12*(1), 96–110.

Shulman, M.E. (1987). *On being a brother: Constructions of the sibling experience*. Unpublished doctoral dissertation, University of Michigan, Ann Arbor.

Vandell, D.L., Minnett, A.M., & Santrock, J.W. (1987). Age differences in sibling relationships during middle childhood. *Journal of Applied Developmental Psychology, 8*, 247–257.

See also earlier bibliographies.

INDIVIDUAL DATA SHEET

Code

E: _____ Day and Date: _____ S–Sex: *M or F*

S: _____ Birthdate: _____ CA: _____

Time Begun: _____ Time Ended: _____ Elapsed Time: _____ Room: _____

The Brother-Sister Questionnaire

There are _____ children in my family of origin (including me).

The OLDEST child is _____ years old. Male or female? (circle one)

The NEXT OLDEST child is _____ years old. Male or female?

The NEXT OLDEST child is _____ years old. Male or female?

The NEXT OLDEST child is _____ years old. Male or female?

The NEXT OLDEST child is _____ years old. Male or female?

(Continue on back if needed)

Put a star (*) next to *your* age. Now put a circle around the age of the brother or sister who is *closest in age* to you. Please indicate in the right hand margin whether any brothers or sisters are stepsiblings, halfsiblings, or adopted siblings. Use the back of this page if there are more than five children in your family.

Now let's read the sentences below about YOU and THAT brother or sister whose age you have circled. Now circle the number from one to five which best describes your relationship living at home together.

		Never True				Always True
1.	We are very much alike.	1 – 2 – 3 – 4 – 5				
2.	We do a lot of arguing or fighting.	1 – 2 – 3 – 4 – 5				
3.	He or she always tries to copy me.	1 – 2 – 3 – 4 – 5				
4.	I would loan money to him or her.	1 – 2 – 3 – 4 – 5				
5.	I get to do things before my brother or sister.	1 – 2 – 3 – 4 – 5				
6.	We like the same sports and games.	1 – 2 – 3 – 4 – 5				
7.	I care a lot about what he or she does.	1 – 2 – 3 – 4 – 5				
8.	He or she cares a lot about what I do.	1 – 2 – 3 – 4 – 5				
9.	We have the same friends.	1 – 2 – 3 – 4 – 5				
10.	We argue a lot about whose turn it is to do things.	1 – 2 – 3 – 4 – 5				
11.	We are good at the same school subjects.	1 – 2 – 3 – 4 – 5				
12.	We like to do the same things.	1 – 2 – 3 – 4 – 5				
13.	We get in about the same amount of trouble.	1 – 2 – 3 – 4 – 5				
14.	When she or he feels happy, I do too.	1 – 2 – 3 – 4 – 5				
15.	We like the same TV shows.	1 – 2 – 3 – 4 – 5				
16.	He or she takes my things without asking.	1 – 2 – 3 – 4 – 5				
17.	We spend a lot of time together.	1 – 2 – 3 – 4 – 5				
18.	We do about the same amount of chores.	1 – 2 – 3 – 4 – 5				
19.	We are very close to each other.	1 – 2 – 3 – 4 – 5				
20.	We usually get along very well.	1 – 2 – 3 – 4 – 5				

21. I would tell my biggest secret to her or him.	1 – 2 – 3 – 4 – 5
22. He or she feels bad when I feel bad.	1 – 2 – 3 – 4 – 5
23. My brother or sister gets blamed more than me.	1 – 2 – 3 – 4 – 5
24. I felt rejected by my brother or sister.	1 – 2 – 3 – 4 – 5
25. He or she tries to keep me away from my friends.	1 – 2 – 3 – 4 – 5
26. He or she always tries to do what I am doing.	1 – 2 – 3 – 4 – 5
27. She or he always gets into my stuff.	1 – 2 – 3 – 4 – 5
28. We are good friends or buddies.	1 – 2 – 3 – 4 – 5
29. I care a lot about what he or she thinks.	1 – 2 – 3 – 4 – 5
30. He or she cares a lot about what I think.	1 – 2 – 3 – 4 – 5
31. If I get something, he or she always wants it too.	1 – 2 – 3 – 4 – 5
32. She or he always makes a mess of my things.	1 – 2 – 3 – 4 – 5
33. He or she shows me how to do bad things.	1 – 2 – 3 – 4 – 5
34. I feel used or taken advantage of by him or her.	1 – 2 – 3 – 4 – 5
35. He or she takes care of me a lot.	1 – 2 – 3 – 4 – 5

TABLE G12.1

FACTOR ITEM SCORES FOR THE BSQ, ONE CHILD

Empathy		Boundaries		Similarity		Coercion	
Item	Score	Item	Score	Item	Score	Item	Score
*2		*3		1		*5	
4		*16		6		23	
7		*26		9		24	
8		*27		10		25	
14		*31		11		33	
17		*32		12		34	
19				13			
20				15			
21				18			
22							
28							
29							
30							
35							
Mean	_____		_____		_____		_____

*Reverse item for scoring.

TABLE G12.2

MEAN BSQ FACTOR SCORES FOR EIGHT GROUPS

Groups		Empathy	Boundaries	Similarity	Coercion
O M m	Mean				
	SD				
O M f	Mean				
	SD				
Y M m	Mean				
	SD				
Y M f	Mean				
	SD				
O F m	Mean				
	SD				
O F f	Mean				
	SD				
Y F m	Mean				
	SD				
Y F f	Mean				
	SD				
Combined					
Older	Mean				
	SD				
Younger	Mean				
	SD				
Males	Mean				
	SD				
Females	Mean				
	SD				
Same Sex dyads	Mean				
	SD				
Opposite Sex dyads	Mean				
	SD				
Total	Mean				
	SD				

Note: OMm refers to the older child, male, with a (younger) male sib; YMf refers to the younger child, male, with a (older) female sib. The first letter refers to the sib status of your subject, the second to the sex of your subject, the third to the sex of the sibling.

TABLE G12.3

2(SIB STATUS) X 2(SEX) X 2(SEX OF SIB) ANOVA FOR THE BSQ EMPATHY SCORES

Source of variation	df	Mean Square	F	p
A Between sib status (O/Y)	1			
B Between sexes (M/F)	1			
C Between sex of sib	1			
A x B	1			
A x C	1			
B x C	1			
A x B x C	1			
Within group (error) N-8				
Total (n–1)				

Repeat this table for each of the other factors—Boundaries, Similarity, Coercion.

TABLE G12.4

INTERCORRELATION OF BSQ SUBSCALES

	Empathy	Similarity	Boundaries	Coercion
Empathy	---			
Similarity	.40***	---		
Boundaries	.17***	.20**	---	
Coercion	−.23***	−.08	.06	---

$N = 202$, p < .05*, p < .01**, p < .001***

Note: The correlations below and to the left of the diagonal are from "The Brother–Sister Questionnaire (BSQ: Psychometric assessment and discrimination of well-functioning from dysfunctional relationships" by S. A. Graham-Bermann & S. E. Cutler, 1994. *Journal of Family Psychology, 8*(2), pp. 224–238. Copyright © by American Psychological Association. Reprinted by permission.

H

A FINAL PROJECT: SUGGESTIONS

The final project often vies in popularity with the infant observation project.

It is a *student-designed* experiment in developmental psychology that can actually be run, or can be limited to a paper design like a grant proposal. Each student can be responsible for his/her own project, or subgroups of students can work together, or the whole class can design one study. The instructor will pace the parts (literature review with references; hypotheses; detailed method section; suggested statistical analysis of results with empty tables; discussion of possible positive and negative results in relation to the literature and theory).

Where do the ideas for an experiment originate? Your readings in this and other psychology courses are one source: Did the researchers omit a variable you think should be investigated? Would different cohorts, or different ethnic groups produce different outcomes and why? Would different test measures or different scoring be consistent with the published results? Is there a deduction from a theory that should be tested? Is there an elaboration or extension of a theory that should be investigated?

An old, personal example: As a graduate student many decades ago, I was interested in Edna Heidbreder's theory and research on thinking, and decided to do my PhD thesis in that area. Her research indicated that concepts were attained in a certain order: objects first, then forms, then numbers. That seemed simplistic to me. I thought that if I added a "level of abstractness" to the stimuli, the order of attainment would change. I bet that using "markmakers" as the object concept instead of buckles would be more difficult for our subjects than number concepts like "2" or "5." It was, and Heidbreder graciously accepted that amendment and extension.

Appendix B lists experiments performed in this lab course over the decades. Although most were class projects designed by me or my assistants, some were student-designed. The final project was occasionally expanded, and run in later semesters as independent research projects, MAs, even PhDs.

Although it is stimulating fun to construct your own tests and stimuli, it often makes more scientific sense to use already published tasks. You don't want to be trying to compare apples and oranges. You need to relate your results to the published literature.

Two topics worth considering are cross-cultural studies and neuropsychology projects.

Cross-Cultural Studies

Interest by psychologists in cross-cultural and subcultural studies has burgeoned in the last few decades. In addition to journals specifically devoted to cross-cultural research and essays, such studies appear in most of our journals and conferences. Subcultural and ethnic research has grown, and an APA division (45) is named the Society for the Psychological Study of Ethnic Minority Issues. There is an International Association for Cross-cultural Psychology.

Despite the difficulties and expense of cross-cultural research, anthropologists, psychologists, sociologists, medical doctors and others have roamed the world, from jungles to mountains, from tiny villages to big cities, investigating many facets of behavior. For example, they have investigated parental values, child-rearing practices, cognitive development, social-emotional development, morality, identity formation, stereotypes, and more. Think of the difficulty in composing culture-fair test instruments, of gaining sufficient trust to run studies in various populations, of training local testers and administrators, of overcoming language differences. Researchers have been forced to drop the bias for generality of their results, regardless of cultural context. Cultural differences are very influential in the development of human behavior and the implications of this process require much more study. The bibliography at the end of this chapter is a mere sample of the books and articles appearing in the literature.

Several trends have recently surfaced in the cross-cultural literature. Parke (2000) points to a focus on *family strengths*, rather than on weakness or deficits in the observed cultures. Another trend is the recognition of *intragroup variability*. Not all members of a group behave or think similarly, and it is important to study these variations.

Most institutional review boards and school principals will not permit students like you to do research that directly compares ethnic groups or races. Bemoaning this to Charles Super recently, he solved our problem easily: Interview grandparents or great grandparents or older neighbors, preferably those born in other countries! Ask questions like: Where were you born (home or hospital)? Who was present? Were you breastfed or bottle fed? Your birth order? Number of sibs?

Ask about child care arrangements, games played and with whom, differences between how you and opposite-sex sib were treated, schooling, clothes, allowances? Chores?

Many helpful and detailed suggestions for such interviews appear in Greene and Fulford (1993). The class can jointly compose the structured interview and limit its scope, if desired, to sex differences, or sibling relations, or family values, for example. Compare and contrast those responses with parallel information from your own cohort.

Neuropsychology

For several decades, I have been urging my psychology students to take neuropsychology and/or neuroscience courses. The brain and nervous system are involved in all behavior, so to fully understand behavior, the brain-behavior relationships should be considered.

Clinical neuropsychology has become a well-recognized discipline over the last five decades. An APA division was established—Clinical Neuropsychology (Division 40), and several national and international journals are devoted to the field. The early work was on adults, mostly adults with disorders.

There was a developing interest in neuropsychological disorders in children, and the theory and research of brain–behavior relationships in adults was followed by the expansion of pediatric neuropsychology in children with disorders. This is slowly expanding to children without disorders. Researchers are interested in the behavior correlates of developmental changes in the nervous system. The frontal lobes of the brain cortex mature over many years, and it is believed they do so in spurts, namely at 7–9 and 11–12 years. Efficient functioning of the frontal lobes is involved in "planning and problem solving abilities, abstract reasoning, mental flexibility, and the capacity to utilize feedback" (Anderson, Anderson, & Lajoie, 1996, p. 55).

Generalization of findings from adults to children is problematic. The central nervous systems of children differ from adults'. Trauma to the head affects the brain differently in children and adults.

Neuropsychology tests have several sources, according to Spreen and Strauss (1998): (a) clinical neuropsychology examination, (b) experimental psychology, (c) neuropsychological research, and (d) clinical psychology. A neuropsychologist does not give one test and write a report. Depending on the domains of behavior he or she is investigating, there are many tests and procedures for each domain. Neuropsychological domains of interest include executive functioning, attention/concentration/orientation/vigilance, receptive and expressive language, sensory–perceptual functioning, motor functioning, visual–spatial analysis and constructional skills, learning and retrieval, academic achievement, personality/social–emotional/adaptive functioning (Yeates, Ris, & Taylor, 2000).

There are many problems and difficulties with neuropsych testing. One has to do with the database: The norms established with adults cannot be easily adjusted for children, and the tests are often unattractive to them. Some recent studies attempt to provide normative data for children (e.g., Archibald & Kerns, 1999), ages 7–12 years, on modified executive functioning measures. A second dilemma is articulated by Obrzut and Hynd (1986): When a child shows impaired performance in some domain, how do we determine whether it is a developmental delay, or a psychiatric disturbance, or a neurological deficit?

A suggestion for your final project is a neuropsychological project: a study of executive function in children 8- and 12-years-old, or children and adults.

Executive function, as you have just read, is a multidimensional construct referring to many higher level cognitive processes like initiation, planning, hypothesis generation, cognitive flexibility, decision making, regulation, judgment, feedback utilization, self-perception, with working memory an important component (Spreen & Strauss, 1998). Given that definition, there are obviously various tests that measure these skills.

Two that will introduce you to neuropsychology measures and that are appropriate and interesting to children and adults are the Tower of London (or the Tower of Hanoi) and the Stroop test.

The *Tower of London* focuses on the planning, working memory, problem-solving, inhibition aspects of executive functioning. The version described in detail by Anderson, Anderson, and Lajoie (1996) is quick to administer, challenging, attractive, and has a range of difficulty levels. The subject is presented with the sample problem of three colored balls (red, blue, white) on three posts of different length. The balls must be moved to match the goal stimulus cards. There are 12 items, and the number of moves for each problem is prescribed. There are rules for manipulating the balls that must be followed. Scores include planning time (before the first ball is touched), solution time, and number of attempts to correct solutions for each of the 12 items. Previous research indicates older children exhibiting shorter solution times and more correct solutions, as you would expect from the development of the frontal cortex.

An alternative is the *Tower of Hanoi*. Although this measure is often used interchangeably with the Tower of London, there is considerable nonshared variance between them, possibly indicating that they may be presenting different cognitive demands (Welsh, Satterlec-Carmell, & Stine, 1999). In Tower of Hanoi, the subjects move different-sized discs across three pegs to match the goal figure in the fewest moves possible. There are 12 TOH problems, 6 three-disk items and 6 four-disk items. Again, there are constraining rules for moving the disks. The scoring procedure differs from the Tower of London. The two tests correlate significantly but moderately.

The *Stroop Test* (see Experiment 4) is used in neuropsychology as a measure of attention/concentration/orientation/vigilance. It "measures the ease with which a person can shift his or her perceptual set to conform to changing demands and suppress a habitual response in favor of an unusual one" (Spreen & Strauss, 1998, p. 213).

Using your two measures, look for age and sex differences on the respective scores, and correlate the Tower of London scores with the Stroop inhibition/interference score.

Selected Bibliography

Cross-cultural

Bakhurst, D., & Shanker, S. (2001). *Jerome Bruner: Language, culture and self*. Thousand Oaks, CA: Sage.

Berry, J. W., Poortinga, Y. H., Dasen, P. R., Sarawathi, T. S., Segall, M. H., & Kagitcibasi, C. (1997). *Handbook of cross-cultural psychology: Theory and method*. Needham Heights, MA: Allyn & Bacon.

Betancourt, H., & Lopez, S. R. (1993). The study of culture, ethnicity, and race in American Psychology. *American Psychologist, 48*, 629–637.

Bjornberg, U. (Ed.). (1991). *European parents in the 1990s: Contradictions and comparisons*. New Brunswick, NJ: Transaction Publishers (Rutgers University).

Bornstein, M. H. (Ed.). (1991). *Cultural approaches to parenting*. Hillsdale, NJ: Lawrence Erlbaum Associates.

Cole, M. (1996). *Cultural psychology: A once and future discipline*. Cambridge, MA: Harvard University Press.

Crystal, D. S., Parrott, W. G., Okazaki, O., & Watanabe, H. (2001). Examining relations between shame and personality among university students in the United States and Japan: A developmental perspective. *International Journal of Behavioral Development, 25*(2), 113–123.

DeLoache, J., & Gottlieb, A. (2000). *A world of babies: Imagined childcare guides for seven societies*. New York: Cambridge University Press.

Demo, D. H., Allen, K. R., & Pine, M. A. (Eds.). (2000). *Handbook of family diversity*. New York: Oxford University Press.

Diener, E., & Suh, E. M. (Eds.). (2000). *Culture and subjective well-being*. Cambridge, MA: MIT Press.

Fisher, C. B., Jackson, J. F., & Villarruel, F. A. (1998). The study of African American and Latin American children and youth. In W. Damon (Gen. Ed.) & R. M. Lerner (Vol. Ed.), *Handbook of Child Psychology: Vol. 1. Theoretical models of human development* (pp. 1145–1207). New York: Wiley.

Garcia Coll, C., Lamberty, G., Jenkins, R., McAdoo, H., Crnic, K., Wasik, B., & Garcia, H. (1996). An integrative model for the study of developmental competencies in minority children. *Child Development, 67*, 1891–1914.

Goodnow, J. J., Miller, P. J., & Kessel, F. (Eds.). (1995). Cultural practices as contexts for development. *New directions in child development, 67*. San Francisco: Jossey-Bass.

Gopaul-McNicol, S., & Armour-Thomas, E. (2002). *Assessments and culture: Psychological tests with minority populations*. Orlando, FL: Academic Press.

Greene, B., & Fulford, D. G. (1993). *To our children's children: Preserving family histories for generations to come.* New York, NY: Doubleday.

Greenfield, P. M., & Cocking, R. R. (Eds.). (1994). *Cross-cultural roots of minority child development*. Hillsdale, NJ: Lawrence Erlbaum Associates.

Greenfield, P. M., & Suzuki, L. K. (1998). Culture and human development. In W. Damon (Editor-in-Chief) and I. E. Sigel and A. Renninger (Vol. Eds.), *Handbook of child psychology, Vol. 4*, (5th Ed., pp. 1059–1112). New York: Wiley.

Harkness, S., & Super, C. M. (Eds.). (1996). *Parents' cultural belief systems: Their origins, expressions, and consequences*. New York: Guilford.

Hill, G. W., IV. (2000). Incorporating cross-cultural perspective in the undergraduate psychology curriculum: An interview with David Matsumoto. *Teaching of Psychology, 27*, 71–75.

Holloway, S. D. (1988). Concepts of ability and effort in Japan and the United States. *Review of Educational Research, 58*(3), 327–345.

Hwang, C. P., Lamb, M. E., & Sigel, I. E. (Eds.). (1996). *Images of childhood*. Mahwah, NJ: Lawrence Erlbaum Associates.

Journal of Family Psychology. (2000). Special issue: Cultural variation in families, *14*(3).

Kagitcibasi, C. (1996). *Family and human development across cultures: A view from the other side*. Mahwah, NJ: Lawrence Erlbaum Associates.

Lamb, M. E., Sternberg, K. J., Hwang, C. P., & Broberg, A. G. (Eds.). (1997). *Childcare in context: Cross cultural perspectives*. Mahwah, NJ: Lawrence Erlbaum Associates.

Lee, Y. (1994). Why does American psychology have cultural limitations? *American Psychologist, 49*, 524.

LeVine, R. A., Dixon, S., Levine, S., Richman, A., Liederman, P. H., Keefer, C. H., & Brazelton, T. B. (1994). *Child care and culture: Lessons from Africa*. New York: Cambridge University Press.

LeVine, R. A., Miller, P. M., & West, M. M. (Eds.). (1994). *Parental behavior in diverse societies*. San Francisco: Jossey-Bass.

Lowe, R. C., & Wilczynski, M. (1994). A cross-cultural study of need for achievement in Italian and American children. *Psychological Reports, 75*(1, pt. 2), Special Issue 590.

Masten, A. S. (Ed.). (1999). *Cultural processes in child development*. Mahwah, NJ: Lawrence Erlbaum Associates.

Matsumoto, D. (Ed.). (2001). *The handbook of culture and psychology*. New York, NY: Oxford University Press.

Mays, V. M., Rubin, J., Sabourin, M., & Walker, L. (1996). Moving toward a global psychology: Changing theories and practice to meet the needs of a changing world. *American Psychologist, 51*(5), 485–487.

Miller, J. G., & Chen, X. (Eds.). (2000). Indigenous approaches to developmental research. Newsletter, *International Society for the Study of Behavioural Development, 1*, (serial No. 37).

Nagayama Hall, G. C., & Okazaki, S. (Eds.). (2002). *Asian American psychology: The science of lives in context*. Washington, DC: American Psychological Association.

Nucci, L. P., Saxe, G. B., Turiel, E. (Eds.). (2000). *Culture, thought, and development*. Mahwah, NJ: Lawrence Erlbaum Associates.

Nuckolls, C. W. (Ed.). (1993). *Siblings in South Asia: Brothers and sisters in cultural context*. New York: Guilford.

Parke, R. D. (2000). Beyond white and middle class: Cultural variations in families—Assessments, processes, and policies. *Journal of Family Psychology, 14*(3), 331–334.

Roopnarine, J. L., & Carter, D. B. (Eds.). (1992). *Parent–child socialization in diverse cultures*. Norwood, NJ: Ablex.

Shweder, R. A., Goodnow, J., Hatano, G., LeVine, R. A., Markus, H., & Miller, P. (1998). The cultural psychology of development. In W. Damon (Editor-in-Chief) and R. Lerner (Vol. Ed.), *Handbook of child psychology, Vol. 1*, (5th Ed., pp. 865–938). New York: Wiley.

Smith, G. E., & Eggleston, T. J. (2003). Examining cross-cultural diversity in psychology classes: Around the world in 15 weeks. *Teaching of Psychology, 30*(1), 54–55.

Sue, S. (1999). Science, ethnicity, and bias. *American Psychologist, 54*, 1070–1077.

Super, C. M., & Harkness, S. (1986). The developmental niche: A conceptualization at the interface of child and culture. *International Journal of Behavior Development, 9*, 545–569.

Sweder, R. A., & Sullivan, M. (1993). Cultural psychology: Who needs it? *Annual Review of Psychology, 44*, 497–523.

Thomas, R. M. (2001). *Folk psychologies across cultures.* Thousand Oaks, CA: Sage.

Whiting, B. B. (Ed.). (1963). *Six cultures: Studies of child rearing.* New York: Wiley.

Whiting, B. B., & Edwards, C. P. (1988). *Children of different worlds: The formation of social behavior.* Cambridge, MA: Harvard University Press.

Worthman, C. W. (1993). Bio-cultural interactions in human development. In M. E. Pereira & L. A. Fairbanks (Eds.), *Juvenile primates: Life history, development and behavior* (pp. 339–358). New York: Oxford University Press.

Wosinka, W., Cialdini, R. B., Barrett, D. W., & Reykowski, J. (Eds.). (2001). *The practice of social influence in multiple cultures.* Mahwah, NJ: Lawrence Erlbaum Associates.

Zhang, L. F., & Sternberg, R. J. (2001). Thinking styles across cultures: Their relationship with student learning. In R. J. Sternberg and L. F. Zhang, *Perspectives on thinking, learning, and cognitive styles* (pp. 197–226). Mahwah, NJ: Lawrence Erlbaum Associates.

Neuropsychology

Anderson, P., Anderson, V., & Lajoie, G. (1996). The Tower of London task: Validation and standardization for pediatric populations. *The Clinical Neuropsychologist, 10*, 54–65.

Archibald, S. J., & Kerns, K. A. (1999). Identification and description of new tests of executive functioning in children. *Child Neuropsychology, 5*(2), 115–123.

Arcia, E., Ornstein, P. A., & Otto, D. A. (1991). Neurobehavioral Evaluation System (NES) and school performance. *Journal of School Psychology, 29*, 337–352.

Baron-Cohen, S., Tager-Flusberg, H., & Cohen, D. (Eds.). (2000). *Understanding other minds: Perspectives from developmental cognitive neuroscience* (2nd Ed.). New York: Oxford University Press.

Bengtson, M. L., & Boll, T. J. (2001). Neuropsychological assessment of the child. In C. E. Walker, & M. C. Roberts (Eds.), *Handbook of clinical psychology* (pp. 151–171). Somerset, NJ: Wiley.

Houghton, S., Douglas, G., West, J., Whiting, K., Wall, M., Langsford, S., Powell, L., Carroll, A. (1999). Differential patterns of executive function in children with attention-deficit hyperactivity disorder according to gender and subtype. *Journal of Child Neurology, 14*(12), 801–805.

Johnson, M. H. (1998). The neural basis of cognitive development. In W. Damon (Editor-in-Chief) and D. Kuhn and R. Siegler, (Vol. Eds.), *Handbook of child psychology, Vol. 2*, (pp. 1–49). New York: Wiley.

Krikorian, R., Bartok, J., & Gay, N. (1994). The Tower of London procedure: A standard method and developmental data. *Journal of Clinical and Experimental Neuropsychology, 16*, 840–850.

Nelson, C. A., & Luciana, M. (Eds.). (2001). *Handbook of developmental cognitive neuroscience.* Cambridge, MA: MIT Press.

Obrzut, J. E., & Hynd, G. W. (1986). Child neuropsychology: An introduction to theory and research. In J. E. Obrzut and G. W. Hynd (Eds.), *Child neuropsychology, Vol. 1, Theory and research*, (pp. 1–12). Orlando, FL: Academic Press.

Ochsner, K. N., & Lieberman, D. (2001). The emergence of social cognitive neuroscience. *American Psychologist, 56*(9), 717–734.

Schnirman, G. M., Welsh, M. C., & Retzlaff, P. D. (1998). Development of the Tower of London - Revised. *Assessement, 5*, 355–360.

Spreen, O., & Strauss, E. (1998). *A compendium of neuropsychological tests: Administration, norms, and commentary* (2nd Ed.). New York: Oxford University Press.

Welsh, M. C., Satterlee-Cartmell, T., & Stine, M. (1999). Towers of Hanoi and London: Contribution of working memory and inhibition to performance. *Brain and Cognition, 41*, 231–242.

Yeates, K. O., Ris, M. D., & Taylor, H. G. (Eds.). (1999). *Pediatric neuropsychology: Research, theory, and practice.* New York: Guilford Press. (See chapter 18, Developmental Neuropsychological Assessment, pp. 405–438.)

Zelazo, P. D., & Muller, U. (in preparation). *Executive function.* Mahwah, NJ: Lawrence Erlbaum Associates.

PART FOUR

APPENDICES

APPENDIX A

Notes for the Instructor

PART ONE—INTRODUCTION; RESEARCH CONSIDERATIONS

A review of the major theoretical and methodological paradigms at the start of the semester is strongly recommended. This can be concise and limited to salient characteristics and concepts, broad comparisons and contrasts, and stands on major issues.

It is difficult within a one-semester term to demonstrate the sequential strategies described in Section 2. By repeating one experiment every couple of years, however, and utilizing the cumulated data, one can approximate some of the designs by judicious choice of grades and subjects. A class discussion of which topics would be most likely to show age versus time of measurement effects is lively and valuable.

If you wish to pursue the "correlation is not causation but maybe" theme, the analysis by Clarke-Stewart (1973) of her Bayley infant scale data in relation to mother's attention has high interest value. Another example of a cross-lagged panel analysis is a study by Bradley, Caldwell, and Elardo (1979), which was performed to determine the direction of effect among three categories of environmental stimulation and Bayley scores at 6, 12, and 24 months.

You can find useful demonstrations and activities in Ware and Johnson (2000). Volume 2 of this handbook includes perception, learning, memory and developmental activities.

It is important to caution students early in the term to pay attention to sex, socioeconomic class, and ethnicity in the research literature. Yoder and Kahn (1993, *American Psychologist, 48*(7), 846–850) warned about the fallacy of the White privileged male norm. If there is time, you may want to discuss how sexism, politics, and ideological rivalries have shaped the field of psychology via funding decisions, faculty appointments, and the media.

APA's ethical principles and code are available on the World Wide Web site: http://www.apa.org/ethics. For more information, contact APA's Ethics Office, (202) 336-5930. A free copy of *Ethical issues in teaching and academic life: Annotated bibliography* (1993), and *Sensitizing undergraduate students to the nature, causes, scope, and consequences of research fraud* (1993), both by Patricia Keith-Spiegel and colleagues, are available from the Office of Teaching Psychology, Georgia Southern University, P.O. Box 8041, Statesboro, GA 30460-8041. (Send return envelope and stamps.) The 2002 Ethical Principles of Psychologists and Code of Conduct is now revised and will be effective June 1, 2003. It appears in the *American Psychologist,* (2002), *57*(12), 1060–1073. Section 8 on Research and Publications has material relevant for your students.

Many relevant films are available for rent from audiovisual centers at major universities. The "Discovering Psychology" series hosted by Phillip Zimbardo (26 episodes, 1990), has been revamped and updated for Fall 2001. It includes a textbook, guides, and a web page. New topics include cognitive neuroscience, cultural psychology, and applying psychology in life. You will find a useful resource in APA (2000), *Videos in Psychology: A resource directory.* Washington, DC: APA.

Videos relevant to the introductory chapter include:

Past, Present, and Promise, #1 (Updated)
Understanding Research, #2
    Both in Discovering Psychology, Annenberg/CPB.
    The second also fits well with Three: D. later in this manual.

APA Divison 2 (Teaching of Psychology) has contributed a free electronic book which covers the latest directions in research across 13 subfields:

Halonen, J., & Davis, S. F. (Eds.). (2002). *The many faces of psychological research in the 21st century.* Division 2, American Psychological Association: Electronic book: www.teachpsych.org

The fifth edition of the APA *Publication Manual* arrived as I was finishing this book. We have reformatted the bibliographies and made a few other changes to conform, but perhaps not all.

The 1982 edition of this manual included the following projects, which I have dropped. These are available, if you wish, from the Copyright Clearance Center, 222 Rosewood Drive, Danvers, Massachusetts 01923:

Experiment 1. Size Constancy pp. 67–86
Experiment 4. Selective Attention pp. 131–156
Experiment 7. Representational Processes: Proportionality pp. 193–204
Experiment 9. Class Inclusion Performance pp. 243–260
Experiment 13. Social Influences on the Muller-Lyer Illusion pp. 333–346
Experiment 15. Achievement Motivation pp. 369–404

I also dropped the Wozniak and Nadelman chapter on Statistical Analysis, Appendix A, (pp. 407–440). Although a prerequisite for this lab course included a prior statistics course, I spent at least five hours a semester reviewing statistical concepts, and helping them understand analysis of variance, in English. My lab assistants and I often did the computer analysis and presented the students with empty or partially filled tables. For this course, I believed that understanding the statistics was more important than the arithmetic.

You may wish to introduce multiple regression methods in lieu of analysis of variance and/or demonstrate how to determine adequate sample size and/or use of Cohen's *Kappa* for assessing agreement in categorical judgments, and the use of confidence intervals.

A discussion of the worth of significance tests, widely used in psychology research, can benefit advanced students. Helpful articles include:

Lachman, S. J. (1993). Statistically significant difference or probable non-chance difference. *American Psychologist, 48*, 1093.

Cohen, J. (1994). The earth is round, $p < .05$. *American Psychologist 49*(12), 997–1003.

Krueger, J. (2001). Null hypothesis significance testing: On the survival of a flawed method. *American Psychologist, 56*(1), 16–26.

If you wish to discuss meta-analyses or path analysis, some references (in addition to the ones in the bibliography) include:

Bentler, P. M. (1987). Structural modeling and the scientific method: Comments on Freedman's critique. *Journal of Educational Research, 12*, 151–157.

Eysenck, H. J. (1995). Meta-analysis is squared—Does it make sense? *American Psychologist, 50*(2), 110–111.

Kline, R. B. (1991). Latent variable path analysis in clinical research: A beginner's tour guide. *Journal of Clinical Psychology, 47*(4), 471–484.

Morris, R. J., Bergan, J. R., & Fulginiti, J. V. (1991). Structural equation modeling in clinical assessment research with children. *Journal of Consulting and Clinical Psychology, 59*(3), 371–379.

Sohn, D. (1995). Meta-analysis as a means of discovery. *American Psychologist, 50*(2), 108–110.

PART TWO—OBSERVATIONAL STUDIES

In the mid-1970s, we often used the DOT, an auditory prompting device with an earjack, for time-sampling studies. For the exercises suggested here, we found a good large watch, clock, or stopwatch sufficient (and cheaper).

B. Infant Observation

The infant project is one of the highlights of the term, according to students' evaluations. Even in semesters when the enrollment has been too large for me to cope with the flood of protocols and I have consequently omitted the home visits, infants of several ages are brought to class early and late in the term. Demonstrating their behavior changes over a 12–week period on Bayley or Piagetian items, having mother wave goodbye and leave the classroom for a few seconds, watching the babies' reactions to the crowded classroom, and assigning a 2-minute live sequential protocol for later reliability scoring—all provide excellent teaching and learning opportunities. When possible, videotape the visit and show the tape just prior to the second visit.

For home visits, it may be best to omit the babies under 3 or 4 months. Many undergraduates do not see enough activity to sustain their interest and do not have the background to discern the subtle reciprocal interactions taking place. Students watching babies about 20 to 36 weeks of age could be alerted to observe the details of prehension and early stages of object concept; second year—language, symbolic play, problem solving.

Classroom training in sequential protocol note taking, with the aid of videotapes or movies, is valuable. You may wish to have half your class pair up and do this exercise with no instruction other than, "Watch everything that happens in these two minutes and get it all down." The other half of the class could be given privately a focus of observation—motor movements or mother–child interactions. All pairs could then score their protocols and see if there is a difference in reliability between the two groups of pairs. Instead of a five-minute sequential protocol, you may designate a different time span. This kind of note taking, however, is very tiring, and the scoring can become tedious to do (and to correct). The value of the home observations and protocols can be immeasurably enhanced by the feedback that the instructor provides the student. Comments like the following, noted in the margin of the written protocols, improves the quality of subsequent protocols:

> "Did you realize that that episode was an excellent example of Piaget's Stage 3A of the development of the object concept?"
>
> "That's the second tertiary circular response on this page. Can you spot the first?"
>
> "What was the mother's tone of voice then?"
>
> "Describe the baby's expression when that happened?"
>
> "What makes you say the child is frustrated?"
>
> "How does that friendliness jibe with the fear of strangers notion?"
>
> "A mother reading this report would get a good picture of what her baby can and cannot do but would not know in which areas of development the baby was precocious, or on target, or delayed."

The issue of feedback to the family needs careful attention on your part. Although my preference is not to show the parents the raw reports or my comments on the reports, the amount and kind of feedback given to the parent who wants feedback (not all do!) needs to be resolved. I do show parents any videotapes taken of the parent and baby, with a running commentary. On the other hand, the student needs to feel free to write what has been observed even if it is, "The mother's comments about the father were negative or neutral, and rarely positive. Examples: "He never bathes B or changes his BM diaper ... I keep telling him not to throw B in the air that way; some game! ... Maybe he'll pay some attention to B when the kid starts walking or talking." Not being a clinician, therapist, or family counselor in a formal relationship with the family, I would not wish to send that paragraph along. A good detailed description of how their baby showed the development of object concept, or some examples of creative problem solving, or a detailed sequence of prehension development seem to be welcome additions to the baby book many families keep.

Class discussions of minisituations, to try in visits 3 and 4 if parents permit, are valuable. See the coding categories used by Zahn-Waxler et al. (1979) and newer ones. Have your class try to construct a coding protocol.

Among the many audiovisual aids suitable for use in connection with this unit are these:

Rock-A-Bye baby. 30 minutes. Time-Life Multimedia.
   Old, but good, film on attachment.

Brazelton Neonatal Assessment Scale.
   Film 1. An introduction (1974). 20 minutes.
   Film 2. Variations in normal behavior (1974). 20 minutes.
      Distributor: Educational Development Center, 39 Chapel Street, Newton, MA 02160

The Bayley Scales of Infant Development Part 1, 52 minutes; Part 2, 56 minutes.
    Psychological Corporation

Infancy and Early Childhood, (1990). One hour.
    Seasons of Life, Annenberg/CPB Multimedia Collection, #1.

Childhood: Great Expectations
    57 min., 1991.
    Part I from the Childhood Series.
    Explores the nature/nurture mutual influences to adolescence in three births in Russia, US, and Brazil.
    WNET/13TV; Ambrose Video Publishing

Audio programs, Seasons of Life series:
    First Words
    Attachment: The Dance Begins
    Both in Annenberg/CPB

Infancy Research Methods, 19 min., 1983.
    Moxley, J.; Indiana University AV Center.
    Presents four methods to study the visual and auditory perceptual abilities of 1 month to 1-year-old infants.

Baby Talk, (Re-edited Nova version), 60 min., 1987.
    British Broadcasting Co-TV; Insight Media.

Life's First Feelings, 58 min., 1986.
    Emotional development of the human infant.
    WGBH Educational Foundation; Coronet Instructional Films.

The "Discovering Psychology" series mentioned earlier has been updated for Fall 2001. It includes several of its 26 episodes that apply to this and later chapters, namely #5—The Developing Child.

For advanced students, Rovee-Collier and Lipsitt have edited volumes 1–10, 1981–1996, on *Advances in Infancy Research*. Volume 7, 1992, includes a symposium on the *Bayley Scales of Infant Development: Issues of prediction and outcome revisited.*

If children beyond infancy are of interest, a film by Meisels and Wiske on identifying children 4–6 years of age who are at high risk for failure can be used: *ESI Early Screening Inventory*, 1989 Edition, Volume 1, 32 minutes. Michigan Media.

C. Observation Projects

Videotapes or films are useful and less time-consuming than field trips in training observer reliability in early stages. Scoring sheets for observer agreement, described in B, when used for even two minutes of specimen records (sequential protocols), will give the students a forceful demonstration of the implications of different sizes of behavior units and of focused versus massive observation. There are countless films that have brief portions suitable for record taking and observer-reliability scoring. A brief video of the nursery school children you will be observing is helpful.

The activity-preferences data described in this chapter can be used for observer-reliability scoring, at either a gross or molecular level. For "gross" scoring, one can see if two observers (recording simultaneously) noted the same number of boys and girls in the *sum* (or mean) column, counting each *whole cell* as the unit for agreement or disagreement. For example, Mary and James, each with a mean of 2 boys and 2.4 girls in the first activity row, have one agreement. Sue—with 3 boys and 2.5 girls, and John—with 2.6 boys and 2.5 girls, have one disagreement. On a more "molecular" level, score for agreement on the number of boys and girls separately. Mary and James then have two agreements, Sue and John have one agreement and one disagreement. Use the formula in "Infant Observation".

In practice, we found reliability for the first exercise extremely high. We settled, finally, on two practice columns and no reliability check. The second and third exercises, however, are more difficult and it is important to give the students some practice in observer reliability as indicated. A discussion in class of the limitations of these projects as run is in order: The need for more practice in observer and scoring reliability, the probability that some children may have been observed by more than one observer, the possible overlap in ages in the younger and older groups.

The TV project can be extended or curtailed by you and/or your class, by adding or omitting observation columns.

Alternate similar observation projects have looked at how aging is portrayed in TV programs and commercials. Books for preschoolers and early elementary-grades can be coded similarly to the TV programs.

We have omitted additional projects necessitating rapid multiple coding during repeated brief observation cycles, because such projects use a very large chunk of the term for extensive training and data collection. Admittedly, such experiences increased our students' respect for empirical articles based on observational methods. In this connection, observational methods such as used by Clarke-Stewart (1973) or Lamb (1976, 1977) and others could profitably be described and discussed in class. Advanced students may wish to pursue some of the issues in observational research by studying Beaty (1990), Irwin and Bushnell (1980), Lamb, Suomi, and Stephenson (1979), Lytton (1971), Pellegrini (1996), or Thomas and Martin (1976).

If any of your advanced or graduate students are interested in ethnographic descriptions, or graphic analysis, refer them to this publication:

Rogoff, B., Mistry, J., Gnc, A., & Mosier, C. (1993). Guided participation in cultural activity by toddlers and caregivers. *Monographs of the Society for Research in Child Development, 58* (8, Serial No. 239).

Murray's law review commentary (see Bibliography) served as the basis for a one-hour video program on television violence, produced for the Great Plains University Consortium, 1995. For information or a copy, e-mail JPM@KSUVM.KSU.EDU.

A comprehensive resource is:

Singer, D. G., & Singer, J. L. (2001). *Handbook of children and the media*. Thousand Oaks, CA: Sage.

Another good resource, limited to TV viewing, is:

Anderson, D. R., Huston, A. C., Schmidt, K. L., Linebarger, D. L., and Wright, J. C. (2001). Early childhood television viewing and adolescent behavior. *Monographs of the Society for Research in Child Development, 66*(1, Serial No. 264).

These high school students had had their early use of television evaluated at age 5.

PART THREE—EXPERIMENTAL STUDIES

D. General Experimental Research Procedures

Retrieval

Bringing a PsycLIT or MEDLINE product to class makes a good demonstration. Give instruction on electronic retrieval. It is also wise to bring some copies of *Psychological Abstracts* and demonstrate how to search for related studies in the author and topic indices. For more information about PsycINFO databases or services, contact PsycINFO User Services, 750 1st St. N. E., Washington, DC 20002, or call (800) 374-2722.

Data Collection and Handling

It is possible, even with few experiments, to sample the elementary-school age range by the end of the semester. Students find these experiences with kindergartners through sixth-graders valuable, despite their relative brevity. Should you wish to change the suggested grades, try to leave an equivalent gap between older and younger groups. Not all the projects can be age-transposed well. As an example, the self-esteem measure is not suitable for older children. The experiments in this manual were chosen with a nonemphasis on hardware, and the apparatus can be built locally and inexpensively. The reaction-time experiment does require a purchased clock, telegraph key, and so on, or can be purchased as a complete efficient unit. When our university closed its campus nursery and elementary and junior high schools, we were forced to resort to the community. The fol-

Program in Child Development
Department of Psychology
University of Michigan

Dear (Name of School) Parents:

This letter is to tell you about the university child study program, with which the schools cooperate, and to ask your help. Your children are being invited to participate by coming once or twice a semester, after school hours, for a brief session (up to half an hour) at (name of) School.

I am well aware that many of you will wish to know something about the program and about me before giving your child permission to participate. For many years, I have been training graduate and advanced undergraduate students in my courses to investigate the growth and development of children. Such training, to be effective, must include observing or working directly with children of various ages from birth on. To accomplish this, we receive (and are very grateful for) the help extended by the local schools and nurseries, and community agencies. The training of our students is not only technical. We are very conscious of the fact that many of them are going into the teaching, social work, medical, or psychological professions. It is, therefore, crucial that they be carefully trained not only in the techniques of research with children but also in the ethics, the limitations, and the implications of such work.

This training program has been described in detail in a published article (1968), which has been left with (name), the principal. The following are examples of some areas we have investigated: age and sex differences in the development of accurate perception of "vertical" and "horizontal," preferences for colors versus forms, "impulsive" versus "reflective" styles of thinking or problem solving, imitation, and verbal control of motor behavior. In the last few weeks, the program has been presented at the (name of school) teaching staff meeting, at the P. T. O. Board meeting, and to administrators of the Ann Arbor Public Schools. The Ann Arbor school system does not direct or supervise the project, but as part of the continuing interaction and relationship with the university, it does cooperate with our program. Detailed descriptions of the purposes, exact procedures, and materials are given to the Ann Arbor schools administrators and the teachers of the grades involved. I should welcome the invitation to attend room group meetings or informal coffee hours during the term, with our pictures and materials, in order to keep you informed about our work. Information on the performance of specific children is not given to the school, teacher, parent, or Board of Education. (Such practice would not be ethical in a training program.)

Appointments with your children would be made in advance, by home telephone; the session would be at (name of) School, under my or my assistant's supervision; the child would be walked home if you so indicated. If you are willing to permit your child to cooperate, please sign the attached form promptly, and return it to your child's teacher with your child.

By way of a "thank you" to the child, she or he may choose an item from our supply of rewards, such as legal pads, index cards, highlighter pens, and similar notions. By way of a "thank you" to the parents, I and my colleagues in the child study program will be happy to speak to your community groups or clubs on any topic within our special competences.

Feel free to call me at my office (phone number) or home (phone number) or write to me c/o (name of school or the University of Michigan) with any questions, criticisms, or suggestions. We do need your cooperation! Thank you.

Cordially,
Lorraine Nadelman, PhD
Associate Professor

lowing page displays a copy of the letter sent to all families in a large public school near the university, with permission from the Board of Education Research Committee. This was accompanied by personal visits to the classroom (with permission from the teachers and principal) to let the children see me and the assistants, to ask for their cooperation, to answer their questions, and to show them sample rewards. The letter and visits combined elicited much positive response, particularly from the middle grades. The youngest are often hesitant, the oldest blasé (bored?) and less eager.

It is important, prior to permitting any telephone calls to homes for specific appointments, to work out precisely how the experiment is to be described to the parent and to the young child. Having your students participate in this process is helpful to them. Avoid the word *experiment* or *laboratory* (*study* or *project* is less emotionally laden). Referring to the instructor as "Miss," "Ms." or "Mr." with young children (and perhaps Professor with parents) is often preferable to "Dr." One does not "use" or "run" a child. Explaining the objective or measures used in an experiment, *in layperson terms*, can be a demanding task.

We have had our students testing in unused classrooms, in stockrooms, in hallways, research trailers, lunchrooms, and so on. Good physical facilities such as we had at Mount Holyoke College, (with dedicated research rooms and one-way mirrors) or as described by Eckerman, Rheingold, and Helwig, (1974) are a boon, and many schools can rival these; but they are not an absolute necessity for a *training* program.

If your subject pool is sufficiently large, it is preferable for each student to test at least two children for each experiment, with supervisor's feedback given before the second child. The supervisor should be evaluating the student experimenter for (a) Preparation, Rapport, Control: Is E relaxed and able to make S comfortable, yet in control? Is E on time? Is E well prepared? (b) Procedure: Does E follow verbatim instructions; correct order and timing, et cetera? Are her data usable?

Often data can be milked more than I indicate in the suggested data analysis accompanying each experiment. You need to consider your depth-breadth priorities when considering how many experiments to run and how deeply to analyze them. At the least, however, students should be encouraged to eyeball the data. It is also helpful to encourage them to consider the different ways in which data might be analyzed *before* they read the "Results" section.

Providing *some* but not all of the data analysis is a pedagogic technique that is appreciated by some of the better prepared students. Even if the statistical background of your students is too weak to turn them on their own profitably, a class discussion of which techniques to use is helpful. Collation of data on Master Data Sheets, even if not strictly necessary for sophisticated computer use, is very useful for perusing and for clarifying the experimental design. Students should pair up to check one another's scoring and entry of data.

Although statistics is a prerequisite for the present version of my lab course, I frequently lecture on the requisite statistics for a particular experiment (in English), then have my assistants run the programs on the university computer system and present the students with finished or almost-finished tables. For ANOVAS, the F column is left for them to finish. In correlation matrices, they need to star the significant rs appropriately. Having them plot the scores in a correlational graph, or showing the computer printout of the graph, assists their understanding of r.

Reports

Although the *APA Publication Manual* is detailed and careful, undergraduate students often find it overwhelming, and it pays to take class time to make explicit how the reports should be written. The quality of the products at the end of the term depends heavily on the quality of oral and written feedback provided to each student earlier in the term. A technique that has worked well is to comment fully on an abstract written by the student and then have the student rewrite it. This can apply to any section of the report that gives particular trouble.

The questions and comments presented in this manual in the "Discussion" sections often range far beyond what is needed or appropriate for a published article. We are trying to use each experiment to sharpen the students' critical evaluative abilities, with regard to both research design and measurement issues and to the relationships of the results to opposing theoretical views.

It is usually necessary to emphasize the differences between References and Bibliographies.

Two videos which are useful early in the term and available from APA Books are:

How to use *PsychLIT* on CD-Rom (1991).
18 minutes, VHS # 3900120. $65.

How to use Psychological Abstracts
    12 minutes, #3900020. $50.
    For your use, there is a special edition of the journal *Teaching of Psychology*, edited by D. F. Halpern and S. G. Nummedal (1995), *Psychologists teach critical thinking*.
    Another useful resource for you is:

> Chastain, G., & Landrum, R. E. (Eds.). (1999). *Protecting human subjects: Departmental subject pools and institutional review boards*. Washington, DC: American Psychological Association.

Bloopers

Early in the term, and when I'm lecturing on experimental design, I bring in "bloopers" for class practice. These are real or fictional very brief descriptions of experiments with an outstanding flaw, for example, no control group, sampling errors, possible curvilinear rather than 2-point linear relationship, ignoring of practice or fatigue effects, counterbalancing needed, correlation is not causation, and so on. Ready-made examples appear in Johnson, H. H., & Solso, R. L. (1971. *An introduction to experimental design in psychology: A case approach*, NY: Harper & Row, and in later editions. Late in the term, the students are given a test made of bloopers, in which they need to point out the design error and what should have been done.

Statistical Analysis

Although we require a statistics course as a prerequisite for this lab course, I always lecture 4–6 hours on the relevant statistics.
    Helpful films include:

> *Against all odds: Inside statistics series*, 1988-1989.
>   26 half-hour programs.
>   Chedd-Augeriers Production Co.; Intellimation.

    We do not, at this level of the lab course, discuss cluster analysis or meta-analysis. A treatment of the latter appears in the *American Psychologist*, February 1995, pp. 108–115 and many new books. Similarly, structural equation modelling requires more subjects than we usually run, and more statistically sophisticated students; if interested, see R. O. Mueller, (1995), *Basic principles of structural equation modelling: An introduction to LISREL and EQS*, Springer Texts in Statistics. Other references that may interest you or graduate students are:

> Eysenck, H. J. (1995). Meta-analysis squared—Does it make sense? *American Psychologist, 50*(2), 110–111.

> Lachman, S. J. (1993). Statistically significant difference or probable non-chance difference. *American Psychologist, 48*, 1093.

> Hoyle, R. H. (1993). On the relation between data and theory. *American Psychologist, 48*, 1094–1096.

> Schmidt, F. L. (1993). Data theory, and meta-analysis: Response to Hoyle. *American Psychologist, 48*, 1096.

> Schmidt, F. L. (1992). What do data really mean? Research findings, meta-analysis, and cumulative knowledge in psychology. *American Psychologist, 47*, 1173–1181.

> Sohn, D. (1995). Meta-analysis as a means of discovery. *American Psychologist, 50*(2), 108–110.

    If you have time, the procedure used by Aberson and colleagues may be interesting and valuable:
> Aberson, C. L., Berger, D. E., Healy, M. R., & Romero, V. L. (2003). Evaluation of an interactive tutorial for teaching hypothesis testing concepts. *Teaching of Psychology, 30*(1), 75–78.

    If you wish an example of cross-sectional, longitudinal, and sequential strategies, see:
> Gatz, M., & Karel, M. J. (1993). Individual change in perceived control over 20 years. *International Journal of Behavioral Development, 16*(2), 305–322.

Additionally, a topic that could use more emphasis in our research training courses is *qualitative research*. See:
 Camie, P. M., Rhodes, J. E., & Yardley, L. (Eds.). (2003). *Qualitative research in psychology: Expanding perspectives in methodology and design*. Washington, DC: American Psychological Association.

E. Psychomotor and Perceptual Behavior

An introduction to this general topic can be found in the VHS Cassette: Sensation and Perception, #7 in Discovering Psychology series, Annenberg/CPB Multimedia Collection. The Teaching Module #3, Sense and Perception provide excerpts from the full cassette.
 A relevant reading for you:

 Gibson, E. J. (2002). *Perceiving the affordances: A portrait of two psychologists*. Mahwah, NJ: Lawrence Erlbaum Associates.

Experiment 1. Age and Sex Differences in Two Reaction-Time Tasks

See Appendix A, Fig. E.1 for wiring of the reaction-time apparatus. If finances permit, ready-made reaction-time apparatus can be purchased.
 Forty trials of either task can be administered in a fairly brief period, usually less than 15 to 20 minutes. The age difference and the difference in reaction-time tasks should reach statistical significance in an experiment with a moderate number of subjects. The 2 X 2 X 2 design would need a minimum of 40 children. The N could

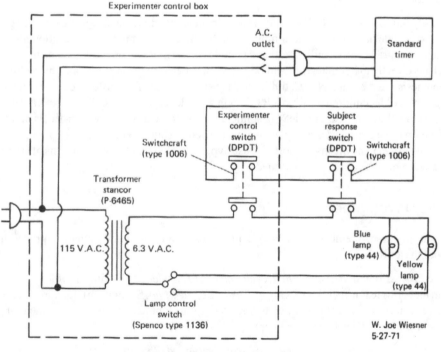

Appendix A, Fig. E1. Reaction-Time Apparatus.

be reduced by ignoring sex and using a 2 task X 2 grade design. We have not found the sex difference in reaction time that Goodenough (1935) reported.

Although we used the means for the 30 simple reaction times and the 15 C-reaction times, it is appropriate to perform the anova on the means of the 15 trials of C-reaction versus the means of those same 15 trial positions of simple reaction time. Adjust the Master Data Sheets and Table 1.1 accordingly.

The between-subjects design was used here for simplicity. Most current reaction-time studies use within-subjects designs where subjects perform under all experimental conditions and the order of conditions is counterbalanced across subjects. In such a case, a repeated measures (for the two tasks) analysis of variance would be used. We have found it expedient to avoid repeated measures designs until later in the semester. The mean rather than the median score for each subject was used in the analysis of variance. See Pachella (1974).

With an advanced class, you may wish to consider additional hypotheses relating to sex X task interaction, or even a sex X task X age interaction.

For data collation make up four master data sheets, one chart for each task-grade group (that is, simple RT-first grade, simple RT-sixth grade, CRT-first grade, CRT-sixth grade. Put girls in the top half of the chart, boys in the bottom half, with some space between. Point out the eight groups of data to the students to illustrate the 2 X 2 X 2 design. The stub heads across the top would read from left to right as follows:

> Experimenter's name
> Child's ID
> Light color
> Mean RT-Practice trials
> Mean RT-30 trials
> Median RT-Practice trials
> Median RT-30 trials
> Standard Deviation-Practice trials
> Standard Deviation-30 trials
> Range-Practice trials
> Range-30 trials

Students newly familiar with ANOVAS may need help understanding that a significant F for grade effects tells them that one grade has a faster reaction time than the other, on simple and C-reaction *together*.

A significant F for grade X task indicates that the grades differ more on one task than on the other. This interaction F relates directly to hypothesis 6. Although the four means in the grade X task interaction may seem to support hypothesis 1 and 2, our ANOVA did *not* test the significance of the difference between those pairs of means: young versus older children on simple RT; young vs. older children on CR-T, et cetera. To do that, you would need to follow the significant grade X task interaction with Scheff or Newman-Keuls or similar tests. Therefore, if the first two hypotheses in the manual were used as stated, without the follow-up statistics, students could simply say that the means supported those hypotheses but that the specific tests of significance (of differences between means) were not performed.

F. Cognitive Development

The projects on attention, memory, interference proneness, and automatic semantic processing can be introduced with these films:

> *Cognitive Processes and Memory/ The Development of Knowledge.* 90 min., 1990.
> > From the series featuring Richard Gerrig, *The Life of the Mind*, Second part, Lecture 4. This discussed the nature/nurture concept in relation to knowledge development and the development of perception in young children. The Teaching Company
>
> *Growing Minds: Cognitive Development in Early Childhood.* 25 min., 1995.
> > Looks at reasoning, perception, and language acquisition. Narrator: Dr. David Elkind. Davidson Films
> *Cognitive Processes*, #10.
> > Discovering Psychology, Annenberg/CPB. This looks into the higher mental processes and the cognitive revolution.

If you wish more information than is present in the Background section, and in the essays preceding Experiment 3 (Theory of Mind) and Experiment 7 (Susan Gelman: Cognitive Development and Language), the following are comprehensive resources:

Cowan, N. (1995). *Attention and Memory: An integrated framework*. New York, NY: Oxford University Press.

Landau, B., Sabini, J., Jonides, J., & Newport, E. L. (Eds.). (2000). *Perception, cognition, and language: Essays in honor of Henry and Lila Gleitman*. Cambridge, MA: MIT Press.

Nelson, C. A., & Luciana, M. (Eds.). (2001). *Handbook of developmental cognitive neuroscience*. Cambridge, MA: MIT Press.

Osherson, D. N. (Series Editor). (1995–1998). *An invitation to cognitive science* (2nd Ed., 4 volumes). Cambridge, MA: MIT Press.

Tulving, E., & Craik, F. M. (Eds.). (2000). *The Oxford handbook of memory*. New York, NY: Oxford University Press.

Wilson, R. A., & Keil, F. C. (Eds.). (1999). *The MIT encyclopedia of the cognitive sciences*. Cambridge, MA: MIT Press.

Piagetian Research

The following three old (but good) films on Piagetian concepts were produced by Davidson Films and are distributed by Sterling Educational Films.

Piaget's developmental theory:
Classification. 17 minutes, rental.
Conservation. 28 minutes, rental.
Formal thought. 32 minutes, rental.

A newer film shows how thinking changes between the ages of five and seven:

Piaget and the Age of Reason, 1990.
From Seasons of Life series, Annenberg/CPB Multimedia Collection

For archival footage of Piaget, and a new film of David Elkind interviewing children of various ages, see:

Piaget's Developmental Theory: An Overview, 1989.
27 min. Davidson Films

If you are teaching a graduate course or very advanced undergraduates, you may wish to consider some of the issues and controversies surrounding stage theories at more depth. Brainerd (1993), for example, considered the phenomenon of *abruptness*, one of the assumed hallmarks of stages, and argues that abrupt-change data can be explained without resorting to stages. He said, "Simpler concepts that are much more closely related to data, such as rules, do quite nicely" (p. 189). He described five arguments against stages.

Brainerd, C. J. (1993). Commentary: Cognitive development is abrupt (but not stage-like). In H. Thomas and A. Lohaus, Modeling growth and individual differences in spatial tasks. *Monographs of the Society for Research in Child Development, 58*(9, Serial No. 237).

Experiment 2. Spatial Perspective-Taking: The Three Mountains Task

Both the children and students like this one, and it is administered easily if the experimenter is well practiced. Scoring is best done with pairs of students in class, with supervision.

Several modifications are possible: (a) Instead of the point system, just use the Piaget stage-scoring and count the frequency of boys and girls in each grade at each stage. Ignore the statistics. (b) Use the point system but increase Part 1 from 11 to 22 points to allow for partial credit (0, 1, 2 points). (c) Just use total scores and ignore the analysis of kinds of errors.

To translate the black-white Fig. F2.3 to colored pictures for Part 2 (Picture Choice) of the spatial perspective task, cut out many triangles of the specified size and color (See Fig. F2.2) and paste them on 10-cm cards in the overlapping fashion indicated. Write A, B, C, D, E, F, respectively on the back of the card. Cards E and F are jokers, in effect (never right).

Mr. Smith (Fig. F2.4) can be mounted on a card with folded wings to hold him upright.

For data collation, make a master data sheet for each grade. Number the children in the left column, with space between the boys and girls. The stub heads across the top would read from left to right as follows:

> Experimenter's name
> Child's ID
> Reconstruction I
>   Interposition
>   L-R
>   Nonegocentric
> Picture Choice
> Position Choice
> Total score
> Piaget stage

Experiment 3. False Belief in Children's Theory of Mind

The false-belief task is short and simple, and a brief practice session among your students should be sufficient before testing a child. It is important that the prescribed wording not be changed: "What does he (she) think is in this box?" and that all students use this same question.

If at all possible, an equal number of boys and girls should be tested. This simplifies the statistical handling. The number of children answering question 2 correctly or incorrectly can then be used with Chi Square or Fisher tests. Otherwise, switch to percentages or proportions.

Because this task is so short, you may wish to consider adding a second task, either a different FB task (change of location) or a test of inhibition like the Stroop. The latter would pick up on an aspect of the executive function (response inhibition) which some researchers relate to FB. (The Stroop test appears in Experiment 4.) See, for example, Carlson and Moses, 2001; Carlson, Moses, and Hix, 1998.

Instead of a Band-Aid box, other familiar containers could be substituted, for example, M & M bag, or Animal Crackers box. It is important for the child to be familiar with and easily recognize the container. For manual data collation, use two master data sheets, one for each age group. Put girls on top half of each chart, boys on bottom half. The stub heads across the top would read from left to right as follows:

> Experimenter's name
> Child's ID
> Q1
>   Score–Correct (Bandaid)
>   Score–Incorrect
> Q2
>   Score–Correct (Bandaid)
>   Score–Incorrect

The critical data are the responses to Question 2, of course, and the statistics are run on those responses. Those data are also used for the figure.

I strongly recommend the Flavell (2000) article for a good overview.

Experiment 4. Age and Sex Differences in Interference Proneness (Stroop Test)

The method of constructing the Stroop stimuli by using plastic label tapes and an embossing device is generally neater and faster than attempting to make incongruously colored words. The resulting colored rectangles with neutral colored incongruous words have been found to produce results virtually identical to those found when the more traditional incongruously colored words are used (Kamlet & Egeth, 1969).

In addition, the instructions to name the colored strip and not the word are more easily understood by children.

If the instructor wishes to save time, the analysis of variance on score CW may be omitted because, by itself, it is not a valid measure of interference proneness. It is useful to discuss in class the types of errors that children make on the Stroop test. However, most investigators have not statistically analyzed the errors made on the test.

With our group of children of above-average intelligence, we had no subjects who could not read the four color words. If an experimenter encounters such a child, testing should proceed with card PC. Students should note how many children in the sample could not read the words; however, *none* of the data from such a subject should be included in any of the analyses.

The administration of the Stroop test is generally quite fast, averaging around seven or eight minutes. The experimenter should note that timing of all three cards begins with the first response, *not* as soon as the child is shown the card. Experimenters should make sure that the child is praised and encouraged after each card, irrespective of the speed of the performance.

The fifth-grade sample may be replaced by any older subgroup that is available. This should still result in a reliable decrease in interference proneness when compared with the third-graders. It should also be noted the first-grade results may differ from Schiller's when the sample is from a population of high intelligence and high reading ability or if the children are tested late in the year. Under these conditions, word-reading speed is usually either equal to or faster than color naming. Also, in contrast to the minimal interference observed by Schiller in the first grade (CW/C ratio of 1.1), a significantly higher mean CW/C score may be obtained. We found a CW/C ratio of 1.45 with a group of high socioeconomic first graders. However, this is still significantly lower than the score obtained with third graders, which is usually 1.75 or greater.

For data collation, make up six master data sheets, one chart for each grade-sex group. Number the children in the left column. The stub heads across the top would then read from left to right as follows:

Experimenter's name
Child's ID
W Score
C Score
CW Score
CW-C
CW/C

We have used the Stroop test frequently in our lab course, and find it a robust task and one the students and children both enjoy.

A Contingency Naming Test has been used as an alternate to the Stroop:

Taylor, H. G. (1988). Learning disabilities. In E. J. Mash (Ed.), *Behavioral assessment of childhood disorders* (2nd Ed., pp. 402–405). New York: Guilford Press.

An article that appears in searches on Reaction time, Stroop, and Picture-Word interference is:

Weiler, M. D., Harris, N. S., Marcus, D. J., Bellinger, D., Kosslyn, S. M., Waber, D. P. (2000). Speed of information processing in children referred for learning problems: Performance on a visual filtering test. *Journal of Learning Disabilities, 33*(6), 538–550.

Experiment 5. Semantic Processing in a Picture-Word Interference Task

This study takes about five minutes per child or adult. Aside from the short time and high interest and topicality, this is one of the few experiments whose effects are very large and reach .01 levels. We have used this task with both undergraduate and graduate experimenters, and an hour of supervised practice is sufficient to diminish experimenter variability.

During practice sessions, standardize the timing (from word "go"); placement of card (flat or on a stand; neither the experimenter nor the child should be holding the card up); marking of errors; and so on. Although we did not analyze errors, it is good note-taking practice to have students record these.

Because both Rosinski and our class found no sex differences, the tabled ANOVA omits sex effects. It is important either that (a) you run a preliminary analysis to confirm the absence of sex effects and report this to your class (as we did); or (b) lacking this step, to emphasize that hypothesis 6 is *not* being tested by the statistical analysis.

To collate the individual data, make up six master data sheets, one for each of the major grade and task (pictures–words) subgroups. The column stubs across the top should read from left to right

Experimenter's name
Child's ID
Time scores: 0%
                   100%
                   Difference

Label the top half of the page *Boys*; the bottom half, *Girls*. Under each sex, divide the space in half again, and label one portion *0%–100% sequence*, and the other portion *100%–0% sequence*. This provides a bird's eye view of the various counterbalancings and suggests other analyses (i.e., sequence of testing effect). Remind the students to be careful with the signs in the Difference column.

Our students criticized the design for omitting a base-line time; that is, although the children practice word or picture labeling on the respective distraction-free card, there is no timed response trial with this card. Their prior experience with the Stroop cards led our students to wonder about the relation of the 100% congruence card to the single image card: Would the superimposed word and picture, albeit congruent, slow or hasten the response? Would the effect be different for the two tasks? If this problem is of interest, the procedure and analysis could be changed accordingly: The adjusted scores for the ANOVA in Table F5.2 could be the difference between the base-line response and 100% congruence and between the base-line response and 0% congruence.

Another possibility is a delayed recognition memory study for words and pictures as a function of age. For example, if initially given a *picture* of a hen, does the child say "yes" to the picture of a hen 24 hours later? Does the child say "yes" to the word *hen* 24 hours later? If given the word *hen* initially, does the picture of a hen elicit "yes" 24 hours later? Are there age differences in these effects?

Experiment 6. The Influence of Category-Blocked and Random Presentation on Free Recall and Clustering

This is a fast (several minutes), enjoyable task for the children. Your students will require supervised practice in presenting and removing the cards at the timed and regular pace, speaking the labels clearly, and writing responses unobtrusively and quickly.

Instead of covering each picture with the next during the presentation, it may be preferable to remove the picture with one hand while presenting the next picture with the other. This removes the child's temptation to look underneath at earlier items.

It is worth the time to score some sample data sheets in class on the board. While the scoring is simple, the opportunities for minor errors abound. Students often mistake the *r* in the ICI index for runs, instead of *pairs* of adjacent items from the same category. They occasionally call $c = 5$, erroneously, even if the child has no items at all from one or more of the categories.

Robinson's ICI formula (1966) is similar to the Moely and Jeffrey formula (1974) that we used.

For the data collation, make up eight master charts, one for each condition-age-sex group (Blocked-Second Grade-Girls; Random-Second Grade-Boys, and so on). The column stub heads across the top would read from left to right as follows:

Experimenter's name
Child's ID
No. Recalled
No. Intrusions
No. Repetitions
No. Categories
No. Vehicles
No. Furniture
No. Food

No. Toys
No. Body parts
Mean per category
No. of runs
Mean length of run
ICI

If you wish to limit the data analysis to amount recalled and clustering score, as outlined in the text, then only three scores are needed on your individual data sheets and master data collation sheets: number recalled, number of categories, and ICI.

If your students however, are interested in differential recall by categories, then a repeated measures ANOVA can be run, with the five separate category scores for each child (vehicles, furniture, etc.) as the repeated measure. In a graduate level class, this is a good place, too, to discuss some of the assumptions of multivariate analysis.

A serious analysis of serial position would be a large undertaking, but a crude illustrative attempt can be made, as follows. Each student can enter on the Individual Data Sheet and then on the Master Data Sheet the answer to the question, Did the child recall the *first* test picture? No or yes. If yes, did child give it as a *first* response, a *last* response, or somewhere *between* the first and last? The same procedure is followed for the *last* presented picture. A comparison of the number of children recalling first item versus last item presented relates to the primacy–recency effects.

Our laboratory course did find significant grade effects with both recall and clustering scores, but the condition effect for our sample reached significance only with the cluster scores. The differences in procedure (particularly one-trial design) are important when interpreting data and relating these data to the literature.

With an advanced class, some attention to Robinson's category clustering index (CCI), as contrasted to his item-clustering index (ICI), would be possible. Robinson (1966) believed that both kinds of clustering indicate that subjects can establish highly structured plans for remembering, and that these different associations are hierarchically organized.

Or, alternatively, one can simplify the experiment by dropping one of the presentation conditions and looking just for age differences. If the developmental implications are not your main concern, simplify by using one age group and retaining the presentation variations. The class may indeed wish to pursue the number and width of categories used instead of the three variables in this chapter. Possibilities abound that will introduce a class to the memory literature and the recall test procedure.

A video on memory is:

Remembering and Forgetting, #9
Discovering Psychology, Annenberg/CPB

Experiment 7. Children's Interpretation of the Word *Big*

This is a complex and sophisticated study, so I would not suggest starting an undergraduate class with this project as their first. The students will need considerable practice in handling the stimuli, laying them out on the same base line, understanding the counterbalancing, and the random presentations. They will also need to be supervised on their use of the master data collection sheets.

For data collation, make four separate master data sheets for

vertical orientation—3-year-olds
vertical orientation—5-year-olds
horizontal orientation—3-year-olds
horizontal orientation—5-year-olds.

On each master data sheet, devote the top half to boy subjects, the bottom half to girl subjects. Number the children in the left column. The stub heads across the top would read from left to right as follows:

Experimenter's name
Child's ID
Correct answers (area responses)

Brownies
   #
   %
People
   #
   %
Rectangles
   #
   %
Combined
   #
   %
Consistency (23 out of 32)—Yes or No; # of items
   Area
   Height
   Salient dimension
Consistent use of a rule by object type (for subjects who did use a rule consistently)
   Area
      Brownies
      People
      Rectangles
   Height
      Brownies
      People
      Rectangles
   Salient Dimension
      Brownies
      People
      Rectangles

This study can, of course, be much simplified by omitting the data and analyses for consistency, and just focusing on the correct (area) responses to the three object types, in the two orientations, for the two age groups. Relevant films include:

Language Development, #6, Discovering Psychology Series, Annenberg/CPB
   Describes how children develop complex language skills, and use language in social communication.

Playing the Language Game, 55 min..
   In The Language Series, Part Two: Acquiring the Human Language. Ways of Knowing, Inc.

Language, 58 min., 1988.
   From *The Mind* Series. How biology and environment interact to enable us to communicate. WNET/13 TV; PBS Adult Learning Service.

Language Development, 20 min., 1972.
   A visit to David Premack's chimpanzee lab, and Noam Chomsky's theory. CRM Educational Films; CRM/McGraw-Hill Films.

Then Sentences, 1990.
   Language in preschoolers. Annenberg/CPB.

For your own background, resources include:

Damon, W., & Daiute, C. (Eds.). (1993). *New directions in child development, Vol. 61, the development of literacy through social interaction*. San Francisco: Jossey-Bass.

Dickinson, D., & Tabors, P. (Eds.). (2001). *Beginning literacy with language: Young children learning at home and school*. Baltimore, MD: Paul H. Brookes.

Robbins, D. (2001). *Vygotsky's psychology-philosophy: A metaphor for language theory and learning.* Kluwer Academic/ Plenum Publishers.

G. The Socialized Child

Self Concept

To emphasize the importance of social context on beliefs and behavior, show the video:

> *The Power of the Situation*, #19
> Discovering Psychology Series, Annenberg/CPB

Experiment 8. Age and Sex Differences in Self-Esteem

It is particularly important, when working with self-esteem measures, for the experimenter to be very comfortable and practiced with the scale and to be relaxed with the child. Note taking, especially, needs to be inconspicuous.

This experiment can be handled at different levels of complexity. At the simpler and briefer end, just have the class administer the test and look for age and sex differences in the total score. Omit the correlational material, or the introduction of relatively difficult issues, as in the Katz and Zigler article. Omit the third set of hypotheses. As time and class sophistication permits, include more of the complexities. It makes a good class exercise to use sex-role stereotypes to make up the third set of hypotheses.

Enough rating figures have been supplied in each manual for one subject. Xerox, trace, or mimeo seven more for each additional child to be tested by each experimenter.

Engel only provides the wording for the happy/unhappy dimension, and permits some freedom in describing the seven dimensions. See if the class is comfortable with our wording for the sample to be tested, and make minor changes as desired, in advance of testing.

Your students should be cautioned repeatedly, in the interest of accurate scoring, about the necessity of labeling each scale and clearly indicating positive and negative poles.

Have the class discuss the sexlessness of the stick figures on the rating sheet. If there is any feeling that "it" is more male than female, it is appropriate to add a skirt to the drawings when testing girls.

For the data collation, make up four master charts, one for each age-sex group. The column stub heads across the top would read from left to right as follows:

> Experimenter's name
> Child's ID and CA
> Scale A (Smart)
>   B (Happy)
>   C (Popular)
>   D (Brave)
>   E (Attractive)
>   F (Strong)
>   G (Obedient)
> Total Self-Esteem score
> Child's mean score

In the far left column, number the children. Under the last tested, draw a horizontal line the width of the chart, and label the next three *rows*:

> Total
> Mean
> Median

In the statistical analyses, the *Total self-esteem* score for each child is used as the data for the analysis of variance. The median of that column will be needed in some of the median tests. Be careful to compute and use the appropriate median for combined groups in the median tests. Four forms for correlation matrices are supplied. If you're obtaining *r*s by computer, and your sample is large, you may wish also to make matrices for Grade *x* boys, Grade *x* girls, Grade *y* boys, Grade *y* girls, with appropriate attention to *n*, *df*, and the correct significance level of *r*.

An exercise the class enjoys is the demonstration and comparison of various measures: Where Are You Game; Thomas Self-Concept Values Test; Coopersmith Self-Esteem Inventory; Children's Self-Social Constructs Tests Preschool Form, Primary Form, 1967; and Self-Social Symbols Tasks, Adolescent Form, 1966 (all three by Long, Henderson, and Ziller).

With a sophisticated class, you may wish to consider a one-way (four-group) Kruskal-Wallis analysis of variance by ranks, if your data appear to have a skewed distribution. (If the value of *H* corrected for ties is significant, the Mann-Whitney *U* tests can then be used for age and sex differences.) The Kruskal-Wallis test is more efficient than median tests in that the scores are converted to ranks and not simply dichotomized as above and below the median. A film you should consider is:

> *The Self*, Updated.
> > The origins of self-identity and self-esteem; beliefs about oneself and the emotional and motivational consequences of those beliefs. The Annenberg/CPB Multimedia Collection, #15.

A new journal has been announced: *Self and Identity* (Psychology Press, c/o Taylor & Francis, Philadelphia). It is the flagship journal for the International Society of Self and Identity. The editor is Mark Leary.

Sex Identity

Both projects that follow are very brief and can be performed as a unit, in the order presented, in under 15 minutes. Each, of course, can also be performed as a separate project, or in conjunction with other experiments than the suggested ones.

You may wish to suggest that your students also read the preceding section, "Self-Concept," as well as the earlier observation project on sex-typed play.

Class discussions on the topic of sex identity are usually quite lively and often begin ranging too widely if not directed. Topics that can be tied to methodological and design and theoretical issues include:

> Would you expect college women to have more masculine preferences than noncollege women? Explain.

> Do you think sex identity may be related to self-esteem? To dependence? To what else? How would the respective theories explain such a relation?

> Do you expect more or less sex typing in America in the next decade? Why?

Students can find much contemporary material in newspapers and magazines on the subject of sex identity. Films that can be shown are:

> *Boys and Girls are Different: Men, Women, and the Sex Difference.* 50 min., c 1995.
> > Investigates the influences of biology and the environment. An ABC News Special, Host John Stossel.

> *The Pinks and the Blues.* 59 min., 1981.
> > Parental and school subtle socialization patterns in fostering gender stereotypes.
> > WGBH Educational Foundation; Live Home Video.

> *Sex and Gender*, #17.
> > Psychological differences and similarities between males and females, and how sex roles reflect social values.
> > Discovering Psychology Series, Annenberg/CPB.

> *Because I Wear Dresses*, 1990.
> > Gender identities.
> > #10 in *Seasons of Life*. The Annenberg/CPB Multimedia Collection.

> *From Images of Males and Females in Elementary School Textbooks*. Feminist Press.
> > This is a 45-minute slide show by Lenore Weitzman and Diane Rizzo. It analyzes the most popular textbooks in science, mathematics, reading, spelling, and social studies according to sex, race, and age.

There is a full-text data base which includes periodicals that focus on women and women's issues, and includes as well regional publications, magazines, newspapers, booklets, etc. It is called *Gender Watch* and can be accessed at www.softlineweb.com/genderw.

Experiment 9. Differential Recall of Sex-typed Material

The recall test administration takes 80 seconds and the child's response, a couple of minutes at most. However, the experimenter needs supervised practice to coordinate the timing, smooth handling of the cards, and clear enunciation of the verbal labels of the items. The experimenter should also practice writing verbatim answers in list form, as fully as consonant with the need *not* to interrupt the subject's flow. A common experimenter error is failure to give the child time to think. There should be at least a five-second pause before prodding the child for *more* recall items.

I have often used this experiment, even with sophomores, as a quick and interesting introduction to research that straddles the cognitive and social domains, and that offers the opportunity to teach repeated measures analysis of variance and the value of the interaction *F.* We usually get significant age effects, no sex differences, and frequently (but not always!) a significant sex of child X sex of item interaction.

A discussion of the validity problems raised by the different methods of choosing items by different researchers (e.g., Fagot, Nadelman, Rabban) interests advanced students.

For data collation, prepare four master data sheets: Grade *x* boys, Grade *x* girls, Grade *y* boys, Grade *y* girls. Column heads should read Experimenters name, childs ID, m, f, total recalled.

Experiment 10. Preference for Sex-typed Material

This is very fast and very easily administrated. Be sure the experimenter knows where to record the identifying number of the card chosen. If the differential recall test (Experiment 9) is also being given, be sure the recall test precedes the preference test.

This portion of the battery is often used by the students in designing their other projects, for example, in relation to TV sex-typed programs; in relation to need for approval (Children's Social Desirability Scale).

One idea is to follow the administration of the preference test with a second administration Bem-style. In the second task, our 40 cards are mixed with some neutral cards, and the child rates *each* item on a 1 to 7 scale like Bem's (1974), or 1 to 5 or 1 to 3, depending on the age of the sample and ability to cognitively differentiate. We can then see how the two scores relate.

Some pains should be taken with rapport, because children hesitate to choose any nonsex-typed items if they are not fully comfortable with the tester and assured of total privacy (confidentiality). Sex of experimenter is a variable of interest but difficult to work with unless your male and female college students are equal in number.

For data collation, prepare master data sheets for each grade-sex group. Column headings should read: Experimenter, child ID, Preference 5, Preference 20.

$$(m/5) \qquad (m/20)$$

Experiment 11. Cooperation and Competition As a Function of Sex of Dyads

The instructions look very complicated, but this is one of the tasks that the children enjoy once they begin playing the game. Students should practice the administration and scoring fully and often on one another before tackling a dyad of children. The child-couples vary from apprehensive to gleeful in their approach to the task, and they vary in their speed of execution. On the average, the instructions, opportunity to practice with the pushpin and scoreboard, and 30 trials take about a 30-minute session with a practiced tester. Some children will speed through in 15 minutes; some serious, deliberate ones will take 45 minutes. We generally pair children from the same classroom.

For a simpler version of this experiment, eliminate the age variable and use children in the one grade, running *t* tests between boy and girl groups on each dependent variable. For a more complex analysis, look at the trial blocks as indicated and/or look at other scores, like the *first move* (responses for trial 1). Krondstadt and Vogt (1976) and Nadelman and Shiffler (1977) also analyzed the frequency of plateau scores (three or more identical response patterns in a row), final total scores, trust, forgiveness, repentance, and so on. These will all need to be entered on your Master Data Sheet if analyses are planned.

Trust: Percentage of times *P* follows *SS*, for each subject, repectively.

Trustworthy: Percentage of times *P* follows *PP*, for each subject, respectively.

Foregiveness: Percentage of times *P* follows *PS*, for Subject 1

                    Percentage of times *P* follows *SP*, for Subject 2.

Repentance: Percentage of times *P* follows *SP*, for Subject 1

                    Percentage of times *P* follows *PS*, for Subject 2

We kept the *P-S* and *S-P* analyses separate since we also used mixed-sex groups (boys paired with girls). If you plan not to use mixed-sex groups or to compare the frequency of response patterns to the individual *first* response or to the individual *final* score, then you may combine the *P-S* and *S-P* frequencies and eliminate one of the four anovas.

To collate the individual data, make up four master charts: second-grade girl pairs, second-grade boy pairs, fifth-grade girl pairs, fifth-grade boy pairs. The column stubs could then read as follows:

		Frequency of					
Experimenter's Name	Child's ID	*PP*	*PS*	*SP*	*SS*	First Move	Final Score
1.	S1	__	__	__	__	_____	_____
	S2					_____	_____
2.	S1	__	__	__	__	_____	_____
						_____	_____

and so on.

An old film on rivalry in same-age peers is:

Childhood Rivalry in Bali and New Guinea. 17 min., 1952. Bateson, G.; Pennsylvania State University.

Experiment 12. Sibling Relationships and Sibling Status: Older or Younger

Although Graham-Bermann had her subjects report on the sibling with whom they had the most conflict, I'm suggesting that your subjects report on the sibling *closest in age* to them. Another alternative is to designate the sibling to whom your subjects *feel closest*.

For a three-way ANOVA, a minimum of five subjects in each of the eight cells is needed (40). If this is impractical with the children available, you can either switch to testing college students, or simplify to a two-way ANOVA by dropping the sex of the sib variable and its related hypotheses. (Significant *F*s on the interactions will require follow-up statistics.) Students find that drawing figures for interactions, for example, the four means in status O/Y x sex, is helpful in stating the results, even if the figure is not included in the finished report.

You may or may not wish to include some of the information derivable from the demography questions on your master data sheets—birth order of your subject, age difference between the subject and her sib, number of children in the family. Add these columns, if you wish, to the ones listed below.

For data collation, make eight master data sheets, for each code group: OMm, OMf, YMm, YMf, OFm, OFf, YFm, YFf. The column heads across the top would read from left to right as follows:

Experimenter
Child's ID or initials (optional)
Child's age
Child's birth order (optional)

Age difference between child and sib (optional)
Number of children (optional)
Mean Empathy score
Mean Boundaries score
Mean Similarity score
Mean Coercion score

When practicing, your students need to articulate clearly and slowly. They need to postpone gently a child's long elaborations of an episode with her sib until the questionnaire is done; then such conversations are fine and can be illustrative.

For a more sophisticated study, use Schachter's sibling deidentification question, "Are you alike or different in personality from your sibling?" Divide your subjects on the basis of their response (Alike or Different), find their respective subscale scores, and run a t test between the two means for each subscale . Do the subjects who said they were like their sibling show a higher Similarity mean score than the subjects who said Different? More Empathy? And so on.

Furman and Buhrmester (1985) designed a Sibling Relationship Questionnaire which has been heavily used. Your students may wish to compare this with Graham-Bermann's.

Researchers are investigating sibling relationships in later life. See, if interested:

Campbell, L. D., Connidis, L. A., & Davies, L. (1999). Sibling ties in later life: A social network analysis. *Journal of Family Issues, 20*(1), 114–118.

Cicirelli, V. G. (1991). Sibling relationships in adulthood. *Marriage and Family Review, 16*(3–4), 291–310.

Gold, D. T. (1989). Sibling relationships in old age: A typology. *International Journal of Aging and Human Development, 28*, 37–51.

H. Final Project: Suggestions

For the last project of the term, we usually have students design a do-able experiment. Sometimes we have subgroups of students create these; more often, we have individual students do their own design. In either case, these projects require much staff time and should probably not be undertaken with oversize class sections. We used to perform the group-designed projects; more recently, we limit effort to paper designs, written in a grant format.

Although the last project, this should be started by midterm at the latest. Students need sufficient supervision to avoid totally blind alleys, grievously flawed designs, ethically or politically sensitive topics or instruments that will not receive clearance in your locale. Some initial help with the bibliography often saves students' time and frustration. Students need to be warned that correlation studies do not usually produce significant results unless the N is very large; studies manipulating independent variables have better payoffs.

Pace the sections of the projects over several months. The initial choice of a topic is difficult for some students. Discuss how one gets ideas, and how one does a library search on that topic for background review material and contemporary articles. The first piece turned in can consist of a brief topic description and tentative bibliography. After discussion with you and/or your assistants, students turn in the Introduction, including their hypotheses and rationale. The detailed Method section follows after your feedback on the preceding section. The Results section indicates how the data will be handled, and should include empty tables. The Discussion section should indicate how the results relate to their hypotheses and to the literature, the implications, and future research steps.

This is a difficult assignment and distinguishes among your students. We have often found that students find it a turn-on, and continue in an independent study or honors course in the following semesters to carry out their research. Some of the studies in Appendix B began from these projects.

The following article may interest you:

Pury, C. L. (2001). Use of in-class lab groups to enrich independent research projects. *Teaching of Psychology, 28*(4), 280-282.

Should your class decide to do cross-cultural interviews, you may wish to look at:

International Society for the Study of Behavioural Development. (2000). *Newsletter:*Indigenous approaches to developmental research, Number 1, Serial No. 37.

Some sources for instruments or tasks to utilize in empirical studies are:

American Psychological Association. *Directory of unpublished mental measures, 7vols.* 1970–1995. Washington, DC: American Psychological Association.

Dunn, L. M., & Dunn, L. M. (1981). *Peabody Picture Vocabulary Test-Revised.* Circle Pines, MN: American Guidance Service.

Impara, J. C., & Plake, B. S. (Eds.). (1998). *The thirteenth mental measurements yearbook.* Lincoln, NB: University of Nebraska Press.

Lindley, P. (Ed.). (2000). *Review of personality assessment instruments (Level B).* Malden, MA: Blackwell Publishing.

Vance, H. B. (Ed.). (1997). *Psychological assessment of children: Best practices for school and clinical settings.* San Francisco, CA: Jossey-Bass (Wiley).

There are also commercial catalogs that provide tests, like *Psychological Corporation*, and *Pro-ed: Psychological Products*.

If you have time in class for a video, order

Cultural Psychology, #26 in Discovering Psychology, Updated edition. Annenberg/CPB

Neuropsychology Project

Some more readings for you:

Gazzaniga, M. S. (Ed.). (2000). *The new cognitive neurosciences.* Cambridge, MA: MIT Press.

Korkman, M. (Guest Ed.). (2001). Normal neuropsychological development in the school-age years. A special issue of *Developmental Neuropsychology, 20* (1).

Letz, R. (1991). Use of computerized test batteries for quantifying neurobehavioral outcomes. *Environmental Health Perspectives, 90,* 195–198.

McClelland, J. L., & Siegler, R. S. (Eds.). (2001). *Mechanisms of cognitive development: Behavioral and neural perspectives.* Mahwah, NJ: Lawrence Erlbaum Associates.

Segal, N. L., Weisfeld, G. E., & Weisfeld, C. C. (Eds.). (1997). *Uniting psychology and biology: Integrative perspectives on human development.* Washington, DC: APA Books.

Welsh, M. C., Revilla, V., Strongin, D., & Kepler, M. (2000). Towers of Hanoi and London: Is the nonshared variance due to differences in task administration? *Perceptual and Motor Skills, 90,* 562–572.

Two videos that are relevant for a neuropsychology project are:

Health, Mind, and Behavior, #23
    Discovering Psychology series-Updated Edition, Annenberg/CPB

Cognitive Neuroscience, #25
    Discovering Psychology series-New, Annenberg/CPB

Concluding Note From the Author

Your feedback would be useful and valuable. Which studies did you perform? What did you and your students appreciate most about this manual? What would you most like to see added, revised, or dropped? Why? Which experiments would you like to see included? Answers from you and/or your students would be greatly appreciated and can be sent to Dr. Lorraine Nadelman, Psychology Department, East Hall, 525 East University Street, University of Michigan, Ann Arbor, Michigan, 48109-1109. Or e-mail to nadelman@umich.edu.

APPENDIX B

List of Experiments

The projects that were performed in the laboratory course in developmental psychology are listed here; the accompanying date indicates when it was first run in our laboratory sections. Most projects included both sexes and several age groups.

Project	First run
Psychomotor and Perceptual Behavior	
Color-form potency	Spring 1952
Reaction time	Fall 1954
Reaction time (2, 4, and 6 second preparatory intervals)	Winter 1971
Verbal control of reaction time	Fall 1968
Verbal control of tapping	Fall 1970
Size constancy	Spring 1952
Stimulus equivalence	Spring 1953
Size discrimination and transposition	Fall 1953
"Tilted Room" adjustment to the vertical and horizontal	Spring 1953
Müller-Lyer illusion	Fall 1954
Perception of abstract time (Cottles Circles Test)	Fall 1978
Time estimation as a function of age, length of time interval, filled and unfilled intervals	Fall 1978
Cognitive Style	
Relations among impulsivity-reflection (Matching Familiar Figures Test), inhibition of motor movement, and intelligence (Peabody Picture Vocabulary Test)	Winter 1969
Verbal control of tapping and impulsivity-reflection	Winter 1972
Relation between persistence, impulsivity-reflection, and ability to inhibit motor movement	Fall 1973
Impulsivity-reflection and interference-proneness	Winter 1976
Relation between impulsivity-reflection and selective attention	Winter 1971
Age and sex differences in field independence (Children's Embedded Figures Test)	Fall 1974
Relation between field independence and spatial egocentrism	Winter 1976

Project	First run
Relation between interference proneness, measured two ways (Stroop and Santostefano Fruit Distraction Test)	Winter 1975
Cognitive and attitudinal rigidity (Luchins water jar task and intolerance of ambiguity questionnaire)	Winter 1976
Relation between cognitive style (impulsivity/reflection) and humor ratings and latency	Fall 1983
Locus of control and impulsivity/reflection in first-born and later-born college students	Fall 1986
Cognitive Development	
Language Behavior (McCarthy)	Spring 1952
Skinner operant conditioning:	
Effect of adult co-worker on bar-pressing	Spring 1952
Regular reinforcement versus fixed ration reinforcement	
Sight of pictures as reinforcement	Spring 1953
Sight of pigeon as reinforcement	Fall 1953
Piaget measures of cognitive development:	
Conservation of amount—clay	Winter 1967
Conservation of number—poker chips	
Cows in the field	
Classification of animals	
Arrangement of number	
Seriation and memory (Piaget)	Fall 1968
Analytic thinking: Field dependence-independence, and Piaget Bottles Test	Fall 1971
Effect of training on Piaget inclusion task	Winter 1969
Proportionality experiment, varying age, and training	Fall 1967
Reversal shift (Kendler)	Winter 1971
Relations among selective attention, ability to inhibit motor movement and intelligence	Fall 1971
Relation between selective attention and interference proneness (central-incidental memory task and Stroop Test)	Fall 1974
Effect of arousal of incidental categories on selective attention	Winter 1977
Proactive inhiition release	Fall 1973
Effect of block and random presentation on recall and clustering	Fall 1975
Effect of meaningfulness on free recall	Fall 1976
Effect on recall of auditory and visual presentation, verbal and motor response	Fall 1978
Relation between interference proneness and recall of pictures and words	Fall 1978
Effect of irrelevant humor on recall	Fall 1978
Automatic semantic processing	Fall 1975
Development of conformity in word association (Brown & Berko)	Fall 1977

Project	First run
Creativity and conformity in word-association	Fall 1978
Cross-age tutoring	Fall 1973
Relation among three perspective-taking tsks (Piaget Mountain task, Flavell 7/4 story, Blindfold task)	Winter 1975
Immediate and delayed recall of aging stereotypes	Winter 1985
Spatial memory in young and middle-aged adults	Fall 1986
Money values and relation to career choice, adjective attribution, and coin-size perception	Winter 1986
Effect of modes of presentation on free recall	Fall 1989

Social Development

Project	First run
Development of moral judgment (Piaget)	Spring 1952
Moral judgment in aggression stories, varying sex of character	Fall 1975
Moral judgment and internal/external locus of control	Winter 1976
Moral judgment, varying intentions, consequences, parental reinforcement	Fall 1977
Moreno social structure studies	Spring 1952
Conflict behavior (Lewin)	Sprint 1953
Sharing behavior with toys: verbal versus "overt"	Spring 1952
Cooperation and sharing behavior (Seals)	
Between "high-" and "low-chosen" children (Moreno)	Fall 1953
Between children of different ages	Fall 1953
Cooperation-competition as a function of sex-group pairings (MM, MF, FF); scissors-paper game in a prisoner's dilemma paradigm	Fall 1974
Cooperation-competition as a function of age pairings (3–3, 3–5, 5–5 grades)	Fall 1975
Effect of limited reward versus rivalry on cooperation (Madsen circle board)	Fall 1975
Effect of set on cooperation-competition	Fall 1976
Relation between cooperation-competition and need for affiliation	Fall 1977
Social influences on Müller-Lyer illusion	Fall 1954
Imitation experiment, varying sex, age, tasks (cognitive and aesthetic), and reinforcement of model	Fall 1967
Effect of peers on a conservation task (2 non-conservers, 1 conserver triads)	Fall 1973
Need for approval from peers and from adults (social desirability scale)	Fall 1975
Play preferences and sex differences in play preferences (observational study)	Fall 1954
Sex differences in play preferences and social interaction (observational study)	Fall 1978
Sex-role preferences: sex and age differences on IT Scale and drawings	Winter 1967
Sex identity: drawings, preference and knowledge of masculine and feminine items	Fall 1968

Project	First run
Sex identity: recall, knowledge and preference for masculine and feminine items	Fall 1969
Sex differences to five kinds of humor	Fall 1974
Sex and age differences in self-concept	Winter 1974
Stability of gender identity	Winter 1974
Body build and social stereotypes (Staffieri)	Winter 1972
Age attribution: (a) as a function of upper and lower facial features; (b) age labeling of photographs of 6-months to 90-year-old people	Winter 1976
Role-taking and communication (Flavell's Sour Grapes task)	Winter 1974
Effects of role-taking experience on communication	Winter 1976
Spatial and social perspective taking and concept development (picture vocabulary)	Fall 1977
TV and sex preferences	Fall 1973
Influence of TV characters as behavior models	Fall 1976
Effect of aggressive and prosocial arousal on response hierarchy to conflict situations	Winter 1977
Relationship between achievement motivation and locus of control (Nowicki-Strickland Scale)	Fall 1974
Achievement motivation (Veroff's tasks) and impulsivity-reflection	Winter 1974
Fear of success and need for approval	Winter 1977
Situational arousal of emotions	Winter 1979
Images of elderly in TV commercials	Fall 1978
Happiness, life satisfaction, and participation in activities (questionnaire, interview)	Winter 1979
Perception of "people" versus "old people"	Winter 1979
Cohort differences in sex-role attitudes of college and middle-aged men	Fall 1982
Self and task concepts of elementary school children in the physical, social, and academic domains	Fall 1982
Sex and age differences in socially directed and object directed play	Fall 1985
Sex-typed play preferences: Test versus observed play	Fall 1981
Effect of cues on sex-stereotyping	Fall 1981
Relation between need for achievement and cooperation–competition	Fall 1981
Sex, age, and "set" effects on need for achievement	Winter 1984
Self-esteem and need for achievement: Sex, age, and birth order effects	Winter 1984
Self-esteem and play behavior	Fall 1988
Fear of success and anxiety in two cohorts	Fall 1985
Career and family choices in two cohorts	Fall 1985
Attitudes toward divorce and its consequences	Winter 1986
Single and traditional families on TV	Fall 1985

Project	First run
Relation between TV-watching and children's prosocial and aggressive responses	Fall 1988
Sex-role stereotyping in two cohorts of books	Fall 1983
Minority representation in two cohorts of children's picture books—1950s and 1970s	Winter 1986
Effect of personalized set on perception of old people	Fall 1984
Relation between empathy and egocentrism in second and fourth graders	Fall 1984
Age and sex differences in children's stereotypes about physical attractiveness	Fall 1988
Relation between TV watching and prosocial/aggressive tendencies in children	Fall 1988
Self-esteem and interaction styles in preschoolers	Fall 1988
Career and family choices in high school and college seniors	Fall 1988
Cartoon character preference in relation to children's aggression	Fall 1989
Age and sex differences in occupational stereotypes	Fall 1989

INDEX